Palgrave Studies in the History of Economic Thought

Palgrave Studies in the History of Economic Thought publishes contributions by leading scholars, illuminating key events, theories and individuals that have had a lasting impact on the development of modern-day economics. The topics covered include the development of economies, institutions and theories.

The series aims to highlight the academic importance of the history of economic thought, linking it with wider discussions within economics and society more generally. It contains a broad range of titles that illustrate the breath of discussions – from influential economists and schools of thought, through to historical and modern social trends and challenges – within the discipline.

All books in the series undergo a single-blind peer review at both the proposal and manuscript submission stages.

For further information on the series and to submit a proposal for consideration, please contact the Wyndham Hacket Pain (Economics Editor) wyndham.hacketpain@palgrave.com.

More information about this series at
https://link.springer.com/bookseries/14585

Mats Lundahl

Twelve Figures in Swedish Economics

Eli Heckscher, Bertil Ohlin, Gunnar Myrdal, Ingvar Svennilson, Axel Iveroth, Jan Wallander, Erik Höök, Bo Södersten, Rolf Henriksson, Ingemar Ståhl, Villy Bergström and Göte Hansson

palgrave
macmillan

Mats Lundahl
Stockholm School of Economics
Stockholm, Sweden

ISSN 2662-6578 ISSN 2662-6586 (electronic)
Palgrave Studies in the History of Economic Thought
ISBN 978-3-030-94326-4 ISBN 978-3-030-94327-1 (eBook)
https://doi.org/10.1007/978-3-030-94327-1

Cover illustration: Lars Johansson/Alamy Stock Photo

This Palgrave Macmillan imprint is published by the registered company Springer Nature Switzerland AG
The registered company address is: Gewerbestrasse 11, 6330 Cham, Switzerland

Preface

In 2015, I published a book of essays called *Seven Figures in the History of Swedish Economic Thought* (Palgrave Macmillan). The seven figures were Knut Wicksell, Eli Heckscher, Bertil Ohlin, Torsten Gårdlund, Sven Rydenfelt, Staffan Burenstam Linder and Jaime Behar. The present volume is a sequel to that book. It deals with Eli Heckscher, Bertil Ohlin, Gunnar Myrdal, Ingvar Svennilson, Axel Iveroth, Jan Wallander, Erik Höök, Bo Södersten, Rolf Henriksson, Ingemar Ståhl, Villy Bergström and Göte Hansson.

As was the case also with *Seven Figures*, the chapters all have their own histories. They have not been written with the book in mind but have been prepared for a variety of occasions. Most of the essays, however, have one thing in common. They present aspects that are not commonly known, especially not to an international audience. Most of the books and articles dealt with were written in Swedish and were never translated. In some instances, the chapters are also based on private letters which were subsequently buried in archives. Putting the essays together offers a selective longitudinal section of Swedish economics during the twentieth century. Several of the pieces deal with what in the *Down Beat* annual jazz polls used to be called 'Talent Deserving Wider Recognition.'

The only part of the book which is vaguely systematic consists of the essays devoted to economics who at some point in their life had a relation to the Industrial Institute for Economic and Social Research [Industriens Utredningsinstitut—IUI]. Together with Benny Carlson I have been, and still am, involved in the writing of the history of the institute—today known as the Research Institute of Industrial Economics [Institutet för Näringslivsforskning—IFN]. These essays have been written together with Benny and their Swedish versions have been collected in our book *Från Värmland till Washington* (Samhällsförlaget, Stockholm, 2020).

As always, when preparing a book, I have put a heavy strain on the librarians of the Stockholm School of Economics, notably Peter Gavelin and Ute Harris. They have born with me with equanimity, always delivered, and time after time demonstrated their ability to dig out the most impossible items. My debt of gratitude to them keeps accumulating. Thanks are also due to the Jan Wallander and Tom Hedelius Foundation and the Tore Browaldh Foundation for financial support.

Djursholm, Sweden
September 2021

Mats Lundahl

PRAISE FOR *TWELVE FIGURES IN SWEDISH ECONOMICS*

"Following the lead of intellectual giants such as Knut Wicksell and Eli Heckscher numerous well-trained Swedish economists became renowned public intellectuals. By applying the economists' toolbox on the most pressing policy issues of the day, skilfully articulated in their native language in a fashion accessible to non-economists, they also became highly influential. In this collection of essays, Mats Lundahl offers an erudite exposé of twelve Swedish economists who conceived of economics as a broad social science and ventured outside the ivory tower. By presenting key parts of their work that is only available in Swedish, this book not only fills some gaps in the picture of the history of Swedish economics, it also inspires new generations of economists to communicate their findings outside their narrow circle of specialists."

—Magnus Henrekson, *Professor of Economics and Senior Research Fellow at the Research Institute of Industrial Economics (IFN), Stockholm*

"Students all over the world ask for more diversity and rethinking in economics. A good start is to learn more about the diversity and thinking of economists in the past. In this book, we learn about twelve Swedish scholars—a bit about their lives and a lot about their economics. Heckscher, Ohlin, and Myrdal are world famous—others are talents deserving wider recognition. Mats Lundahl brings them all to life in an excellent overview."

—Karl Ove Moene, *Professor of Economics, University of Oslo*

"Mats Lundahl is a master of biographical essays and has published several books in English, Swedish, French and Spanish on economists and musicians. In *Twelve Figures in Swedish Economics* he returns with new material on Eli Heckscher and Bertil Ohlin, who were earlier presented in *Seven Figures in the History of Swedish Economic Thought* (2015), and also presents ten new economists: Gunnar Myrdal, Ingvar Svennilson, Axel Iveroth, Jan Wallander, Erik Höök, Bo Södersten, Rolf Henriksson, Ingemar Ståhl, Villy Bergström and Göte Hansson.

Lundahl has met most of the twelve economists and some of them were his close friends. Therefore, he is able to give colourful and penetrating portraits that would not have been possible with the help of only written sources. His personal style makes the reading a great pleasure at the same time as you learn a lot both about the individuals and their subjects."

—Bo Sandelin, *Professor Emeritus of Economics, University of Gothenburg*

Contents

CHAPTER 1

Introduction: Twelve Figures in Swedish Economics

Far too many of my younger economists have a static view of our profession. The only publications that count are the contemporary ones. Anyone who reads an article (books are not read, since they don't count) more than five years old is out of his mind, and those relatives of Gerontius who delve into works from the twentieth century should be sent to the nuthouse as quickly as possible. The youngsters have their feet firmly on the ground, unlike those of us in the older generation who consider it a privilege to be able to stand on the shoulders of the giants from the generations that preceded our own.

Hopefully, the situation will change with age. Histories of economic doctrines are still published, even though the subject largely appears to have disappeared from the university curricula. There are good reasons why we should strive for a future resurrection. Economics is a science where many—arguably the majority—problems are 'perennial.' They have not been invented during the last five years, but centuries, or even millennia, ago. The economic problem is that of making the best use of scarce resources, and this problem has been the companion of humankind ever since Adam and Eve.

This, in turn, means that people have thought of how to solve the problem of scarcity since time immemorial. That is what is known as the history of economic doctrines. The wheel has already been invented and

M. Lundahl, *Twelve Figures in Swedish Economics*, Palgrave Studies in the History of Economic Thought, https://doi.org/10.1007/978-3-030-94327-1_1

if we want to produce better, more efficient varieties of it, it may not be a bad idea to go back in time and see how the more or less ancient wheelmakers reasoned. Some of their ideas we have accepted. They are part of the mainstream tradition. There is, however, no guarantee—*pace* evolutionary game theory—that it is always the best solutions that have been handed down to us. For reasons that may or may not be rational, some solutions are forgotten as times change, but times may change again, and then it may be rewarding to look back and see what the past may hide. From time to time, old and forgotten ideas are resurrected and used for rethinking our current doctrines.

The above is a plea for more history of doctrines in economics. Of course, this philosophy is behind many writings in the field. The present book is a case in point. By bringing out some writings by twelve Swedish economists from the early twentieth century to our own time it can hopefully make a modest contribution to the joy of exploration and discovery of the thought of those who preceded us. Like all thought, these writings mirror the time when they were written. Keynesian economics is unthinkable without the depression, and the story of growth and development economics is intimately related to the reconstruction after the second works war and the independence of the colonies in the Third World. In a similar fashion, the writings of the economists included in the present volume are the children of the state of Swedish society at various times.

The book deals with twelve economists who in different ways found their own subjects and who in the vast majority of cases took part in the Swedish debate on the economic, social and political issues of their time. All of them began in academia or at the Industrial Institute for Economic and Social Research [Industriens Utredningsinstitut], a private institute specialized in applied research—the only one of its kind in Sweden—but thereafter their careers differed widely: a reflection of the economics scene in the country. Seven of them became full professors at some Swedish university. Three of them in addition pursued a political career. Two became cabinet ministers and one in addition party leader. One became deputy governor at the Swedish central bank: the Riksbank, another managing director of one of the most important Swedish banks, another managing director of the Federation of Swedish Industries and yet another head of the planning department at the Ministry of Finance. The idea behind the book is to present a dozen essays which one way or another portray the twelve economists in settings that reveal something about both their personalities and their works.

The works of the economists dealt with here form part of the trajectory described by Swedish economics since the breakthrough of the neoclassical approach during the last quarter of the nineteenth century. They bring out the story of the beginning of neoclassical international trade theory through the works of Eli Heckscher and Bertil Ohlin and tell the tale of the rise of the so-called Stockholm School of economists, through the writings of Gunnar Myrdal and Ingvar Svennilson, dealt with here.

They also provide an account of the creation and contribution of the Industrial Institute for Economic and Social Research [Industriens Utredningsinstitut]. Svennilson, Axel Iveroth, Jan Wallander, Erik Höök, Villy Bergström and Rolf Henriksson were all, in one way or the other, related to its activities. The institute for a number of years was the only institution concentrated on empirical economic work, mainly, but not exclusively, topics related to the Swedish industrial sector. It produced high-class academic products but, as testified by its history and the people portrayed here, it also prepared alumni for high-level positions in the private and public sectors of the Swedish economy.

Finally, our story brings out the work of three economists at Lund University: Bo Södersten, Ingemar Ståhl and Göte Hansson. The former two became known to a wider audience mainly through their participation in the public debate, as critics of the conventional wisdom, whereas Göte, when not doing research, concentrated his energy on institution building, both in Lund and Tanzania, and cooperation with the Swedish foreign aid agency.

The essays collected in the present volume bear witness to the diversity of the Swedish economics profession from the interwar period to the 2000s. All the people dealt with were people who ventured outside the ivory tower. They indeed did academic research, but they also conceived of economics as a broad social science, a science that should produce research results that could be brought to bear on important issues outside the university campus. About half of them are well known in Sweden but not internationally Much of what they wrote was in Swedish. Hopefully, the present volume can to some extent contribute to changing this fact and to fill some gaps in the picture of the history of Swedish economics. My protagonists are all acquaintances well worth to make—in their own right.

Eli Heckscher and Bertil Ohlin: The Origin of Their Theorem

The Heckscher–Ohlin theorem is one of the most well-known theorems in international trade. It states that countries will export goods that make intensive use of their abundant factors and import goods that make intensive use of their scarce factors. The theorem owes its origin to a 1919 article by Eli Heckscher on foreign trade and income distribution.[1] Heckscher (1879–1952) was a bit of a Janus's face, since he straddled both economics and economic history. He is the father of the latter as a separate discipline in Sweden[2] and during his entire professional life, he strove to marry the two branches of the social sciences.[3] Economics needed historical empirical material to make sense, and in order to arrive at an understanding of economic history, it was necessary to apply the economic theory.

Heckscher dealt with economics mainly during his younger years. With time, he was drawn more and more into economic history, and it was in the latter field that he became internationally famous for his works on the Continental System[4] and mercantilism.[5] The process culminated with his monumental work on the economic history of Sweden, a work that was not fully completed at the time of his death in 1952.[6] His article on foreign trade had been written in Swedish and was not published in English until 1949, and then only incompletely.[7]

Chapter 2 investigates where Heckscher's inspiration for writing his classic article came from. His sources were threefold. In the first place, he had been involved in a controversy over the Swedish tariff on sugar which raged just before the outbreak of the first world war. Secondly, he had reviewed a book by his colleague Fritz Brock on what the later called 'solidary' tariffs—tariffs uniformly levied on all imports. Lastly, and most importantly, he had published a book of essays which among other things

[1] Heckscher (1919).

[2] Lundahl (2015, Chapter 7).

[3] Ibid., Chapter 6.

[4] Heckscher (1922).

[5] Heckscher (1935a).

[6] Heckscher (1935b, 1936, 1949a, 1949b).

[7] Heckscher (1949c).

contained a chapter on the sugar tariff. The chapter was criticized by Knut Wicksell, who argued that Heckscher's plea for a reduction did not take into account the effects on population (emigration). Thus, Heckscher had dealt with problems of foreign trade before 1919 and as he acknowledged himself, it was Wicksell's criticism that made him write his pathbreaking article.

Exactly like Eli Heckscher, Bertil Ohlin (1899–1979) presents a dual picture, but in his case that of the economist and the politician. Whereas the Swedes think of him as the perennial opposition leader (for the Liberals), the international community sees him as the world-famous economist: the recipient of the Sveriges Riksbank Prize in Economic Sciences in Memory of Alfred Nobel. Ohlin contributed both to international trade and macroeconomics. He was one of the leading exponents of the so-called Stockholm School of economists, an expression coined by himself, who worked in parallel with Keynes, but with a methodology of their own, on problems related to unemployment and stabilization and who—like Keynes—advocated interventions in the market economy instead of *laissez-faire*.

Bertil Ohlin's contributions to the Heckscher–Ohlin theorem and the related factor-price equalization theorem were elaborated in a 'cascade' trilogy which consisted of his licentiate thesis, his doctoral dissertation and his *magnum opus*, *Interregional and International Trade*.[8] As was the case with Heckscher's article, the first two were written in Swedish and not translated into English until several decades later.[9]

Ohlin's main contribution was that he approached the problem of what determines the pattern of international trade within a general equilibrium framework. In the first volume of his memoirs, he offers the story of how he arrived at his idea, during a walk on Unter den Linden in Berlin in 1920, getting a kind of a *Eureka!* experience.[10] The accepted view has been that he then understood that he could combine Heckscher's idea of factor proportions with the general equilibrium approach, which he had been exposed to through his teacher Gustav Cassel.[11] However, as it seems, Ohlin did not incorporate Heckscher's views until he was well on

[8] Ohlin (1922, 1924, 1933).

[9] Ohlin (1991, 2002).

[10] Ohlin (1972, p. 79).

[11] Cassel (1918).

his way with his work, so most likely, what dawned on him in Berlin was simply the idea of formulating his problem within the general equilibrium framework.

Gunnar Myrdal on Method

Gunnar Myrdal (1898–1987) was Bertil Ohlin's contemporary. Like Ohlin, he was a member of the Stockholm School and like Ohlin he received the Sveriges Riksbank Prize in Economic Sciences in Memory of Alfred Nobel. Myrdal was elected a Member of Parliament for the Social Democrats on two occasions, in the 1930s and 1940s, and he served as Minister of Trade from 1945 to 1947.

Myrdal began his career as a more or less conventional economist, emphasizing central theory. However, with time, he increasingly turned into an interdisciplinary researcher on the one hand and an iconoclast on the other, a researcher who worked in the intersection between mainly economics and sociology and to some extent also political science. He repeatedly stated that the conventional demarcations between the various branches of social science were artificial. There was no such thing as purely economic or sociological problems, only problems. Myrdal became skeptical of formal model building, preferring institutional explanations of social phenomena instead.

As could be expected, Gunnar Myrdal throughout virtually his entire career struggled with methodological issues, regardless of the issue at stake. The point of departure was virtually always what he perceived of as shortcomings of mainstream economic theory. Chapter 3 of the present work constitutes an attempt to follow Myrdal's methodological development from his doctoral dissertation in 1927[12] to *Asian Drama*[13] and *The Challenge of World Poverty* in 1968 and 1970, respectively.[14]

Myrdal's views on the economic methods developed in steps. In his doctoral dissertation, which dealt with price formation, he took issue with the static character of the neoclassical theory. It excluded the influence of expectations, a dynamic element which certainly influenced the actions of both consumers and producers. His next methodological step was a

[12] Myrdal (1927).

[13] Myrdal (1968).

[14] Myrdal (1970).

highly unconventional one. Myrdal had become increasingly irritated by the tendency of the older Swedish generation of economists to present political views as incontrovertible scientific truths and decided to write a polemic pamphlet. However, as so often with him, the topic grew, and he ended up examining the entire Western tradition of economics from the Enlightenment to his own time.[15] The works of the great economists were full of hidden value premises which inflicted a bias on their analysis, and which had better be brought out into the open. Normative economics must rest on explicitly stated value premises, a prescription which Myrdal later would extend to positive economics as well.

Myrdal's third methodological step is connected to the first one. In what, via one Swedish[16] and one German[17] edition, would eventually become *Monetary Equilibrium*,[18] he criticized Knut Wicksell's formulation of the cumulative process which is behind upward or downward movements in the price level.[19] From the present point of view, however, is not the contents of Myrdal's criticism, but rather the fact that he accepted the principle of dynamic, circular cumulation, a concession that would have a fundamental impact on his own work in completely different areas.

Myrdal's next two—interrelated—steps were taken more or less simultaneously. During the first half of the 1930s, he became convinced of the importance of institutions as social determinants. The second step was the advocacy of social engineering, a step intimately connected with his insistence on explicit value premises. These were in turn fused with the principle of circular, cumulative causation in a holistic framework where all variables are affected by and affect each other, something that must be taken into account when you want to reform society by changing its institutions. The urge for reform came to the forefront in the book on Swedish population problems that Gunnar published together with his wife, Alva, in 1934,[20] and which was not in any way limited to the population question proper, but which called for a radical reform of most

[15] Myrdal (1930), English translation, Myrdal (1953).

[16] Myrdal (1931).

[17] Myrdal (1933).

[18] Myrdal (1939).

[19] Wicksell (1936, p. 10), German original, Wicksell (1898).

[20] Myrdal and Myrdal (1934).

aspects of Swedish society. The book became the starting point for the construction of the modern welfare society in Sweden.

The population book was the mere forerunner of a far more ambitious effort: *An American Dilemma*.[21] Myrdal spent the early war years in the United States after having received an invitation by the Carnegie Corporation to head a major investigation of the racial problem there: the position of blacks in American society and their relations with the whites. His work rested on a series of explicitly formulated value premises, what Myrdal termed the 'American Creed': democracy, equality, freedom, fair opportunity and the rule of law, and the analysis stressed the circular, cumulative interaction between the economic level of blacks, their standards of intelligence, ambition, health, education, decency, manners, and morals; and discrimination of blacks by whites. Needless to say, Myrdal ended up with a call for deep, planned social reform, true to his insistence on the importance of social engineering.

A decade after the publication of his American masterpiece, Myrdal brought his methodological apparatus to bear also on inequalities between countries and the workings of the international economy, in a series of three books: *An International Economy*, *Development and Under-Development* and *Economic Theory and Under-Developed Regions*.[22] There, he investigated how national and international factors interacted to create low-income levels and large inequalities within developing countries and large income gaps between the latter and the developed nations.

Gunnar Myrdal's methodological effort culminated in *Asian Drama* and *The Challenge of World Poverty*,[23] where he made an attempt to lay bare the mechanisms which created poverty in the countries of South Asia, the interaction between six sets of variables: output and incomes, conditions of production, conditions of living, attitudes toward life and work, institutions and policies. Again, the analysis was guided by a set of explicit value premises—modernization ideals—rationality, development and planning for development, rise of productivity, rise of levels of living, social and economic equalization, improved institutions and attitudes, national consolidation, national independence, political democracy,

[21] Myrdal (1944).

[22] Myrdal (1956a, 1956b, 1957).

[23] Myrdal (1968, 1970).

democracy at the grassroots, social discipline and 'democratic planning.' The planning element was particularly important. The South Asian countries would not be able to escape from their poverty unless a concerted effort, guided by rational planning, was made. They needed a 'big push.'

Gunnar Myrdal was not only an economist or a social scientist. He was also a political activist who felt compelled to provide advice on practical reform matters and who took an active part in politics and government himself. Over the years, his role increasingly became that of a preacher—a preacher whose visions rested on an elaborate view of how social problems should be approached—a view which had taken four decades to shape.

The Swedish Planning Issue: Ingvar Svennilson

Chapters 4–8, and partly also Chapters 10 and 11, are devoted to economists employed at or otherwise related to Industrial Institute for Economic and Social Research [Industriens Utredningsinstitut, IUI]. This institute was founded at the initiative of J. Sigfrid Edström, the managing director and subsequently chairman of the board of ASEA, according to a story which forms part of the folkloristic heritage of the institute, after a meeting between Edström and the Swedish Prime Minister Per Albin Hansson, where the latter pointed out that the voice of the business community was by and large absent in the political debate. Edström thought the issue over and began planning an institute that could gather information that could be useful in such a context.

The institute began its operations in 1939. In 1941, Ingvar Svennilson (1908–1972) became its director. His appointment turned out to be a hit, for Svennilson made sure that the IUI was converted into an independent institute focused on research in the best academic tradition, on themes that were of interest for the business community, but which were mainly decided by the researchers themselves and published without any strings attached, a tradition which the institute has managed to preserve to the present day.[24] (In 2006, the name was changed to The Research Institute of Industrial Economics—Institutet för Näringslivsforfskning—IFN.)

Chapter 4 deals with one of Ingvar Svennilson's main interests: economic planning. He wrote his doctoral dissertation on planning by the

[24] For a presentation of Svennilson at the IUI, see Carlson and Lundahl (2014, Chapter 7).

business firm, in 1938,[25] and after the outbreak of the second world war, he became increasingly involved with planning on the national level—naturally enough, given the immediate strain put on the Swedish economy by the outbreak of the war and the disruptions inflicted on international trade. For Svennilson, planning was an exercise in economic dynamics, a means for reducing the uncertainty with respect to the future, both at the level of the firm and at the level of the national economy. It interfered with the market mechanism and had to be coordinated with macroeconomic policy.

While planning stood out as a natural component of a wartime economy, after the end of the war, it became a hotly debated issue in Sweden.[26] One of the participants in this debate was Svennilson. His views did not remain static but changed as the times did. Between 1941 and 1949, the emphasis shifted from wartime to peacetime and long-term planning. Svennilson stressed the exceptional conditions imposed by the war, when the military needs had to be prioritized, which called for strict planning and rationing of scarce raw materials, and cooperation between the government and the business community.

Planning might also be necessary after the war when a recession could set in, and the structure of firms could need a 'rationalization.' The preparation of the return to peacetime conditions contributed to this need as well, and the government to that end appointed a Commission on Postwar Planning, generally referred to as the Myrdal commission, since it was chaired by Gunnar Myrdal, which, on the initiative of Myrdal and Svennilson suggested the creation of an investment council with representatives from government agencies and business organizations to coordinate investment with the swings of the business cycle. The task of the council was limited to advisory duties and it appears to have worked well for both sides. Still, it became a bone of contention in the debate. Images of both Nazism and Communism were conjured up by some of its opponents.

As the war drew to an end, the economic environment gradually changed, which called for a different approach, as Sweden gradually went back to normalcy: more supportive measures and fewer prohibitions and restrictions. The government would have to back private initiatives in

[25] Svennilson (1938).

[26] See Lewin (1967), for an overview.

a positive fashion. Svennilson advocated a looser 'framework planning,' instead of the centralized approach that characterized the war years, where discussion and negotiation should be used to bridge the gap between the necessary control and decentralization.

When the peace finally arrived, the planning discussion changed again. The opposition to planning took on more elaborately organized forms and the tension with the interests of the labor movement became evident. Ingvar Svennilson at this point had become convinced that the extent of planning could and should not be pushed too far—not beyond the stage of establishing a loose framework within which the market forces should be allowed to operate. Planning could be employed to decide the location of industries, for example, but not their production. Also, international trade might have to stay regulated for some time, but as soon as the circumstances permitted, the controls should be relaxed.

When it comes to planning issues, Ingvar Svennilson is, however, most well known for his pioneering involvement with long-term planning. He was in charge a government committee covering the recovery years 1947–52/53—what became the first long-term survey of the Swedish economy—and he proposed an investigation of the period up to 1960 to the board of the Industrial Institute for Economic and Social Research which in due time resulted in a number of important reports. In 1949, Svennilson left the IUI to conduct a study of economic trends for the Economic Commission for Europe in Geneva, an endeavor which ended up producing his well-known *Growth and Stagnation in the European Economy*.[27] When he returned to Sweden, indicative long-term planning had already become an integral tool of Swedish economic policy and Svennilson immediately was drafted as chairmen for three more long-term economic surveys in the 1950s and 1960s.

Ingvar Svennilson managed to balance successfully between the Social Democracy and the business community, maintaining one foot in each camp as it were, without arousing any hard feelings. He was clever enough not to get stuck in any preconceived notions but constantly pondered and revalued his position, moving in an increasingly liberal direction as the effects of the war petered out.

[27] Svennilson (1954).

A Young Man in the Swedish Diplomatic Service: Axel Iveroth

The first secretary of the Industrial Institute for Economic and Social Research was Axel Iveroth (1914–1993).[28] He was recruited in 1939, the year after he graduated from the Stockholm School of Economics. Before arriving at the IUI, Iveroth had worked at a shirt factory and at the Swedish Broadcasting Corporation, where he continued to work until 1941, in parallel with his work at the IUI.

Iveroth was responsible for the first major research project at the institute: a study of small-scale industry which he carried out from 1939 to 1941, a period during which he was also drafted into military service.[29] He produced a well-written book that can still be read with pleasure, and it enjoyed a wide readership when it was issued. The study covered both handicrafts and small-scale industry proper and Iveroth managed to produce a vivid, partly even fascinating, report which mixed history with an economic analysis of the strengths and weaknesses of the sector and its future prospects which made it accessible to people with only rudimentary knowledge of economics.

Iveroth was an efficient secretary. During his work on the small-scale industry, he developed a wide contact net and a thorough knowledge of Swedish industry which he used to the benefit of the IUI, developing and deepening the tradition that the research at the institute should be carried out in collaboration with the business community. In the end, Iveroth stood out as a godsend for the institute.

In the summer of 1944, at the age of 30, Axel Iveroth left the IUI to become an industrial attaché at the Swedish legation in Washington, DC. This, however, did not mean that he cut his ties with the institute. On the contrary, he regularly reported back to the institute in letters to its director, Ingvar Svennilson, letters written by a young man who completely lacked respect for incompetent seniors, of which there were many both in the Swedish diplomatic service and among those from the business community who visited the United States during the time he was stationed there, from 1944 to 1945. Iveroth's letters offer an interesting mixture of his own everyday chores and trivial problems, his attempt

[28] For details about Iveroth and his time at the Industrial Institute for Economic and Social Research, see Carlson and Lundahl (2014, Chapter 5).

[29] Iveroth (1943).

to meet the pent-up needs of the Swedish economics research community as a result of the disruptions due to the war, his observations and remarks about the Swedish diplomatic representation in Washington, New York and Chicago, and his direct encounters with the American business community and its organizations.

Washington, DC was a bit of a hellish place, not least due to the summer heat. Iveroth was thrown smack, dab in the middle of it. He provides a colorful picture of what he had to endure and how he tried to cope with it. On the one hand, he had to cope with the hot Washington summer, which affected him physically, on the other hand, he soon found out that he did not have the time that he needed to produce enough economic reports of sufficient quality and assemble enough books and printed material that could be sent home to his fellow economists who needed to stay in contact both with theoretical developments on the other side of the Atlantic and with the development of the American economy during the war.

Being an industrial attaché, Iveroth felt an urge to tackle the problem of Swedish-American relations on the level of the business communities in the two countries and to that end made a point of visiting American companies and industrial organizations. The American interest in Sweden was to be reckoned with but channels had to be developed outside the inefficient Swedish diplomatic representation, from company to company and from branch organization to branch organization. The Swedes by and large lost a golden opportunity, the international chamber of conference organized by the United States Chamber of Commerce in November 1944, a conference where the Swedish representation left a lot to be desired and hence did not accomplish too much.

Iveroth made a brilliant career after his return to Sweden. Over the years, the Industrial Institute for Economic and Social Research would turn out a large number of people who had spent a number there and acquired a competence that prepared them for life both inside and outside academia: as future professors, high-level civil servants inside and outside Sweden, company directors, journalists and consultants. Axel Iveroth was one of the first examples of this. He went on to the Swedish Employers' Confederation, the cement industry in Sweden and abroad, and finally to the position as managing director of the Federation of Swedish Industries. All this time, he preserved his IUI heritage, a heritage which culminated with his participation in the creation in 1948 of the Center for Business and Policy Studies [Studieförbundet Näringsliv och Samhälle, SNS], an organization modeled on the IUI. Iveroth was its chairman 1948–60.

Ingvar Svennilson Goes West

To stay in contact with the United States was of utmost importance for the Industrial Institute for Economic and Social Research. It was mainly there that the theoretical development of economics took place and the US economy in many respects was ahead of the Swedish one. It must also be kept in mind that the IUI was the only institute of its kind in Sweden, so the much-needed impulses that could contribute to the evolution of its research had to come from abroad. During his stay in Washington, Axel Iveroth had tried to convince Ingvar Svennilson to make a study tour to America. The trip, however, did not materialize until Iveroth had returned home. Svennilson came to the United States in February 1947 and stayed until May. Chapter 6 provides an account of his journey and a later (1960) journey to Cuba.

Svennilson made efficient use of his American tour. It began in Boston, with Harvard where he met its formidable faculty: Gottfried Haberler, Joseph Schumpeter, Edward S. Mason, John Henry Williams, Edward Chamberlin, Sidney Alexander and Paul Samuelson. True to the spirit of the IUI—that research should be undertaken in cooperation with the business community—Svennilson also visited some of the most important American industrial corporations, interacting with their managing directors and visiting their factories. He was impressed by their efficiency, which was, however, lowered in the instances where the trade unions had grown strong. Also, the basic conditions of the American industry differed considerably from those prevailing in Sweden, so in the end, Svennilson concluded that Sweden did not have all that much to learn from the United States. He continued to the universities of Chicago, Northwestern, UCLA, Berkeley and Cornell before he went back home.

Svennilson shared his American experience with the Swedish public in one journal article and four newspaper articles. In the former, he argued that The United States had an enormous need for industrial investment, something that by and large had been neglected since the beginning of the 1930s. In his first newspaper article, he took issue with Gunnar

Myrdal's prediction that the US would be hit by a postwar overproduction crisis.[30] Myrdal had not reckoned with the American consumer and what he had had to forsake during the war. The second article dealt with the influence of the trade unions and the attempts to balance their influence and that of the employers. The third surveyed issues of social care and income equalization and the last one dealt with the American economic policy environment and its organization. Altogether, Svennilson's reports clearly demonstrate that his American excursion had been eminently worthwhile.

Ingvar Svennilson returned to the United States in 1960, after having left the IUI for the Economic Commission of Europe in 1949. During this visit, he also received an invitation to go to Cuba, which he did for almost two weeks, together with his family. By and large, his Cuban trip was a vacation trip, but Svennilson also wrote an extremely interesting letter back home, to Jan Wallander, who was at the time the head of the IUI. Exactly like Axel Iveroth, he wanted to keep in touch with the institute.

Svennilson's Cuban report testifies to his ability to observe society. He arrived on the island not much more than a year after Fidel Castro had assumed command, at a point in time when the political future of Cuba was still in the scales. Svennilson had big eyes and ears. He knew no more about the country when he arrived than any other Swede, but he rapidly picked up on what was happening. The core of his letter is an attempt to understand the political stance of Fidel Castro, who at the time had not yet made it into the Communist camp.

Svennilson provides a clear-sighted account of Castro's behavior and the forces pulling him toward the left, notably the influence of Che Guevara. He paints a shorthand portrait of Havana and the Cubans and demonstrates that he had understood the economic problems of the country, notably the transition that it was undergoing from a market economy to a centrally planned economy, a transition that had just begun but the importance of which Svennilson managed to capture, and he analyzes the uneasy relation of Cuba with the United States.

[30] Myrdal (1944b).

Deep in the Heart of Värmland: Jan Wallander and the Class Society

Jan Wallander (1920–2016) is remembered in Sweden mainly as managing director (1970–78) and chairman of the board (1978–91) of Handelsbanken, one of our leading banks, where he changed the organizational culture in a way which deviated markedly from that of most other Swedish banks, for example by abolishing budgeting and by introducing a bonus system which covered all the employees of the bank, and not simply the top brass.

The present Chapter 7, however, deals with another, less well known, aspect of Jan Wallander's life, that of the researcher.[31] (Wallander always preferred the title of associate professor to that of managing director.) After studies at Stockholm College between 1941 and 1944—statistics, economics and political science—he was recruited by Ingvar Svennilson as a researcher at the Industrial Institute for Economic and Social Research. The following year, 1945, the institute was approached by the Uddeholm corporation. The latter—a forestry company—had problems with its personnel in Värmland. The lumberjacks left the forests for other jobs and the company was looking for methods that would allow it to keep its workforce. The responsibility for the project fell on the twenty-five-year-old bachelor of arts Jan Wallander.

Wallander spent a year on fieldwork in the Klarälven valley in Värmland, 1945–46, for what would in the end become his doctoral dissertation.[32] The latter essentially is a study in economic demography. Wallander mapped the flows of people out of and into the forest districts. This task required interviewing 983 individuals in 255 households. The original plan was to have university students conduct the interviews, but the power of attraction of the Värmland forests was far too low, so Wallander had to make the interviews himself together with three collaborators.

Part of the original field notes has survived. Chapter 7 uses these and some of Wallander's writings elsewhere to put together a sociological picture of a society that was dominated by the Uddeholm corporation,

[31] Wallander's early life and his time at the IUI is dealt with in Carlson and Lundahl (2019), mainly Chapters 7–9.

[32] Wallander (1948). The story of the work on the dissertation is found in Carlson and Lundahl (2014, Chapter 15).

from the top—the managing director of the omnipotent company—to the bottom—the local elderly poor. Wallander and his collaborators got to meet a cross-section of the people who lived in the area. The field notes provide a vivid picture of their environment, their daily chores, their place in an extremely hierarchic society, their hopes and frustrations and their relations to the Company, in short, a picture of a complete microcosmos. They are full of—completely candid—reflections of what the interviewers saw during various parts of the year.

The field experience in Värmland was an experience that Jan Wallander would never forget. He came from a Social Democratic family in Stockholm, but a family which belonged to the top of the Social Democratic establishment. As an adolescent Jan had met some of the leading figures in the Swedish labor movement. The Värmland experience was completely different. There, he met the rank and file of the party and could piece together a picture of what formed their social and political views of life.

Through the field notes, the reader gets to take place of precisely this. The vast majority of the interviewees generously supplied information of what the Uddeholm community looked like through their eyes, the workers about how they felt that they were treated by the company and the company directors of what they thought about the working habits of their laborers and their demands. With few exceptions, all the people that the Wallander team met were directly or indirectly dependent on the company and its activities, a company governed by patriarchal values and principles—for better and for worse—and where the behavior of certain bosses bred resentment among the workers and contributed to the decision to vote with the feet: either to leave the Klarälven valley or to opt for an industrial job in the area. In his memoirs, Wallander writes about the importance of his year in Värmland—an experience that stayed with him for the rest of his life.

The Swedish Public Sector: Erik Höök

The size of the public sector in Sweden has been the subject of an extensive and heated discussion since the 1960s. The sector grew especially since the beginning of the 1970s, while employment in the private sector shrank. This went on until the 1990s when the tide began to turn.[33]

[33] See e.g. Bjuggren and Johansson (2009).

One of the most debated issues has been what made the sector grow. Was growth a result mainly of political decisions or did demand factors play a major role?

What by and large triggered the debate was Erik Höök's (1920–1997) doctoral dissertation from 1962, *Den offentliga sektorns expansion* [The Expansion of the Public Sector],[34] a work which dealt with the period 1913–58. Höök had studied social sciences, including economics, in Uppsala, where he graduated in 1946 and continued to the licentiate degree there in 1954. He was recruited to the Industrial Institute for Economic and Social Research in 1948 and remained there until finishing his PhD in 1962. Before embarking on his five-year study of the expenditure share of the public sector he worked on a number of issues related to this subject, such as consumption, the service sector, child allowances, taxes and pensions. When he left the institute, Höök became head of the planning department at the Ministry of Finance, where he was responsible for the work on the long-term economic surveys. Between 1976 and 1985, he was the managing director of Jernkontoret.

Höök's work on the public sector began in 1957 and continued with a visit to the United States in the spring of 1958 in order to take stock of newer theories of the public sector. The year 1959 was spent on gathering statistics and during 1960, Höök analyzed the different expenditure areas.

In 1962, the dissertation was ready. Höök had been inspired mainly by the large project about consumption in Sweden which had been carried out at the IUI under the leadership of Ragnar Bentzel but also by Erik Dahmén's views of industrial structural transformation and Erik Ruist's productivity studies.[35] The theoretical foundation of Höök's study is, to the extent possible, the conventional consumption theory where the consumption of goods and services (including public ones) is determined by incomes, relative prices and consumer tastes. Höök discussed two types of expenditures: those complementary to private expenditures (e.g. roads and cars) and those that had been transferred from the private to the public sector (mainly social care). The overall income increase in Sweden had, in Höök's view, made for a smooth and steady demand-driven expansion of the public sector.

[34] Höök (1962).

[35] For an account of these, see Carlson and Lundahl (2019, Chapters 2, 12–13 and 15), respectively.

When Erik Höök defended his dissertation, he received strong criticism from both his opponents, Göran Ohlin and Ulrich Herz, who both found his thesis outrageous. The expansion of the public sector was supply, not demand, driven, propelled by political visions. Nevertheless, his work, they stated, provided a valuable contribution to financial statistics. The examination committee shared their views and awarded him a *cum laude*. The same viewpoints by and large appeared in the daily press and the professional journal reviews, and ten years later, when Höök applied for a chair in social policy at Stockholm University (which he did not get).

In the longer run, the main trace left by Höök's dissertation was his meticulous handling of the statistical material. This was cited in later studies of the public sector, while his views of the driving forces behind its expansion were quickly pushed into the background. What happened in the 1960s and thereafter was mainly the result of the political factors on the supply side.

Economics as Polemics: Bo Södersten

Bo Södersten (1931–2017) described a somewhat unusual professional trajectory. He came from a mineworker family in Dalarna but got the opportunity to study and graduate from high school, before he began to study economics and related subjects at Uppsala University. There he finished a licentiate degree with a thesis on the long-run development of the Swedish foreign trade.[36]

Thereafter, Bo moved to Stockholm University, for PhD studies, where, in 1964, he defended a theoretical dissertation on the effects of economic growth on foreign trade, with growth specified both as factor accumulation and technical change.[37] During the rest of the 1960s, after moving to Lund, he applied for various professorships before he finally got a chair in Gothenburg in 1971, and from there, he moved on to a chair in international economics in Lund in 1977. During this period, he worked on the books that he considered to be his best work: *International Economics*, the first modern textbook in the area—a work

[36] Södersten (1959).

[37] Södersten (1964).

that became a commercial success for several years, since it had no competitors.[38]

Bo Södersten was prone to get involved in polemics. Most of the time, he provoked the fights himself. His first major conflict came when he began to deal with the housing market. In 1963, he took issue with a book by Ragnar Bentzel, Assar Lindbeck and Ingemar Ståhl, which advocated deregulation of the Swedish housing market.[39] This led to a very long conflict with Lindbeck. That was, however, only the beginning. In 1978, he made the headlines after publishing a book that demonstrated that homeowners made substantial gains simply by living in their houses, since house prices increased rapidly over time, a fact not widely appreciated by the beneficiaries.[40]

Another controversial subject introduced by Bo was labor-managed firms. He was a convinced Socialist who had written a number of ideological essays, and when the idea that the workers and not the capitalists should be the ones running companies, he immediately grasped it and wrote extensively about it. His attempts to convince the Social Democratic Party of its excellence, however, fell through. The party leadership rejected it.

Bo's specialty was international economics, but the chair in Lund included development economics as well, so Bo also wrote shorter pieces on countries Cuba, Chile, Botswana, Swaziland and Namibia. At the same time, he produced a number of anthologies on various aspects of the Swedish economy.

Bo Södersten had a political heritage from home. His father, a mineworker, had been an active Social Democrat, and Bo shared his conviction. During his time in Uppsala, he had been a member of the Social Democratic student club, he had been a member of the editorial board of the Social Democratic journal *Tiden*, he had written extensively on Socialist subjects and he had spoken several times in political contexts. All this served to prepare him for his next step in life: that of the politician. In 1979, Bo was elected to Parliament for the Social Democrats. He remained there until 1988. His Parliament years, however, did not turn out the way he wanted. Bo was too much of an individualist to accept the

[38] Södersten (1970).

[39] Bentzel et al. (1963).

[40] Sandelin and Södersten (1978).

party discipline and he frequently got into conflicts with senior politicians. The result was that he never got the ministerial portfolio that he aspired to.

Bo's failure in Parliament turned him into a stern critic of his party. After leaving Parliament, he became more of a Liberal than a Social Democrat. This was manifested in a long series of critical newspaper articles on economic and social topics which one way or another were related to his old party. Article writing became more important than the production of academic articles and books. Bo wrote extensively on economic policy, he criticized what he thought was a completely oversized, low-productivity public sector and he claimed that the Social Democrats had made no contribution to the creation of the opulent modern Swedish society. Bo also criticized the Swedish pension system, defended nuclear power, condemned the child daycare system, pushed for university reform and criticized the Swedish immigration policy and the abuses of the Swedish welfare system, a system that needed reforms. He did not hesitate to accuse the Social Democratic party of centralization and breeding of incompetence, and he even suggested that a number of policy issues should be removed from Parliament and handled by experts instead. Swedish politics suffered from a number of systemic defects, most of all the decay of the welfare state.

It is difficult to know what drove Bo. He had made it from the mining community where he grew up to the top of the academic hierarchy, but that was not enough. It is obvious that his failure in Parliament had a lot to do with what he wrote. He never became minister, something that he resented very much. That prevented him from becoming a celebrity and he attempted to make up for that by constantly sticking his neck out with provoking articles on controversial subjects, to the detriment of his academic activities. Bo was a complex person who easily turned people off by his comments, but the people he liked he fully supported. You had to know how to handle him, but if you did, it was easy to like him.

Economic Doctrines: Rolf G. H. Henriksson

Arguably, the most knowledgeable person with respect to the Swedish history of doctrnes was Rolf G. H. Henriksson (1937–2020). He was a veritable encyclopedia for the period extending from Knut Wicksell to the late Stockholm School: Erik Lundberg and Ingvar Svennilson. Rolf worked in the intersection between economics and economic history, with the history of doctrines as the common denominator.

Rolf did his undergraduate studies at the Stockholm School of Economics, majoring in economics, for teachers like Bertil Ohlin, Erik Dahmén and Arthur Montgomery, persons who he would later also write about. In 1960, he left Stockholm for Northwestern University in Evanston, Illinois, where he began PhD studies, and later, the University of Texas at Austin, where he became an assistant professor. Rolf, however, was not quite satisfied with Austin, so he went back to Stockholm in the mid-1960s.

In 1969, Rolf Henriksson got his PhD at Northwestern, on a dissertation on the Swedish emigration to the United States between 1860 and 1910.[41] He worked with an approach inspired by Knut Wicksell, but a very personal one: a model where emigration determines the supply of labor which is determined by the emigration and the capital stock by the labor force through its savings. Rolf analyzed the effects on the capital-labor ratio of the economy of emigration and savings, concluding that the negative effects of emigration on the labor force were stronger than the reduction of savings, so the ratio increased. He also argued that wages increased as a result of emigration, due to the increased capital-labor ratio and changes in efficiency. Emigration also stimulated the structural transformation of the economy, since the emigrants mainly came from stagnating branches, and because it stimulated entrepreneurship. Altogether, the wave of emigration from Sweden to the United States was likely to have resulted in higher welfare at home.

The bulk of Rolf's writings after his dissertation dealt with the history of economic doctrines, mainly from a biographical perspective. He wanted to write the biography of Eli Heckscher, but unfortunately, no book came out of his efforts. What he produced were a few essays that all have in common that they map Heckscher's life and his dual role as an economist and an economic historian. Two contributions deviate from this pattern. The first one, co-authored by Mats Lundahl, deals with Heckscher's constant preoccupation with methodology.[42] The second provides a detailed account of Heckscher's early years as a social scientist.[43]

[41] Henriksson (1969).

[42] Henriksson and Lundahl (2003).

[43] Henriksson (2006).

Rolf wrote a book chapter on the conception of Bertil Ohlin's doctoral dissertation in connection with a symposium on the occasion of the centennial of Ohlin's birth.[44] More importantly, however, he on several occasions dealt with the life and works of Erik Lundberg. He edited a book on Lundberg's period as director of the National Institute of Economic Research [Konjunkturinstitutet], and a volume of Lundberg's articles, he provided a thoroughly researched biography and a bibliography of his works for an internationally published book on Lundberg and he dealt in detail with Lundberg's licentiate thesis. Another economist to whom Rolf devoted a great deal of attention was Erik Dahmén. He was one of the editors of the festschrift for Dahmén's seventy-fifth birthday, he wrote a chapter in another book to Dahmén, published five years later, and as he had done with Lundberg, he wrote a piece on the works of the very young Dahmén.[45]

Rolf Henriksson also continued the research on economic institutions begun with his work on the National Institute of Economic Research with pieces on the Political Economy Club and the Swedish Economic Association. Most important, however, was his only published book, on the Industrial Institute for Economic and Social Research, where he tells the story of the foundation of the institute in 1939 and its first years, until 1943.[46]

Rolf Henriksson was a very thorough researcher—too thorough. His urge to penetrate everything written about a subject before he put anything on paper himself acted as a formidable brake on his productivity. His collected output is not large. Given his erudition, this was a pity. He conveyed so much in face-to-face conversations, but when it came to writing his ideas down he always hesitated, too often to the point where things came to nothing.

Deregulation of Agriculture: Ingemar Ståhl

Ingemar Ståhl (1938–2014) was one of those brightly shining young comets that became professors at an early age: in his case 33, at Lund

[44] Henriksson (2002).

[45] See Chapter 10 for references.

[46] Henriksson (1990).

University in 1971.[47] He had grown up in Stockholm and studied social sciences at Stockholm College, with economics as his main subject. He also spent a year at Oslo University. Ingemar was an active Social Democrat who made useful contacts with people who would make it to the top of the party hierarchy. He got involved in no less than seven different government committees in the 1960s: indexation, financing of university studies, defense program budgeting, energy, defense costs, education and ports. The first of these assignments also led to his licentiate thesis on portfolio choice.[48] (He never wrote any doctoral dissertation. It was a pity that he got his chair before.) During the same period, he participated in the writing of a widely debated book on the regulation of the Swedish housing market together with Ragnar Bentzel and Assar Lindbeck.[49]

Ingemar's works during the 1960s and early 1970s were anchored in the welfare economic tradition, but during the same time, he also began to be exposed to a different research approach. It was Ingemar Ståhl who introduced public choice in Sweden. This he did in a survey of the theory, some of which he applied to the Swedish mixed economy.[50] He would later apply his newly acquired insights to agriculture, housing and labor market issues. During the same period, partly as a result of his conversion from welfare economics to public choice, he also underwent a political conversion, from Social Democracy to Liberalism.

One of the most important contributions that Ingemar Ståhl made to the public choice analysis of the Swedish economy was his analysis of the regulation of Swedish agriculture. The latter had been subject to administrative interventions ever since the first world war. The interwar period in particular had seen the introduction of politically motivated measures designed to 'correct' the outcome of the actions of producers and consumers in the market. To be able to push their active employment policy through the Parliament, the Social Democrats had to strike the deal which in Swedish political history is known as the 'cow trade'

[47] For biographies of Ingemar Ståhl, see Jonung (2018) and Jonung and Jonung (2018, 2020).

[48] Ståhl (1964).

[49] Bentzel et al. (1963).

[50] Ståhl (1977).

with the Agrarian Party, a deal which led to tariff protection for Swedish agricultural products.[51]

Protectionism continued to dominate the Swedish agricultural policy also after the end of the Second World War. The farmers' organizations had managed to build a strong position with plenty of political clout. A number of government committees were appointed to look into possible changes of policy, but they all had in common that they had been given terms of reference that only allowed for a choice between different types of regulations. The main purpose of the policy was to keep farmer incomes up, and to that end, the issue of deregulation was never raised. The economist committee members regularly filed dissenting opinions but to no avail. Two influential books, by Odd Gulbrandsen and Assar Lindbeck, which clarified the welfare consequences of the policy, in spite of a widespread readership, could do nothing to change the situation.[52]

The above was the situation when Ingemar Ståhl made his appearance on the Swedish agricultural scene, in 1984, with a book written together with Olof Bolin and Per-Martin Meyerson, *Makten över maten*, translated as *The Political Economy of the Food Sector: The Case of Sweden*.[53] The public choice analysis in that book (written by Ingemar) differed completely from everything that had been published on the subject before, in that it laid bare the positions of each of the interest groups involved. And it posed the 'forbidden' question: What would happen if the Swedish agricultural sector—not just production but also the later stages in the commercialization chain—was deregulated?

It was clear that the agricultural policy which had been in use during the postwar period had not contributed to the fulfillment of two of its proudly professed goals: efficiency in production and food security. The farmer income target had dominated completely. This was a well-known fact, but nothing had been done to change it. Ingemar analyzed the reasons in terms of a game between interest groups, with the farmer organizations as the dominant one. They were the ones favored by the regulations. If the latter were abolished, the Swedish surplus production would disappear, food prices would be reduced, the capital requirements

[51] The history of agricultural protection in Sweden is dealt with in Hedlund and Lundahl (1985).

[52] Gulbrandsen and Lindbeck (1966, 1969).

[53] Bolin et al. (1984), English version, Bolin et al. (1986)

for new farms would be lowered and the policy would become more transparent.

The farmer interests reacted strongly to the analysis, suggesting that Ingemar and his two colleagues did not understand how the agricultural sector worked and that deregulation would be tantamount to catastrophe for the sector. They were, however, fighting a losing battle, for the prevailing mood within the governing Social Democratic party had begun to change, and in 1991, Sweden changed its food policy with the introduction of a market-based food policy. The farmers, however, lost only in the short run, for at the end of 1994, Sweden joined the European Union whose Common Agricultural Policy made the former Swedish regulations almost resemble free trade.

A Moose Hunter at the Riksbank: Villy Bergström

Villy Bergström (1938–2018) never failed to impress the people who met him. There was nothing artificial about him. Villy was as natural and sincere as could be, never politically correct, and always proffered his own opinion in a straightforward way. He came from the Horndal in Dalarna, famous for the 'Horndal effect,' the technical progress later known as learning by doing. As the family moved to Grängesberg, Villy became the classmate of Bo Södersten's nephew Lars Ramqvist, who would become the chief executive officer and chairman of the board of Ericsson. It was Bo who inspired Villy to take up the study of economics.

This he did at Uppsala. He began there in 1959, with statistics for Herman Wold, and then moved on to economics and Tord Palander. Both professors were known to be great eccentrics, difficult to deal with, but Villy, who had been a convinced Social Democrat from his early youth, felt that he needed economics in order to understand society better and to underpin his political views. Hence, after his graduation, he decided to go on and get a licentiate degree, under the auspices of Ragnar 'Naja' Bentzel, Palander's successor.

Villy's licentiate thesis dealt with his favorite topic: Swedish economic policy. It combines a historical survey with a presentation of the economic theory of economic policy and an attempt to evaluate the Swedish policy between the two world wars and during the postwar period.[54] Economic

[54] Bergström (1969).

policy was close to Villy's heart, and he would maintain his interest in it during his entire life, as a means for changing society in a socialist direction.

Villy's thesis was written in connection with his association with the Industrial Institute for Economic and Social Research in Stockholm, but he also taught economics at Uppsala, where he continued his studies toward a doctorate. His doctoral dissertation dealt with industrial investment in Sweden after the second world war.[55] Although formally published as a monograph, it consisted of four separate chapters which today would have been turned into journal articles: a survey of the rules governing the industrial capital formation, a model of the capital cost of industrial firms, estimates of production functions and factor demand functions, and finally, disaggregated estimates of investment demand.

Villy defended his doctoral dissertation in 1981 when he also was awarded the title of *docent* [associate professor]. The work on the dissertation had dragged out. The reason was simple: Villy's interest in politics, made him undertake frequent detours from the academic road. He was a member of the editorial team of *Tiden* and that of *Ekonomisk Debatt* and he was engaged in the yearly surveys of Swedish economic policy carried out by Center for Business and Policy Studies [Studieförbundet Näringsliv och Samhälle, SNS].

Villy also participated in the debate about the wage-earners' funds proposed by the trade union movement in 1971, which aimed at increased worker company ownership, and which became a red-hot topic over the next few years. Villy published his own analysis of them in the book *Kapitalbildning och industriell demokrati* [Capital Formation and Industrial Democracy],[56] a book where he made the connection between the funds and the old Social Democratic call for industrial democracy and increased worker influence. A few years after the publication of this book, by claiming that nominally independent economists were in fact hostile to the labor movement, in a publication celebrating centenary of the Swedish Economic Association, Villy managed to aggravate Assar Lindbeck to the point where the latter decided to leave the association.[57]

[55] Bergström (1982).

[56] Bergström (1973).

[57] Bergström (1977).

Already before defending his dissertation, Villy left academia, first for the National Institute for Working Life, until 1984, and thereafter to head the newly created Trade Union Institute for Economic Research, where he remained until 1995 when he became the editor in chief of the daily *Dala-Demokraten*. His last active years, between 1999 and 2005, he spent as a deputy governor at the Riksbank, where his contract stipulated that he had the right to take time off for the yearly moose hunt.

You could not cheat Villy. He was a keen observer who reported what he saw. He never demonstrated his ability better than when he visited North Korea in 1971 as a member of a three-man delegation of Swedish Socialists. The visit resulted in a strangely dualistic book where one member fell back almost entirely on Kim Il-sung's collected works, while Villy contrasted the official rhetoric with the poor on-the-ground reality that he saw with his own eyes—two completely different worlds.[58]

All Too Soon: Göte Hansson

Göte Hansson (1950–2012) was my student and one of my main collaborators. I supervised his dissertation, we wrote and supervised together, we shared an interest in development economics and Africa, and he was my boss when he was chair of the department of economics in Lund. Göte had a strong analytical ability which he brought out in his main works. His specialty was international economics, which naturally made him use general equilibrium theory extensively.

After finishing a bachelor of arts with economics, mathematics, and information processing, Göte wrote his doctoral dissertation on social clauses in international trade, a topic which had become widely discussed in the early 1970s. The debate was, however, characterized less by analytical and factual insights than by emotional and political standpoints.[59] A social clause means that exporting countries undertake to observe certain minimum standards as far as working conditions, etc. are concerned. If not, the importing countries have the right to introduce tariffs and other impediments to trade. Göte's contribution was that on the one hand, he analyzed the economic effects of differently formulated social clauses on the incomes of various groups in the economies of the countries trading

[58] Bergström and Wickman (1972).

[59] Hansson (1983).

with each other and on the other hand compared them with the effects of traditional protectionist measures. His dissertation was an essay in political economy which allowed him to draw conclusions with respect to the likelihood that social clauses would contribute to the improvement of working standards.

Göte's next book dealt with a theme that was related to that of his dissertation and which used the same methodology. The theme was international harmonization of economic policy as a measure above all to increase the efficiency of the international allocation of resources—another widely discussed topic.[60] Göte analyzed six different areas of harmonization: trade policy, technical standards, working conditions, environmental policy, fiscal policy and monetary policy. In the same way as in the book on social clauses he deduced the effects of harmonization on the welfare of different groups and discussed the probability that harmonization would be introduced in each of these cases.

The step from social clauses to development economics was a small one. When the Swedish International Development Authority (SIDA) in the late 1980s commissioned a few university economics departments to do macroeconomic country studies, Göte undertook to analyze Ethiopia, a country which had been experienced the effects of a Socialist command economy of the Soviet type and which at the time was involved in an effort to restructure its economy along more market-oriented lines. He wrote close to a dozen studies on the subject, culminating with his book *The Ethiopian Economy 1974–94:* Ethiopia Tikdem *and After*,[61] where he dealt with the results of the Socialist policy and the probable effects of the different proposed reform measures.

Having analyzed Ethiopia, it was natural that Göte would also be allotted Eritrea when the latter became independent in 1993. He made four studies for Sida on different economic and political aspects of the new country: the effort to build the state, the liberalization of the economic system which Eritrea had inherited from Ethiopia, the development of the economy and the political and economic tensions with Ethiopia.

Göte Hansson obtained his professorship in international economics at Lund University in 1997, after a process that brought out some of the worst instincts of some of his colleagues. A number of professors who

[60] Hansson (1990).

[61] Hansson (1995).

had nothing to do with the appointment undertook a concerted, orchestrated, effort to prevent him from getting the chair, but failed. Göte was a skilled economist and also a skilled administrator. He served as head of the economics department in Lund and as subdean and dean of the faculty of social sciences and was also involved in three instances of international university cooperation, most notably with economic institutions in Dar es Salaam and Arusha in Tanzania. Unfortunately, his time on earth was cut short by carcinoid, an intestinal tumor which metastasized to the liver, which he, however, managed to keep at bay during twenty years before he left us in 2012—all too soon.

References

Bentzel, Ragnar; Lindbeck, Assar and Ståhl, Ingemar (1963), *Bostadsbristen: En studie av prisbildningen på bostadsmarknaden*. Stockholm: Almqvist & Wiksell.

Bergström, Villy (1969), *Den ekonomiska politiken i Sverige och dess verkningar*. Stockholm: Industriens Utredningsinstitut and Almqvist & Wiksell.

Bergström, Villy (1973), *Kapitalbildning och industriell demokrati. Socialdemokratiska perspektiv*. Stockholm: Tidens förlag.

Bergström, Villy (1977), 'Nationalekonomerna och arbetarrörelsen', in: Jan Herin och Lars Werin (eds), *Ekonomisk debatt och ekonomisk politik: Nationalekonomiska Föreningen 100 år*. Stockholm: Norstedts.

Bergström, Villy (1982), *Studies in Post-War Swedish Industrial Investments*. Uppsala: Studia Oeconomica Upsaliensia.

Bergström Villy and Wickman, Kurt (1972), *Bilder från Nordkorea*. Stockholm: Tidens förlag.

Bjuggren, Carl Magnus and Johansson, Dan (2009), 'Privat och offentlig sysselsättning i Sverige 1950–2005', *Ekonomisk Debatt*, Vol. 37, No. 1, 41–53.

Bolin. Olof; Meyerson, Per-Martin and Ståhl, Ingemar, under medverkan av Kjell-Åke Brorsson, Ingemar Haraldsson och Ewa Rabinowicz (1984), *Makten över maten: Livsmedelssektorns politiska ekonomi*. Stockholm: Studieförbundet Näringsliv och Samhälle.

Bolin, Olof; Meyerson, Per-Martin and Ståhl, Ingemar, with contributions by Kjell-Åke Brorsson, Ingemar Haraldsson and Ewa Rabinowicz (1986), *The Political Economy of the Food Sector: The Case of Sweden*. Stockholm: SNS Förlag.

Carlson, Benny and Lundahl, Mats (2014), *Ett forskningsinstitut växer fram: IUI från grundandet till 1950*. Stockholm: Ekerlids Förlag.

Carlson, Benny and Lundahl, Mats (2019), *Ett forskningsinstitut expanderar: IUI från 1950 till 1966*. Stockholm: Ekerlids Förlag.

Cassel, Gustav (1918), *Theoretische Sozialökonomie*. Leipzig: C.F. Winter.

Gulbrandsen, Odd and Lindbeck, Assar (1966), *Jordbrukspolitikens mål och medel*. Stockholm: Industriens Utredningsinstitut.

Gulbrandsen, Odd and Lindbeck, Assar (1969), *Jordbruksnäringens ekonomi*. Stockholm: Almqvist & Wiksell.

Hansson, Göte (1983), *Social Clauses and International Trade*. London and Canberra: Croom Helm; New York: St. Martin's Press.

Hansson, Göte (1990), *Harmonization and International Trade*. London and New York: Routledge.

Hansson, Göte (1995), *The Ethiopian Economy 1974–94:* Ethiopia Tikdem *and After*. London and New York: Routledge.

Heckscher, Eli F. (1919), 'Utrikeshandelns inverkan på inkomstfördelningen. Några teoretiska grundlinjer', *Ekonomisk Tidskrift*, Vol. 21, No. 2, 1–32.

Heckscher, Eli F. (1922), *The Continental System: An Economic Interpretation*. Oxford: Clarendon Press.

Heckscher, Eli F. (1935a), *Mercantilism*. London: George Allen & Unwin.

Heckscher, Eli F. (1935b), *Sveriges ekonomiska historia från Gustav Vasa. Första delen. Före Frihetstiden. Första boken. Medeltidshushållningens organisering 1520–1600*. Stockholm: Albert Bonniers förlag.

Heckscher, Eli F. (1936), *Sveriges ekonomiska historia från Gustav Vasa. Första delen. Före Frihetstiden. Andra boken. Hushållningen under internationell påverkan 1600–1720*. Stockholm: Albert Bonniers förlag.

Heckscher, Eli F. (1949a), *Sveriges ekonomiska historia från Gustav Vasa. Andra delen. Det moderna Sveriges grundläggning. Första halvbandet*. Stockholm: Albert Bonniers förlag.

Heckscher, Eli F. (1949b), *Sveriges ekonomiska historia från Gustav Vasa. Andra delen. Det moderna Sveriges grundläggning. Andra halvbandet*. Stockholm: Albert Bonniers förlag.

Heckscher, Eli F. (1949c), 'The Effect of Foreign Trade on the Distribution of Income', in: Howard S. Ellis and Lloyd A. Metzler (eds), *Readings in the Theory of International Trade*. London: George Allen & Unwin.

Hedlund, Stefan and Lundahl, Mats (1985), *Beredskap eller protektionism? En studie av beredskapsmålet i svensk jordbrukspolitik*. Malmö: Liber Förlag.

Henriksson, Rolf G.H. (1969), *An Interpretation of the Significance of Emigration for the Growth of Economic Welfare in Sweden, 1860–1910*. PhD thesis. Evanston, IL: Northwestern University.

Henriksson, Rolf G.H. (1990), *Som Edström ville – hur IUI blev till*. Stockholm: Industriens Utredningsinstitut.

Henriksson, Rolf G.H. (2002), 'Eureka Unter den Linden: A Reinterpretation of Ohlin's Early Contributions to the Heckscher-Ohlin Theme', in: Ronald Findlay, Lars Jonung and Mats Lundahl (eds), *Bertil Ohlin: A Centennial Celebration (1899–1999)*. Cambridge, MA and London: MIT Press.

Henriksson, Rolf G.H. (2006), 'The Making of the Economic Historian: Eli F. Heckscher, 1897–1904', in: Ronald Findlay, Rolf G.H. Henriksson, Håkan Lindgren and Mats Lundahl (eds), *Eli Heckscher, International Trade, and Economic History*. Cambridge, MA and London: MIT Press.

Henriksson, Rolf G.H. and Lundahl, Mats (2003), 'Inledning', in: *Janusansiktet Eli Heckscher: Nationalekonom och ekonomisk historiker*. Texter i urval av Rolf G H Henriksson och Mats Lundahl. Stockholm: Timbro.

Höök, Erik (1962), *Den offentliga sektorns expansion: En studie av de offentliga civila utgifternas utveckling 1913–1958*. Uppsala: Almqvist & Wiksell.

Iveroth, Axel (1943), *Småindustri och hantverk i Sverige*. Stockholm: Industriens Utredningsinstitut.

Jonung, Christina and Jonung, Lars (eds) (2018), *Ingemar Ståhl – en ekonom för blandekonomin*. Stockholm: Dialogos.

Jonung, Christina and Jonung, Lars (eds) (2020), *Ingemar Ståhl. A Market Liberal in the Swedish Welfare State*. Stockholm: Dialogos.

Jonung, Lars (2018), 'Ekonomporträtt: Ingemar Ståhl 1938–2014', *Ekonomisk Debatt*, Vol. 46, No. 5, 61–73.

Lewin, Leif (1967), *Planhushållningsdebatten*. Stockholm: Almqvist & Wiksells Tryckeri AB.

Lundahl, Mats (2015), *Seven Figures in the History of Swedish Economic Thought: Knut Wicksell, Eli Heckscher, Bertil Ohlin, Torsten Gårdlund, Sven Rydenfelt, Staffan Burenstam Linder and Jaime Behar*. Houndmills, Basingstoke and New York: Palgrave Macmillan.

Myrdal, Gunnar (1927), *Prisbildningsproblemet och föränderligheten*. Uppsala and Stockholm: Almqvist & Wicksells Förlag.

Myrdal, Gunnar (1930), *Vetenskap och politik i nationalekonomien*. Stockholm: P.A. Norstedt & Söners Förlag.

Myrdal, Gunnar (1931), 'Om penningteoretisk jämvikt. En studie över den "normala räntan" i Wicksells penninglära', *Ekonomisk Tidskrift*, Vol. 33, Nos. 5–6, 191–302.

Myrdal, Gunnar (1933), 'Der Gleichwichtsbegriff als Instrument der geldtheoretischen Analyse', in: Friedrich A. Hayek (ed.), *Beiträge zur Geldtheorie*. Wien: Julius Springer.

Myrdal, Gunnar (1939), *Monetary Equilibrium*. London: William Hodge & Co.

Myrdal, Gunnar, with the assistance of Richard Sterner and Arnold Rose (1944a), *An American Dilemma: The Negro Problem and Modern Democracy*. New York and London: Harper & Brothers Publishers.

Myrdal, Gunnar (1944b), *Varning för fredsoptimism*. Stockholm: Albert Bonniers Förlag.

Myrdal, Gunnar (1953), *The Political Element in the Development of Economic Theory*. London: Routledge & Kegan Paul.

Myrdal, Gunnar (1956a), *An International Economy: Problems and Prospects*. New York: Harper & Brothers Publishers.

Myrdal, Gunnar (1956b), *Development and Under-Development: A Note on the Mechanism of National and International Economic Inequality*. Cairo: National Bank of Egypt.

Myrdal, Gunnar (1957), *Economic Theory and Under-Developed Regions*. London: Gerald Duckworth & Co.

Myrdal, Gunnar (1968), *Asian Drama: An Inquiry Into the Poverty of Nations*. 3 Volumes. New York: The Twentieth Century Fund.

Myrdal, Gunnar (1970), *The Challenge of World Poverty: A World Anti-Poverty Program in Outline*. New York: Pantheon Books.

Ohlin, Bertil (1922), *Det interregionala bytets teori*. Stockholm: Licentiate thesis, Stockholms Högskola [Stockholm College].

Ohlin, Bertil (1924), *Handelns teori*. Stockholm: AB Nordiska Bokhandeln.

Ohlin, Bertil (1933), *Interregional and International Trade*. Cambridge, MA: Harvard University Press.

Ohlin, Bertil (1972), *Bertil Ohlins memoarer: Ung man blir politiker*. Stockholm: Bonniers.

Ohlin, Bertil (1991), *The Theory of Trade*, in: Harry Flam and M. June Flanders (eds), *Heckscher-Ohlin Trade Theory*. Cambridge, MA and London: MIT Press.

Ohlin, Bertil (2002), 'The Theory of Interregional Exchange', in: Ronald Findlay, Lars Jonung and Mats Lundahl (eds), *Bertil Ohlin: A Centennial Celebration (1899–1999)*. Cambridge, MA and London: MIT Press.

Sandelin, Bo and Södersten, Bo (1978), *Betalt för att bo: Värdestegring och kapitalvinster på bostadsmarknaden*. Stockholm: Rabén & Sjögren.

Södersten, Bo (1959), *Studier i den långsiktiga utvecklingen av svensk utrikeshandel*. Uppsala: Nationalekonomiska institutionen vid Uppsala universitet.

Södersten, Bo (1964), *A Study of Economic Growth and International Trade*. Stockholm: Almqvist & Wiksell.

Södersten, Bo (1970), *International Economics*. London and Basingstoke: Macmillan.

Ståhl, Ingemar (1964), *Risk- och avkastningsförändringars verkningar på portföljsammansättning, konsumtion och produktion*. FOA P Rapport C 129. Stockholm: Försvarets forskningsanstalt, Planeringsbyrån.

Ståhl, Ingemar (1977), 'En ekonomisk teori för blandekonomin', in: *Erfarenheter av blandekonomin. Uppsatser och diskussioner vid Dahmén-symposiet om den svenska blandekonomin, Saltsjöbaden 18–19 oktober 1976*. Stockholm: Skandinaviska Enskilda Banken.

Svennilson, Ingvar (1938), *Ekonomisk planering: Teoretiska studier*. Uppsala: Almqvist & Wiksells Tryckeri AB.

Svennilson, Ingvar (1954), *Growth and Stagnation in the European Economy*. Geneva: United Nations Economic Commission for Europe.
Wallander, Jan (1948), *Flykten från skogsbygden: En undersökning i Klarälvsdalen*. Stockholm: Industriens Utredningsinstitut.
Wicksell, Knut (1898), *Geldzins und Güterpreise. Eine Studie über den Tauschwert des Geldes bestimmenden Ursachen*. Jena: Verlag von Gustav Fischer.
Wicksell, Knut (1936), *Interest and Prices: A Study of the Causes Regulating the Value of Money*. London: Macmillan and Co.

CHAPTER 2

The Inspiration for the Heckscher–Ohlin Theorem

Is it actually true that Isaac Newton arrived at his theory of gravity by seeing an apple fall from a tree in his mother's garden in Lincolnshire in 1666? And did it really hit him on the head? I don't know and, as it seems, nobody else knows for sure either. Newton left no written account of the alleged event, but only mentioned it several decades later to other persons.[1] Where does this leave us? Certainly with a good and picturesque story—but is it true? Who cares anyway? True or untrue, it provides a good metaphor for physics classroom use. Maybe we had better leave it at that.

What inspires scientific and artistic work? I guess that the only plausible answer to that question is that it varies and that it is due to the particular circumstances of each case. As is well known, love relations or otherwise intimate partnerships are capable of inspiring and stimulating creativity. The anthology *Significant Others: Creativity and Intimate Partnership*, edited by Whitney Chadwick and Isabelle de Courtivron,[2] contains the following formidable list of twosomes: Camille Claudel and Auguste Rodin, Sonia and Robert Delaunay, Clara and André Malraux, Vanessa Bell and Duncan Grant, Virginia Woolf and Vita Sackville-West, Leonora

[1] Notably to his first biographer, William Stukeley (2004). Cf. also Connor (2010).

[2] Chadwick and de Courtivron (1993).

M. Lundahl, *Twelve Figures in Swedish Economics*, Palgrave Studies in the History of Economic Thought, https://doi.org/10.1007/978-3-030-94327-1_2

Carrington and Max Ernst, Frida Kahlo and Diego Rivera, Kay Sage and Yves Tanguy, Anaïs Nin and Henry Miller, Lillian Hellman and Dashiell Hammett, Jasper Johns and Robert Rauschenberg, Simone and André Schwartz-Bart, Lee Krasner and Jackson Pollock.

The list is limited to art and literature, but it is not difficult to find examples also in economics. The prime Swedish case—and the best documented—is of course Alva and Gunnar Myrdal, who inspired each other and often wrote together for almost a lifetime,[3] but it is not hard to find other examples. The book *Par i vetenskap och politik: intellektuella äktenskap i moderniteten* [Couples in Science and Politics: Intellectual Marriages in Modernity], edited by Annika Berg, Christina Florin and Per Wisselgren,[4] among others deals with six couples involving economists: in addition to the Myrdals, Knut Wicksell and Anna Bugge, Gustaf and Oskara Steffen, Gustav and Johanna Cassel, Eli and Ebba Heckscher, and finally, Karin Kock and Hugo Lindberg.[5]

In the cases listed above, the cause–effect relationship runs from the people to the work. It is, however, also conceivable that it runs in the opposite direction: that a work stimulates an artist, a writer, a musician or a scientist in the process of creation. Could the arts provide inspiration for economic writing? My colleague Tönu Puu—economist and baroque viol builder—has raised the fundamental issue of 'the basic unity of all creative activities: arts, crafts, and sciences.'[6] We should hence not be afraid to delve into the relationships between these three activities.

[3] See e.g. Myrdal and Myrdal (2003), Vinterhed (2003) and Hederberg (2004).

[4] Berg et al. (2011).

[5] The international scene of course abounds with similar relations, e.g. John Stuart Mill and Harriet Taylor and Milton and Rose Friedman, to name but two. Writing the present essay, I have had my own partner. I have benefited—immensely, as always—from the view of my rooftop terrace in Torremolinos, Spain, looking at a most spectacular show that Mother Nature has chosen to offer to me: the August moon rising out of the Mediterranean: a slight slice of orange peel coming out of the sea, growing bigger and bigger and bigger; in just a few minutes you have a whole orange, gradually rising, first producing an orange colored and later, a silvery, path in the water as the moon itself turns from orange to silver. I don't know how many times I have witnessed this hypnotic scene, but it easily beats any piece of human art. Looking into the eyes of the Man in the Moon, as he makes it out of the sea, always puts you into a contemplative mood which, in my case, has certainly made it easier to face Heckscher and Ohlin as well.

[6] Puu (1990, p. 19). Cf. also Puu (2006).

The Heckscher–Ohlin Theorem

The present essay has been written on the occasion of the inauguration of the Heckscher-Ohlin room at the Stockholm School of Economics—a room that has been converted from a traditional venue for lunches and dinners filled with oil paintings of former professors at the school to an 'art' room, dominated by a large-scale work by Jens Fänge, where the only vestiges of its former appearance are the two portraits of Eli F. Heckscher and Bertil Ohlin. The writing of the Heckscher–Ohlin theorem is literally on the wall, as it were.

What is commonly known as the Heckscher–Ohlin theorem is usually presented in the textbooks in its standardized two-by-two-by two version: two countries, with the same production technologies, both producing the same two goods with the aid of two factors of production with production functions that are linearly homogeneous, not displaying any economics of scale. The two factors are commonly thought of as capital and labor, mobile inside each country but not across national borders. In this setting, trade is caused by differences in factor endowments between the two countries. The demand side is neutralized by assuming uniform, homothetic preferences. (Consumers with different incomes, but facing the same prices, will demand goods in the same proportions.) The theorem states that each of the two countries will export the good which uses its relatively abundant production factor intensively and import the good using its relatively scarce production factor intensively.

The above is not the way that Heckscher and Ohlin formulated their analysis.[7] As is often the case in economics, later generations of economists picked up their ideas and steeped them into a different form, a form more suitable for mathematical formalization.[8] Eli Heckscher and Bertil Ohlin, however, provided the fundamentals, the original ideas, the source of inspiration for the following generations of international

[7] Heckscher's formulation is in Heckscher (1919b), English translation in Heckscher (1991), Ohlin's progressively in Ohlin (1922)—English translation Ohlin (2002)—Ohlin (1924)—English translation Ohlin (1991)—and Ohlin (1933). For an overview of the contributions of Heckscher and Ohlin, respectively, see the essays in Findlay et al. (2002, 2006). Cf. also Flam and Flanders (1991) and Lundahl (2015b).

[8] A parallel case is that of Keynes. See Leijonhufvud (1968). The reformulation of Heckscher's and Ohlin's ideas is due to Abba Lerner, in an unpublished seminar paper from 1933 (published later as Lerner, 1952) and Paul Samuelson (Stolper and Samuelson, 1941; Samuelson, 1948, 1949).

trade theorists, Heckscher in his famous 1919 article, 'The Effect of Foreign Trade on the Distribution of Income' (in Swedish), and Ohlin in his cascading trilogy, *The Theory of Interregional Exchange* (1922), *The Theory of Trade* (1924) (both in Swedish) and *Interregional and International Trade* (1933). Without these works there would not have been any theorem—however formulated. Bertil Ohlin received the Sveriges Riksbank Prize in Economic Sciences in Memory of Alfred Nobel in 1977, together with James Meade. Eli Heckscher died on 23 December 1952. Had he been alive in 1977, Ohlin would have shared the prize with him, not with James Meade.

Heckscher and Ohlin inspired the redecoration of the Heckscher–Ohlin room at the Stockholm School of Economics. But what inspired Heckscher and Ohlin when they developed the ideas that with time became known as the Heckscher–Ohlin theorem in the canon of economics? Was it art? Unfortunately, given the occasion, it was not. To the extent that this is possible, the remainder of the present essay will spell out the real sources of inspiration for Heckscher and Ohlin. Let us begin with Heckscher.

Heckscher's Sources of Inspiration: The Sugar Tariff Issue

Eli Heckscher's interest in theoretical issues of international trade began with his involvement in the contemporary Swedish discussion of protectionism, mainly on two occasions. The first was the debate on tariffs that took place in Sweden on the eve of World War I. In the late nineteenth century, Sweden had followed the 'German' pattern of agricultural protectionism, a policy that led to increased food prices in general. (Grain tariffs had been introduced in 1888.)[9] The tendency had continued during the following decades in most of Western Europe. Heckscher condemned the system:

> The real, true, situation with respect to the treaty situation of the latest decades has been that it has simply constituted a pretext for *increasing* tariffs in virtually all countries. On the pretext of having to 'arm' yourself for the negotiations, a number of new or increased tariff rates have been adopted. […] … it does not require too much intelligence to understand

[9] Schön (2014, pp. 177–178).

that the adversary ... would do the same. In the best case, the outcome thus would be the same situation as prevailed before the negotiations began, i.e. status quo; in the worse, and more common, cases, however, both countries ended up with *higher* tariffs than before the beginning of the game. A more distinct mock battle than the one represented by this system during the twentieth century is certainly hard to find.[10]

In 1913, the Social Democrats tabled a proposal in Parliament that urged a reduction of the general tariff level by 10% in order to keep the general price level down.[11] The sugar tariff level stood out as notoriously high. At the time, a rate of between 40 almost 47%, depending on the world market price—between four and five times the average Swedish tariff level—was imposed on refined sugar.[12] Beet sugar production had begun in Sweden in the 1850s and the output of raw sugar had increased almost 80-fold from the late 1870s to 1913. The industry had been protected throughout this period.[13]

In November 1911, Heckscher had given two lectures on the relationship between tariff policy and trusts.[14] Two years later, he published his ideas in an article in *Ekonomisk Tidskrift*.[15] This article focused mainly on the sugar tariff. Heckscher was irritated, because the 'public opinion,' which he equated with the press,[16] had come out against the reduction proposal. The 'sugar war' was on.[17] Heckscher saw it proper 'for the scientists to whose field the question belongs' to step in and state their opinion.[18] Their verdict should, however, 'if possible be kept within the boundaries of science without looking askance at what is politically

[10] Heckscher (1919a, pp. 32, 33).

[11] Brock (1917, p. 7).

[12] Ibid., p. 8.

[13] SOU 1924:38, pp. 135–144, gives the details.

[14] Heckscher (1913), note, p. 1.

[15] Heckscher (1913).

[16] Heckscher (1913, p. 8).

[17] Herlitz (2002, p. 485).

[18] Heckscher (1913, p. 1).

feasible. The politicians ought to do something useful too and the scientists damage themselves by usurping their [work].'[19] Having said that, he immediately revealed his theoretical bent:

> Attempts to produce a purely scientific judgement of a concrete economic question are very easily condemned as 'theoretic'. But what do you actually mean by that? Either the reasoning is valid, and then it does not matter if it is theoretic, or else it is unsustainable and then it is enough to demonstrate that. The only really practical exercise consists in presenting things as they are, not just as they seem to be, according to your ability. Only the former has any importance and only in the context of the former does science serve any purpose.[20]

This was the approach that Heckscher brought to bear on the sugar tariff issue. A reduction of the tariff level could not be discussed simply from the technical tax point of view. On the contrary, the issue had 'released a host of false economic conclusions of the most elementary kind.'[21] Heckscher saw it as his task to demonstrate why the sugar tariff had been questioned.

The sugar tariff article deals with several issues: the relation between tariffs and trusts, i.e., between tariffs and monopolies, the arguments against the reduction of the sugar tariff, the impact of tariffs on profitability and the economic effects of a reduction of the sugar tariff. From the present point of view, the central part of the article is the discussion of the pro-tariff arguments and of the effects of a tariff reduction. The arguments that Heckscher deals with are those presented in the daily newspapers. 'In the process, no named newspapers will be cited; only the adduced arguments will be scrutinized—if nobody wants to acknowledge them, so much the better.'[22]

The main pro-tariff argument was formulated in terms of employment. '... the most common argument seems to be that the tariff reduction causes a great deal of *factories* – and according to one source also railroads – *to be closed and workers to be unemployed.*' Heckscher did not accept the argument. '... it ought to be obvious even for a relatively

[19] Ibid.

[20] Ibid.

[21] Ibid., p. 2.

[22] Ibid., p. 8.

little trained economic brain,' he wrote, 'that no loss will arise through the concentration.' Ever since Sweden could obtain the same result with fewer factories and workers, those workers and factories had been redundant. During this entire time, Sweden had been making an economic loss every year, 'as a result of the uneconomic organization of the industry.' Whatever these factors of production could earn elsewhere after leaving the sugar industry would constitute a net gain for the economy. '... *even though the tariff reduction does not lead to any other result than the closure of unnecessary factories it will be gainful and increase the national income by freeing capital and labor*,' wrote Heckscher.[23]

Heckscher took exception to the claim that sugar protection would create employment for workers in other industries (especially construction) that would otherwise be seasonally unemployed. This, he argues, was a false argument. The marginal productivity of the seasonally unemployed in sugar production was zero:

> The said argument fails to take into account the fundamental fact that the workers, economically speaking, *are* redundant, in the sense that the same result would be achieved without them, and that thus there is no economic value of their being occupied in their otherwise idle time. If you want to formulate this incontrovertible train of thought in paradoxical terms you could say that it would be better for the economy that those who are redundant in the sugar industry, e.g. those from the construction industry, use their free time to play football instead of working in the sugar factories; for they would thus be occupied with something that would invigorate them more, and no addition to the national income will be forthcoming in either case.[24]

The third argument in favor of the sugar tariff was that the state, the sugar beet growers and the sugar processing industry would all make a loss from a reduction. Again, Heckscher disagreed. He put these losses against the consumer gains that would arise through lower prices and higher sugar consumption, 'because the sugar industry, like any other industry, only exists in order to serve this [the consumer] interest; and it is simply in order to cater to this interest that the [sugar] industry has

[23] Ibid., p. 9.

[24] Ibid., p. 10.

enjoyed tariff protection during many years.'[25] Heckscher even attributed a higher nutritional value to sugar than to the traditional Swedish hard rye bread, since its price per 1,000 calories was more than 17% lower.[26] 'And to this then comes the fact that sugar has a pleasure value, which, to be sure, cannot be measured, but which most people would tend to think of as being substantially higher than that of hard rye bread.'[27]

Heckscher must have loved sugar[28]:

> The easiest way of seeing the importance of this is by thinking of coffee and tea, whose nutritional value is zero, but the taxation of which at any rate is taken very seriously. As a matter of fact, the nutritional value of the cup of coffee is doubled if you put two sugar lumps into it instead of one, and hence only by making sugar cheap can you give coffee drinking a positive value from the point of view of physiology. 'Candy lovers' thus seem to have good reasons for their taste.[29]

Heckscher considered the sugar tariff to be a case of protection of an infant industry, i.e. of an industry that in the long run would be capable of producing at a competitive price but which during a transition period needed protection in order to increase its productivity and lower its costs. 'The connection between ... [the] development [of the beet sugar industry] and the tariff policy cannot be directly proved; but its existence must be regarded as highly probable, and beet sugar must hence, for good reasons, be considered one of the most incontrovertible creations of the infant industry tariff policy.'[30]

Having said this, Heckscher, however, hastened to add that for an industry to deserve protection, it must prove that at some point it will be able to do without it. The industry must pass what is known as Mill's test. Protection should, in other words, be only temporary. 'Nobody can be "brought up" his entire life, and when you have reached the mature age of the Swedish sugar industry, of around thirty years, the time ought soon

[25] Ibid., p. 12.

[26] Ibid.

[27] Ibid., p. 13.

[28] He always kept a bowl with candy on his desk (Heckscher et al., 2005, p. 490).

[29] Heckscher (1913, p. 13).

[30] Ibid.

to have come when you have to demonstrate the usefulness of the education that you have received.'[31] But this was precisely what Heckscher saw as the main problem with all tariffs. They were difficult to get rid of, and even to reduce, once they had been introduced.[32]

One of the consequences of a reduced tariff level on sugar would of course be that some sugar workers would lose their jobs. It had hence been suggested that they should enjoy unemployment benefits. Heckscher was completely against it:

> If there is anything that more than all else would lead to discontent and hence to emigration, it is ... to give people who are capable of working support as long as they don't work and do nothing to deserve it, since all work will thereafter become too difficult for them, and when the support at some point must come to an end, they have lost all inclination to take the trouble. It is hence difficult to imagine anything more truly anti-social, i.e. more prone to destroy the character traits needed by society.[33]

Heckscher thought of unemployment benefits as a solution 'borrowed from the medieval monasteries' and instead wanted the public employment offices to get in contact with the sugar companies and see to it that the redundant workers could be transferred to other branches.[34] It is obvious that he was an economist who preferred market solutions to public interventions.

By the same token, he was in favor of free trade. Heckscher sternly defended it in the public debate. '... the *consumer interest* must be the only final determinant in all economic discussions,' he wrote in a pamphlet published the same year as his famous paper on international trade—in 1919. 'That consumption, in the widest sense of this word, is the only real task of economic life constitutes a truth about which all economists who deserve their name agree.' Production was for Heckscher completely subservient to consumption. Its only task was to serve the latter and it did not serve any purpose in itself. The lack of understanding of this simple fact was 'lacking to an astonishing extent among people less trained in economics, and the havoc wrought by it is serious in many

[31] Ibid., pp. 13–14.

[32] Ibid., p. 3.

[33] Ibid., p. 26.

[34] Ibid., p. 27.

areas, but perhaps nowhere worse than precisely when it comes to the tariff issue.'[35] Free trade allowed a country to make the best use of its productive resources. By using them to produce goods that can be exported—goods that can be produced relatively cheaply at home—and importing such goods that can be produced only at a relatively high cost, a country maximizes the value of its total consumption. Arguing in terms of domestic employment amounted to misunderstanding the situation completely:

> It follows immediately ... how completely you misunderstand the order of things if you assume that the question of importing or not importing is a question of *employing domestic or foreign workers*. Importing actually means that you employ domestic workers in the export industries through which the imports are paid, and viewing imports as prone to take the bread out of the mouths of the workers of your own country amounts to a complete violation of reality.[36]

'Solidary' Tariffs: Fritz Brock

Heckscher dealt with the tariff issue in yet another context. In 1918, he reviewed a book by Fritz Brock on the subject. Brock was a strange bird among Swedish economists. 'Few economists today have heard of him, and hardly anyone has read anything by him. The few posthumous remarks are harsh,' writes Eskil Wadensjö.[37] Brock succeeded David Davidson as a professor in Uppsala in 1921, and according to the grapevine, he immediately stopped publishing. '... he laid down his pen, never to pick it up again,'[38] and he did not take on any students. The statement is, however, apocryphal. As Wadensjö demonstrates, Brock taught regularly and published around thirty works after his appointment. He, however, did not supervise any doctoral students, and over time, his published contributions became increasingly scarce.[39]

[35] Heckscher (1919a, p. 3). Heckscher (1915) also opposed the use of tariffs to stimulate domestic production of strategic goods—notably food—in the situation where imports may be cut off as a result of for example armed conflict.

[36] Heckscher (1919a, pp. 8–9).

[37] Wadensjö (1994, p. 15).

[38] Quoted by Jonung (1992, p. 241).

[39] Wadensjö (1994, p. 16).

Brock was seen as an eccentric by his contemporaries. 'He became a source of anecdotes and gradually got into conflicts with more and more of his colleagues' [...] 'A contributing factor in this respect was his vitriolic pen, even if the people he debated with were not far behind in this respect.'[40] One of those people was Eli Heckscher. It was to be expected. Heckscher was notoriously conflictive himself. He managed to antagonize virtually all the Swedish economists of his time: those in the elder generation, those in his own generation and those in the younger generation.[41] When Brock applied for the chair that had been held by Davidson, Heckscher operated behind the stage to get Gösta Bagge to apply as well. He managed to convince Bagge, but in the end, the latter withdrew his application, since he got a chair in Stockholm which he preferred.[42]

Heckscher and Brock had been at each other's throats before. The conflict had begun in 1916 with an attack by Brock on Heckscher's views of progressive taxation, and over the years, the tone of the—long-lasting—debate between the two became more and more acrimonious.[43] The next issue was the tariff question. In 1913, Brock had written an article on 'solidary' tariffs (equal tariffs on all products) which had invited criticism by Knut Wicksell.[44] This was followed by a number of other articles between 1914 and 1917, and when Brock the latter year collected his tariff essays in a book,[45] Heckscher stepped in and reviewed it, with no love lost.[46] As Rolf Henriksson has pointed out, Brock's 'theoretical treatment seems to have provoked Heckscher,'[47] who thought that some of it dealt with an utterly unlikely situation. 'Brock's writings on tariffs

[40] Ibid., pp. 24, 25.

[41] Lundahl (2015a).

[42] Wadensjö (1993, p. 17).

[43] See ibid., pp. 23–24, for details and references.

[44] Ibid., p. 21 gives the references.

[45] Brock (1917).

[46] Heckscher (1918c).

[47] Henriksson (2001, p. 13). Henriksson (2001) is a longer manuscript version of Henriksson (2002). Since the manuscript is much more detailed and carefully argued than the eventual book chapter and contains discussions of issues not retained in the shorter version I have chosen to use the longer version throughout.

were in general provocative to Heckscher by running counter to much of the received doctrine.'[48]

This is not the place to provide an exhaustive account of either Brock's book or Heckscher's review of it. What is of interest in the present context is mainly those of Brock's arguments that are directly connected with Heckscher's interests. The first of these is the one presented in Brock's 1913 article,[49] reprinted as the first chapter in the book. Apparently inspired by Bismarck and the German pro-tariff lobby that demanded the same rate of protection for all national branches of production,[50] Brock analyzed the effects of such a system and its abolition on the structure of the economy and on the general price level, a problem related to the 1913 Social Democratic parliamentary proposal, and hence also to Heckscher's interest in the tariff issue.[51]

Brock argued that it was impossible to protect all branches at the same time. The system amounted to nothing but free trade in disguise, only that it was costlier. Neither exports nor imports would be affected. Production costs would increase in absolute terms, but relative costs would not change. Brock assumed that the international demand for export products was very strong. Hence, exports would not be affected. Imports would, however, initially be reduced. This would, in turn, lead to an inflow of money (gold) from abroad which would serve to push up the domestic price level. Domestic import-competing producers would then have to pay more for their inputs, which in turn would serve to wipe out the initial protective effect of the tariff on their outputs.

The increased price level produced by the 'solidary' tariff system would not hurt anyone, according to Brock, provided that the prices of all goods and services had increased in the same proportion and provided that they thereafter remained stable. What might hurt the working classes was continued increases in the price level, increases that were faster than the increases of nominal wages. A stable 'solidary' tariff system that had

[48] Henriksson (2001), note, p. 13.

[49] Brock (1913).

[50] 'System der Solidarität der protektionistischen Interessen' (Brock, 1917, p. 189).

[51] In all probability, Heckscher must have been aware of Brock's 1913 article, as it dealt with a theme that occupied him at the time. However, Henriksson (2001, p. 13), has advanced the hypothesis that Heckscher may have been motivated to read Brock closely by reading a seminar paper by Bertil Ohlin (1918) on grain tariffs.

been in place for a number of years did not play any part in the inflation process, as Brock saw it. The latter was a result of overproduction of gold. Hence, he concluded, a 'solidary' tariff system could not be blamed for hurting the workers. The Social Democratic tariff reduction proposal could not be justified by arguing that it was in their interest.

Heckscher did not like Brock's analysis of the 'solidary' tariff system at all. He argued that it was unsuccessful and 'hence hardly deserves to be reprinted.'[52]

> Very little is gained by discussing the consequences of a situation which very closely resembles an economic impossibility, and the fact that ignorant legislators of all parties have believed that a solidarity system can be created should have called for information about the correct circumstances rather than for an analysis that will presumably strengthen their erroneous views.[53]

Heckscher did not share Brock's conviction that a 'solidary' tariff system was nothing but free trade in disguise. The tariffs had to be paid by those branches—the export branches and related branches such as shipping—that could not profit from the domestic price increases. These would lose production factors to other branches and hence shrink. Heckscher considered Brock's assumption of strong foreign demand for export goods 'anything but convincing.' It belonged to 'the most unlikely' of situations since it could never apply to all exports of a country.[54]

The central chapter of Brock's book, as Heckscher saw it, dealt with the economic consequences of tariffs. Although Brock was prone to defend tariffs, he basically came out right, i.e., against protection. While tariffs could benefit single countries, they hurt the world economy as a whole. For Heckscher, the essential contribution of the chapter was the discussion of the relation between tariffs and monopolies—a question that Heckscher had dealt with himself in his 1913 essay. However, in hindsight, given the title of Heckscher's 1919 essay, the most interesting part in the present context is what Brock had to say about the effects of tariffs

[52] Heckscher (1918c, p. 323).

[53] Ibid.

[54] Ibid., p. 324.

on the distribution of income.[55] '... as you could predict, no important results are obtained on this point,' wrote Heckscher, sarcastically.[56] In his argument, Brock came back to the effects of a reduction of the level of food tariffs. On the one hand, this will make bread cheaper for the workers, but it will also reduce the price of land and hence make farmers substitute land for labor. This will, in turn, lead to rural–urban migration and hence increase the cost of housing in the cities and make 'the advantage of cheaper bread fairly illusory for a large part of the working population.'[57] Hence, you should think twice before advocating a reduction in the protection of agricultural products. Heckscher saw the sequence sketched by Brock as a mere theoretical possibility, but not more. In practice, a gradual, relatively slow, reduction of the tariff level in combination with suitable urban planning and development of intraurban communications would counteract the tendency for the price of urban land to increase.[58]

Wicksell's Criticism

After preaching the virtues of free trade, a logical second step for Heckscher must have been to investigate what determines which products a country exports and imports, respectively. His discussion of tariffs predisposed him for this, as it were. As Harry Flam and June Flanders have pointed out, it is 'unlikely' that he had not thought of theoretical trade issues at the time.[59] Heckscher had had several other occasions. His empirical inspiration did not just stem from the tariff issue. The most important of his historic publications at the time, the Swedish edition of *The Continental System*,[60] dealt with trade issues and mercantilism in the context of Napoleon's blockade of England, and during World War I, he analyzed trade problems caused by the war, both in his private

55 'This was no doubt an early penetration of that theme which must have tuned his mind considerably onto his later famous treatment ...' (Henriksson, 2001, p. 13).

56 Heckscher (1918c, p. 324).

57 Brock (1917, p. 53).

58 Brock (1919) replied to Heckscher's review in *Ekonomisk Tidskrift* 1919 and Heckscher (1919c) retorted in the same issue.

59 Flam and Flanders (1991, p. 8).

60 Heckscher (1918b), English translation, Heckscher (1922).

capacity and as a member of a government commission set up to examine the policy measures called for by the wartime economic conditions—a commission which had been proposed by Heckscher himself.[61]

However, none of these circumstances did, in fact, constitute the immediate reason for Heckscher's writing of the 1919 article. In 1918, he collected a number of essays in a book called *Svenska produktionsproblem* [Swedish Production Problems].[62] He then included a revised and shortened version of his sugar tariff piece. The book was reviewed by Knut Wicksell.[63] The review was very critical. Wicksell argued that Heckscher's opus displayed two main defects. Firstly, Heckscher did not deal with the social distribution problem, i.e. with income inequalities. The second, and according to Wicksell, even more serious, shortcoming was that Heckscher was ignoring the population problem completely.

This is not the place to deal in detail with Wicksell's criticism. The important part of it from the present point of view is that he linked the population problem to the analysis of foreign trade. Blinded by his enthusiasm for free trade, Heckscher had not taken into account that free trade might lead to falling wages and emigration. As always, Wicksell was concerned with the effects of population growth.[64] '… labor may be, and is of course always in some sense "scarce", but if it is *so little* scarce that wage rate determined by its scarcity does not even suffice to defray the worker's necessary cost of living – what happens then, and what should happen?'[65]

Wicksell's answer was that the workers might emigrate. He used 'a concrete example, which although it constitutes a great exaggeration, is not completely inconceivable or absolutely unlikely,' to drive home his point, an argument that, as Ronald Findlay has noted, foreshadows the modern theory of Dutch Disease.[66] Wicksell assumed that the price of

[61] Morell (2006, p. 461). Heckscher (1915) argued against the use of tariffs to stimulate domestic production of strategic goods—notably food—in the situation where imports may be cut off as a result of for example armed conflict.

[62] Heckscher (1918a).

[63] Wicksell (1919).

[64] The population problem occupied Wicksell during his entire career. See Lundahl (2005) for a detailed discussion.

[65] Wicksell (1919, p. 16).

[66] Ibid., p. 17, Findlay (1995, p. 3). The modern formulation of the Dutch Disease argument is due to Corden and Neary (1982). Wicksell's example was hardly 'a great

iron ore or wood increased in relation to the price of processed industrial goods and food to the point where mine- and landowners would find it most profitable to export only raw ore and unprocessed or little processed wood products. In the extreme case, it would even be profitable to let forests grow on fields and meadows. Provided that the price increase was not too large, deindustrialization and retreat of the agricultural frontier might, argued Wicksell, 'under the pressure of falling wages' be counteracted by a more intensive use of the best arable land and 'perchance by a few still surviving industrial branches.' If, on the other hand, the increase was large, 'under free competition, the greater part of the population would be forced to emigrate or, by other means, reduce its size.' Wicksell did not advocate tariffs. He stated that he shared Heckscher's conviction that perpetual protection was not the way out but hastened to add that 'an argument that wholly disregards such consequences can hardly be considered satisfactory.'[67]

That it was Wicksell's criticism that inspired Heckscher to write his famous 1919 article is beyond doubt. In the very opening paragraph, Heckscher wrote:

> The immediate reason for the following remarks is a review that Professor Wicksell was kind enough to write a year ago[68] of my book *Swedish Production Problem* [sic]. Although Wicksell and I have reached a different conclusion on at least one important point, I have nevertheless profited greatly form his criticism – apart from that proferred in his review – in a number of ways. It is not my intention to follow Professor Wicksell's article too closely, however, since it seems to me that the problem can be discussed more fruitfully in more general terms. The importance of the subject and the surprisingly scant attention so far paid to it in the theoretical literature tend to make a theoretical study of it particularly useful and also tempting: it may prove entirely possible to explain the actual nature of foreign trade and its effects more fully than has been done up to now.[69]

exaggeration.' He had been concerned with the effects of population growth since the beginning of the 1880s, and what he was describing resembles the situation in Sweden during the years of heavy emigration during the late nineteenth century.

[67] Wicksell (1919, p. 17). For an overview of Wicksell's previous writings on foreign trade, see Herlitz (2002, pp. 482–485).

[68] The 1919 issue of *Ekonomisk Tidskrift* did not appear until the following year.

[69] Heckscher (1991, p. 44). As Ronald Findlay (1995, p. 1) has pointed out, after Ricardo's development of comparative advantage and Mill's analysis of the determinants

As noted by Flam and Flanders, implicit in Wicksell's example is the difference in factor proportions between different nations and production sectors. 'Missing is the concept of comparative advantage based on relative factor endowments and factor proportions in production as well as the concept of the equalization of factor prices between nations through commodity trade. These were left to Heckscher to derive.'[70] The bulk of his pathbreaking article deals precisely with this.

Toward the end of his article, Heckscher took direct issue with Wicksell's analysis of international trade and emigration. To the extent that Wicksell's example only dealt with a process that would lower the wage rate, he agreed with it. The possibility that it might also result in emigration, however, he saw as far-fetched. The prices of the raw materials exported by Sweden are determined in the world market:

> If Professor Wicksell starts from a point of free exchange of commodities as well as mobile factors, which must be assumed, then all factor prices are initially also at the world average. There is subsequently an increase in the scarcity of raw materials abroad and with it necessarily higher foreign rent on land, etc., and a decrease of the foreign wage rate. Sweden then has lower rents but higher wages than prevail abroad and consequently exports more raw materials and imports more manufactures, for example. This leads eventually to *the same* change in factor prices in Sweden and abroad; when this has taken place, exchange no longer increases. Here too equilibrium is restored and there is no reason for emigration since wages are not higher abroad than in Sweden. Increased demand for a country's natural resources does not in itself result in labor having a lower price inside the country than outside, and since it does not, there is clearly no reason for it to emigrate.[71]

In fact, Heckscher argued, an increase of the price of raw materials could lead to immigration instead of emigration, since it would result in an increased demand also for labor in the raw material producing sector.

of the terms-of-trade, not much happened in the theory of international trade until Heckscher wrote his article.

[70] Flam and Flanders (1991, p. 8).

[71] Heckscher (1991, p. 65).

Given its relative abundance of raw materials, Sweden would then attract labor to the industries exporting them.[72]

At the end of his analysis of Wicksell's argument, Heckscher once more thanked his older colleague for having inspired his article—in terms that suggest that he was completely aware of the importance of his own endeavor:

> If this reply to Professor Wicksell's statement holds up, there is no one I can thank more than him because it is through the criticism he has been willing to direct at my endeavors that I have been able, at least in part, to think through these hitherto neglected aspects of international trade.[73]

Bertil Ohlin's Contribution

As the foregoing has hopefully demonstrated, Eli Heckcher's road to his 1919 article can be traced—in a somewhat heuristic fashion. What about Bertil Ohlin? Heckscher's 1919 paper is a 'work of genius,' writes Paul Samuelson.[74] He originated both the factor proportions approach to international trade—what is commonly known as the Heckscher–Ohlin theorem—and the factor-price equalization theorem—that even in the absence of factor mobility across international borders, trade will equalize factor prices between countries.

What could Ohlin possibly add to this? According to Harry Flam, his contributions were not on par with those of Heckscher: 'Taking the central propositions of modern Heckscher-Ohlin theory as the yardstick, it is clear that Ohlin did not add anything to what Heckscher had already done. […] The irony is that had Heckscher's paper been published in English in 1919, it is less likely that Ohlin would have been associated with the Heckscher-Ohlin theory by name, though he made the theory known to the world and played an important role in developing it.'[75]

[72] The publication of Heckscher's 1919 article was followed by a further exchange between Wicksell (1920a, 1920b) and Heckscher (1920), see also Herlitz (2002, pp. 491–495) and Lundahl (2015b, pp. 112–113), for English summaries. This exchange, however, falls outside the scope of the present essay.

[73] Heckscher (1991, p. 66).

[74] Samuelson (1982), note p. 38.

[75] Flam (1993, pp. 147, 152).

In a sense, this is true, for Heckscher had his own version, what I have elsewhere referred to as the 'Heckscher theorem':

> The existence of trade with Heckscher … rests on two pillars. 'The prerequisites for initiating international trade may … be summarized as *different relative prices of the factors of production in the exchanging countries,* as well as *different proportions between the factors of production in different commodities*, he writes.[76] This is Heckscher's formulation of the 'Heckscher-Ohlin theorem', and here, factor intensity is not defined in terms of relative factor endowments but in terms of relative *prices.*[77]

The above, however, does not in any way belittle what Ohlin did. 'His [licentiate] thesis dealt largely with the same topic as my paper in the Davidson festschrift but considerably more systematically and successfully,' wrote Eli Heckscher himself in a letter to the future director of the International Monetary Fund, Per Jacobsson, in July 1922.[78]

Paul Samuelson is also quite adamant with respect to Ohlin's contributions.[79] 'Ohlin will live forever as one of the great innovators in the theory of international trade,'[80] he writes. 'To say that Bertil Ohlin lives on in the Valhalla of great contributors to the theory of international trade is to say much, for trade theory has always been the queen realm of economic theory.'[81] Furthermore:

> It also says much to claim that Ohlin's name belongs on the same shelf with such names in the field of international trade as Hume, Torrens, Ricardo, J.S. Mill, [Hans von] Mangoldt, Marshall, Taussig, and Edgeworth. If Alfred Nobel's will had provided for prizes in economics beginning in 1901 along with the prizes in physics, chemistry, medicine, literature, and peace, I think that by 1940 Bertil Ohlin would have received one either by

[76] Heckscher (1991, p. 48).

[77] Lundahl (2015b, p. 108).

[78] Letter from Eli Heckscher to Per Jacobsson, 7 July 1922, quoted by Henriksson (2001, p. 4).

[79] Cf. also Caves (1978) for a similar view.

[80] Samuelson (1982, p. 33).

[81] Ibid., p. 36.

himself, or sharing one with either or both of Jacob Viner and Gottfried Haberler or with Eli Heckscher.[82]

... it is an injustice to his 1933 classic to think of it as simply a stepping stone between the original article of Heckscher and the two-by-two (or n x r) models of Stolper-Samuelson or Lerner-Samuelson'[83]

I find that Ohlin definitely did go beyond Heckscher. Heckscher gives shrewd conjectures, but he never presented a complete model and necessarily lacked cogent proofs of the key theorems latent in his model. [...] Ohlin's appendix [I to the 1933 book] ... does bring to completion, not the Heckscher system, but rather the Heckscher-Ohlin system![84]

Flam as well recognizes, that once you venture outside the strict limits of Heckscher's original approach, Ohlin indeed made a contribution, in the same spirit as Heckscher, precisely by stretching and extending the Heckscher setting:

... Ohlin received the fundamental ideas from Heckscher ... and Ohlin's contribution to international trade theory was to recognize the revolutionary character of these ideas, integrate them with general equilibrium, neo-classical price theory, and to increase our understanding of Heckscher's model by making it more general and by applying it to a large number of cases of empirical relevance. This was no lesser achievement.[85]

Ohlin's contribution was to recognize the importance and originality of Heckscher's model, to demonstrate its workings in great detail, using many real-world examples, to generalize it by introducing factor mobility and financial capital flows in conjunction with real flows of commodities, capital and labour, and to investigate the implications of the model's assumptions and of his own generalizations. Ohlin was motivated by what he saw as the unrealism of many of Heckscher's assumptions and conclusions. Fixed and internationally immobile factors were prime targets among the assumptions, and factor-price equalization among the conclusions.[86]

The original part of Ohlin's contributions is the analysis of international capital movements, in particular of balance of payments adjustments,

[82] Ibid.

[83] Ibid., p. 38.

[84] Ibid., note, p. 38.

[85] Flam (1993, p. 143).

[86] Ibid., p. 148.

where he integrated real and monetary aspects and used his own concept of buying-power as a powerful tool.[87]

Thus, maybe we had better to talk about 'Heckscher-Ohlin economics' in a broader sense than limiting the attention to the narrower 'Heckscher-Ohlin theorem.' Whichever way, the names of Heckscher and Ohlin will be forever interwoven in the theory of international trade.

Ohlin's Sources of Inspiration: Studies in Lund and Stockholm

How did Ohlin arrive at his views? What inspired him? In the foregoing, we have followed the development of Eli Heckscher's interest in international trade. Ohlin's road to his doctoral dissertation and his later *Interregional and International Trade* went through a number of problems related to international economics.

Bertil Ohlin began his studies of economics at the University of Lund in 1915, at the tender age of 16, mainly for Emil Sommarin, but he also attended Knut Wicksell's lectures during the last year before retiring—unfortunately on agrarian policy, not least in Germany. 'It appeared as completely uninteresting to me, and apparently also to the lecturer.'[88] (Wicksell's lectures were offered to law students.) As it seems, Ohlin's exposure to international economics in Lund was minimal. Wicksell's *Lectures*,[89] which he no doubt must have read, contain little trade theory. Bastable's *The Theory of International Trade*[90] was included in the reading list for higher credits in economics, but only as optional reading, and as Rolf Henriksson has pointed out, 'there is no reason to presume that Ohlin had delved especially into trade theory in his Lund studies.'[91]

After finishing his Bachelor's degree at the age of eighteen, in 1917, Bertil Ohlin moved to Stockholm, to study economics and business administration at the Stockholm School of Economics. Apparently, it was the presence of Eli Heckscher there that attracted him:

[87] Ibid., p. 143.

[88] Ohlin (1972, p. 46).

[89] Wicksell (1911, 1915).

[90] Bastable (1903).

[91] Henriksson (2001, p. 11).

> Sometime during 1916, I saw in the newspaper a picture of a bearded younger man. He had written a book about 'The Economics of the World War'; his name was Eli Heckscher, professor at the Stockholm School of Economics. The short newspaper review made me think of continuing my studies at the Stockholm School of Economics, after finishing my degree at Lund, in order to broaden my knowledge, which seemed to me to be too concentrated on theoretical issues.[92]

In Stockholm, Ohlin attended the economics seminar led by Heckscher. His first own presentation there, in 1918, dealt with grain tariffs.[93] It was mainly an empirical analysis of the Swedish experience. However, Ohlin also discussed the effects of protection of agriculture in a two-sector (agriculture and industry) setting, 'but there was no focus on the factor market dimension in a manner inviting the analytical preconceptions of the later Stolper-Samuelson treatment of the problem.'[94] Possibly, he was 'already at this stage ... groping in the direction of the later H-O theory,'[95] although at the time he lacked the necessary theoretical background.

Ohlin increasingly turned to international economics. In 1919 and 1920, he worked for the Tariff and Treaty Committee [Tull- och traktatkommittén], in the tariff section, studying the impact of tariffs on bricks, glass and rubber.[96] These studies were empirical and historical, of three small industries. As Henriksson has argued, their relative insignificance did not invite any analysis steeped in the general equilibrium framework. Ohlin's approach was 'more in the direction of partial industrial dynamics.'[97]

At the time of his work in the Tariff and Treaty Committee, Ohlin had, however, been thoroughly exposed to general equilibrium analysis. In May 1919, Gustav Cassel presented his *Theoretische Sozialökonomie*[98] at a meeting of the Political Economy Club [Nationalekonomiska klubben]

[92] Ohlin (1972, p. 54).

[93] Ohlin (1918).

[94] Henriksson (2001, pp. 11–12).

[95] Ibid., p. 12.

[96] Ohlin (1972, pp. 64–69).

[97] Henriksson (2001, p. 14).

[98] Cassel (1918).

which Ohlin attended.[99] This fundamental, synthetic, book used a general equilibrium approach.[100] Ohlin reviewed the book in *Svenska Dagbladet*, under the heading 'An Economic Standard Work.'[101] As may be deduced from the title of Ohlin's review, the latter was very positive. Ohlin was duly impressed, but he noted that Cassel's analysis dealt only with a closed economy. 'Naturally, this should not be taken as a signal that at this time, Ohlin understood the strategic role the conception of the income distribution would hold in a general theory of trade. Such a theory as an inherent analytical promise inherent in the Casselian approach was apparently not yet within Ohlin's purview,' writes Rolf Henriksson. However, at the same time he notes that 'it may be taken as a significant fact that Ohlin here recorded precisely the gap that he was later trying to fill.'[102]

The conclusion is inevitable: Cassel's *magnum opus* provided important input to Ohlin's future work in international trade theory—both because of what it contained and because of what it lacked. It was from Cassel that Ohlin got his basic analytical approach. He was himself the first person to acknowledge this. In the preface to *The Theory of Trade* he wrote:

> Unfortunately, there is no universally accepted theory of price determination that can constitute a basis for a theory of interlocal trade. However, differences between various authors are probably less important than is often assumed. On the whole, most modern authors adopt a general equilibrium approach. This principle seems to have been given its most consistent and lucid formulation by Cassel.[103] The approach here adheres closely to his system, in that it attempts to build upon that basic formulation a theory of interlocal trade directly connected to the general theory of price determination. [...]

[99] Ohlin (1972, p. 59).

[100] Cassel had of course been inspired by the founding father of general equilibrium theory, Léon Walras, but as usual, in his writings, he did not acknowledge his (heavy) intellectual debt.

[101] Ohlin (1919a).

[102] Henriksson (2001, p. 16).

[103] There is no Walras entry in Ohlin's (1924) bibliography.

> The origin of this research was an attempt to extend Cassel's system of equations of price determination in *one* market to that of several trading countries.[104]

Ohlin did, however, not embark on the course that would establish his international reputation as an economist immediately. In 1920, he became Cassel's graduate student at Stockholm College [Stockholms Högskola] where he remained until the end of 1924, after receiving his licentiate degree in 1922 and his doctorate in 1924. During these five crucial years, he received a number of influences that would be decisive for his work in the theory of international trade during this period.

Unter den Linden

As far as the inspiration for Ohlin's work in international trade theory is concerned, as Rolf Henriksson has pointed out, already as a student, Ohlin 'was strikingly self-reliant and it would be misleading to attempt to explain his achievements as mainly a product of the guidance he obtained.'[105] In the first volume of his memoirs, Ohlin offers his own version of how he arrived at his approach to international trade. In 1921, 'I began writing on the foundations of a to some extent new approach to foreign trade theory, the inspiration for which I had received during a walk on Unter den Linden in Berlin in 1920.'[106] What did he mean by this cryptic statement? The generally accepted version is succinctly summarized by Harry Flam and June Flanders:

> The idea that came to Ohlin during his walk in Berlin was to combine Cassel and Heckscher. Cassel had neoclassical general equilibrium for a single economy, Heckscher a neoclassical theory of international trade. Ohlin's idea was to extend Cassel's paradigm to international equilibrium with trading economies, where the reasons for trade were those given by Heckscher.[107]

[104] Ohlin (1991, p. 76).

[105] Henriksson (2001, p. 2).

[106] Ohlin (1972, p. 79). The exact date is not known. Ohlin was in Germany between the beginning of April and late May or early June 1920 (Henriksson, 2001, p. 26).

[107] Flam and Flanders (2002, p. 176).

The conventional view of what happened to Ohlin during his walk on Unter den Linden has been challenged by Rolf Henriksson.[108] In 1921, Ohlin published an article about equilibrium exchange rates in *Ekonomisk Tidskrift*,[109] and Henriksson claims that what he calls Ohlin's 'Eureka' experience dealt with exchange rate determination and not with the real side of international trade.

> It is rather astonishing that initially, before settling on the topic as we know it, Ohlin contemplated a seemingly quite different topic, the theory of the exchange rate. There is no exchange rate in the [licentiate] thesis and it only plays a marginal role as a specific theme in the [doctoral] dissertation. Exchange rate issues are quite far from the real theory of trade as considered both generally in the H-O themes as well as specifically in Heckscher's seminal paper. Nor is the theory of exchange rates integrated into Cassel's version of the equilibrium system.[110]

Ohlin's concern with exchange rate determination should be seen mainly as part of an endeavor to come to grips with Sweden's economic problems after the end of World War I. Henriksson has the story:

> Ohlin's ambitions to reach a breakthrough with the issue of the exchange rate were due to his apparently strong desire to explain the acute unfolding of events in Sweden's economic turmoil and his eagerness to reach conclusions of immediate interest on policy issues. ... the prevailing exchange rate theory did not offer what he needed in order to take a stand on the current economic policy issues. There was a central controversy with much confusion between Wicksell and other economists as regards the price-level goal of short-term economic policy interventions with bearings also on the exchange rate developments. The heated discussion related to the use of the discount rate was also confused. Here, views diverged when the exchange rate was over or undervalued by the market. This created a conflict of goals in situations when there was a need to influence both the price level and the exchange rate.[111] [...]
>
> Thus, in the following years of Swedish price level drama, Ohlin would constantly search for an adequate exchange rate theory. He wanted to be

[108] Henriksson (2001, 2002).

[109] Ohlin (1921).

[110] Henriksson (2001, pp. 5–6).

[111] Ibid., p. 23.

'on top' of that problem, not only in the seminar room but also in the open economic policy debate.[112]

Ohlin's analysis was presented in the *Ekonomisk Tidskrift* article in the spring of 1921, at the end of a process that had extended over a few years[113]:

> It should be noted that Ohlin's failure to come to terms with the theory of the exchange rate quickly enough was an important inducement to further efforts. Ohlin recognized that the understanding of the movement of the exchange rate in the monetary turmoil of the time was an essential part of his ability to analyze current developments more generally. This presented him with a challenge that remained an acute concern of his until the spring of 1921 when he eventually made the sought for breakthrough also on that problem.[114]

Thereafter, however, Ohlin by and large turned his back on exchange rate problems. In a letter to Heckscher from late November 1923, he wrote: 'I intended at the outset—spring 1921—again to write on the theory of exchange rates, but found that I had to go more deeply and take up the theory of international trade.'[115] Henriksson conjectures that 'the query into international trade might simply be posed as a more in-depth exploration of the determinants of the exchange rate.'[116] He claims that the latter may have been Ohlin's ultimate goal:

> ... the hunch one gets ... is that the pursuit of the real theory of international trade, as an autonomous analytical problem area, might only be a temporary slip-off from the ulterior goal of illuminating the monetary dynamics. It might, in fact, only have meant a postponement of that ultimate task.[117]

[112] Ibid., p. 24.

[113] Ohlin (1921).

[114] Henriksson (2001, p. 24).

[115] Letter from Bertil Ohlin to Eli Heckscher, 22–24 November 1923, quoted by Henriksson (2001, p. 5).

[116] Henriksson (2001, p. 6).

[117] Ibid.

If so, it hardly matters. It does not shed any light at all on the Unter den Linden event. Ohlin did not follow up the exchange rate path in his work for the licentiate degree and his doctorate. In a letter to Heckscher from Grenoble written in May 1921, he relates how he, for the first time, had read John Stuart Mill's analysis of exchange rate determination[118] and discovered that Mill had anticipated his own results. 'Had I not known that I had never held that book in my hand, I would have been tempted to believe that I had subconsciously copied his presentation ...'[119] Nevertheless, writes Ohlin, the reading 'made me think anew on the theory of exchange rates and I began to reconsider if I ought not return to my idea of spring last year to write the licentiate thesis on that.'[120] In the end, however, he chose not to. 'Ohlin was apparently not satisfied with having hit on a solution independently of earlier work through a procedure that might in itself be of scientific value. He wanted to make a contribution in a more substantive sense.'[121] Ohlin's reading of Mill made him abandon exchange rate determination as a topic for his licentiate thesis.[122]

Heckscher and Ohlin

Obviously, under the aegis of Cassel, Ohlin must have submerged himself into the nitty-gritty of general equilibrium analysis. A review is one thing—a working grasp of the matter is another. This goes without saying. But Cassel was not the only one influencing Ohlin. In the meantime, the same year as Ohlin became Cassel's student, Eli Heckscher had published

[118] Mill (1848).

[119] Letter from Bertil Ohlin to Eli Heckscher, 15 May 1921, quoted by Henriksson (2001, p. 8).

[120] Ibid.

[121] Henriksson (2001, p. 8).

[122] Ibid., p. 9. Ohlin had also played with the idea of writing his thesis on the relation between exchange rate movements and productivity changes but apparently gave this up for a 'somewhat chivalrous' reason. In 1920, Gunnar Westin Silverstolpe had published an article (Silverstolpe, 1920) where he stated his intention to deal with this subject. In a letter to Heckscher dated 15 May 1921, Ohlin wrote: '... I think it is unpleasant to block the way for Silverstolpe who is dealing with these questions. Surely, we began about the same time (my draft where the reasoning on productivity is developed dates from that time) but he has been working on them continuously and has therefore, in a sense, the right of way' (cited by Henriksson, 2001, pp. 8–9).

his pathbreaking article about international trade. Of course, Ohlin had read it. The paper had been published in a special issue of *Ekonomisk Tidskrift*, a *Festschrift* volume dedicated to David Davidson, and Ohlin had contributed to the issue himself, with an article about the quantity theory of money in the Swedish economic literature.[123]

To what extent Heckscher's paper influenced Ohlin when he wrote his licentiate thesis and doctoral dissertation is, however, a somewhat moot point. '... the core of ... [Ohlin's] trade theory, the emphasis on the importance of factor endowments and factor intensities in production, is there in the licentiate thesis.'[124] In the latter, Ohlin points directly to Heckscher: 'This leads to the question of the reason for the differences in comparative costs and prices of goods, an issue hardly dealt with in most studies.'[125] He cites Heckscher directly in the footnote to this sentence and comes back to him once more in a discussion of goods requiring different factor proportions.[126]

It is, however, quite possible that Heckscher's influence was mainly indirect. In the preface to his doctoral dissertation, Ohlin stresses the influence that Cassel had on him but downplays the importance of Heckscher:

> Although the point of departure is completely different [Cassel's general equilibrium system], the results of the attempt (presented in chapter III) exhibit important similarities to Heckscher's treatment in 'The Effect of Foreign Trade on the Distribution of Income,' published one year earlier in *Ekonomisk Tidskrift*, 1920 ... There is no doubt that the author was unconsciously influenced by Heckscher's paper, both at this and later stages of the work. The influence of this pathbreaking paper, both conscious and unconscious, has surely been particularly decisive in the development of the material in chapters I-III.[127]

[123] Ohlin (1919b). That Ohlin read Heckscher's paper carefully is beyond doubt. Hans Tson Söderström is the proud owner of Ohlin's copy of the *Festschrift*, full of annotations by Ohlin.

[124] Flam and Flanders (2002, p. 190).

[125] Ohlin (2002, p. 146).

[126] Ibid., p. 152 and note 19, p. 173.

[127] Ohlin (1991, p. 76).

After reading the first version of Ohlin's licentiate thesis, Heckscher had complained about the latter's failure to refer to his 1919 article in a satisfactory manner.[128] In a letter to Heckscher, written in November 1923, Ohlin explained how he had arrived at his results. After reading Cassel's work a second time, he had extended the Cassel framework to cover two countries instead of one:

> Thus, I arrived at the equation systems which are reproduced in my licentiate thesis and my present manuscript. … 'Trade cannot arise if relative commodity prices are the same': That far I had come at the beginning of August 1921 without having seen your paper since the spring of 1920, when I read it carefully twice. As I now set out to explore what the above proposition implied with respect to factor prices. I remembered your paper … (and that you had found two cases, 1) relative factor prices are equal and 2) something about the proportions (of factors of production) in different commodities of which I did not have a clear memory.)[129]

According to Ohlin, it was not until this point that he looked at Heckscher's paper and found that some of their results (but not all) coincided:

> Concerning the causes for trade or rather the conditions for its absence, an analysis of the equations could not possibly yield more than one result. Although I was no doubt greatly assisted by my partly subconscious knowledge of your results, I hold that I had reached my results from a completely different point of departure. To say that I had taken your results and changed them a little is surely not to describe the development correctly.[130]

Ohlin, however, pays Heckscher his dues for factor-price equalization. 'My dependence on your paper is much greater as regards the effects of trade. When I wrote on that, I had again read your paper and, besides,

[128] Henriksson (2001, p. 4).

[129] Letter from Bertil Ohlin to Eli Heckscher, 22–24 November 1923, cited by Henriksson (2001, p. 5).

[130] Ibid.

had never after the first reading lost sight of your enormously important conclusion that trade equalizes the scarcity of factors of production.'[131]

As Henriksson has demonstrated, Heckscher and Ohlin had little contact during the crucial year of 1919 when Heckscher wrote his paper. The latter was on sabbatical leave and the letters that he exchanged with Ohlin did not deal with foreign trade.[132] When the paper was published in the Davidson *Festschrift*—Heckscher received the issue on 20 February 1920—Ohlin, as already mentioned, read it twice, but this does not necessarily mean that it had any impact on the work that he was to initiate the following year:

> ... this should not make us infer too much about Ohlin's interest in or his absorption of its contents. Reading the paper twice was probably a minimum necessity in order to understand it. This was not only a profound text, it also entailed seeming inconsistencies and employed the most tedious numeral algebra, a trying passage even for the modern reader.[133]

Thus, if we are to believe Ohlin—and I don't see any reason not to—he set out independently to derive his results and did not read Heckscher in the context of his own work until at a later stage of his research, more than a year after Unter den Linden. By the same token, it probably means that Heckscher's research did not form any part of what came to Ohlin during his walk. On the other hand, to imply, as Henriksson does, that the experience dealt with exchange rates completely contradicts Ohlin's own words: 'a to some extent new approach in *foreign trade theory*.'[134] Henriksson's monetary conjecture certainly sounds far-fetched, especially as he chooses to label the event a 'Eureka' experience, 'as seemingly a bolt out of the blue.'[135] This only leaves Cassel. Remember what Ohlin states in the preface to his doctoral dissertation, which I have already cited: 'The *origin* of this research was an attempt to extend Cassel's system of

[131] Letter from Bertil Ohlin to Eli Heckscher, 22–24 November 1923, cited by Henriksson (2001, p. 18).

[132] Henriksson (2001, pp. 16–17).

[133] Ibid., p. 18. Or, as Herlitz (2002, p. 488) puts it, 'Heckscher usually worked with what might be called a homemade casuistry built up by numbers.'

[134] Ohlin (1972, p. 79), emphasis added.

[135] Henriksson (2001, p. 3).

equations of price determination in *one* market to that of several trading countries.'[136]

It is clear enough. Could it simply be that the Eureka experience entailed dropping exchange rate theory and taking up the determinants of trade in the Cassel framework of general equilibrium instead? Ohlin may have had his mind set on the problem of exchange rate determination during his stroll, when he was suddenly—in a Eureka fashion—reminded of Cassel's general equilibrium system and the possibility of using it for a thesis on real trade theory.

Bertil Ohlin began his work on international trade in June 1921.[137] His work was, however, interrupted by military service the very same month, so his licentiate thesis was not ready until the beginning of April 1922, after obtaining two weeks of special leave for its completion directly from the Prime Minister, Per Albin Hansson.[138]

From Harvard to Copenhagen and Beyond

In the summer of 1922, Bertil Ohlin left Sweden for a year of studies in the United States. His later colleague at the Stockholm School of Economics, Torsten Gårdlund, has argued that, in Sweden, Ohlin suffered from a lack of qualified theoretical teaching. '... in his fairly detailed memories about his year in Lund, Bertil speaks only about how he listened to elementary lectures' by Emil Sommarin, and in Stockholm, although marginally better, the situation also left a great deal to be desired. 'During the years 1917 to 1919 Bertil no doubt learned a good deal by following Heckscher's seminars—but less from Heckscher's lectures in general theory. [...] Bertil had, in my opinion, comparatively little to learn from Heckscher, and he completed his study of economics by reading literature in the field.'[139] Gårdlund's conclusion is clear: it was not until Ohlin got a possibility to study abroad that he was able to fill out this lacuna:

136 Ohlin (1991, p. 76). Emphasis added on *origin*.

137 Ibid., p. 18.

138 Ohlin (1972, pp. 78–79).

139 Gårdlund (2002, p. 49).

> It is my impression – or rather my conviction – that in these early years, Bertil regretted that he had never had the chance to follow a first-rate course in economic analysis – as a whole or in part treated by specialists. In the summer of 1922 he got the chance to take up such studies abroad, however.[140]

Ohlin went to Harvard for a year, where he obtained a Master of Arts degree. The courses that he took there included international trade and international financial relations, for John Williams, an economist who took a critical stance toward classical trade theory, and general economic theory for Frank Taussig.[141] Ohlin also got in touch with Jacob Viner, from the University of Chicago,[142] who let him read the manuscript of his *Canada's Balance of International Indebtedness 1900–1913*.[143] He made use both of this and of Williams' *Argentine International Trade under Inconvertible Paper Money 1880–1900*[144] in his doctoral dissertation, where also much more space is devoted to the presentation of classical trade theory (even more in his 1933 book). 'This steady development may have been due, inter alia, to the Harvard influence,' suggest Flam and Flanders.[145]

Ohlin came back to Sweden, at the end of 1923, after a visit to Cambridge in the fall, which was, however, cut short by a severe eye inflammation, which also precluded him from working on his doctoral dissertation. He had planned to publish it in English, but since a chair in economics had fallen vacant in Copenhagen, and Heckscher had advised him to apply for it, at the beginning of April 1924, Ohlin began dictating a shorter version in Swedish—around 170 pages—which was finished—and printed—in the record time of seven weeks. Ohlin defended it in May, got the chair in Copenhagen in December, ahead of Erik Lindahl, and began his tenure there in January 1925.[146] He was twenty-five years old.

[140] Ibid., p. 50.

[141] Ohlin (1972, p. 86).

[142] Expressed above all in Williams (1929).

[143] Flam (1993, p. 145). Viner's book is Viner (1924).

[144] Williams (1920).

[145] Flam and Flanders (2002, p. 181).

[146] Ohlin (1972, pp. 90–96). For the chair and for Ohlin in Copenhagen, see Topp (2002).

In 1933, the last brick of the Heckscher–Ohlin building was put in place as Ohlin finally got his work published in English, in vastly expanded form: *Interregional and International Trade*—617 pages.[147] The extension and modification of this building was to occupy the next couple of generations of trade theorists. It was not until the advent of the 'new trade theory' at the end of the 1970s and the early 1980s that an alternative to the factor proportions approach began to be built—and then largely on the foundations of one of the side tracks of Ohlin's work—increasing returns.[148]

* * *

Alluding to the introduction of the present essay, it may be argued that Eli Heckscher and Bertil Ohlin also constituted an intellectual twosome. In his long essay on Ohlin, Rolf Henriksson emphasizes not only the importance of Heckscher for Ohlin, but also the importance of Ohlin for Heckscher.[149] The latter's regard for the former was high. In his 1922 letter to Per Jacobsson, he was outspoken: 'I consider Ohlin to be the leading economist of the next generation …'[150]

However, Ohlin was not above criticism in Heckscher's eyes. On the contrary: when Ohlin succeeded him as professor of economics at the Stockholm School of Economics in 1929 (and Heckscher got a chair in economic history), Heckscher, who was a die-hard moralist, was under the impression that Ohlin for a while was earning a double salary—both from Copenhagen and Stockholm, and attacked him for that, and when Ohlin began his political career in the Liberal party, he blamed him for neglecting his teaching duties and tried to stop him from getting a requested leave of absence from the school.[151]

All's well that ends well, but everything does not end well. The personal friendship of Heckscher and Ohlin came to an end in 1935. After a meeting of Nordic economists in Oslo in June, where the two clashed over the issue of planning, which was in full swing at the time, Heckscher

[147] Ohlin (1933).

[148] Cf. e.g. the confessions of Paul Krugman (2002).

[149] Henriksson (2001, pp. 12–14).

[150] Cited by ibid., p. 4.

[151] Lundahl (2015a, pp. 164–165).

labeled Ohlin—since 1934 the leader of the Liberal Party Youth League—a political opportunist who, by declaring openness to arguments, would swallow whatever the party in power (the Social Democrats) chose to decide, called him a Social Democrat at heart and recommended him to join that party instead. Ohlin, in turn, contended that Heckscher was no Liberal, but a Conservative with an inclination to do 'less than honest things.' From then on, the personal relationship between Heckscher and Ohlin was frozen. Heckscher announced the end of it and Ohlin set for future 'collegial treatment.' 'None of my disciples have interested me as much as you, I have not gone out of my way as much for anybody else – and nobody else has caused me such disappointment,' wrote Heckscher to his former student.[152] In his memoirs, Ohlin, in turn, resented the rupture: '… to say the least, it felt sad that my personal relations to a man that I still admired very much and who during more than ten years had helped me so much as had Eli Heckscher, deteriorated radically during the first years of the 1930s and thereafter remained strongly limited.'[153]

That was the end of a beautiful friendship.[154]

Published in Pierre Guillet de Monthoux and Robert Stasinski (eds), *The Heckscher-Ohlin Room*. Stockholm: Stockholm School of Economics Art Initiative, 2018. Reprinted by permission.

Acknowledgements Thanks are due for bibliographical assistance to Peter Gavelin and Erik and Oscar Lundahl, and for constructive comments on a draft version by Benny Carlson and Christina Rapp Lundahl. The usual disclaimer applies.

References

Bastable, C.F. (1903), *The Theory of International Trade*. Fourth edition. London: Macmillan and Co.

Berg, Annika; Florin, Christina and Wisselgren, Per (eds) (2011), *Par i vetenskap och politik: intellektuella äktenskap i moderniteten*. Umeå: Borea.

Brock, Fritz H:son (1913), 'Om dyrtid, arbetslöner och solidartullar', *Statsvetenskaplig Tidskrift*, Vol. 16, No. 5, 276–294.

[152] Carlson (2018, p. 74).

[153] Ohlin (1972, p. 272).

[154] But hardly the beginning of love.

Brock, Fritz H:son (1917), *Om tullarne samt om den lämpligaste metoden för vår sockerbeskattning*. Stockholm: Albert Bonniers Förlag.

Brock, Fritz (1919), 'Om tullarne. Ett genmäle', *Ekonomisk Tidskrift*, Vol. 21, No. 1, 48–50.

Carlson, Benny (2018), *Swedish Economists in the 1930s Debate on Economic Planning*. Cham: Palgrave Macmillan.

Cassel, Gustav (1918), *Theoretische Sozialökonomie*. Leipzig: C.F. Winter.

Caves, Richard E. (1978), 'Bertil Ohlin's Contributions to Economics', *Scandinavian Journal of Economics*, Vol. 80, No. 1, 86–99.

Chadwick, Whitney and de Courtivron, Isabelle (eds) (1993), *Significant Others: Creativity and Intimate Partnerships*. London and New York: Thames and Hudson.

Connor, Steve (2010), *The Core of Truth Behind Sir Isaac Newton's Apple*. https://www.independent.co.uk/news/science/the-core-of-truth-behind-sir-isaac-newtons-apple-1870915.html. Downloaded 23 June 2018.

Corden, W. Max and Neary, J. Peter (1982), 'Booming Sector and De-industrialization in a Small Open Economy', *Economic Journal*, Vol. 92, No. 368, 825–848.

Findlay, Ronald (1995), *Factor Proportions, Trade, and Growth*. Cambridge, MA and London: MIT Press.

Findlay, Ronald; Henriksson, Rolf G.H.; Lindgren, Håkan and Lundahl, Mats (eds) (2006), *Eli Heckscher, International Trade, and Economic History*. Cambridge, MA and London: MIT Press.

Findlay, Ronald; Jonung, Lars and Lundahl, Mats (eds) (2002), *Bertil Ohlin: A Centennial Celebration (1899–1999)*. Cambridge, MA and London: MIT Press.

Flam, Harry (1993), 'Bertil Ohlin's Contributions to International Economics', in: Lars Jonung (ed.), *Swedish Economic Thought: Explorations and Advances*. London and New York: Routledge.

Flam, Harry and Flanders, M. June (1991), 'Introduction', in: Harry Flam and M. June Flanders (eds), *Heckscher-Ohlin Trade Theory*. Cambridge, MA and London: MIT Press.

Flam, Harry and Flanders, M. June (2002), 'The Young Ohlin on the Theory of Interregional and International Trade', in: Ronald Findlay, Lars Jonung and Mats Lundahl (eds), *Bertil Ohlin: A Centennial Celebration (1899–1999)*. Cambridge, MA and London: MIT Press.

Gårdlund, Torsten (2002), 'Bertil Ohlin as a Friend and Colleague', in: Ronald Findlay, Lars Jonung and Mats Lundahl (eds), *Bertil Ohlin: A Centennial Celebration (1899-1999)*. Cambridge, MA and London: MIT Press.

Heckscher, Eli F. (1913), 'Tullpolitik och trustväsen med anledning af förslaget om sockertullens sänkande', *Ekonomisk Tidskrift*, Vol. 15, No. 5, 1–29.

Heckscher, Eli F. (1915), *Världskrigets ekonomi: En studie af nutidens näringslif under krigets inverkan*. Stockholm: Handelshögskolan.

Heckscher, Eli F. (1918a), *Svenska produktionsproblem*. Stockholm: Albert Bonniers Förlag.

Heckscher, Eli F. (1918b), *Kontinentalsystemet*. Stockholm: P.A. Norstedt & Söner.

Heckscher, Eli F. (1918c), Review of Fritz H:son Brock. *Om tullarne samt om den lämpligaste metoden för vår sockerbeskattning*, *Ekonomisk Tidskrift*, Vol. 20, 323–327.

Heckscher, Eli F. (1919a), *Tullsystemets framtid*. Stockholm: Kooperativa Förbundets Förlag.

Heckscher, Eli F. (1919b), 'Utrikeshandelns verkan på inkomstfördelningen. Några teoretiska grundlinjer', *Ekonomisk Tidskrift*, Vol. 21, No. 2, 1–32.

Heckscher, Eli F. (1919c), 'Svar', *Ekonomisk Tidskrift*, Vol. 21, No. 1, 50.

Heckscher, Eli F. (1920), 'Råvaruexport och utvandring', *Ekonomisk Tidskrift*, Vol. 22, 172–178.

Heckscher, Eli F. (1922), *The Continental System: An Economic Interpretation*. Oxford: The Clarendon Press.

Heckscher, Eli F. (1991), 'The Effect of Foreign Trade on the Distribution of Income', in: Harry Flam and M. June Flanders (eds), *Heckscher-Ohlin Trade Theory*. Cambridge, MA and London: MIT Press.

Heckscher, Eva; Heckscher, Einar; Heckscher, Sten and Heckscher, Ivar (2005), 'A Portrait of Our Grandfather', in: Ronald Findlay, Rolf G.H. Henriksson, Håkan Lindgren and Mats Lundahl (eds), *Eli Heckscher, International Trade, and Economic History*. Cambridge, MA and London: MIT Press.

Hederberg, Hans (2004), *Sanningen, inget annat än sanningen: Sex decennier ur Alva & Gunnar Myrdals liv*. Stockholm: Atlantis.

Henriksson, Rolf G.H. (2001), *Eureka unter den Linden: A Reinterpretation of Ohlin's Early Contributions to the Heckscher-Ohlin Theme*. Unpublished manuscript, Department of Economics, Stockholm University.

Henriksson, Rolf G.H. (2002), 'Eureka unter den Linden: A Reinterpretation of Ohlin's Early Contributions to the Heckscher-Ohlin Theme', in: Ronald Findlay, Lars Jonung and Mats Lundahl (eds), *Bertil Ohlin: A Centennial Celebration (1899–1999)*. Cambridge, MA and London: MIT Press.

Herlitz, Lars (2002), 'Wheat and Wood: Wicksell, Heckscher, and the Theory of Foreign Trade, 1896–1920', *History of Political Economy*, Vol. 34, No. 2, 479–498.

Jonung, Lars (1992), 'Economics, the Swedish Way 1889–1989', in: Lars Engwall (ed.), *Economics in Sweden*. London and New York: Routledge.

Krugman, Paul (2002), 'Was It All in Ohlin?', in: Ronald Findlay, Lars Jonung and Mats Lundahl (eds), *Bertil Ohlin: A Centennial Celebration (1899–1999)*. Cambridge, MA and London: MIT Press.

Leijonhufvud, Axel (1968), *On Keynesian Economics and the Economics of Keynes: A Study in Monetary Theory*. New York: Oxford University Press.
Lerner, Abba P. (1952), 'Factor Prices and International Trade', *Economica*, NS, Vol. 19, No. 73, 1–15.
Lundahl, Mats (2005), *Knut Wicksell on Poverty: 'No Place Is Too Exalted for the Preaching of These Doctrines'*. London and New York: Routledge.
Lundahl, Mats (2015a), 'Eli Heckscher and the Colleagues: The Role of Personality for Economic History', in: *Seven Figures in the History of Swedish Economic Thought: Knut Wicksell, Eli Heckscher, Bertil Ohlin, Torsten Gårdlund, Sven Rydenfelt and Jaime Behar*. Houndmills, Basingstoke and New York: Palgrave Macmillan.
Lundahl, Mats (2015b), 'Foreign Trade and Exchange Rates: The Theoretical Contributions of Eli Heckscher to International Economics', in: *Seven Figures in the History of Swedish Economic Thought: Knut Wicksell, Eli Heckscher, Bertil Ohlin, Torsten Gårdlund, Sven Rydenfelt and Jaime Behar*. Houndmills, Basingstoke and New York: Palgrave Macmillan.
Mill, John Stuart (1848), *Principles of Political Economy*. London: J.W. Parker.
Morell, Mats (2006), 'From Wartime Provisioning to Barbarous Prosperity: Eli F. Heckscher's Investigations of Food Consumption in Early Modern Sweden', in: Ronald Findlay, Rolf G.H. Henriksson, Håkan Lindgren and Mats Lundahl (eds), *Eli Heckscher, International Trade, and Economic History*. Cambridge, MA and London: MIT Press.
Myrdal, Alva and Myrdal, Gunnar (2003), *De blå kuverten: Kärleksbreven juli 1919 – augusti 1920*, utgivna av Yvonne Hirdman. Hedemora: Gidlunds Förlag.
Ohlin, Bertil (1918), *Spannmålstullarna*. Stockholm: Seminar paper, vinterterminen 1918, Nationalekonomiska seminariet B, Stockholm School of Economics.
Ohlin, Bertil (1919a), 'Ett nationalekonomiskt standardverk', *Svenska Dagbladet*, 28 May.
Ohlin, Bertil (1919b), 'Kvantitetsteorin i den svenska litteraturen', *Ekonomisk Tidskrift*, Vol. 21, No. 2, 99–146.
Ohlin, Bertil (1921), 'Växelkursernas jämviktsläge', *Ekonomisk Tidskrift*, Vol. 23, 29–37.
Ohlin, Bertil (1922), *Det interregionala bytets teori*. Stockholm: Licentiate thesis, Stockholms Högskola (Stockholm College).
Ohlin, Bertil (1924), *Handelns teori*. Stockholm: AB Nordiska Bokhandeln.
Ohlin, Bertil (1933), *Interregional and International Trade*. Cambridge, MA: Harvard University Press.
Ohlin, Bertil (1972), *Bertil Ohlins memoarer: Ung man blir politiker*. Stockholm: Bonniers.

Ohlin, Bertil (1991), *The Theory of Trade*, in: Harry Flam and M. June Flanders (eds), *Heckscher-Ohlin Trade Theory*. Cambridge, MA and London: MIT Press.

Ohlin, Bertil (2002), 'The Theory of Interregional Exchange', in: Ronald Findlay, Lars Jonung and Mats Lundahl (eds), *Bertil Ohlin: A Centennial Celebration (1899–1999)*. Cambridge, MA and London: MIT Press.

Puu, Tönu (1990), 'On the Unity of Arts, Crafts, and Sciences: Reflections of an Economist and Violmaker', *Journal of Cultural Economics*, Vol. 14, No. 1, 19–34.

Puu, Tönu (2006), *Arts, Sciences, and Economics: A Historical Safari*. Berlin: Springer.

Samuelson, Paul A. (1948), 'International Trade and the Equalization of Factor Prices', *Economic Journal*, Vol. 58, No. 230, 168–184.

Samuelson, Paul A. (1949), 'International Factor Price Equalization Once Again', *Economic Journal*, Vol. 59, No. 234, 181–197.

Samuelson, Paul A. (1982), 'Bertil Ohlin: 1899–1979', *Journal of International Economics*, Vol. 12, No. 1 (supplement), 33–49.

Schön, Lennart (2014), *En modern svensk ekonomisk historia: Tillväxt och omvandling under två sekler*. Fjärde upplagan. Lund: Studentlitteratur.

Silverstolpe, Gunnar (1920), 'Ricardo och växelkursen', *Ekonomisk Tidskrift*, Vol. 22, 281–295.

SOU 1924:38, Finansdepartementet, *Tull- och traktatkomitténs utredningar och betänkanden XXXVI. Betänkande angående tullskyddssystemets verkningar i Sverige före världskriget, Del II*. Stockholm: Isaac Marcus' Boktryckeri-Aktiebolag. https://data.kb.se/datasets/2015/02/sou/1924/1924_38%28libris id_14181136%29.pdf. Downloaded 3 August 2018.

Stolper, Wolfgang and Samuelson, Paul A. (1941), 'Protection and Real Wages', *Review of Economic Studies*, Vol. 9, No. 1, 58–73.

Stukeley, William (2004) [1752], *Memoirs of Sir Isaac Newton's Life*. http://www.newtonproject.ox.ac.uk/view/texts/normalized/OTHE00001. Downloaded 23 June 2018.

Topp, Nils-Henrik (2002), 'Bertil Ohlin in Copenhagen', in: Ronald Findlay, Lars Jonung and Mats Lundahl (eds), *Bertil Ohlin: A Centennial Celebration (1899–1999)*. Cambridge, MA and London: MIT Press.

Viner, Jacob (1924), *Canada's Balance of International 1900-1913*. Cambridge, MA: Harvard University Press.

Vinterhed, Kerstin (2003), *Kärlek i tjugonde seklet – en biografi över Alva och Gunnar Myrdal*. Stockholm: Atlas.

Wadensjö, Eskil (1994), 'Fritz Brock – An Eccentric Economist', in: *Research 1993, Annual Report and Program*. Uppsala: Department of Economics, Uppsala University.

Wicksell, Knut (1911) *Föreläsningar i nationalekonomi. Första delen: Teoretisk nationalekonomi. Häft. I.* Andra, omarbetade upplagan. Lund: Berlingska Boktryckeriet.

Wicksell, Knut (1915) *Föreläsningar i nationalekonomi. Första delen: Teoretisk nationalekonomi, Häft. II, Om penningar och kredit.* Andra, tillökade upplagan. Stockholm: C.E. Fritzes Hofbokhandel (i distribution).

Wicksell, Knut (1919), 'Heckscher, E.F., *Svenska produktionsproblem*', *Forum*, Vol. 6, No. 2: 16–17, No. 3, 29–31.

Wicksell, Knut (1920a), 'Frihandel och utvandring', *Ekonomisk Tidskrift*, Vol. 22, 124–125.

Wicksell, Knut (1920b), 'Råvaruexport och utvandring', *Ekonomisk Tidskrift*, Vol. 22, 229.

Williams, John H. (1920), *Argentine International Trade Under Inconvertible Paper Money 1880–1900.* Cambridge MA: Harvard University Press.

Williams, John H. (1929), 'The Theory of International Trade Reconsidered', *Economic Journal*, Vol. 39, No. 154, 195–209.

CHAPTER 3

Gunnar Myrdal on Poverty and Circular, Cumulative Causation

The present essay deals with Gunnar Myrdal's analysis of poverty, as applied to Sweden in the 1930s, the United States at the beginning of the 1940s, the international economy in the 1950s and South Asia in the 1960s. It also traces the development of the methodology which he applied in his main works, from the late 1920s to the beginning of the 1970s. As Paul Streeten has pointed out, 'Methodological questions occupied Myrdal's thought throughout his life,'[1] and his methodology is absolutely central to what he wrote on poverty and social policy.

When fully developed, Myrdal's analysis rested on five interrelated pillars. One is the principle of circular dynamic, cumulative causation, which in turn is based on the assumption that the analysis must be dynamic, and not static. The third is the conviction that the analysis must be carried out within an institutional framework. The remaining two pillars are explicit value premises and social engineering.

[1] Streeten (1992, p. 120).

M. Lundahl, *Twelve Figures in Swedish Economics*, Palgrave Studies in the History of Economic Thought, https://doi.org/10.1007/978-3-030-94327-1_3

Dynamics

In his doctoral dissertation from 1927, *Prisbildningsproblemet och föränderligheten* [The Price Formation Problem and Economic Change],[2] Gunnar Myrdal made an attempt to extend the static neoclassical price theory. He was inspired by the formulation provided by his teacher, Gustav Cassel, who considered prices to be established by the interaction of three factors: demand as a function of price, the technical conditions of production and the available means of production.[3] Cassel was also concerned with the dynamics of price formation, through the influence of such exogenous factors as population growth on the three 'immediate' determinants, but never incorporated it into any explicit analysis.[4]

Myrdal took upon himself to fill the void 'to a certain extent,'[5] by working expectations with respect to the future into the analysis of price formation. '... the price formation takes place in human minds. Thus, notions of the degree of probability of future changes and in addition valuations of the very moment of uncertainty in these notions will exert an influence on price formation at the present time.'[6] To this he added the existence of time lags in the reaction of the allocation of production factors to changes in demand and supply—'stickiness'—and risk. The interaction between the present and the future, as Myrdal saw it, worked in two directions, forwards in time through the impact of actually realized prices on future prices, and backwards, though anticipations:

> It is the latter problem which is the primary one from the theoretical point of view. Because it is this price formation situation, where the anticipations have contributed to the outcome, which is hit by the changes and which then develops into a new one. The investigation of the former problem in other words requires that the latter problem is solved.[7]

[2] Myrdal (1927).

[3] Cassel (1923, p. 152).

[4] Hansson (1982, pp. 30–32).

[5] Myrdal (1927, p. 4).

[6] Ibid., p. 8.

[7] Ibid., p. 21.

In other words, Myrdal's problem was 'how equilibrium values and prices are determined in a world in which expectations form part of the data upon which decisions are taken.'[8]

We will stop here. This is not the place to go into the details of Myrdal's analysis of the price formation process. We simply note that from the very beginning of his academic career he was concerned with dynamic, as opposed to static, analysis.

Wicksell's Cumulative Process and Myrdal's Adaptation of It

Four years after his thesis defense, Myrdal was to extend his insistence on dynamics into the use of cumulative causation. The occasion was his critique and extension of a mechanism introduced by Knut Wicksell. One of the things that Wicksell is best known for is his cumulative process, the process which sets off upward or downward movements in the price level. In his original formulation, he took as his point of departure what he called the natural rate of interest. It was introduced in *Interest and Prices*:

> There is a certain rate of interest which is neutral with respect to commodity prices, and tends neither to raise nor to lower them. This is necessarily the same as the rate of interest which would be determined by supply and demand if no use were made of money and all lending would be effected in the form of real capital goods. It comes to much the same thing as the current value of the *natural interest on capital*.[9]

In the second volume of his *Lectures on Political Economy* (Swedish original: Wicksell, 1906), Wicksell changed his definition: 'The rate of interest at which *the demand for loan capital and the supply of savings* exactly agree, and which more or less corresponds to the expected yield on the newly created capital, will ... be the normal or natural real rate.'[10] According to Wicksell, there is no reason why we should expect the normal or natural rate of interest to coincide with the bank lending rate. If banks lend at an interest rate which diverges from the natural one,

[8] Seccareccia (1992, p. 154).

[9] Wicksell (1936, p. 10), German original: Wicksell (1898).

[10] Wicksell (1935, p. 193).

the price level will change. Suppose that the lending rate of interest falls below the real rate. Then, producers benefit from lending and will expand their production and investment. This will in turn expand the demand for goods and services used for investment and set off a process where the price level will increase.

Wicksell saw the process as a cumulative one: 'It is ... frequently the case that quite a small fall in the [lending] rate of interest would *immediately* bring about a much greater rise in prices. The price which can be paid for goods obtained by means of credit is higher the longer the period during which the credit is utilized.'[11] (In the case of an increased lending rate, producers will make losses and be discouraged from investing, etc.) Carl Uhr explains the logic in his *Economic Doctrines of Knut Wicksell*:

> In fact, if the process is of long duration, it may accelerate in its later stages, or, as he put it, 'create its own draft.' This would happen if entrepreneurs (who are usually assumed to make decisions for the future on the expectation of the continuation of current prices), after having experienced some rounds of price increases, begin to make their decisions on expectations of increasing prices. In such cases speculation is aroused and prices may reach great heights. The process itself may then terminate in a crisis. As increasing production maladjustments, overextension of investment in various branches of the economy, etc., engender doubts concerning the continuation of further price increases.[12]

Alternatively, the banks (sluggishly) adjust their lending rates or some exogenous change brings an end to the process.

Knut Wicksell's idea of cumulative causation was picked up, criticized, extended and brought to bear on completely different issues by Gunnar Myrdal from the 1930s to the 1970s. Myrdal began with an immanent critique of Wicksell, developed gradually in a Swedish, a German, and, finally, an English version of what in the end became *Monetary Equilibrium*.[13] By immanent critique, Myrdal meant a critique which, based on Wicksell's assumptions examined the inner consistency of his reasoning. He focused on Wicksell's central notion: the normal rate of interest.

[11] Wicksell (1936, p. 91).

[12] Uhr (1962, p. 233).

[13] Myrdal (1931a, 1933b, 1939).

Myrdal took issue with the fact that Wicksell had chosen to define monetary equilibrium in a threefold way. The normal rate of interest coincides with the lending rate and at the same time equates savings and investment and ensures that the price level remains constant. Myrdal discussed whether these three conditions are compatible with each other. He argued that Wicksell's analysis was too simplified, that—in the same way as with price formation—it is necessary to include anticipations in the reasoning and that the analysis must be carried out in the context of a monetary economy.

More interesting than Myrdal's criticism from the present point of view, however, is the fact that Myrdal accepted Wicksell's notion of a cumulative process:

> On one point ... Myrdal absorbed Wicksell without significant modification, namely the conception of a 'cumulative process.' With respect to the problem at hand, this could be defined as a '*dynamic deviation in one direction or the other from a monetary equilibrium*.' And he added that 'the essential feature of the process is a shift in production which brings with it an increased production of real capital if the dynamic process has an upward direction and a decreased production if the process has a downward trend.'[14]

Gunnar Myrdal was to extend the cumulative process into circular causation as well and make use of the principle in his later works. We will come back to this.

The Problem of Value Premises

Already before Myrdal took issue with Wicksell's formulation of the cumulative process, he had begun to develop his third pillar, the one dealing with value premises. In 1930, he published *Vetenskap och politik i nationalekonomien* [English translation, *The Political Element in the Development of Economic Theory*].[15] In this book, 'one of the most famous methodological treatises in economics,'[16] Myrdal attacked his

[14] Barber (2008, p. 26). The two quotations are from Myrdal (1939, pp. 29 and 31, respectively).

[15] Myrdal (1930, 1953).

[16] Velupillai (1992, p. 137).

colleagues for posing as objective scientists in situations where they in fact were spreading value-laden statements which lacked a solid scientific foundation, using them to formulate economic policies.

Myrdal investigated the development of the mainstream of economics from the Enlightenment to his own time, uncovering the underlying assumptions and value judgements—elements that were seldom spelled out explicitly or discussed. Not that he condemned normative economics. Economic science is to a large extent an instrumental science and Myrdal wanted to construct a 'technology of economics' that could be of help when it came to designing policy interventions. In the English version of the book he explained what he meant: 'a scientific theory of how policy can serve concrete interests.'[17]

The question was how this could be achieved. In 1930, Myrdal still thought that objectivity was possible to some extent. 'Economists are on safe ground as long as they describe actual events and their causal connections, and as long as they examine the effects of certain clearly defined "interventions" under specified conditions,'[18] that is, as long as they work within what is conventionally known as 'positive' economics. Once we move into the field of normative recommendations, however, complications arise, since interests are likely to differ. The solution of the normative problem was to bring the value premises that govern policy decisions out in the open. The technology of economics 'should always formulate its value premises explicitly in concrete terms and relate them to the actual valuations of social groups …'.[19]

However, in the second edition of *Vetenskap och politik*, from 1972, Myrdal claimed to have been methodologically naïve when he wrote the first edition. 'Now I know … that value premises are necessary already when it comes to observing reality, establish the facts and the causal relations between facts.'[20] Already in his inaugural lecture for the Lars Hierta chair in economics and finance, on *The Changing World View in Economics*, in 1935, Myrdal took his views on explicit value premises one step further.[21] There was no way to escape the aprioristic. Biases would

[17] Myrdal (1953, p. 196).

[18] Ibid., p. 198.

[19] Ibid., p. 204.

[20] Myrdal (1972, p. 13).

[21] Myrdal (1935a).

creep as much into positive economics as into normative investigations. In order to receive an answer, you must pose a question, but the question was a result of a choice which hence to a certain extent determined the answer. The way out was to work with an explicit set of value premises—a conviction that permeated all his subsequent scientific work. These value premises must be chosen consciously and methodically.

In an opening address to the British Sociological Association in 1953, Myrdal came back to his insistence on a conscious and consistent set of explicit value premises: 'They cannot be a priori self-evident or generally valid. They should be chosen, but not arbitrarily, for the choice must meet the criteria of relevance and significance to the society we live in.'[22] For a premise to be relevant it must correspond to 'the interests and ideals of actual persons and groups of persons.' Significance, in turn, refers to 'valuations which are held by substantial groups of people or by small groups with substantial social power.'[23]

The conscious and rational selection of value premises constitutes the foundation upon which policy formulation must rest. 'When the value premise is chosen and defined, it will, in combination with the analysis of facts, permit rational policy conclusions. These conclusions are rational because they are ... hypothetical. They only spell out the logical policy implications of the selected value premise in a known context of reality.'[24] It is only under these circumstances that it is possible to arrive at rational economic policy making based on feasible goals.[25]

Gunnar Myrdal came back to the issue of value premises in a small book in 1969. He then focused on three possible sources of bias in social science research and how to avoid them: (1) the heritage of earlier writings which contain normative and teleological notions (2) the influence of the society where the researcher lives and works and (3) the researcher's own personality.[26] The solution, as always, was to make the value premises governing the investigation explicit. The method chosen by Myrdal has important consequences for economic analysis:

[22] Myrdal (1958, p. 52).

[23] Ibid., pp. 157, 158.

[24] Ibid., pp. 48–49. Cf., however, Rosier (1992).

[25] Myrdal (1953, p. 206).

[26] Myrdal (1969, pp. 3–4).

> ... [It] leads us to conclude that it is impossible to distinguish clearly ends from means, or positive economics from normative economics. This is not, however, a condition that we can try to avoid, since it constitutes part of the very essence of any social science. It is ... utopian to believe in a value-free political economy.[27]

A Programmatic Article and Active Economic Policy

Gunnar Myrdal and his wife Alva spent the academic year 1929–1930 in the United States. They arrived there just before Black Thursday, 29 October 1929, the beginning of the Great Depression. What they saw was something that would stay with them for the rest of their lives: abject poverty and extreme inequality:

> It was in the United States, as a result, that Alva and Gunnar Myrdal claimed to have wakened up politically. Even apart from the Depression, they were profoundly shaken by the brutal contrasts between millionaires and slum dwellers that they now witnessed. In Sweden, there was already greater equality and local communities along with government agencies had long provided support for those in need. To see such great poverty and such injustice toward racial and religious minorities radicalized both of them.[28]

Their US experience would soon be converted into a call for action on the home front. In 1932, the year when he joined the Social Democratic Party, Gunnar Myrdal published a programmatic article: 'Socialpolitikens dilemma [The Dilemma of Social Policy].'[29] After the First World War, Swedish social policy had developed considerably. But, argued Myrdal, it fit neither the Liberal nor the Socialist ideology. It was a compromise between the two. Myrdal discerned an opening rift between the two ideologies. The very expansion of the scope of social policy served to create increasing expectations with respect to its results, in terms of nutrition, health care, education and housing.

[27] Peltier (1992, p. 188).

[28] Bok (1992, p. 7).

[29] Myrdal (1932a, 1932b).

Myrdal felt that the increasing demand for decent housing among the poor would trigger a class conflict of interest—precisely the conflict that social policy was supposed to defuse. According to the Liberal ideology, assistance had to be given on such conditions that it did not decrease the willingness of the individuals to tackle their situation themselves. This was the dilemma of social policy as viewed from the Liberal camp. The Socialist ideology with respect to social policy was facing a dilemma as well. Myrdal saw 'a risk that the workers would begin to regard social policy as mere patches on the rags, and that they would again turn their attention to more radical change – a change of the "system".'[30] He pointed out that social policy in Sweden hitherto had dealt exclusively with symptoms and called for a more or less radical prophylactic policy instead. Such a policy would be down to earth. 'Its romanticism is that of the engineer.'[31] It would be 'radical in the sense that it calmly presupposes very deep-going reforms of the social "system", which is hence no longer respected as the foundation of the "reforms", since the reforms to a large extent are directed toward the change of precisely this foundation.'[32]

The new approach rested on planning. Economic planning means that you are prepared to push the measures far enough for them to have maximum efficiency, whichever the measures happen to be and regardless of their purpose. 'The more radical social policy is precisely the planned economy variety of social policy.'[33] As Myrdal stated in 1980, 'Planning is changing institutions.'[34] The Liberal market economy was a static, unrealistic construction, while the planning advocates shared a dynamic, realistic view of society and its institutions.

The same approach showed up in other contexts. The year before the publication of 'Socialpolitikens dilemma,' 1931, in the book *Sveriges väg genom penningkrisen* [Sweden's Road through the Monetary Crisis], Myrdal stressed the importance of a monetary policy 'that is *possible* given the actual circumstances and *desirable* from the point of view of

[30] Myrdal (1932b, p. 21).

[31] Ibid., p. 25.

[32] Ibid., p. 28.

[33] Ibid., p. 31.

[34] Angresano (1997, p. 159).

the economic interests and the political views of different groups of citizens.'[35] Its efficiency was dependent on fiscal and social policy measures. Most important was to increase production. The welfare of the Swedes rested on that and Myrdal argued that in order to preserve and develop 'the democratic and private capitalist character sector of the Swedish economy' and preserve the smooth function of the system of checks and balances in Swedish society a measure of planned economy had to be added, at least for the time being.[36]

In 1932, Myrdal was appointed to the official Committee on Unemployment. The following year, he was asked by the Social Democratic Minister of Finance Ernst Wigforss to produce a memorandum endorsing the use of an expansionist fiscal policy to combat unemployment. This became the theoretical foundation of an active government policy. It advocated the use of public works to make use of the otherwise unemployed, stimulate production and increase government revenues. 'Public works, in contrast to relief payments, result in increased production. [...] It is only when the scope for public works is exhausted that relief payments for those still unemployed are motivated.'[37]

Myrdal extended his reasoning in *Finanspolitikens ekonomiska verkningar* [The Economic Effects of Fiscal Policy], published in 1934. There he also stressed the interventionist nature of economic policy measures and the '*necessarily political character of public finance*,' which constituted a part of the institutional framework of the market economy.[38] Myrdal's reasoning rested on the social engineering perspective. The goal of public economic policy was to change the process of price formation in such a way as to make it meet public goals by changing the institutional framework within which the private sector had to work. In the public finance context, revenues were a function of the desired expenditures, and the latter were in turn determined by their economic and social consequences, and not by profitability.

[35] Myrdal (1931b, p. 9).

[36] Ibid., p. 127.

[37] Myrdal (1933a, p. 75).

[38] Myrdal (1934, p. 14).

Circular Causation and Institutions

In his 1935 inaugural lecture, Myrdal hinted that economic analysis needed a holistic approach:

> In a coherent economic policy, there exist no longer any special problems; all special problems are interconnected. The consequence of this for economic research and education is that specialist knowledge is of little value. [...] The study of economics hence to an increasing extent will be a study of the entire economy.[39]

Myrdal had by then begun to build up his latter-day conviction that in the study of society you have to take into account that all the variables that constitute it interact in a circular (and cumulative) fashion.[40] As a young man, he looked down on the American institutionalists like Thorstein Veblen, John R. Commons and Wesley C. Mitchell. The latter two were still alive and Myrdal met them. Looking back at his visit thirty-eight years later he stressed that at the time he 'was not converted to what was then called "the new economics",'[41] a conviction that was strengthened during the early 1930s:

> ... the courageous trend in the late Twenties toward an institutional approach had a brief existence in the United States. What I believe nipped it in the bud was the world-wide economic depression. Faced by this great calamity, we economists of the 'theoretical' school, accustomed to reason in terms of simplified macro-models, felt we were on top of the situation, while the institutionalists were left in the muddle. It was at this stage that economists in the stream of the Keynesian revolution adjusted their theoretical models to the needs of the time, which thus gave victory much more broadly to our 'theoretical' approach.[42]

However, in just a couple of years, Gunnar Myrdal was to change his methodological approach. The 'technology of economics' that he had in mind in *Vetenskap och politik i nationalekonomien* would not necessarily be

[39] Myrdal (1935a, pp. 37–38).

[40] Carlson (2013) provides a chronological account of the findings of a number of accounts of Myrdal's conversion to institutionalism.

[41] Myrdal (1978a, p. 771).

[42] Myrdal (1974, p. 7).

accepted by the decision makers. The ruling constellations were not given once and for all, however. There was no need to take the institutional setting—'the legal order, and the customs, habits, and conventions, which are sanctioned, or at least tolerated, by that legal order'—for granted.[43] The political struggle was very much about the institutional setup. Myrdal hence called for the inclusion of institutional change into the economic analysis. 'An inquiry into economic interests should therefore treat the whole institutional set-up as a variable. It should also examine to what extent any groups are sufficiently powerful to bring about institutional changes throughout the price system.'[44]

Being involved in a number of government commissions in the 1930s forced Gunnar Myrdal to concentrate on practical social issues which most of the time were multidimensional and called for practical solutions based on several social sciences, solutions that involved reform of institutions. He has himself described his change of course:

> Meanwhile, I had become an institutional economist. In Sweden I became involved in social equality problems, which I found could not be handled scientifically except by broadening the approach to all human relations. In 1938 I accepted responsibility for a study of race relations in the United States, and this took me farther away from conventional economics. I found myself writing a book about the entire American civilization, with stress on various aspects relevant from the viewpoint of the largest of the disadvantaged groups here.
>
> From then on more definitely I came to see that there are no economic, sociological, or psychological problems, but just problems, and they are all mixed and composite. In research, the only permissible demarcation is between relevant and irrelevant conditions. The problems are regularly also political and, moreover, must be seen in historical perspective.[45]

James Angresano offers the following characteristic of the approach:

> Myrdal's perspective towards an economy was evolutionary-institutional. He viewed the economy not as a static entity, but as an ongoing process comprised of the aggregate of institutions which perform economic functions and determine economic conditions. These institutions behave

[43] Myrdal (1953, p. 196).

[44] Ibid., pp. 196–197.

[45] Myrdal (1978a, p. 772).

> according to working rules, many of which are established by authorities who allocate scarce resources while answering questions pertaining to production and distribution of goods and services. Working rules establish rights and duties of the economy's participants, and serve to create order among conflicting interests while strengthening the social process for coordinating economic (as well as social, political, and cultural) matters by outlining the boundaries of behavior for economic activity. Societies establish institutions and working rules in an attempt to achieve order – predictability without rigidity and flexibility without chaos.[46]

Formal rules establish the rights and duties of both the individuals and the state and they establish the property rights system within which the economic transactions take place. Informal rules (attitudes and opinions) in turn provide a basis for the establishment of formal rules by expressing the views of the citizens on the conditions that ought to prevail in society and on the existing conditions.

Social Engineering: The Population Issue

Gunnar Myrdal's interest in methodological issues predated his interest in poverty but during the 1930s, he began to produce works which touched social problems directly. The first item of this kind was a book written together with his wife, Alva: *Kris i befolkningsfrågan* [Crisis in the Population Question].[47] Birth and population growth rates were low in Sweden, although not uniformly so. The poor kept breeding too large families while middle class people actively reduced their fertility. If nothing was done, the country ran the risk of embarking upon the journey to extinction of the Swedish population. Unemployment was higher than ever, in the middle of the depression. Catastrophe was lurking around the corner.

In a 1935 pamphlet, Myrdal made a succinct statement of the reasons why an active population policy was needed.[48] Fertility had declined to a level that would lead to a future decline of the population. Myrdal did not believe that the concomitant increase of the capital-labor ratio would lead to increased wages and reduced unemployment. The population decline

[46] Angresano (1997, pp. 1–2).

[47] Myrdal and Myrdal (1934).

[48] Myrdal (1935b).

would also reduce production, the future, smaller, generations would have to support an increasing number of elderly and this would lower their own living standard. That people opted for fewer children was not strange. There was a tradeoff between more children and an increased material standard, but this, in the long run would be self-defeating.

Myrdal regarded the decline of the population as a cumulative process:

> ... it is very doubtful whether a reduction of the population, once it has gathered momentum, can ever be broken at any population level. The issue *may* then not be that of a certain reduction of the population, which may perhaps not be so serious, but of an increasing, ever downward depopulation tendency, a movement towards the extinction of the population.[49]

The Myrdals put the problem into a wider, social, context.[50] In order to break the downward spiral, social reform measures were needed. The population could not be allowed to grow unless the economic and social conditions of the poor were improved. This called for deep-going social engineering measures. The only way of simultaneously solving the problem of a potentially declining population and reducing poverty was the combination of thorough reform of the Swedish society and a redistribution of incomes. Solving the poverty problem would create room for more people. The new social policy should aim at the reduction of the risks that threatened the livelihood of the population and at securing employment and incomes for the families and contain measures that reduced the costs of having children. Incomes should be redistributed from people without children or with few children to families with more children as well as from richer to poorer people.

Their project did not end there, however. It was part of a deep-going effort to change Swedish society. It was an effort to create a modernity hitherto unheard of in Sweden.[51] The ambition of the Myrdals went far beyond the solution of the population problem. In the revised edition of their book, from 1935, they bluntly stated:

[49] Ibid., pp. 10–11.

[50] See Carlson (1990), for a thorough discussion.

[51] A detailed account of Alva and Gunnar Myrdal's project in the wider modernity context prevailing in Sweden at the time is provided by Etzemüller (2014).

> For us the problem is: depopulation or social reform. And the program becomes: a new society permeated by social solidarity, where the entire nation to an increasing extent recognizes its shared responsibility for the children who will constitute the next generation. Only through the gradual realization of this society it will become possible to gradually destroy the narrow individualism that currently poisons every aspect of the life of our people and threatens its very existence.[52]

The most important reform issue was that of guaranteeing a satisfactory living standard for the families. Unless employment and subsistence risks could be substantially reduced and incomes increased, '*all other measures to increase marital fertility will be futile*.'[53] Families needed economic security if they were to have more children. The entire labor force—including the women—had to be put to productive work. This called for legislation and new forms of childcare: collective forms, 'large nurseries,' i.e. daycare centers.

But this was not enough. In order to guarantee the reproduction of the Swedish population, a 'rather radical redistribution of incomes between families with different child support burdens and different incomes' was required,[54] This social solidarity, in combination with a prophylactic population policy that could serve to 'improve the quality of the human material,' was necessary in order to ensure that the Swedish population once more would 'find it worthwhile to reproduce itself.'[55]

The social recipe presented by the Myrdals involved a number of specific family policy measures: subsidized housing, an improved nutrition standard, health care at no cost to the families, and an educational system that rewarded cooperation among the pupils instead of promoting docile submission on the one hand and rugged individualist capitalism on the other.

The programmatic book by the Myrdals became the point of departure for 'virtually all the components of the welfare policy that were brought to the fore during the ... following decades.'[56] Gunnar was drafted to a number of government commissions on social issues between 1933 and

[52] Myrdal and Myrdal (1935, pp. 16–17).

[53] Myrdal and Myrdal (1934, p. 187).

[54] Ibid., p. 11.

[55] Ibid.

[56] Gustafsson (1987–1989, p. 151).

1938. Most important, however, in 1935, after the debate that followed the book, the Swedish government appointed a commission to deal with the population issue. Myrdal joined the commission, which worked until 1938. Needless to say, with his restless energy, Myrdal became the primus motor of the commission, which allowed him to turn his ideas with respect to social engineering into practice and which laid the foundation for the modern Swedish population policy. He was the main or the only author of several of the reports published by the commission, but he did not take any part in the drafting of the last reports, after a fallout with Nils Wohlin, the formal leader of the commission.

The population issue became the starting point for a large social reform program in Sweden, the realization of Prime Minister Per Albin Hansson's idea about the 'People's Home [folkhemmet],' what internationally became known as 'the Swedish model.'[57] As William Barber puts it, 'The architecture of the Swedish welfare state was ... put in place under the smokescreen of the population argument.'[58]

In a short article from 1937, Myrdal stressed that 'the social problem still is ... *mass poverty*.'[59] In order to improve the lot of the poor, he advanced the same recipe as in the 1934 book: a combination of social policy and income transfers. He spoke of 'consumption socialism.' By seeing to it that the transfers took the form of public subsidies of housing, health care and education, it would be easier to improve the situation of the poor than by providing mere cash. In the end, such a policy would also contribute to the production increases—the economic growth—that were necessary to come to grips with poverty in a sustainable way.[60]

An American Dilemma

In 1937, Gunnar Myrdal received an invitation from Frederick Keppel, the president of the Carnegie Corporation in New York, to lead an investigation of the 'Negro problem' in the United States—the position of blacks in American society and the relations between whites and blacks.

[57] Gustafsson (1998, p. 623).

[58] Barber (2008, p. 59).

[59] Myrdal (1937, p. 4).

[60] Gunnar Myrdal returned to the population issue in his 1938 Godkin Lectures at Harvard (Myrdal, 1962a).

Myrdal accepted and, in September 1938, left Sweden for the United States together with his family and the statistician Richard Sterner, who would become one of the members of his team. Myrdal and Sterner began their work with a two-month tour through the American South, where at the time the vast majority of blacks were disenfranchised, to get first-hand on-the-ground experience before they began reading the relevant literature.[61]

In the preface to the study, Myrdal spells out the all-embracing terms of reference:

> The study ... should aim at determining the social, political, educational, and economic status of the Negro in the United States as well as defining opinions held by different groups of Negroes and whites as to his 'right' status. It must, further, be concerned with both recent changes and current trends with respect to the Negro's position in American society. Attention must also be given to the total American picture with particular emphasis on relations between the two races. Finally, it must consider what changes are being or can be induced by education, legislation, interracial efforts, concerted action by Negro groups, etc.[62]

Gunnar Myrdal put together a team of six researchers plus thirty-one independent scholars and thirty-six assistants for work on different themes. The team members produced draft manuscripts,[63] but in the end, Myrdal wrote the entire text with Sterner and Arnold Rose, who figure as co-authors in the book. In August 1942, the manuscript was finished: a monumental study of almost 1,500 pages. Given the limits of the present essay, it is impossible to go into any details of this incredibly impressive study—arguably the best Myrdal ever wrote. What matters in the present context is how Myrdal viewed the 'Negro problem,' how he analyzed it and how he purported to solve it.

[61] Myrdal's own account of the work with the book is found in Myrdal (1987), a book dictated during the last years of his life. For a brilliant scholarly account of the history of *An American Dilemma*, see Jackson (1990).

[62] Myrdal (1944a, pp. x–xi).

[63] Several were published as books, most notably that by the social anthropologist Melville Herskovits (1941).

The 'Negro Problem'

At the time when Myrdal began his study, the 'Negro problem' was viewed mainly as an economic problem. In one sense, it was true. Poverty among blacks was one of the main ingredients of the racial issue. In 1932, the worst year of the depression, black unemployment in the major cities could run as high as 50 percent and in 1935, one-third of the black population was on relief. In the South, low agricultural prices made poor black tenant farmers face the unpalatable choice of either leaving agriculture or trying to survive on drastically reduced incomes.[64]

Myrdal himself offers a succinct summary evaluation of the appalling living conditions of the American blacks:

> The economic situation of the Negroes in America is pathological. Except for a small minority enjoying upper or middle class status, the masses of American Negroes, in the rural South and in the segregated slum quarters in Southern and Northern cities, are destitute. They own little property; even their household goods are mostly inadequate and dilapidated. Their incomes are not only low but irregular. They thus live from day to day and have scant security for the future. Their entire culture and their individual interests and strivings are narrow.[65]

The blacks were concentrated in the poorest part of the country, the South, in agriculture, which was a depressed industry. They seldom owned land but were sharecroppers or wage laborers. Few worked outside the agricultural sector, and if they did, it was in low-paid services or in unskilled jobs in manufacturing. And unemployment rates were much higher, proportionally, among blacks than among whites. At the same time, in the South, blacks were considered to be inferior to whites. Myrdal asked why this was so. He described them not as a class or a race, but as a 'caste':

> Myrdal's use of caste developed from his conception of Negro status as being determined by whites. If whites refused to intermarry with blacks, if they confronted blacks with insuperable social barriers that did not exist for white immigrant groups, then, Myrdal reasoned, the term *caste* was justified. Myrdal deployed the word *caste* to highlight the contradiction

[64] Myrdal (1944a, pp. 2–3).

[65] Ibid., p. 205.

between the American ideology of open competition and the practice of excluding Afro-Americans from rising freely in the white class system.[66]

According to the conventional American wisdom of the time, racial prejudice would disappear as economic and social standards improved among whites and blacks. Myrdal, however, thought of this as simplistic. He reintroduced the moral element into the discussion. The United States was an eminently moralistic society, he argued. A Liberal set of values, rooted in the Enlightenment, in Christianity and in English law, of which all Americans were conscious, existed. These principles Myrdal called the 'American Creed'. They constituted the foundation of American nationalism and they encompassed democracy, equality, freedom, fair opportunity and the rule of law.

However, it was precisely here that Myrdal saw the 'American Dilemma.' The American Creed built on 'high national and Christian precepts,' but 'the valuations on specific planes of individual and group living' often diverged substantially from the former.[67] This created a conflict within the individual, which in turn affected his behavior, making him pay lip service to the ideals in a number of concrete situations. The 'Negro problem' was an outstanding case in point. Myrdal argued that it was necessary 'to give *primary* attention to what goes on in the minds of white Americans.'[68] He did not stop there, however:

> In addition to making his argument about the conflict in the minds of white Americans, Myrdal presented a structural argument that a conflict between the American creed and racial discrimination existed within American institutions. He presented the case against scientific theories of inherited differences in intelligence and temperament among the races; he marshaled an enormous array of evidence to show discrimination in the economy, political system, and courts; he sketched a disturbing picture of the damage that segregation and racial discrimination inflicted on blacks; and he analyzed competing strategies within the black protest movement.[69]

[66] Jackson (1990, p. 220).

[67] Myrdal (1944a, p. xlvii).

[68] Ibid., p. li.

[69] Jackson (1990, p. 186).

Explicit Value Premises

Gunnar Myrdal spent two appendices in *An American Dilemma* on the problem of values and value premises. The danger of biased results was exceptionally high in the case of the 'Negro problem.' Myrdal identified six possible classes of scientific biases in the case of the American race problem: the scale of 'friendliness' to blacks, the scale of 'friendliness' to the South, the scale of radicalism-conservatism ('*In a sense this is the master scale of biases in the social sciences*'), the scale of optimism–pessimism, the scale of integration-isolation (the tendency to treat the race problem in isolation from the total complex of problems in American society), and, finally, the scale of scientific integrity (the degree to which the scientist is prepared to state 'plainly and clearly' unpopular conclusions.[70] The value premises that Myrdal himself chose for *An American Dilemma* were precisely what he called the American Creed.

Circular, Cumulative Causation

The terms of reference pointed directly to the need for an analytical method that cut across all the social sciences, and Myrdal had it. In *An American Dilemma*, he applied the approach that he had originally encountered in Wicksell's monetary writings: that of circular cumulative causation. Although he had played with the idea before, it was in this book that he wholeheartedly embraced for the first time the idea of a total view of an economic and social problem in terms of a circular and cumulative process—rejecting the notion of stable equilibrium—where all the constituent parts interacted with each other. In this process, no single part was more important than the other. Economic, social, cultural and moral factors all had to be brought into the picture to explain the situation. It was their interaction that made for the outcome. Myrdal identified three groups of factors which all reinforced each other in a cumulative fashion so as to keep the blacks at the bottom of American society but which could also interact in the opposite direction:

> The scheme of causal interrelation is as important in explaining why Negroes are so poor and in evaluating the wider social effects of Negro poverty. The dynamics of the problem is this: A primary change, induced

[70] Myrdal (1944a, p. 1040).

or unplanned, affecting any one of the three bundles of interdependent causative factors – (1) the economic level; (2) standards of intelligence, ambition, health, education, decency, manners, and morals; and (3) discrimination by whites – will bring changes in the other two and, through mutual interaction, move the whole system along in one direction or another. No single factor, therefore, is the 'final cause' in a theoretical sense.[71]

An American Dilemma constituted an important methodological step for Myrdal. Applied to the 'Negro problem':

Throughout this inquiry, we shall assume a general interdependence between all factors in the Negro problem. White prejudice and discrimination keep the Negro low in standards of living, health, education, manners and morals. This, in its turn, gives support to white prejudice. White prejudice and Negro standards thus mutually 'cause' each other. If things remain about as they are and have been, this means that the two forces happen to balance each other. Such a static 'accommodation' is, however, entirely accidental. If either of the factors changes, this will cause a change in the other factor, too, and start a process of interaction where the change in one factor will continuously be supported by the reaction of the other factor. The whole system will be moving in the direction of the primary change, but much further. This is what we mean by cumulative causation.[72]

It does not matter where you start. The entire system will be set in motion in the same direction as the original change and furthermore feeds back on the latter.[73]

[71] Ibid., p. 208.

[72] Ibid., pp. 75–76.

[73] As Trevor Swan (1962) later demonstrated, the process is not necessarily cumulative (unstable). It may as well converge to a stable equilibrium. The situation may be depicted in a diagram with black standards on the y-axis and white prejudices on the x-axis. Swan draws two linear reaction curves: aa (the reaction of black standards to a change in white prejudices) and bb (the reaction of white prejudices to a change in black standards) and shows that for the unstable situation to arise the bb line must cut the aa curve from below. This describes the situation where a single equilibrium exists. Swan, however, considers that situation unrealistic (Swan, 1962, pp. 424–425):

The unstable equilibrium case – *bb* cutting *aa* from below – seems *too* unstable to serve even as a 'simplified' mental model' for many purposes. The slightest breeze can puff Uncle Tom's cabin either into the heaven of White brotherhood or into

An American Dilemma is divided into eleven very detailed 'parts,' each one with a number of variables which interact with each other. In the first, Myrdal presents his approach and introduces his value premises. The second deals with various facets of 'race' and the third with the black population and its migration. The long fourth part scrutinizes the place of blacks in the American economy with particular emphasis on discrimination. Next, the race issue is analyzed as a political problem and in the sixth part the functioning of the American justice system. Two parts analyze social inequality and social stratification and another two deal with various

> the limbo of extinction. The stable case – *bb* cutting *aa* from above – seems *too* stable. Only a permanent shift in the structure of social forces can change the equilibrium point. Is there no counterpart in the model for our instinctive feeling that an initial 'explosion' of some kind – a war or depression, a rape or a lynching – may disrupt a pre-existing stable equilibrium and lead to an entirely new social situation?

Swan suggests that there may instead be limiting factors that work to stop cumulation (Swan, 1962, p. 425):

> When the Negroes (on the average) approach the standards of the Whites, some of the latter grow jealous and any further improvement in Negro standards causes little reduction of White prejudice, and may even cause it to increase; on the other hand, when the Negroes are very poor the White stomach for prejudice is satiated and perhaps compassion is aroused.

If similar limiting factors are present in the black community as well, the aa curve, looked at from the y-axis, may be S-shaped and the bb curve looked at from the x-axis may have the shape of an inverted S. Then the two curves twist around each other and produce a situation with three equilibrium points. In the high one, white prejudices are weak and black standards high. In the low one, white prejudices are strong and black standards are low. These two points are stable equilibria. Any departures from there will generate reactions that bring the system back to the original equilibrium. The intermediate point, with mid-level white prejudices and black standards, on the other hand, is unstable. Any departure from it will send the system either to the high-level or low-level equilibrium.

This, in turn, has consequences for the possibility of using social engineering. Using the undesirable low-level equilibrium, as the starting point, the first one consists in finding measures that lift the aa curve until the unstable equilibrium point is converted into a point of tangency between the two curves. In that case, the system becomes stable downwards, but unstable upwards, which allows for measures that lead to a cumulative upward movement until the desired high-level equilibrium point is reached. The second case assumes that the curves are unchanged. This requires a push which is big enough to move the system all the way from the unstable equilibrium to the stable high-level point. According to Swan, the multiple equilibrium situation constitutes a much better description of the real world than Myrdal's original suggestion in *An American Dilemma*.

aspects of black leadership and the black community. The last part of the book is forward-looking. It explores the trends in race relations and black economic and social status in the light of the wartime experience.

Social Engineering

Myrdal made it clear from the beginning that he was after the *solution* of the 'Negro problem.' His study would be concerned with social engineering. This conviction grew stronger during the course of the work, notably after Myrdal's visits to the South. As Walter Jackson observes, 'After Myrdal saw the desperate poverty of most Afro-Americans, the system of legalized segregation and discrimination, and the racial violence in the South, the research project became a challenge of the utmost personal importance to him.'[74]

The existence of circular, cumulative causation, Myrdal noted, had a practical corollary. It opened for the possibility of effecting an upward push on the overall situation of blacks through any of the variables in the system, although in practice no rational policy would work by changing a single factor: 'the rational refutation of so-called panaceas.'[75] By the same token, it was bound to encourage the reformer. Myrdal was optimistic. The war effort constituted a positive influence. The United States had to defend the idea of equality between the races in the face of Hitler's attempt to exterminate the Jews, and this, in turn, made it more difficult to maintain racial discrimination at home. Myrdal thought that he saw a coming change and invoked the American Creed, which in the end he hoped would overcome racial prejudice. In the preface to *An American Dilemma* he wrote:

> When looking back over the long manuscript, one main conclusion – which should be stressed here since it cannot be reiterated through the whole book – is this: that *not since Reconstruction has there been more reason to anticipate fundamental changes in American race relationships, changes which will involve a development toward the American ideals.*[76]

[74] Jackson (1990, p. 132).

[75] Myrdal (1944a, p. 77).

[76] Ibid., p. xix.

Walter Jackson calls *An American Dilemma* 'one of the most influential works of social science ever written in America.'[77] It sold more than 100,000 copies, and William Barber refers to it as 'one of the few works of scholarship to alter the course of history.'[78] Myrdal abstained from making specific recommendations with respect to how the racial problem should be solved. 'He regarded social engineering as the "supreme task of social science." Yet he saw his task in *An American Dilemma* as laying the analytical groundwork for new social policy rather than proposing particular legislation or outlining new policies in detail.'[79] Still,

> *An American Dilemma* exerted a powerful influence on American intellectuals, the educated reading public, and policymakers for twenty years after its publication. Myrdal's book played a key role in the campaign against disenfranchisement and segregation in the South; it convinced many whites that modern social science supported racial equality; it framed the question as a moral issue; and it helped to build some support for social engineering to lift the mass of blacks out of poverty.[80]

Not only that, the rest, as is well known, is history. In his very detailed book about the reactions to *An American Dilemma* and the aftermath of its publication, David Southern stresses the importance of Myrdal's work in court decisions: 'By 1954 Myrdal's name had become a household word in the halls of justice.'[81] The most famous case in which *An American Dilemma* cited was *Brown v. Board of Education of Topeka*, the same year in the Supreme Court:

> In the historic *Brown* case of 1954, Chief Justice Earl Warren declared that segregated schools harmed black children. As evidence for this crucial assertion, the chief justice, speaking for a unanimous Supreme Court, alluded to 'modern authority.' Warren specified this authority more fully in the controversial footnote 11, in which he cited seven social science

[77] Jackson (1990, p. xi).

[78] Barber (2008, p. 64).

[79] Jackson (1990, p. 187).

[80] Ibid., p. 310. For extensive accounts of the reception of *An American Dilemma* in the United States, see Southern (1987) and Jackson (1990). Myrdal's own retrospective is found in Myrdal (1987).

[81] Southern, (1987, p. 128).

studies. The famous footnote concluded with the words: 'And see generally Myrdal, *An American Dilemma* (1944).'[82]

The Supreme Court decided that school segregation was unconstitutional, and two years later, racial segregation in buses was outlawed. Myrdal's role in these and similar events was beyond doubt:

> The numerous racial breakthroughs after 1944 elevated Myrdal to the status of a prophet in his own time. Hope sprang forth like flowers in spring with the integration of the armed forces, the Supreme Court's ruling on the desegregation of schools, the sit-ins, the freedom rides, and the first significant civil rights legislation in Congress since Reconstruction.[83]

American Poverty Revisited: *Challenge to Affluence*

In 1962, Gunnar Myrdal came back to the poverty problem of the United States, in a book called *Challenge to Affluence*. There, he noted that an 'under-class' was developing rapidly in the country:

> ... changes [...] are under way to trap an 'under-class' of unemployed and, gradually, unemployable and underemployed persons at the bottom of a society, while for the majority of people above that layer the increasingly democratic structure of the educational system creates ever more real liberty and equality of opportunity, at least over the course of two generations.[84]

Myrdal made clear that the number of people (millions) who risked falling into abject destitution was decreasing as a result of increasing productivity and improvements in the educational system. This coin, however, also had a reverse. New production methods called for better education across the board, i.e. also among those at lower echelons in the job hierarchy. 'This process has continued steadily downwards, first to middle positions and then to ever lower strata of employees in industry and commerce, until it is now beginning to make unskilled and many

[82] Ibid., p. 127.

[83] Southern (1987, p. 189).

[84] Myrdal (1962b, p. 34).

skilled workers redundant.'[85] Following the logic of circular, cumulative causation, the very poverty of the bottom strata excluded them from education and hence pushed them deeper into poverty and permanent unemployment.

> The unemployed will be forced to live in the slums or, more probably, they will always have lived in the slums. Whatever the regulations are, the schools will be bad in the slums as they will be in the districts where the backwoods farmer lives. And the whole way of life in the crowded slum quarters in the cities or the rural slum districts will be destructive for the will and ability to advance in life.[86]

Many of the poor belonged to minority groups. '... the Negroes are still "the last hired and first fired".'[87] Their unemployment rate was three times the average. 'There is an ugly smell rising from the basement of the stately American mansion.'[88]

Again, Myrdal's solution of the poverty problem may be described as a piece of social engineering. He argued that in order to achieve full employment in a sustained way, investment in education, training and retraining of workers must be made an integral part of the strategy. Growth and reduction of poverty must be aimed for at the same time. In order to stimulate aggregate demand, large-scale redistributional reforms were urgently called for. '*Never in the history of America has there been a greater and more complex identity between the ideals of social justice and the requirements of economic progress.*'[89]

This twofold expansion, in turn, called for comprehensive long-range planning where all the plans for particular areas were integrated into an overall plan for the entire economy:

> Once America has decided that it wants to inaugurate a policy leading to rapid and steady economic growth, this implies the necessity of long-range economic planning. There will always be questions to answer: growth *of what* and *for what*, and growth *at what cost* – in the latter respect, not only

[85] Ibid., p. 37.

[86] Myrdal (1962b, p. 42).

[87] Ibid., p. 44.

[88] Ibid., p. 49.

[89] Ibid., pp. 64–65.

economically but in terms of changing institutions and human relations in case they do not all go in the desired direction and are not part of the growth that is aimed at.[90]

Myrdal's approach was ambitious, to say the least:

[The] various strands of government policy do not fall into place in the big puzzle without detailed planning in all the various fields: public construction work, spatial and vocational reallocation of the labor force, education, training and retraining, social security of different types, changed taxation on the federal, state, and municipal level, agricultural policy, wage and price policies, and so on. New drafts of city plans and transport systems will have to be produced.[91]

The International Dimension of Poverty

Gunnar Myrdal returned to Sweden from the United States in 1942, but already the following year he was back as financial counselor at the Swedish embassy in Washington, DC. His task was to study the situation of the US, the country's future prospects and planning efforts. Upon returning home, in 1944, he published a book which became slightly notorious, *Varning för fredsoptimism* [Beware of Peace Optimism],[92] because it predicted a depression during the coming years—a prediction that turned out to be completely mistaken. The same year, he once more became a member of the First Chamber of the Swedish parliament and was appointed chairman of the Swedish Commission for Economic Postwar Planning, a commission which he dominated to such an extent that it became popularly known as 'the Myrdal commission.'[93]

In 1945, upon the dissolution of the wartime government of national unity, he became Minister of Trade, a position which he had to leave in 1947, after a series of unfortunate events for which Myrdal was blamed by the public opinion: the revaluation of the Swedish krona in 1946, a speech by Myrdal to the Swedish Economic Association [Nationalekonomiska

[90] Ibid., p. 83.

[91] Ibid., p. 84.

[92] Myrdal (1944b).

[93] For an extensive discussion of the work of the commission and Swedish economic policy during Myrdal's term as Minister of Trade, see Appelqvist (2000).

föreningen] the same year where he revealed that the government was contemplating the introduction of quantitative import restrictions and the conclusion of a trade agreement with the Soviet Union which included sizeable export credits. Justly or unjustly, he had to resign as minister.

In 1947, Gunnar Myrdal became executive secretary of the newly established United Nations Economic Commission for Europe in Geneva, where he worked to facilitate east–west trade and supervised the production of economic surveys of the economic problems of Europe. He would remain there until 1957.[94] However, and more importantly, he also spent much of the 1950s working on problems related to poverty and inequality on the international level and on the relation between polarization between regions within a country and polarization between countries. This resulted in a 'trilogy': *An International Economy*, *Development and Under-Development: A Note on the Mechanism of National and International Economic Inequality*, usually referred to as his Cairo lectures, and *Economic Theory and Under-Developed Regions* (or *Rich Lands and Poor*).[95]

In *An International Economy,* Myrdal, the internationalist, began by lamenting the lack of international integration and noting the trend toward greater international inequality. The richer countries were progressing while the poorer ones were either stagnating or retrogressing. Neither international migration, capital movements, nor trade had been able to overcome this trend. 'Immigration from the poorest regions, with the largest amount of surplus labor, is excluded in almost all receiving countries by statutory or administrative color bars.'[96] The underdeveloped countries were receiving extremely little private capital from abroad, but private investment was not their primary need. It was infrastructure. Myrdal argued in favor of increased international aid. Bilateral capital flows would not do, since they were strongly influenced by all kinds of political considerations on part of the donors. 'Only by insulating … the ultimate receiver of financial aid from the contributor will it to some extent be possible to remove the political element from this international

[94] For Myrdal's ECE activities, see e.g. Jackson (1990, pp. 320–32), and Appelqvist (2014, pp. 63–68).

[95] Myrdal (1956a, 1956b, 1957a, 1957b).

[96] Myrdal (1956a, p. 93).

redistribution of resources, or at least keep to a minimum elements of demagogy, log-rolling, and pressure politics.'[97]

International trade, in turn, did not at all have the properties that orthodox trade theory postulated. Above all, it did not lead to any factor price equalization. '... instead of an equilibrium, as the theory of international trade would demand, we are facing *a cumulative process away from equilibrium in factor proportions and factor prices, engendered by international trade* ...'.[98]

The main problem of the poor countries was the lack of internal integration, which in turn made their bargaining power in the international arena weak. Myrdal dreamed of a 'world government' which could work to further the interests of the poor:

> When international integration is held as an ideal, the corresponding political image, carried to its logical perfection, is a world state under a world government, directed by a democratic process in which, directly or indirectly, all people participate. Such a world government would have good reason to instigate policies which, viewed from the *status ex ante* position, discriminated in favor of the great majority of backward peoples.[99]

A world government, however, was nowhere to be found. The countries of the Third World had to find their own development strategies, and development was not a matter of just economics. Myrdal observed that the economic progress of the advanced countries had gone hand in hand with profound changes in the social fabric. These interacted with economic development, in the usual circular way:

> ... the gradual attainment of attainment of national integration had its essential base in these noneconomic changes: increased social mobility both locally and within the entire national community, which opened up the avenues for competition and individual advance; intensified social cohesion and practical solidarity in the nation as a whole, which formed the basis for the coming into force of rules that applied to the entire community and for the sharing within the whole nation of the burden of common expenditure; increased participation of all the citizens, on local and national

[97] Ibid., p. 124.

[98] Ibid., p. 225.

[99] Ibid., p. 4.

> levels, in the political responsibility of controlling the social processes. It was though such changes that greater equality of opportunity was gradually attained. Economic development was in many ways a driving force, but it was itself made possible and continuously sustained by all the other socially integrating forces.[100]

The need for social change was even more pressing in the contemporary underdeveloped countries, where the social structures were frequently rigidly closed. Such change entailed redistribution of incomes and wealth. Myrdal called for land reform and progressive taxation, educational reform and a health care system that did not simply cater to the rich. He also stressed the importance of a population policy that served to reduce birth rates. Otherwise, the advances in medicine that served to reduce death rates would simply increase poverty and human suffering. The development program also entailed a proper balance between efforts in different sectors. Development did not amount just to industrialization. Increasing productivity in agriculture served not only to increase the incomes of poor peasants, but also to create a market for domestically produced manufactured goods. The same message would be repeated a decade later, in *Asian Drama*.[101]

The poor countries needed a proper commercial policy, and Myrdal analyzed the issue from the point of view of their interest. He advised them to maximize the value of their exports, since the ability to export determined the ability to import the capital goods that were necessary for their development effort. These countries were exporters of primary goods, usually not more than one or two, which in turn raised the question of the long-run development of the prices of these goods vis-à-vis that of manufactures. The solution recommended by Myrdal was diversification of exports, into goods with high-income elasticities of demand, if possible into manufactured goods. The latter was not an easy task, however, since it meant competing with the efficient producers in the already industrialized countries. Diversification also entailed increased use of capital goods, which had to be imported. This made it necessary to restrict imports of non-essential goods, notably luxuries, which called for interventions in the market mechanism. The accumulation of domestic capital, in turn, made it necessary to restrict domestic consumption.

[100] Ibid., p. 169.

[101] Myrdal (1968).

Higher standards of living could be achieved mainly in the longer run, since they rested on the creation of more production capacity.

The Cairo Lectures

In October 1955, Gunnar Myrdal gave the National Bank of Egypt Fiftieth Anniversary Commemoration Lectures in Cairo.[102] The theme he chose was that of national and international inequalities, a theme which of course was intimately related to the poverty issue, and which he had also dealt with in *An International Economy*. His point of departure was once more 'the very large and steadily increasing economic inequalities inequality between developed and under-developed countries.'[103] The per capita income of the latter was only a fraction of that of the former and some of these countries had even moved backwards.

Myrdal wanted to explain the pattern that he observed and once more resorted to his idea of circular, cumulative causation. The traditional theory of international trade, in his view, could not explain the disparities. It was conceived in terms of stable equilibrium and pointed to equalization of incomes. Instead, Myrdal suggested, the analysis would have to concentrate on the quality of the factors of production and the effectiveness of their use in different uses. The notion of stable equilibrium was false. The economic system is '*not steering towards such a position at all but, rather, is continuously en route away from it*' in the cumulative fashion sketched in *An American Dilemma*.[104] His claims were extraordinarily strong: 'I have suggested that the principle of interlocking, circular interdependence within a process of cumulative causation has validity over the entire field of social problems.'[105] Referring, first, to the problem of regional differences within a country, Myrdal stated that the market mechanism normally would cause inequality, not equality. It would cluster economic activities in certain localities while leaving the rest of the country in a backwater. The expanding regions would attract migrants from other areas and capital would flow there as well. The same was true with respect to trade, and industries would be concentrated in

[102] Myrdal (1956b).

[103] Ibid., p, 7.

[104] Ibid., p. 18.

[105] Ibid., p. 25.

the richer regions while the poorer ones would remain agricultural. So would infrastructure, including health and education. All this constituted what Myrdal first termed backsetting effects, later changed to backwash effects, in an extended version of his lectures, which is the term that we will use here.[106]

Myrdal, however, did not exclude the possibility of development in certain regions. Against the backwash effects he set 'spread effects':

> It is natural that around a main centre of expansion a whole surrounding region is more or less taken into the stride as it becomes spurred ahead by increasing outlets of agricultural products and stimulated to technical advance and rational business conduct all around. There is also another line of 'spread' to localities farther away, where favourable conditions exist for producing raw materials for growing industries. These and all other localities, where new starts are being made and happen to succeed, become in their turn, if the expansionary momentum is strong enough to overcome the Backsetting Effects, new centres of self-sustained economic expansion.[107]

However, the spread effects tended to be weak, the weaker the poorer the country. They were a function of the level of development and their relative weakness contributed to the maintenance of the vicious spiral in underdeveloped countries. In richer countries, on the other hand, they were strong enough to push the development process:

> A high average level of development in a country is followed by improved transportations and communications, higher levels of education and a more dynamic communion of ideas and values, which all tend to strengthen the forces for the spread of economic expansion. [...] sustained and rapid progress becomes an almost automatic process when a country has once reached a high level of development.[108]

The cumulative process will not run forever. Malthusian checks on the growth of the population, via increased death rates, are likely to provide a brake on the fall of the living standard (possibly counteracted by advances in medicine which reduce death rates so as to increase the

[106] Myrdal (1957a, 1957b).

[107] Myrdal (1956b, p. 31).

[108] Ibid., pp. 32–33.

misery). At the other end of the income scale, industry may become too concentrated and generate external diseconomies of congestion with concomitant cost increases. With an almost Marxist twist, Myrdal also suggested that demand may be slackening in a 'maturing' economy, which in turn may require new markets or increased government expenditure. Factor prices may increase to the point where the established regions find it difficult to compete with emerging ones.

Myrdal also introduced the state into his scheme of circular, cumulative causation. In the richer countries the welfare state had been realized to a varying degree, and this in turn served to improve the lot of the poor and reduce the extent of regional inequality. Richer regions have to pay the expenditure on the poorer. 'In the poorer countries, on the other hand, market forces have been given a relatively freer play, when their effects to create regional inequalities have not been actually supported and magnified by built-in feudal and other inegalitarian institutions and power structures aiding the rich in exploiting the poor.'[109]

Myrdal next moved from interregional to international income disparities. '... on the whole, in recent decades the economic inequalities between developed and under-developed countries have been increasing.'[110] On the international level as well, he argued, trade acts to widen the income gap instead of making it converge. Trade had destroyed the handicraft sectors in many poor countries by flooding the latter with cheap imports, promoting instead the exports of primary commodities which meet an inelastic demand in international markets as well as strong price fluctuations. In addition, the strong population growth in poor countries creates a large supply of cheap labor which in turn tends to make the fruits of technical progress in the export branches accrue to the importer countries in the form of low prices while the wage level in the exporting countries will remain low. Capital movements would not provide any solution to this dilemma, since by and large, investors tended to prefer to put their money into the already developed country.

Myrdal did not deny that international trade and transportation could generate spread effects in underdeveloped countries, but these effects, he claimed, would largely be limited to the export–import ports and their

[109] Myrdal (1956b, p. 37).

[110] Myrdal (1957a, p. 6).

immediate surroundings. It would result in isolated enclaves rather than in a chain of positive effects extending into the regions.

Myrdal did not think much of the possibility of reducing international inequalities through international organizations. The latter were weak and toothless, 'in the main only propaganda fora and, in addition, media for diplomatic contacts between governments and for consultations.'[111] Instead, he recommended poor countries to resort to a rational nationalism, taking '*any and all measures which, on the ground of good reasoning, can be proved to enhance its own economic welfare*.'[112]

The development strategy had to rest on a national development plan. 'It is now commonly agreed that an under-developed country should have a national economic development policy. Indeed, it should have an overall, integrated national plan, as is also urged by everybody,' wrote the convinced social engineer.[113] The intrinsic deficiencies in poor countries made it necessary for the state to assume a number of functions which in developed economies could be left to private business. In particular, it had to ensure increased investment. As most economists in the mid-1950s, Myrdal felt that the road to economic growth and development went through increased capital formation:

> There is no other road to economic development than a forceful rise of the part of the national income which is with-held from consumption and devoted to investments, and this implies a policy of utmost austerity – so independently of whether the increased savings are engendered through high levels of profits to be ploughed back in industrial expansion or through increased taxation.[114]

The alternative to this heroic attempt was continued economic and cultural stagnation or retrogression.

When it came to the plans themselves, Myrdal argued that they could not be conceived in terms of the prevailing or expected market prices, since the latter provided no indication of what the economy would need in the future, in particular when it came to large, indivisible infrastructural investments that were to ensure the viability of industries that would be

[111] Myrdal (1956b, p. 58).

[112] Ibid., p. 59.

[113] Ibid., p. 62.

[114] Ibid., p. 64.

created only in the future. The market prices could not handle external economies. The plans would have to be political documents and welfare would have to be defined by the political process. Myrdal instead called for a blueprint in real terms of the entire process of cumulative causation that would lead up to the desired future result.

> A whole cumulative process has to be blue-printed in terms of concrete investment projects and their effects: on the volume of production in various lines, on consumption, on the employment of workers and natural resources, on health, education and the productiveness of labour, and so on, in various sectors and in different years, with main attention focused on the circular causal interactions between all the factors in the system. The plan must also determine the concrete state interferences to be applied to the markets in order to assure that the process really comes off and develops as planned.[115]

Myrdal was completely aware that this was not easy: 'I stress the need that the plan should be founded on study, and indeed study of some of the least accessible functional relationships in the social system: namely the coefficients of circular causation between all the factors in the system.'[116] No objective criteria were available, that could guide the planning process. On the contrary, the choice of ends and means was a policy choice 'reached in terms of national development goals as determined by the political process.'[117]

As he had demonstrated in *An International Economy*, Myrdal was under no illusion that the politico-administrative equation was an easy one to solve. The 'perfect' state regularly assumed by planning advocates was not to be found in the poor countries. The entire machinery had to be set up more or less from scratch:

> Underdeveloped countries have to attempt to create an efficient and honest political and administrative machinery without much in the way of legal traditions. And time does not allow them a purgatory era of economic liberalism; *they have to reform their politics and their administration at the*

[115] Myrdal (1957a, p. 88).

[116] Ibid., p. 86.

[117] Ibid., p. 89.

same time as the state is increasingly compelled to handle vast public funds and run business on a large scale.[118]

The planning principle applied to international trade as well. Myrdal called for a dynamic theory of comparative costs and he considered that underdeveloped countries could call for unilateral trade liberalization in developed countries, 'on rational grounds.'[119] 'The theory of international trade and, indeed, economic theory generally, were not worked out to serve the purpose of explaining the reality of economic under-development and development.'[120]

The skepticism with respect to the traditional theory of international trade applied in particular when it came to the imports of capital goods necessary for the creation of a manufacturing industry. If these were larger than what the country's exports allowed, imports of consumption goods must be restricted in order to create room for the necessary strategic imports. This required government intervention in the pattern of international trade. Myrdal also invoked the infant industry argument. Protection of local industries would give these a chance to compete in the domestic market and grow.

Finally, Myrdal commented on the need for technological change. The 'one advantage' that these countries had was 'our accumulated scientific knowledge,' upon which they could draw.[121] This knowledge, however, could not be used as a simple blueprint, but they would have to adjust and accommodate techniques through independent research so that they suited their own values and conditions.

Beyond the Welfare State

In *Beyond the Welfare State*, published in 1960, Myrdal came back to the need for planning in the Third World countries. The latter were in a situation that differed substantially from that of the industrialized world. 'Indeed,' writes Myrdal, 'it is very unlikely that they will develop much,

118 Myrdal (1956a, p. 204).

119 Myrdal (1956b, p. 74).

120 Myrdal (1957a, p. 9).

121 Myrdal (1956b, p. 76).

or at all, if the state does not take a much bigger responsibility for engendering development, than was taken by the state during the industrial revolution in Western countries.'[122] This, in turn had consequences for the role and timing of planning:

> By the very logic of the under-developed countries' situation, planning becomes programmatic in its approach. [...] In the under-developed countries, the idea precedes its realization. As economic development cannot be expected to come by itself, planning becomes a precondition for development, not, as in the Western countries, a later consequence of development and all other changes which accompanied it. The under-developed countries are thus compelled to undertake what in the light of the history of the Western world appears as a short-cut.[123]

In the Third World, according to Myrdal, planning had to anticipate public policy making. 'It does not grow out of the necessity to coordinate such policies as have already been initiated.'[124] Planning even had to encompass the 'building up of institutions for self-government, collective bargaining and cooperation,'[125] since in stagnant societies, these institutions did not come into existence spontaneously.

Asian Drama

When Gunnar Myrdal left the Economic Commission for Europe in 1957, he embarked upon a mammoth study that would keep him busy for a decade. This study was what would become *Asian Drama*—a work that dealt with Pakistan, India, Ceylon, Burma, Malaya, Thailand, Indonesia and the Philippines, and to a lesser extent, Cambodia, Laos and South Vietnam.[126] Myrdal's approach and perspective were grandiose: in the end 2,284 pages. The work was a natural successor to both *An American Dilemma* and the works on international economic issues of the previous decades, in the sense that it centered on poverty.

[122] Myrdal (1960, p. 88).

[123] Ibid., p. 89.

[124] Ibid., p. 90.

[125] Ibid., p. 98.

[126] Myrdal (1968).

The extent of poverty, not only in South Asia, but in all the ex-European colonies, was overwhelming. In a 1963 lecture Myrdal stated:

> ... I do not hesitate to state that the large masses of these peoples live in the most abject poverty, with a standard – in all conceivable ways – which is so low that people in the rich countries are hardly capable to imagine. And this standard is not improving, at least not with any noticeable speed. The income gap between the rich and the poor countries of the world, which has grown during a hundred years, is now growing faster than ever.[127]

The slow development in those countries that displayed any development at all had slowed down even further, and in the others stagnation or retrogression, was the rule. Domestic inequalities loomed large and very few effective reforms had been carried out to change this sad fact. The political development of the poor countries was not necessarily positive. Many of them had entered the road toward more authoritarian government, frequently with army backing. Myrdal's conclusions breathed pessimism:

> *We are probably entering a very critical period in the history of the underdeveloped countries*. They will feel increasingly disillusioned in their efforts to bring about economic development. Several of them will suffer a deterioration of the general standard of living, especially for the vast majority. Radical changes may occur in the form of government and the political system of these countries, and you have to reckon with numerous conflicts between neighboring countries. At least in some parts of the underdeveloped world the political development will not proceed in the direction that that we would desire.[128]

The above was the theme that Gunnar Myrdal would extend and develop in *Asian Drama*. This is the work that brings Myrdal's methodological tenets to their logical climax. There he merges the five pillars that had grown in his mind since the late 1920*s*: explicit value premises, institutionalism, dynamic analysis, circular, cumulative causation and social engineering. The three volumes of *Asian Drama* on the one hand deliver a formidable critique of the approaches that characterized contemporary thinking on development economics and on the other hand attempt to

[127] Myrdal (1964, p. 25).

[128] Ibid., pp. 31–32.

put together an approach that leaves no stone unturned, no connection unexplored. The attempt ranges from a mapping of economic and social conditions in eleven South Asian countries, through a circularly causal, historical analysis of how their contemporary attitudes and institutions had been created, to a call based on explicitly stated value premises for physical dynamic planning, encompassing most of society, to bring about change in a cumulative fashion. Never was Gunnar Myrdal more institutional than in *Asian Drama* and never was he more acerbic in his judgment of conventional wisdom. As he puts it himself, 'If the book has any degree of originality, it is as a total composition and in the insistence upon following the basic institutional approach through to its consequences.'[129] Myrdal presented what he thought of as very good reasons for approaching the poverty problem of South Asia in institutional terms:

> Not only is the social and institutional structure different from the one that has evolved in Western countries, but, more important, the problem of development in South Asia is one calling for induced changes in that social and institutional structure, as it hinders economic development and as it does not change spontaneously, or, to any very large extent, in response to policies restricted to the 'economic' sphere.[130]

Asian Drama is a kaleidoscope of South Asia and its problems. The work is divided into six different main parts, each one long enough to constitute a book on its own: political problems, economic realities, planning, labor utilization, population size and population quality. In each, Myrdal mapped the prevailing situation, the forces that had caused it, the indigenous forces calling for change, not least nationalism, and the main events that had taken place after independence, politically, country by country, economically, topically arranged, population and its utilization in the different sectors of the economy, the structural division of the economy the evolution of the economy as a whole, living standards and inequality, size and composition of foreign trade and capital movements and, finally, differences in initial conditions.

[129] Ibid., pp. xii–xiii.

[130] Ibid., p. 26.

The Mechanisms of Poverty

Exactly like in *An American Dilemma*, Myrdal's view of the world of South Asia rested on the notion of circular, cumulative causation. He conceived of the situation in each South Asian country as a social system.[131] The system consisted number of conditions that were causally interrelated, so that a change in one would cause changes in the others. Myrdal classified the conditions in six broad categories: (1) output and incomes; (2) conditions of production; (3) conditions of living; (4) attitudes toward life and work; (5) institutions and (6) policies. '… *the movement of the whole social system upwards is what all of us in fact mean by development*.'[132] In the same way as in *An American Dilemma*, a change in any of the six conditions will trigger changes in the others in a cumulative fashion. There is a big difference between *An American Dilemma* and *Asian Drama*, however. In the former book Myrdal argued that once the cumulative process had been set in motion there were no forces that would push the system back toward its original position. In *Asian Drama* he allows for factors that may act as a brake on cumulation or even ensure that the cumulative process does not begin. Even though, theoretically, it was conceivable that the system would be moving in one direction or another, this is not what is likely to be observed in the real world:

> In sharp contrast to this expectation are not only the common experience of 'low-level equilibrium' in underdeveloped countries and the serious obstacles to development policies, but more generally the astonishing stability of most social systems in history. … The great bulk of historical, anthropological, and sociological evidence and thought suggests that social stability and equilibrium is the norm and that all societies, and underdeveloped societies in particular, possess institutions of a strongly stabilizing character. In view of these findings the real mystery is how they can escape from equilibrium and can develop.[133]

Myrdal made a distinction between three types of forces that make for stagnation: time and inertia (mainly attitudes and institutions); independent counteracting forces (e.g. population growth) and counteracting

[131] Ibid., pp. 1859–1860.

[132] Ibid., p. 1868.

[133] Ibid., p. 1871.

forces released by development (like soil erosion produced by increased agricultural production). For a cumulative process to be set in motion it is not enough that the factors composing the social system interact. The strength of the interaction must be large enough and the speed of the reactions must be high.

The Need for Planning

Myrdal again insisted on social engineering as the solution to the poverty problem. Planning should proceed in steps. First, adequate knowledge of the relevant conditions, their causal connections and their coefficients of change should be gathered. Second, a set of adequate value premises to guide the planning process in a direction that allows for an upward movement on all counts must be chosen. The actual value premises used by Myrdal for his study were all related to the desire of modernization, essentially along Western lines, of the South Asian societies: rationality, development and planning for development, rise of productivity, rise of levels of living, social and economic equalization, improved institutions and attitudes, national consolidation, national independence, political democracy, democracy at the grass roots, social discipline and 'democratic planning.'[134]

Myrdal insisted that planning constitutes the only rational way of breaking out of the traditional society. If we divide the forces at work into two groups, factors promoting development or underdevelopment on the one hand, and the standard of living or level of development on the other, Myrdal's account indicates that the South Indian societies were caught in a stable equilibrium at a low level of development as a result of the interaction of the two kind of forces. Some kind of 'big push' was required that would bring the social system beyond a new, unstable, equilibrium at a higher level of development with stronger development promoting forces. Failure to do so would simply push the system back to the original position, whereas moving beyond the unstable higher equilibrium would create a virtuous spiral that would in its turn end in yet another—high-level—equilibrium of the stable kind.

As Myrdal expressed it: '*There is economy in the big push*. Smaller efforts mean waste. [...] For the planning effort to be efficient, 'the efforts have

[134] Ibid., Chapter 2.

to be larger than a critical minimum, but also … *directed simultaneously at a great number of conditions, concentrated within a short period of time, and applied in a rationally coordinated way.*'[135] The necessary change of non-economic variables must be tackled as well. Furthermore, Myrdal argued that the planning must be carried out in physical terms, since the use of the prevailing market prices would be of no use in a situation where it comes to tracing the cumulative interaction of economic and non-economic variables over time.

Myrdal devoted six chapters of *Asian Drama* to planning. 'The basic principle in the ideology of economic planning is that the state shall take an active, indeed the decisive, role in the economy …'[136] One chapter is devoted to 'democratic planning': in the first place, the active participation of the masses in the preparation and implementation of plans, and secondly, the requirement that this participation should be voluntary. People must 'alter their attitudes toward life and work … and cooperate to improve society and its institutions.'[137] The issue of voluntariness was particularly difficult. According to Myrdal, there was little hope for rapid development in South Asia without greater social discipline throughout society, all the way down to the village level. This would not be achieved without regulations backed by compulsion, but the entire institutional and attitudinal structure worked to block such regulations. In addition, the South Asian states were 'soft states,' in the sense that they required.

> … extraordinarily little of their citizens. There are few obligations either to do things in the interest of the community or to avoid actions opposed to that interest. Even those obligations that do exist are enforced inadequately if at all. The low level of social discipline is one of the most fundamental differences between the South Asian countries today and Western countries at the beginning of their industrialization.[138]

The use of plans also called for operational controls of the private sector. This posed a dilemma. Private ventures were desirable and had to be supported by the authorities, but adherence to the planning ideology

[135] Ibid., p. 1901.

[136] Ibid., p. 709.

[137] Ibid., p. 851.

[138] Ibid., p. 896.

had often led to the adoption of far too many administrative discretionary controls, and regulations call forth attempts to avoid them, which in turn leads to more regulations, etc. In the end, an 'odd situation' was created, where '*most officials have to devote most of their time and energy to limiting or stopping enterprise.* This is like driving a car with the accelerator pushed to the floor but the brakes on.'[139] The situation produced other undesirable results as well. Those enterprises which succeeded in maneuvering among the—mainly discretionary—controls could reap extraordinarily high profits, in a situation characterized by monopolies, oligopolies and vested interests—a situation that frequently degenerated into sheer corruption.

Underutilization of Labor

Asian Drama is an exercise in criticism, but not exclusively. The 'constructive core' of the work deals with the use and quality of the human factor. As Myrdal saw it, the main reason for underdevelopment and poverty in South Asia was the underutilization and the low productivity of the labor force. He questioned the validity of such 'Western' terms as unemployment and underemployment, especially in the context of agriculture. In industrialized countries the unemployed want to work and macroeconomic policies that stimulate aggregate demand can be used to increase employment. In South Asia this was far from always the case. The fundamental fact was that labor was underutilized, either because it was idle or because, when working, it produced very little, and macroeconomic policies could do very little to change this fact:

> Instead, the bulk of the labor force is embedded in a climatic, social, cultural, and institutional matrix that not only tends to perpetuate present low levels of labor utilization, but also resists rapid and immediate adaptation to novel and unfamiliar ways of living and working. Idleness and low labor efficiency depend upon institutions, custom and tradition, attitudes toward work and leisure – including taboos and inhibitions related to status and to the participation of women in work. Moreover, the relevant attitudes are set in a framework of institutions, and the relationship between attitudes and institutions is mutually reinforcing.[140]

[139] Ibid., p. 925.

[140] Ibid., pp. 999–1000.

Myrdal focused on three ratios: participation (working members in the labor force), duration (the number of hours worked per working member) and labor efficiency (the output per man hour worked). He proceeded sector by sector. First, he provided an account of the consequences for labor utilization of agricultural institutions and behavior which 'places a high premium on abstention from productive work.'[141] Participation rates were low, the duration of the work year was shortened by holidays and ceremonies, and incentives to put increase the work effort were lacking. '... income and levels of living could ... be improved substantially by a larger and more intensive labor input.'[142]

The Non-Agricultural Sectors

The non-agricultural sectors in South Asia were small, but Myrdal nevertheless devoted a fair amount of attention to them, since he considered them less tied to tradition and custom and more amenable to contribute in the effort to break through the constellation of factors that kept South Asia in poverty. He held that it was impossible to increase incomes without industrialization, especially given the high rate of population growth everywhere.

To rely on exports of manufactured goods was difficult. The world market was not easy to penetrate and the South Asian countries had chosen to fall back on import substitution in the domestic markets. These markets were, however, small. In addition, import substitution had typically been generated by a strained foreign exchange situation. The development of manufacturing required imports of capital goods, so the substitution usually took place in the less 'essential' markets for consumer goods, which were afforded protection. The latter type of goods was hardly those that would contribute the most to the planned development recommended by Myrdal. The choice of techniques posed yet another problem. While the South Asian countries could in principle draw on the accumulated technical knowledge developed in the West, techniques there had been developed in a situation of labor scarcity, whereas in Asia labor was abundant, and even using labor-intensive techniques, the industrial sector would not absorb large numbers of workers. It would simply be

[141] Ibid., p. 1070.

[142] Ibid., p. 1092.

too small for that in the foreseeable future. The spread effects generated by manufacturing were likely to be weak and geographically concentrated.

The case for industrialization rested heavily on the modernization ideals. The latter were, however, not shared by everybody. 'Traditionalists of all shades ... share several convictions. They believe that village crafts should be encouraged ... and that modern industrial products – particularly imported consumer goods – should be viewed with suspicion.'[143]

Acknowledging the fact that the 'traditional ideology would not go away easily, Myrdal examined how village crafts on the one hand and modern small-scale industry on the other could be rationally supported. In the former case, productivity would have to be increased by the provision of improved tools and simple machines and by improved organization of production and marketing. Part of the solution, however, lay outside the cottage industry sector. The main market for such goods was to be found in the agricultural sector and the extension of it hence depended critically on income increases there. Protection would also be required, Myrdal argued, since most of the craftsmen had no alternative employment.

Small-scale industry—industries larger than family enterprises, using hired labor—was a different matter. It could be used to decentralize industrialization and required less capital than large-scale firms. Ideally, large and small industries should complement each other. Small firms could deliver inputs to large firms and work as service establishments to the latter. They could also obtain some of the inputs they used to produce finished goods from the large-scale sector. Like the craft sector, the small-scale industries, however, did not have their fate entirely in their own hands, and unless they could export, advancing across a broad front required increased domestic incomes that led to a widening of the market.

Myrdal did not see any immediate modernization of industrial production in South Asia: 'The case for protecting and promoting the craft industries in the villages of South Asia is a strong one, particularly in the poorer countries,' he wrote. The lack of alternative employment made this the only way of improving the productivity and income of the village craftsmen. Myrdal predicted that two types of smaller industries would coexist for several decades: a modern large- and small-scale sector, which would not absorb much labor, and a cottage industry sector that would

[143] Ibid., p. 1208.

use techniques that resembled the traditional ones and which would be much larger.

Myrdal cautioned, however, against leaving the traditional part of the economy to its time-honored practices. Both agriculture and crafts should be induced to adopt modern, more productive techniques, 'but these should be deliberately chosen to take account of the present vast underutilization of labor and the rapid growth of the labor force.'[144] This, in turn, called for fresh research on labor-intensive technology able to absorb more of the growing labor supply.

Agricultural Reform

The last component in Myrdal's call for a better labor utilization was the elaboration of an agricultural policy. Agriculture was the most important sector. 'Fundamentally, it is in this sector that the battle for long-term economic development in South Asia will be won or lost.'[145] The underutilization of labor in agriculture was substantial. Many did not work, or worked very little and when they worked, they did not produce much. The traditional institutions stood in the way of a rational use of the agricultural labor force.

To increase agricultural production was paramount. Food imports were increasing since domestic production failed to keep pace with the growth of the population, in a situation where in most countries the calorie intake was already low. Yields were low, but Myrdal was hopeful that they could be increased with the aid of modern scientifically based agricultural technology and an increased labor input. Mere price increases would not do the trick, he argued, since much of the marketable surplus was extracted by moneylenders and landowners through mechanisms dictated by power and tradition. Myrdal pointed to a number of measures for increasing production: increases of the cultivated land, conversion of grazing lands to cultivated plots through cultivation of fodder crops, new seed varieties, irrigation, fertilizers, and possibly also mechanization. Technological reforms were exceedingly important, because they allowed for an improved utilization of labor.

[144] Ibid., p. 1239.

[145] Ibid., p. 1241.

Agricultural change is, however, not only a function of inputs and technology. As always, Myrdal stressed the importance of institutional reform. Land reforms had been undertaken only at a modest scale and absentee landowners were a strong force to be reckoned with.[146] Another necessary measure was the legal protection of tenant rights against the landowners: security of tenure and limitation of the share of the latter group in the harvest cooperation among villagers to increase production and equality had failed. Myrdal's verdict was harsh. The existing power structures frequently manipulated the cooperatives to their own benefit. Credit cooperatives did not serve the poorest. They had to do what they always had done: turn to moneylenders who charged very high-interest rates. Community development efforts had also tended to favor the wealthy. Altogether, Myrdal considered the cooperative farming efforts abortive.

When Myrdal summed up the achievements of agricultural policy reform in South Asia after World War II, he was forced to conclude that, if anything, the situation in South Asian agriculture had deteriorated. The measures had in the main strengthened the well-to-do upper strata in the villages and worsened the situation of the sharecroppers and landless at the bottom.[147] Myrdal argued that for labor utilization and production to increase in the long run, it was essential to promote social and economic equality. A very radical change in the approach to agricultural policy making was required, but he had little hope. The politicians were simply not responsive.

Nevertheless, he set out to sketch some of the measures. His approach rested on a radical redistribution of land in favor of the actual tillers. Myrdal rejected that this would lead to reduced production because the new landowners would be less experienced than the old ones. The land was owned in large chunks but cultivated in small, in most cases by tenants, and they were experienced cultivators—much more so than the absentee landowners.

Myrdal was also skeptical about the argument that the new owners would lack capital. Draft animals and tools could be pooled. Myrdal was convinced that the redistribution of land would provide an incentive to do a more careful job on the farm. A redistribution was also likely to create

[146] Ibid., p. 1241.

[147] Ibid., p. 1367.

a more receptive environment to technological change and improved produce prices in the longer run. In the short run, on the other hand, the marketable surplus might shrink, since the part of the tenants' output that was formerly appropriated by landowners and moneylenders, and put on the market, would now be consumed on the farms.

Myrdal also feared that the traditional structures would take over. The main danger was that many new landowners would be indebted to moneylenders at the outset and when their credit standing improved through the ownership of the land, they would be tempted to borrow more, mortgaging their land and in the end losing it. Myrdal therefore advocated a radical cancellation of old debts and a prohibition against moneylending, mortgaging and sales of land.

In spite of all the virtues that Myrdal saw in the radical land redistribution approach, he was, however, not convinced that it would work. He therefore also discussed radical land consolidation, nationalization, in a cooperative setting, to obtain an optimum farm size and make it possible to realize the economies of scale inherent e.g. in irrigation works. However, in order to be efficient, cooperative farming would require compulsory membership. In the end, Myrdal ruled out both radical land redistribution and radical land consolidation—as doctrinaire. 'With considerable hesitation,'[148] he came out in favor of a third strategy that could be employed to break down the traditional status hierarchy which acted as a tremendous obstacle to a fuller utilization of labor, a strategy that turned some of his previous reasoning on its head.[149]

What Myrdal suggested was to rely on the progressive peasant proprietors and privileged tenants in the villages for the intensification and modernization of agriculture. These were the groups that had taken advantage of the existing government initiatives and they were the ones responsible for whatever production increases that had taken place. Their efficiency had, however, 'not been adequately recognized and rewarded.'[150] Myrdal called on the governments to lay down a firm policy 'in favor of capitalist farming by allowing and encouraging the progressive cultivator to reap the full rewards of his enterprise and labor, while approaching the fundamental issues of equality and institutional

[148] Ibid., p. 1378.

[149] Ibid., pp. 1378–1379.

[150] Ibid., p. 1379.

reform from a different angle and by different policy means.'[151] Myrdal recommended a tax that heavily penalized idle landownership and the prohibition of land sales to non-farming non-residents. This constituted a radical 'land reform' in the sense that landowners were encouraged to become cultivators and it would constitute a step toward the abolition of the sharecropping system. The scheme should also include the gifts of small plots of individually owned land to the poor landless to increase their income and to increase their incorporation into the market economy. Myrdal called his approach 'a modified form of welfare capitalism for agriculture.'[152]

In the end, however, he was pessimistic with respect to the future development of South Asian agriculture. Myrdal recognized that his suggestion was hardly likely to be accepted by the politicians. They were likely to continue to propose allegedly egalitarian reforms without substantial content. At the same time, the vested powerful interests at the top of the village structure would continue to do their best to frustrate genuine reform efforts. This was a gloomy prediction indeed, for the sector that Myrdal considered central in the development process of South Asia.

Population Problems

The last two parts of *Asian Drama* are devoted to an analysis of population growth and population quality. The first deals with the population explosion, 'the most important social change that has taken place in South Asia in the post-war era.'[153] Mortality was declining while fertility tended to remain constant. This tended to increase the dependency burden of those in working age and to depress incomes since the modern sectors of the economies expanded only slowly. Both effects called for birth control measures.

The population question also had a qualitative aspect, summarized by Myrdal in terms of health and education. 'Poor health conditions are intimately linked with almost every aspect of life in South Asia,' he bluntly

[151] Ibid., p. 1380.

[152] Ibid., p. 1383.

[153] Ibid., p. 1530.

asserted,[154] and he noted the likely favorable effects of better health on productivity but also its tendency to increase the rate of population growth.

According to Myrdal, education had a double purpose. It should provide knowledge and skills, but modern education was also central when it came to changing attitudes and institutions inimical to economic and social development, but in South Asia it did not work that way. '… there is a traditional contempt for manual work and the educated tend to regard their education as the badge that relieves them of any obligation to soil their hands.'[155] This explained the existence of 'educated unemployed' and was a serious obstacle to development. A Western engineer was prepared to use his hands. His Indian counterpart was not.

Myrdal stressed the importance of literacy—functional literacy—as an instrument for disseminating knowledge and for development in general. However, adult education had not been given any prominent place in the plans for educational reform in South Asia. The formal school system displayed a number of deficiencies: repetition of classes, lack of attendance, high drop-out rates, low quality of teachers, low teacher salaries, low social status of teachers, overly theoretical curricula, lack of teaching materials. The primary schools provided insufficient preparation for pupils going on to secondary education. The extent of vocational education was small, due not least to a lack of qualified vocational teachers, but not only that. The aversion to manual work also played an important role.

Tertiary education had expanded in South Asia, but Myrdal found indications of considerable waste in the system: repetition and failure to graduate. Also, the allocation between different fields of study did not match either the demand situation or the needs posed by the development effort. It produced a large number of 'generalists' trained in law or humanities, who tended to end up in the bureaucracy, while engineers, doctors, agricultural technicians and teachers, who were instrumental in the development process, were scarce. The quality of university education was low, somewhere on the level of secondary education in most European and North American countries.

The entire educational system was selective, in favor of the well-to-do and against the students coming from disadvantaged families. This was

[154] Ibid., p. 1553.

[155] Ibid., p. 1646.

partly for economic reasons, but demand factors were also responsible. Lower-class parents rarely saw the need for education of their children. 'The talk of the "hunger for education" in the villages is largely a romantic illusion, most of all in the poorest countries of the region ...'[156] Myrdal called for a radical educational reform inserted into the national development plans. Issues like 'the low quality and standards of schooling, the wastage and misdirection, and, in particular, the question of equality, which is interwoven in every quantitative and qualitative problem in South Asia,' had to be dealt with.[157] Education should be planned as an integrated whole, in terms of quality and continuity. Special attention had to be paid to the education and the social status of the teachers and to the attitudes to schooling of the pupils and their parents, to prepare them to meet the requirements of development.

The Challenge of World Poverty

Asian Drama ends there. Due to the length of the work, Myrdal chose not to present any comprehensive strategy of development for the South Asian countries. That task he saved for another book, published in 1970: *The Challenge of World Poverty*, with the subtitle *A World Anti-Poverty Program in Outline*.[158] He stressed the political nature of the book:

> This is a *political* book and should thus, according to my philosophy, be directed not only to experts, officials, and professional politicians but to interested persons among the general public. I have therefore labored to make my message as direct and simple as possible, though without giving up my intention that my policy recommendations should stand out as rational conclusions from facts and explicitly stated value premises. I have taken no political or diplomatic precautions but have tried to speak as plainly and frankly as I can.[159]

Myrdal again stated that it was not possible to limit the analysis to economic factors. The only permissible demarcation was between relevant and less relevant factors. The value premises were the same as those in

156 Ibid., p, 1801.

157 Ibid., p. 1812.

158 Myrdal (1970).

159 Ibid., p. xi.

Asian Drama: the modernization ideals. The traditional valuations were static and could not be used for determining goals for planning. '... *the idea of seeking the goals for development in these valuations amounts to abstaining from rational planning.*'[160]

In *The Challenge of World Poverty* Myrdal very strongly came back to the issue of equality as a prerequisite for development. He noted the fact that all the governments in South Asia endorsed equality, but at the same time he lamented the passivity of the masses. Poverty and inequality bred each other. Still, the masses stood out as '*mostly passive, apathetic, and inarticulate.*'[161] This was a serious matter, since Myrdal was convinced that 'the radical reforms which are needed *must be carried out by the underdeveloped countries themselves.*'[162] '*To become important, the egalitarian ideals need pressure from below*. And that is exactly what is missing in most underdeveloped countries.'[163]

The Challenge of World Poverty very much reads like a summary of *Asian* Drama, but not completely. Myrdal singled out four different 'internal' reform issues: agriculture, population, education and the 'soft' state. The industrialization issue, which had occupied an important place in *Asian Drama*, on the other hand, was played down.

Myrdal based his conclusions with respect to agriculture on the low yields prevailing in the sector and the low rate of labor utilization there. This was the result of a primitive agricultural technology. Techniques had to be modernized in such a way as to fit the factor proportions prevailing in the Third World. This in turn called for research, and Myrdal saw research as '*one of the strategically most important requirements for foreign aid from the developed countries.*'[164] The development of agriculture rested on the 'capitalist welfare solution' that he advocated in *Asian Drama*: encouragement of the efforts of progressive landowners and privileged tenants and at the same time development of measures that could serve to protect the contemporary landless in the villages and provide them with small plots of land.

[160] Ibid., p. 29.

[161] Ibid., p. 62.

[162] Ibid., p. 254.

[163] Ibid., p. 76.

[164] Ibid., p. 98.

Myrdal was utterly skeptical to 'technocratic' solutions in agriculture. During the time that had passed between *Asian Drama* and *The Challenges of World Poverty,* the so-called Green Revolution had become a big issue. The use of high-yielding seed varieties was advocated in some optimistic circles, notably the WHO, as a panacea. Myrdal pointed out that productive use of the 'miracle seeds' required a number of complementary inputs, like fertilizer, water and pesticides, increased weeding, etc. More important, however, he felt, was that it diverted the attention from the necessary institutional agrarian reforms. The mere introduction of the new seeds was likely simply to strengthen the position of the reactionary interests that dominated the villages: landowners and moneylenders, and hence increase the extent of inequality instead of reducing it.

Myrdal's recommendations with respect to population policy were simple. High rates of population growth threatened the living standard. They hence had to be brought down, and the only way to do that was to work on the birth rates. Myrdal saw no other way of neutralizing the negative effects of rapid population growth than a vigorous public policy to spread birth control.

The main problem of the educational sector, as Myrdal saw it, was qualitative. The European powers had created educational systems that effectively kept the vast majority of the population out and cemented the barrier between them and the upper classes. The situation had not changed much after independence. Myrdal called for adult literacy education, both as a goal in itself and as a means for making the school education of children more efficient, but this required a fundamental change of attitude among the 'educated' classes. Throughout the school systems, the quality of the education was low and the number of absentees, repeaters and drop-outs were high. Myrdal reiterated the demands that he had made in *Asian Drama,* for improved teacher quality, more vocational education and fewer 'generalists.' The rapid increase of secondary and tertiary education, which took place at the expense of primary education, must be stopped, but possibly, in the short run, given the severe lack of qualified teachers, the enrollment of children in primary education might also have to be cut down—but only temporarily, until the teacher situation improved.

Myrdal also expanded his analysis of the soft state considerably from *Asian Drama* to *The Challenge of World Poverty.* The '… *underdeveloped countries are all, though in varying degrees, "soft states",*'[165] which could be exploited for personal gain by the economically, socially and politically powerful. This attitude, in turn, had spread to all strata of the population and had produced a general inclination to resist public controls. This constituted a formidable obstacle to development since, argued Myrdal, development was impossible without social discipline, and the latter could not be achieved without legislation, regulations and compulsion, all of which tended to be blocked by the vested interests of those on top of the economic and social pyramid. The professed desire to change this state of the arts had led to very little change. The entire political, legal and administrative system was heavily biased against the poor.

Even though it was difficult to measure, Myrdal pointed out that the degree of corruption was much higher in the South Asian countries than in the Western developed countries and he furthermore claimed that practically everything that had taken place after independence in those countries had served to create greater incentives to and greater opportunities for corruption, 'particularly large-scale graft by politicians and higher officials but spreading downward to petty bribery.'[166]

It was obvious to Myrdal that one of the most important tasks of the countries of the Third World was to combat corruption. Large-scale administrative reform was called for, including the scaling-down of the public administration, which at the time was characterized by the employment of people who lacked both competence and integrity. The situation was almost hopeless. The countries of the Third World had to fight rampant corruption when everything in their societies tended to feed corruption. Myrdal, however, saw no other choice than a crusade against corruption if the development effort should not be jeopardized. The efforts had to begin at the top, with ministers, higher officials and businessmen in collusion with these groups, for it was at the top that corruption originated. Unfortunately, such efforts must be accomplished by the countries themselves, even though the developed countries could attempt to put pressure on them to do so. Western companies could abstain from the use of bribes as part of their business practice.

Turning to the role of the developed countries, these could exert an influence by the choice of which countries to assist and of the purposes

[165] Ibid., p. 208.

[166] Ibid., p. 234.

for which aid should be given. Myrdal's vision was that of '*close cooperation between the Western developed countries and the progressive forces in underdeveloped countries.*'[167] He warned against direct private investment by Western business interests in countries where no reforms were undertaken, because the natural allies of such interests were the ruling oligarchies. This simply amounted to '*a direct continuation of colonial policy and, indeed, the justification for the label "neo-colonialism" often thrown at Western enterprise.*'[168]

The position of the Third World countries with respect to foreign trade and capital movements was not only precarious, but also deteriorating. Myrdal repeated his analysis from *Asian Drama* of the systematic bias of the international markets against them and their tendency to contribute to increasing internal inequality. The prospects of traditional exports were not bright, and it was exceedingly difficult to develop exports of manufactured goods. As a result, the gap between these countries' import needs and their export revenues was widening, and neither portfolio investments nor direct investments were of the magnitude necessary to bridge the gap. The result was that the underdeveloped countries were becoming increasingly indebted.

Myrdal called on the developed countries to change their trade policies in such a way as to counteract the 'natural' mechanism of international trade by promoting imports from the Third World. His—utopian—vision was one of international solidarity:

> Abolishing the policies in developed countries that are adverse to the underdeveloped countries, and, still more, initiating policies that would help them positively, assume that people in the former countries would accept, to one degree or another, the conception of a *welfare world*. [...] this can be done with little or no real sacrifice in the long run.[169]

In practice, however, virtually nothing had been done. Myrdal's verdict was harsh:

> It is a fact that, as yet, *no Western developed nation has made any real sacrifices in shouldering aid obligations to underdeveloped countries. Neither*

[167] Ibid., p. 262.

[168] Ibid., pp. 263–264.

[169] Ibid., p. 298.

have they been prepared, on the whole, to abstain from even minor trading advantages that can be shown to be of real long-term interest to a developed country.[170]

The aid flows from the developed countries were completely unsatisfactory according to Myrdal. The official statistics were completely unreliable. They even included military aid and business transactions and much of the aid was tied. Myrdal contrasted American behavior, which primarily saw to the political and economic interest of the United States, and Swedish behavior: The only reason the Swedes had for providing aid was '*the moral one of solidarity with people in distress.*'[171] Aid policies had to rest on moral grounds. In order to get away from narrowly defined, selfish, national interests, Myrdal wanted the aid to be channeled through multilateral, intergovernmental organizations.

America and South Asia in Retrospect

In *Against the Stream*, a book collecting a number of critical essays on economics from the beginning of the 1970s,[172] Gunnar Myrdal anew dealt with the situation in the United States and India—the two main objects of his poverty studies. The American dilemma had not been solved. 'The whites continually live in moral confusion. They proclaim ideals that are bluntly disobeyed in their daily life.'[173] Instead of trying to come to grips with the dilemma, the United States had lapsed into 'the shameful McCarthy era.'[174] On the international scene, it led to a policy of containment of Communism which culminated in the disastrous Vietnam war.

At home, the war on poverty of John Kennedy and Lyndon Johnson had come to nothing. The living conditions for desperately poor slum dwellers, a third of whom were blacks, were not improving much and in some localities were deteriorating. Myrdal noted that there were many vested interests that prohibited reform, but in spite of all the anomalies he

[170] Ibid., p. 313.

[171] Ibid., p. 363.

[172] Myrdal (1974).

[173] Ibid., p. 305.

[174] Ibid., p. 269.

observed, he still preferred not to let himself be pessimistic with respect to the United States. The perennial moral philosopher argued that the country had a tremendous burden of debt vis-à-vis its poor people and warned that if it were not paid it might lead to grave social disturbances and risks for democratic government. The remedy was found in radical reforms based on the American Creed. The general community interests had to be opposed to unhampered individualism. '… liberty [should not] be allowed to mean that a majority of the people is left free to become ever more affluent, while a minority, and a large minority, is pressed down into an alienated underclass.'[175]

In spite of Myrdal's repeated insistence that he was not pessimistic with respect to the future of his beloved America it is difficult to escape a feeling of despair when you read his texts from the 1970s. In the case of India, his feelings were more mixed, wavering between optimism and pessimism. A mere handful of years had passed since the publication of *Asian Drama*, so the need for reform remained. The situation was complicated by the fact that India and Pakistan had just fought the thirteen-day war had led to the independence of Bangladesh in 1971. What was called for was mutual de-armament and friendly cooperation in the region. Pakistan and India had got new leaders in the recent past. Zulfikar Ali Bhutto had become President in the former country and Indira Gandhi become Prime Minster in India in 1966. Myrdal considered both bent on internal reforms. He recognized that to 'liquidate mass poverty and at the same time to spur economic development' was a Herculean task, but India would not have a good future without undertaking the effort. Revolutions 'from above' were anything but common and seldom successful, but the opposite—reform driven from below—was not an alternative:

> The poor, on their side, are downtrodden, hungry, illiterate, and disfavored in regard to education, health, and everything else. And to them it must be even more difficult to see and feel their rational interest in specific reform proposals. The masses are not rational on questions greater than their daily worries. Unfortunately, it is a fact that the masses are normally passive to the point of submission. Many may even consider their lowly status in society to be ordained by God, or the gods, and by their karma.[176]

[175] Ibid., p. 289.

[176] Ibid., p. 260.

The opponents to reforms had a tremendous advantage of experience, not least in terms of covert action, through collusion and corruption. Myrdal hinted at the existence of an 'Indian dilemma' in the context of reform policy making:

> India has become the one country in the world that has succeeded in marrying excellent declarations for greater equality agreed upon by almost everybody, including, since the fight for independence, the clamor for a 'social and economic revolution,' with policies that in practice have not prevented ever greater inequality. The mental state of most intellectually alert persons in India contains serious signs of schizophrenia, with which they apparently manage to live happily and undisturbed.[177]

Myrdal warned against the introduction of merely cosmetic reforms which would leave the privilege structure unchanged. Indira Gandhi had to face short-sighted vested interests, both within her own Congress Party and on the state and municipal levels, but reform was indispensable, 'radical reforms introduced from above but supported by pressure from below, instigated by education of the masses. The more actual alternative to an effective radical reform is to allow mass poverty to remain and even to encompass an ever larger part of the population.'[178]

The Preacher

Gunnar Myrdal remained true to his ideals all his life, notably the call for reforms and greater equality which he had been stressing since the beginning of the 1930s. From the early 1970s, his role became increasingly that of the preacher. Thus, in 1974, he wrote:

> ... conditions in underdeveloped countries, and the suggested radial reforms, have one trait in common. They concern crucial aspects of inequality of opportunity, and the reforms are all intended to work toward creating greater equality. The underlying thesis is that bringing about greater justice by wisely planned egalitarian reforms ... would also enhance the possibilities for growth and development. Indeed, domestic reforms

[177] Ibid., p. 262.

[178] Ibid., pp. 264–265.

along these lines are a by far more important requisite for their rapid and sustained development than any favors obtained from abroad.[179]

Equality was also the theme that Gunnar Myrdal chose for his Nobel lecture in March 1975, having been awarded the Sveriges Riksbank Prize in Economic Sciences in Memory Alfred Nobel (together with Friedrich Hayek) the year before. The lecture to a large extent focused on the unwillingness of the developed countries to provide aid to the Third World. In the United States, as Myrdal had pointed out several times before, aid-giving was motivated largely by the American national interest, interpreted mainly in political, strategic and military terms, rather than by humanitarian concerns. The amount of aid was on decline and the aid statistics were the same misleading old ragbag as ever, making no difference between military spending and public grants. Myrdal considered that all this had contributed to the increasing unpopularity of aid in the United States and contrasted the situation there and some of the allied countries in Western Europe with Sweden, the Netherlands and Canada, where the humanitarian solidarity ideal prevailed. He thought that the situation in the United States could be improved if appeal were made 'to the humanitarianism and fundamental decency of the ordinary American. I cannot believe that Americans are basically less charitable than Swedes.'[180]

The importance of aid had increased in recent years, since the world economy had been undergoing a number of changes which had affected the economic situation of the Third World countries in different ways which had made the latter call for a New International Economic Order with far-reaching concessions from the First World. The formation of OPEC (Organization of the Petroleum Producing Countries) and the concomitant oil price hike had made the oil-producing countries better off, but the vast majority of underdeveloped countries were oil importers and were hence suffering a setback in their development efforts. This situation was in turn compounded by a food crisis caused by bad crops in many countries and a deliberate reduction of the food surpluses in countries like the United States, Canada and Australia. The oil price increase in addition had led to increased fertilizer prices. The deteriorating standard of living was also worsened by continued high population growth in

[179] Ibid., p. 119.

[180] Myrdal (1975, p. 419).

the Third World, which in the limit threatened to provoke a Malthusian situation where death rates would increase.

Myrdal took moral issue with the high consumption of both food and other goods in the industrialized world. Economic growth in the West would have to be channeled into a different direction, one which allowed for a transfer of resources to poor countries on a much larger scale. '*The blunt truth is that without rather radical changes in the consumption patterns in the rich countries, any pious talk about a new world economic order is humbug.*'[181] Myrdal pointed out that there was a risk that the new world order would simply become 'another conventional formula' without content.[182] In his lecture, he also came back to the need for deep-going economic and social reform inside the Third World countries, in the interest of real equality instead of mere lip service.

When he gave the first Félix Neubergh Lecture at Gothenburg University in 1977, Myrdal's theme was the failure of international cooperation. He lamented the fact that, with few exceptions, international organizations had proved to be inefficient and could not point to any practical results of their work. At the time, the world was in the middle of the stagflation crisis, but hardly any efforts at all had been made to find a common solution. '...the plain truth is that each single country, big or small, has been left to steer its course independently. The pretended international cooperation has been a sham.'[183]

The lack of international cooperation was visible not only in the industrialized world but also showed up with respect to the international equality issue: the disposal of resources between developed and underdeveloped countries. With the exception of the oil producers, the latter had been hit hard both by the oil price rise following the foundation of OPEC, by bad harvests which had made increased food imports necessary, and by the crisis in the developed economies which had led to a decreased demand for their export goods. Myrdal, as always, pointed to the need for domestic reforms, notably of power institutions and of the agricultural sector where the majority of the population in the Third World had to make their living. However, he also pointed to the futility of calling for a New Economic World Order. Given the unwillingness

[181] Ibid., p. 424.

[182] Ibid., p. 430.

[183] Myrdal (1978b, p. 31).

of the bigger industrialized countries to provide genuine financial aid to the Third World, Myrdal concluded that 'the discussions of a new world economic order will continue to be ... relatively empty of results ...'.[184]

Again, Myrdal perceived a moral dilemma among the Western countries, based on the same kind of double standards as in America. On the practical level, their professed egalitarian ideals proved to be empty. 'I often wonder how they can help [not] feeling schizophrenic. They apparently succeed in keeping their general international declarations and their national policies in separate noncommunicating baskets.'[185]

For his contribution to a 1978 conference in Saltsjöbaden, outside Stockholm, on the world economic order, Myrdal chose as his theme 'Need for Reforms in Underdeveloped Countries', basically repeating his previous statements.[186]

The Wisdom of Hindsight

Around this time, Gunnar Myrdal began to change some of his views of how to reduce world poverty. As Paul Streeten has pointed out, 'At the end of his life he turned against development aid and development cooperation, and said in an interview that the world "was really going to hell in every possible respect." But he remained cheerful, adding, "We must not let the injustices of the world take over".'[187]

In 1984, the World Bank issued the first volume of *Pioneers in Development*, a book dedicated to the economists who created development economics in the 1940s and 1950s. Ten of them were invited to write retrospective essays on their work. Gunnar Myrdal was one of them. His piece dealt with international inequality and foreign aid. He called it 'an account of growing pangs of conscience.'[188] His pangs were mainly related to the aid issue:

[184] Ibid., p. 45.

[185] Ibid., p. 46.

[186] Myrdal (1981).

[187] Streeten (1992, p. 114). Streeten is presumably referring to the interview with Myrdal made by James Angresano in 1980: 'Of course, now the world is going to hell. [...] Nevertheless you should not give up' (Angresano, 1997, p. 160).

[188] Myrdal (1984, p. 151).

> At the beginning of my research interest in the development problems of the underdeveloped countries, I gave unqualified support to the idea that the developed countries should give financial assistance for their development. In my own country, Sweden, I have been active urging a relatively generous and untied aid program for this purpose. Development aid gradually reached the level, sometimes declared to be a goal, of 1 percent of the national income, and it was planned to reach even higher in the future. Recent happenings in the underdeveloped countries and in the world at large, however, have caused me to doubt whether I was right. Political problems have a moral kernel, and questions of aid are essentially dependent on moral judgment.[189]

Myrdal painted a grim picture of what had taken place in recent years. The available statistics exaggerated growth rates in the Third World. Development efforts were increasingly concentrated on industrialization, in spite of the fact that the manufacturing sector could only employ a small share of the population. Agricultural productivity was low and the surplus population in the countryside migrated to cities where no regular jobs were to be found:

> The result is increasing mass poverty. Famine becomes an ever more crushing problem. There are indications that the children of the poor who survive starvation come to suffer from retarded brain development and will be a hopeless subclass of mental cripples. This increases the damage caused by the lack of primary education or by schooling that is insufficient or maldirected.[190]
>
> As I see it, poverty in the underdeveloped countries is now almost everywhere increasing and becoming extreme.

At the same time the amount of financial aid from developed to underdeveloped countries was low, shrinking and increasingly tied. Myrdal argued in favor of a redirection of aid toward the poorest in the poorest countries, away from industrial projects, and also toward counties hit by catastrophes. He also recommended strict control of the employment of the aid funds. 'Given the undesirable qualities of the governments in most underdeveloped countries' these governments, should not be allowed to

[189] Ibid., p. 151.

[190] Ibid., pp. 160–161.

decide their use and should not administrate them.[191] Myrdal wanted more aid to be channeled through non-governmental organizations, such as the Red Cross, since the latter in his opinion were less prone to be influenced by political considerations. He summed up his new position:

> ... the aid-giving governments should insist upon effectively controlling the use of aid in an underdeveloped country. They should do so even if it would increase the costs of administering aid. In developed countries such guarantees would increase the willingness among ordinary people to give aid. If that type of aid-giving in the interest of the poverty-stricken ever came to be common practice, it would even be one element encouraging more democratic rule in some underdeveloped countries.
>
> For these reasons, I now criticize myself for not having changed my views on aid to underdeveloped countries until the shocks experienced in the present world economic crisis.[192]

Finally, Myrdal once more dealt with the increasing demands for a 'new international economic order' coming from the governments in the Third World. He saw these demands as a non-issue that simply served to divert the attention from the need for domestic reforms. The developed countries were too polite to push for this, and the other side had taken advantage of the situation. 'Under these conditions, by directing their interests so exclusively to this rather inconsequential issue, the underdeveloped countries have, I believe, turned demands for a new economic world order into a sort of alibi for not reforming the way in which they are governed.'[193]

Epilogue

As it were, Gunnar Myrdal exaggerated the plight of the Third World countries before the onset of the world recession in the 1970s. As Hla Myint pointed out in his comment to Myrdal's recollections, between 1950 and 1975, the per capita income of the underdeveloped countries

191 Ibid., p. 162.

192 Ibid., pp. 162–163.

193 Ibid., pp. 164–165.

grew with 3 percent per annum on average, 'an impressive achievement in the face of a rapid population growth of over 2 percent.'[194] Myint attributed Myrdal's pessimism to the fact that Myrdal was in love with his own model and he did not share Myrdal's old pessimism with respect to the effects of international trade on the Third World countries, but instead argued in favor of an outward-looking development strategy, based on an equilibrium exchange rate and relative product and factor prices that reflected relative scarcities, combined with appropriate institutional reform—a policy like the one that had been pursued by several countries in Southeast Asia: Thailand, Malaysia and the Philippines, and above all the four 'tigers,' Singapore, Hong Kong, Taiwan and South Korea. These countries had succeeded in increasing their per capita income levels which were approximately equal to those of the South Asian countries in the 1950s to levels two or three times higher than those prevailing in the latter two or three decades later. Myrdal chose to ignore that.

Time would prove Myint to be right and Myrdal wrong. The story of the South Asian economies of India, Bangladesh and Sri Lanka, during the following thirty-five years, is to a very large extent (although not completely and not evenly) a success story. These economies did not plunge deeper and deeper into poverty the way that Myrdal wanted us to believe they would. More than fifty years have now passed since the publication of *Asian Drama*, and as the overwhelming evidence in the recent volume published to commemorate that occasion demonstrates, events took a turn which deviated completely from the somber one predicted by him.[195] As Deepak Nayyar points out in his introduction, the economic significance of Asia has witnessed a phenomenal change. Between 1970 and 2016, the share of Asia in world GDP increased by 21 percentage points—from less than 10 percent to about 30 percent—due to high growth rates in the Asian countries and its share of world manufacturing value added increased from a mere 4 to 41 percent.[196] This is not the place to go into the statistics and details of the process. The reader is referred to Nayyar's excellent volume. The point to be made simply is that Myrdal failed completely to predict the course of history. Above

[194] Ibid., p. 167.

[195] Nayyar (2019a).

[196] Nayyar (2019b, pp. 7–8).

all, he failed to appreciate the ability of foreign trade and investment to spur development. He wrote at a time when 'export pessimism' was the prevailing mood.

Does this mean that *Asian Drama* is a book to be discarded? The answer is no. Famous economists are notorious for delivering the wrong predictions. Myrdal is definitely not alone. The value of his analysis of South Asia, and of poverty issues in general, rather lies in his methodology—the theme of the present essay—and the boldness with which he questioned established 'truths' and approaches, not only in *Asian Drama*.[197] During his entire professional life, he wrestled with method problems and designed his own, original approach to the study of poverty. What is still alive today is his insistence on the importance of institutions, his holistic approach, as expressed in the notion of circular, cumulative causation, i.e. his focus on interdisciplinary research—that there is no such thing as a purely 'economic' problem and his insistence on explicit value premises, although mainly among heterodox economists. With the exception of the role of institutions for economic development, his influence on the mainstream has been decidedly weaker.

And then, Gunnar Myrdal deserves credit for remaining an optimist all his life. Being a truly international citizen, his vision of social policy and his vision of the welfare state that he so earnestly desired encompassed the entire planet. In one of his last books of essays he wrote:

> In the distant future perspective, I believe … that the human valuations that in the developed countries have brought us on the road toward the welfare state cannot halt at national boundaries. Nothing less than a welfare world corresponds to the valuations upon which our domestic social policy has been founded.[198]
>
> I cannot be defeatist on this score.

* * *

I met Gunnar Myrdal on a single occasion: in Lund, on 7 June 1979, after having defended my PhD thesis on the Haitian economy a week before. Then he asked me: 'Have you read my Monetary Equilibrium*?' I replied that I had, since I had used the idea of circular, cumulative causation in*

[197] Stewart (2019).

[198] Myrdal (1974, p. 50).

my book.[199] *'Well', said Myrdal, 'that's a book about Wicksell, a book that Wicksell himself could have written, if only he had thought as clearly as I.'*

References

Angresano, James (1997), *The Political Economy of Gunnar Myrdal: An Institutional Basis for the Transformation Problem*. Cheltenham and Lyme, NH: Edward Elgar.

Appelqvist, Örjan (2000), *Bruten brygga: Gunnar Myrdal och Sveriges ekonomiska efterkrigspolitik 1943–1947*. Stockholm: Santérus Förlag.

Appelqvist, Örjan (2014), *The Political Economy of Gunnar Myrdal: Transcending Dilemmas Post-2008*. London and New York: Routledge.

Barber, William J. (2008), *Gunnar Myrdal: An Intellectual Biography*. Houndmills, Basingstoke and New York: Palgrave Macmillan.

Bok, Sissela (1992), 'Introduction', in: Gilles Dostaler, Diane Ethier and Laurent Lepage (eds), *Gunnar Myrdal and His Works*. Montreal: Harvest House.

Carlson, Allan (1990), *The Swedish Experiment in Family Politics: The Myrdals and the Interwar Population Crisis*. New Brunswick, NJ and London: Transaction Publishers.

Carlson, Benny (2013), 'Gunnar Myrdal', *Econ Journal Watch*, Vol. 10, No. 3, 507–520.

Cassel, Gustav (1923), *The Theory of Social Economy, Vol. 1*. London: T. Fisher Unwin.

Etzemüller, Thomas (2014), *Alva and Gunnar Myrdal: Social Engineering in the Modern World*. Lanham, MD: Lexington Books.

Gustafsson, Bo (1987–1989), 'Myrdal, Karl Gunnar', in: Göran Nilzén (ed.), *Svenskt biografiskt lexikon*, Vol. 26, 144–160. Stockholm: Norstedt.

Gustafsson, Bo (1998), 'Ekonomporträttet: Gunnar Myrdal (1898–1987)', *Ekonomisk Debatt*, Vol. 26, No. 8, 617–627.

Hansson, Björn A. (1982), *The Stockholm School and the Development of Dynamic Method*. London: Croom Helm.

Herskovits, Melville J. (1941), *The Myth of the Negro Past*. New York and London: Harper & Brothers Publishers.

Jackson, Walter A. (1990), *Gunnar Myrdal and America's Conscience: Social Engineering and Racial Liberalism, 1938–1987*. Chapel Hill, NC and London: University of North Carolina Press.

Lundahl, Mats (1979), *Peasants and Poverty: A Study of Haiti*. London: Croom Helm.

[199] Lundahl (1979, Chapter 3).

Myint, Hla (1984), 'Comment' to Gunnar Myrdal, 'International Inequality and Foreign Aid in Retrospect', in: Gerald M. Meier and Dudley Seers (eds), *Pioneers in Development*. New York: Oxford University Press.

Myrdal, Alva and Myrdal, Gunnar (1934), *Kris i befolkningsfrågan*. Stockholm: Albert Bonniers förlag.

Myrdal, Alva and Myrdal, Gunnar (1935), *Kris i befolkningsfrågan*. Folkupplaga (Tredje, omarbetade och utvidgade upplagan). Stockholm: Albert Bonniers förlag.

Myrdal, Gunnar (1927), *Prisbildningsproblemet och föränderligheten*. Uppsala and Stockholm: Almqvist & Wiksells Förlag.

Myrdal, Gunnar (1930), *Vetenskap och politik i nationalekonomien*. Stockholm: P.A. Norstedt & Söners Förlag.

Myrdal, Gunnar (1931a), 'Om penningteoretisk jämvikt. En studie över den "normala räntan" i Wicksells penninglära', *Ekonomisk Tidskrift*, Vol. 33, No. 5–6, 191–302.

Myrdal, Gunnar (1931b), *Sveriges väg genom penningkrisen*. Stockholm: Bokförlaget Natur och Kultur.

Myrdal, Gunnar (1932a), 'Socialpolitikens dilemma I', *Spektrum*, Vol. 2, No. 3, 1–13.

Myrdal, Gunnar (1932b), 'Socialpolitikens dilemma II', *Spektrum*, Vol. 2, No. 4, 13–31.

Myrdal, Gunnar (1933a), *Konjunktur och offentlig hushållning. En utredning*. Stockholm: Kooperativa förbundets bokförlag.

Myrdal, Gunnar (1933b), 'Der Gleichwichtsbegriff als Instrument der geldtheoretischen Analyse', in: Friedrich A. Hayek (ed.), *Beiträge zur Geldtheorie*. Wien: Julius Springer.

Myrdal, Gunnar (1934), *Finanspolitikens ekonomiska verkningar*. Stockholm: Kungl. Boktryckeriet. P.A. Norstedt & Söner.

Myrdal, Gunnar (1935a), 'Den förändrade världsbilden inom nationalekonomin', in: Gunnar Myrdal and Herbert Tingsten, *Samhällskrisen och socialvetenskaperna*. Stockholm: Kooperativa förbundets bokförlag.

Myrdal, Gunnar (1935b), 'Inledningsanförande', in: *Debatt i befolkningsfrågan*. Stockholm: Kooperativa förbundets bokförlag.

Myrdal, Gunnar (1937), 'Massfattigdomen och dess avskaffande', *Frihet*, Vol. 21, No. 9, 4–5.

Myrdal, Gunnar (1939), *Monetary Equilibrium*. London: William Hodge & Co.

Myrdal, Gunnar, with the assistance of Richard Sterner and Arnold Rose (1944a), *An American Dilemma: The Negro Problem and Modern Democracy*. New York and London: Harper & Brothers Publishers.

Myrdal, Gunnar (1944b), *Varning för fredsoptimism*. Stockholm: Albert Bonniers förlag.

Myrdal, Gunnar (1953), *The Political Element in the Development of Economic Theory*. London: Routledge & Kegan Paul.
Myrdal, Gunnar (1956a), *An International Economy: Problems and Prospects*. New York: Harper & Brothers Publishers.
Myrdal, Gunnar (1956b), *Development and Under-Development: A Note on the Mechanism of National and International Economic Inequality*. Cairo: National Bank of Egypt.
Myrdal, Gunnar (1957a), *Economic Theory and Under-Developed Regions*. London: Gerald Duckworth & Co.
Myrdal, Gunnar (1957b), *Rich Lands and Poor: The Road to World Prosperity*. New York: Harper & Brothers.
Myrdal, Gunnar (1958), 'The Relation Between Social Theory and Social Policy, in: *Value in Social Theory: A Selection of Essays on Methodology*. London: Routledge & Kegan Paul.
Myrdal, Gunnar (1960), *Beyond the Welfare State*. London: Gerald Duckworth & Co.
Myrdal, Gunnar (1962a), *Population: A Problem for Democracy*. Gloucester, MA: Peter Smith.
Myrdal, Gunnar (1962b), *Challenge to Affluence*. New York: Pantheon Books.
Myrdal, Gunnar (1964), *Vår onda värld*. Stockholm: Utrikespolitiska institutet and Rabén & Sjögren.
Myrdal, Gunnar (1968), *Asian Drama: An Inquiry into the Poverty of Nations*. 3 Volumes. New York: The Twentieth Century Fund.
Myrdal, Gunnar (1969), *Objectivity in Social Research. The 1967 Wimmer Lecture, St. Vincent College, Latrobe, Pennsylvania*. New York: Pantheon Books.
Myrdal, Gunnar (1970), *The Challenge of World Poverty: A World Anti-Poverty Program in Outline*. New York: Pantheon Books.
Myrdal, Gunnar (1972), *Vetenskap och politik i nationalekonomin*. Ny omarbetad upplaga. Stockholm: Rabén & Sjögren.
Myrdal, Gunnar (1974), *Against the Stream: Critical Essays on Economics*. London and Basingstoke: Macmillan.
Myrdal, Gunnar (1975), 'The Equality Issue in World Development'. *Swedish Journal of Economics*, Vol. 77, No. 4, 413–432.
Myrdal, Gunnar (1978a), 'Institutional Economics', *Journal of Economic Issues*, Vol. 12, No. 4, 771–783.
Myrdal, Gunnar (1978b), *Increasing Interdependence Between States but Failure of International Cooperation*. Gothenburg: Gothenburg University.
Myrdal, Gunnar (1981), 'Need for Reforms in Underdeveloped Countries', in: Sven Grassman and Erik Lundberg (eds), *The World Economic Order: Past and Prospects*. London: Macmillan.

Myrdal, Gunnar (1984), 'International Inequality and Foreign Aid in Retrospect', in: Gerald M. Meier and Dudley Seers (eds), *Pioneers in Development*. New York: Oxford University Press.

Myrdal, Gunnar (1987), *Historien om an American Dilemma*. Stockholm: SNS Förlag.

Nayyar, Deepak (ed.) (2019a), *Asian Transformations: An Inquiry into the Development of Nations*. Oxford: Oxford University Press.

Nayyar, Deepak (2019b), 'Rethinking *Asian Drama*: Fifty Years Later, in: Deepak Nayyar (ed.), *Asian Transformations: An Inquiry into the Development of Nations*. Oxford: Oxford University Press.

Peltier, Jacques (1992), 'Myrdal and Value Loaded Concepts', in: Gilles Dostaler, Diane Ethier and Laurent Lepage (eds), *Gunnar Myrdal and His Works*. Montreal: Harvest House.

Rosier, Michel (1992), 'On the Hypothetical Character of "Moral Premises"', in: Gilles Dostaler, Diane Ethier and Laurent Lepage (eds), *Gunnar Myrdal and His Works*. Montreal: Harvest House.

Seccareccia, Mario (1992), 'Wicksellianism, Myrdal and the Monetary Explanation of Cyclical Crises', in: Gilles Dostaler, Diane Ethier and Laurent Lepage (eds), *Gunnar Myrdal and His Works*. Montreal: Harvest House.

Southern, David W. (1987), *Gunnar Myrdal and Black-White Relations: The Use and Abuse of* an American Dilemma, *1944–69*. Baton Rouge, LA and London: Louisiana State University Press.

Stewart, Frances (2019), 'Myrdal's Methodology and Approach Revisited', in: Deepak Nayyar (ed.) *Asian Transformations: An Inquiry into the Development of Nations*. Oxford: Oxford University Press.

Streeten, Paul (1992), 'Myrdal, the Man and the Theorist', in: Gilles Dostaler, Diane Ethier and Laurent Lepage (eds), *Gunnar Myrdal and His Works*. Montreal: Harvest House.

Swan, Trevor W. (1962), 'Circular Causation', *Economic Record*, Vol. 38, No. 83, 421–426.

Uhr, Carl G. (1962), *Economic Doctrines of Knut Wicksell*. Berkeley, CA: University of California Press.

Velupillai, Kumaraswamy (1992), 'Reflections on Gunnar Myrdal's Contributions to Economic Theory', in: Gilles Dostaler, Diane Ethier and Laurent Lepage (eds), *Gunnar Myrdal and His Works*. Montreal: Harvest House.

Wicksell, Knut (1898), *Geldzins und Güterpreise. Eine Studie über den Tauschwert des Geldes bestimmenden Ursachen*. Jena: Verlag von Gustav Fischer.

Wicksell, Knut (1906), *Föreläsningar i nationalekonomi II: Om penningar och kredit*. Stockholm: Fritzes.

Wicksell, Knut (1935), *Lectures on Political Economy. Volume II: Money*. London: George Routledge and Sons.

Wicksell, Knut (1936), *Interest and Prices: A Study of the Causes Regulating the Value of Money*. London: Macmillan and Co.

CHAPTER 4

Ingvar Svennilson on Economic Planning in War and Peace

(with Benny Carlson)

During the transition from a wartime to a peacetime economy in the mid-1940s, Sweden experienced a heated debate on economic planning in which a number of Sweden's leading economists were involved. In 1941, Ingvar Svennilson, a member of the so-called Stockholm School of economists, became the head of the Industrial Institute for Economic and Social Research, founded by Swedish industry. During the following years he wrote extensively on the issue of economic planning. Although this issue was ideologically explosive, he managed to strike a balance which earned him respect in most camps. His focus gradually shifted from central planning during the war, toward framework planning and indicative planning after the war, when he designed the first Swedish long-term survey.

This essay is partly based upon the chapters on Svennilson in a volume on the Industrial Institute for Economic and Social Research [*Industriens Utredningsinstitut*] from its foundation up to 1950 (Carlson and Lundahl, 2014). The work on this volume was funded by the Jan Wallander, Tom Hedelius and Tore Browaldh foundations. We are grateful for constructive comments—some pretty detailed—from two anonymous referees.

M. Lundahl, *Twelve Figures in Swedish Economics*, Palgrave Studies in the History of Economic Thought, https://doi.org/10.1007/978-3-030-94327-1_4

Sweden has experienced two fierce battles over the issue of economic planning [*planhushållning*]: one during the Great Depression in the 1930s and another in the 1940s, during the transition from the wartime to the peacetime economy. Both battles were triggered by Social Democratic initiatives. In the latter case, the igniting spark came in 1944 with the Swedish labor movement's postwar program. The world war had forced a great deal of planning and regulation upon the Swedish economy, naturally enough, since the production apparatus had to be adjusted to the fact that Sweden was partially cut off from international trade and could even be drawn into the war. The majority of the population had thought of this as a temporary disturbance and it had not caused much ideological strife. The Social Democrats, however, saw the new-won planning experience as an opportunity for a 'harvest' and a promise for the future, as demonstrated by the following passage from their postwar program, where society is synonymous with state:

> The wartime economy has revealed the immense scope for intensive production when the labor force and the material assets are employed under the direction of society and for the purposes which society determines. The war economy has taught lessons for the peace as well. We do not have to resign ourselves to unemployment, and we can abolish destitution, provided that the productive power which the war revealed us to possess is used with similar expedience for peacetime purposes. The main task before us is to coordinate economic activities into a planned economic system so that the labor force and the material assets are utilized for efficient production all the time. Such coordination ought to take place under the direction of society and should be so arranged that private interests are subordinated to the goals for which we strive collectively.[1]

Ernst Wigforss, the Social Democratic Minister of Finance, was in the frontline of the debate both during the 1930s and the 1940s. He was joined by a number of politicians across the ideological spectrum. Other participants came from the trade union movement and the business community, and several Swedish economists (some of whom were also politicians) were also engaged. The leading planning advocates among the economists during the 1930s were Gunnar Myrdal and Karin Kock (Social Democrats) and Bertil Ohlin (social Liberal). The leading opponents

[1] Arbetarörelsesens efterkrigsprogram (1945, p. 4).

were Gustav Cassel and Eli Heckscher (classic Liberals), who anticipated many of the arguments in Friedrich von Hayek's *The Road to Serfdom*[2] (1944), and Gösta Bagge (Conservative). During the 1940s, Myrdal, Kock, Heckscher and Bagge continued to be deeply involved in the debate. Ohlin moved in the classic Liberal direction, especially after becoming leader of the Liberal Party in 1944, and Cassel's voice fell silent when he died in 1945.

Why Svennilson?

A great deal has been written about the Swedish debate on economic planning in the 1940s, primarily by political scientist Leif Lewin,[3] and on the arguments of the economists involved.[4] There is, however, one prominent Swedish economist who wrote extensively on economic planning, but to whom not much attention has been paid in retrospect: Ingvar Svennilson.[5]

Ingvar Svennilson (1908–1972) was a member of the younger generation of the Stockholm School of economists. The existence of such a 'school' was suggested by Ohlin in 1937 in an effort to show that Swedes had launched ideas about countercyclical and expansionary economic policies in parallel with and independently of John Maynard Keynes, who had published his *General Theory* in 1936.[6] Ohlin considered Myrdal, Erik Lindahl and himself to be the older generation of the school and the younger generation included economists like Svennilson, Erik Lundberg and Dag Hammarskjöld.[7]

[2] Hayek (1944).

[3] Lewin (1967).

[4] E.g. Carlson (1994), Appelqvist (2000).

[5] Svennilson is only mentioned *en passant* by Lewin (1967, pp. 202, 337) and not at all in Villy Bergström's (1977) account of the economists' reactions to the labor movement's postwar program. Bergström's picture of a deep rift between the economists and the labor movement was strongly criticized both by Assar Lindbeck (1978) and Bertil Ohlin (1978), and both of them mentioned Svennilson among the economists who 'collaborated' with the labor movement. Excellent portraits of Svennilson are painted in Lundberg (1972) and Persson and Siven (2009), (2010).

[6] Keynes (1936).

[7] Ohlin (1937).

Between 1938 and 1940, Svennilson worked—with Lundberg—for the National Institute of Economic Research [Konjunkturinstitutet][8] and for the State Industrial Commission [Statens Industrikommission], which had been created in 1914 to facilitate industrial production during World War I. This commission was abolished in 1920 but was resurrected in 1939 to allocate raw materials and regulate industrial production during World War II.

In 1941, Svennilson became the director of the Industrial Institute for Economic and Social Research [Industriens Utredningsinstitut, IUI], which had been founded by the Federation of Swedish Industries [Sveriges Industriförbund] and the Swedish Employers' Confederation [Svenska Arbetsgivareföreningen] two years before. He was thus confronted with the somewhat delicate task of having to handle issues of economic planning in the middle of the war at the same time as he was the leader of an organization founded and funded by Sweden's industrial employers. Svennilson, however, managed to cope with this task and Lundberg has concluded that no one in Sweden has succeeded like Svennilson in being 'involved over long periods of time in both camps—the Swedish Social Democratic Government camp on the one side and the private industrial camp on the other—while keeping his high reputation as an independent research worker'.[9] Svennilson was 'respected in all political camps', as Mats Persson and Claes-Henric Siven put it.[10]

In due time, Svennilson would be well known in Sweden for his initiation of a series of long-term surveys [långtidsutredningar] and also internationally recognized for his *magnum opus* from 1954, *Growth and Stagnation in the European Economy*, written at the request of the United Nations Economic Commission for Europe, which dealt mainly with the period between 1913 and 1938.[11]

As Lundberg noted, Svennilson, 'from the very beginning [had] a strong interest in the theory and application of *economic planning*—both on the micro (firm) and on the level of central Government'.[12] The title of Svennilson's doctoral dissertation from 1938 was *Ekonomisk planering*

[8] Henriksson (1987).

[9] Lundberg (1972, p. 314).

[10] Persson and Siven (2010, p. 33).

[11] Svennilson (1954).

[12] Lundberg (1972, pp. 317–318).

[Economic Planning].[13] It dealt with corporate planning and was decisive for the future direction of his career:

> The ideas behind the dissertation were always with him. How do you plan when the world is uncertain and your environment may hold many different matters in store? How do you allow for the successive dissipation of uncertainty and how will this affect the timing of different investments? This is the perspective of the individual firm. For society, you must add the possibility of reducing the uncertainty with respect to the future through coordination of corporate investments – and Svennilson argued that in this context government has an important role to fulfil.[14]

In his dissertation, Svennilson defined planning as part of dynamic economic analysis. 'In the atemporal, static theory only the coordination of *simultaneous* actions is dealt with. The problem of *economic planning* also encompasses the *coordination of actions during different future time periods* in a plan.'[15] Action parameters are defined as the quantities which may be determined by the decision-making units. An action consists in fixing the value of an action parameter during a shorter or longer time span,[16] and the planner has to indicate '*how under given circumstances the immediate actions are determined as parts of a plan of possibly much longer duration*'.[17] In his more popular writings on planning, the ones that concern us in the present context, Svennilson did not define planning explicitly, but there is nothing in them to suggest that he had a different definition in mind in these.

Planning is part of a wider spectrum of interventions designed to interfere with the unregulated working of the market mechanism. These include different types of regulations as well as fiscal and monetary policies designed to influence aggregate demand and unemployment. Today, it may seem as if these policies can be sorted into different compartments. However, during the 1940s, the decade when our 'story' unfolds, conditions were somewhat different. Back then, the main ideological battle was about more or less government control over the economy. Economists

[13] Svennilson (1938).

[14] Persson and Siven (2010, pp. 32–33). See also Persson and Siven (2009).

[15] Svennilson (1938, p. 19).

[16] Ibid., pp. 27, 18.

[17] Ibid., p. 20.

striving for more state control—like Myrdal and other members of the Stockholm School of economists—were engaged along all these economic policy frontiers. Even if they themselves could perhaps make clear distinctions between these frontiers, their opponents could or would not. In the first line of opposition were the classical Liberals, Cassel and Heckscher. Since the early 1930s they had argued against government plans and interventions. Cassel maintained that one intervention would lead to another in a never-ending sequence and that monetary policy was the only way to stabilize the economy without succumbing to more or less complete state control. Heckscher thought that the fiscal stabilization policies of the Stockholm School or Keynesian brand would lead to a permanent expansion of the state since economic contractions would regularly be met with increased government expenditure, while economic expansions would be met with tax hikes.[18]

At first sight, it may also seem as if planning, regulation, fiscal and monetary stabilization policies follow a declining scale of state intervention. This is, however, hardly the case. Piecemeal regulation of industries or public works programs can be much more interventionist than planning. The 'lightest' form of planning, so-called indicative planning, is clearly one of the least intrusive policies in the toolbox. This kind of planning has often been associated with French planning policies after World War II. However, it was launched already by Herbert Hoover, US Minister of Trade 1921–1928 and President 1929–1933. He used economic information and conferences to coordinate activities within business life to combat economic waste—and to forestall direct government intervention.[19]

The core of the Swedish debate was to what extent the economy had to be planned and to what extent it could be left to the market. The purpose of the present essay is to examine how Svennilson managed to strike a balance in this respect, between government and industry, between plan and market—and how he revised his position over time—when dealing with different aspects of economic planning during and after World War II.

The spotlight will be on Svennilson, while numerous other participants in the debate on economic planning will be relegated to the

[18] Carlson (1994).

[19] Barber (1988), Hoover (1952).

background or left out of sight. The aim is neither to provide an account of the different standpoints on economic planning held by other Swedish economists nor to relate Svennilson's views to the international debate about planning versus markets which had been going on since the times of Vilfredo Pareto, other than *en passant*, when called for by the context. These debates cannot easily be condensed into a short article but should preferably be dealt with in book-length format. The views of a single important, and somewhat overlooked, actor, however, *can*, although in the case of such a prolific author as Svennilson the focus obviously has to be on matters of principle instead of on minute details.

The focus will furthermore be on the eight-year period from 1941 to 1949, when Svennilson as head of the Industrial Institute for Economic and Social Research, an organization funded by organizations representing employers and industry, had to navigate along the brink of an ideological abyss. This period covers powerful shifts between wartime, peacetime and long-term planning.

Before plunging headlong into Svennilson's writings on economic planning, we must position him somewhat more precisely in relation to the other Stockholm School economists. Myrdal, Lindahl, Lundberg and Svennilson had in the late 1920s and early 1930s worked for Bagge in a Rockefeller-funded project on wages, national income and cost of living in Sweden. Bagge, Lundberg and Svennilson produced a voluminous work on *Wages in Sweden, 1860–1930*,[20] which according to Lundberg established Svennilson as 'the pioneer' within the research field of structural change.[21] Svennilson's interest in this field was inevitably strengthened by his position as head of an organization focused on investigating industrial conditions, and by the exceptional wartime resource allocation problems. With Johan Åkerman, he became the leading Swedish proponent and practitioner of structural analysis. He thus deviated somewhat from the tradition of the Stockholm School economists who were not sympathetic to Åkerman's endeavors.[22] During his lectures, Ohlin even used

[20] Bagge et al. (1933), (1935).

[21] Lundberg (1972, p. 314). Svennilson and Lundberg cooperated and complemented each other through their fields of interest—structural change and business cycles, respectively—while at the same time they were stern professional competitors.

[22] Jan Petersson (1987, p. 191) notes similarities between Åkerman and Svennilson, particularly regarding the role of expectations, but concludes that in the end Svennilson's approach did not 'strike Åkerman's fancy'.

to say: 'When I hear structure, I release the safety catch of my gun.'[23] On the other hand, Svennilson's interest in dynamic theory, stabilization and planning was very much in line with the activities pursued by other members of the school. He was 'personally close' to Myrdal but in political terms closer to Ohlin.[24]

> This meant that, within the frame of a free market economy, he advocated a rather large space for economic policy: active business cycle policy, income equalization through the tax system and coordination of corporations' expectations (and thereby their investments) through the long-term surveys.[25]

Wartime Planning

In May 1940, before taking up his position at the Industrial Institute for Economic and Social Research, Svennilson addressed foreign journalists on industrial planning during the current crisis.[26] He stated that central planning had been a heated issue for a long time, but that the war had changed the picture. After its outbreak, 'men of practical life'—business leaders and engineers—agreed that production had to be planned and coordinated to satisfy military needs and to supply the Swedish industry with raw materials when the shipping blockade made imports difficult.

In a radio address the following year, Svennilson spoke about industrial production in the service of the national economy during the blockade.[27] He outlined negative and positive methods which could be used during 'the planned economy within the industrial area, which is now attempted.' The negative method was simply to cut the consumption of scarce raw materials. The positive method consisted in replacing scarce materials with more abundant ones and increasing the domestic production of

[23] As told by Rolf Henriksson (6 April 2017), who was once Ohlin's student. The quote is a paraphrase of 'When I hear *culture* ...', usually, but falsely, attributed to Hermann Göring. It actually stems from Act1, Scene 1 of Nazi writer Hanns Johst's (1890–1978) drama *Schlageter* (1933): '*Wenn ich Kultur höre ... entsichere ich meinen Browning*' (Wikipedia, 2017).

[24] Persson and Siven (2010, p. 33).

[25] Ibid.

[26] Svennilson (1940).

[27] Svennison (1941a).

raw materials. To carry out this task it had been necessary to launch the State Industrial Commission where industry and government had been united in a 'personal union'; leading industrialists had filled many of the leading positions within this government agency. Still, when Svennilson, in a debate in the Swedish Economic Association, argued in favor of taxes on items like housing and cars in order to free resources for government and military production,[28] a leading Swedish daily newspaper brought out the heavy artillery and wrote, somewhat derogatorily, that he had shown 'the face of the planned economy.'[29]

Svennilson also discussed 'social control of business,' inspired by John Maurice Clark's book with the same title.[30] He noted that government control over business had increased in all countries, although the Russian, German and US experiments had received most attention. The increase was a direct result of the war experience but government interventions were now so deeply rooted 'that there can hardly be any doubt that we are facing a development which will continue also after the war.'[31] In Sweden, the extent of government control over business had been limited, although Sweden was regarded as a precursor when it came to designing fiscal and monetary policy measures to cope with the swings of the business cycle. 'However, the framework which state and society have drawn up around the freedom of action of the business community has been much more restrictive than before.'[32] This had held back private initiatives. Hence, new government interventions were needed to stimulate them.[33] The government agency, which, according to Svennilson, could help private business along, was the State Industrial Commission. Its ambition was not to nationalize production but to help private firms to develop through 'information, deliberations and negotiations between different parties.'[34] In this process, industrial associations had to play a

[28] Nationalekonomiska föreningen (1941, pp. 20–21).

[29] *Dagens Nyheter* (1941).

[30] Clark (1926).

[31] Svennilson (1941b, p. 1).

[32] Ibid., p. 3.

[33] This kind of reasoning amounts exactly to what critics of economic planning, like Cassel, as already mentioned, had predicted as the outcome of planning: one intervention will lead to another in a never-ending process.

[34] Svennilson (1941b), p. 9.

key role, which would increase the room for maneuver for 'the industrial leadership.'[35]

Another article by Svennilson on the planned industrial economy, published in late 1941 as the war expanded from a European war to a world war,[36] foreshadows the heated debate on economic planning that would begin a couple of years later. He begins by viewing Sweden during the war as an interesting laboratory experiment:

> The war has forced new organizational forms, which come close to what is usually labeled economic planning, into existence in the industrial arena. When such an extraordinary opportunity is offered in the economic field to witness, as it were, an experiment with the organization of business, one should not refrain from taking advantage of the experiences which only experiments of this kind can offer.[37]

Svennilson discussed '*the centralization of business leadership*.'[38] In principle, complete centralization was 'a relatively simple matter'[39] and it had its advantages. Central agencies could make corporations take up new lines of production, they could remove technical and economic obstacles and encourage new endeavors through risk-sharing. Centralization, however, also had drawbacks. It made it difficult to get information about local conditions, it took longer to react when conditions changed, and if the freedom of business leaders to act was limited in one area, their actions might be disturbed in other areas as well. Even though economic planning had its disadvantages, Svennilson concluded that it 'must be desirable to coordinate different parts of business life as much as possible [...] if one strives for maximum efficiency.'[40]

Somewhat later, one of Svennilson's colleagues at the Industrial Institute for Economic and Social Research, Erik Dahmén, argued that one government intervention would lead to another and that the result would

[35] Ibid., p. 12.

[36] Even if this article was published in late 1941, it is not possible to say exactly when it was conceived; Svennilson does not refer to any actual events.

[37] Svennilson (1941c, p. 295).

[38] Ibid., p. 297.

[39] Ibid., p. 300.

[40] Ibid., p. 307.

be ever increasing planning.[41] Svennilson and Dahmén were both 'structural researchers,' working at the same institute, but their viewpoints differed. Svennilson, who was steeped in the tradition of the Stockholm school, was prepared to accept rather far-reaching government interventions, but Dahmén was not. Perhaps, in a somewhat loose way, it may be claimed that Svennilson represented the position of Keynes and Dahmén the position of Hayek in the prelude to the ideological battle over the planned economy, although Keynes' interest in interventions centered on fiscal and monetary policy, not on economic planning per se.

Looking ahead, Svennilson argued for planning to counter a possible postwar recession like the one Sweden and the world had experienced after World War I.[42] The key was rationalization through cooperation in business. The war had demonstrated how economies of scale could be obtained by standardization, limitation of the number of products, specialization and concentration of production to fewer units, although this could also hamper the development of new goods. In this article, Svennilson thus 'coined the expression "*structural rationalization*" [...] [which] was used extensively in Sweden during the whole postwar period.'[43] According to Rolf Henriksson, the book by Svennilson and Erland Waldenström was the first contribution to the discussion on postwar planning that would soon begin.[44] Svennilson favored cooperation between industry and government, although he came 'dangerously close' to socialist thinking.

This danger was noted by Axel Brunius, editor of *Industria*, a journal published by the Federation of Swedish Industries. He thought that Svennilson was concerned with productive efficiency only, which meant that the distribution of goods would turn almost into 'forced feeding.'[45] When Svennilson stressed the need for cooperation between companies,[46] Brunius did not hesitate to refer to Soviet style planning, whereupon Svennilson objected that Swedish firms hardly suffered from gigantomania but, if anything, were too small.

41 Dahmén (1942).

42 Svennilson and Waldenström (1942).

43 Lundberg (1972, p. 315)

44 Henriksson (1990, p. 169).

45 Brunius (1942, p. 905).

46 Svennilson (1943).

Planning for the Peace

In the fall of 1942, when the war events pointed to a victory for the Allies, the issue of preparing the Swedish economy for peacetime conditions came to the fore. The government authorities were, however, fully occupied with topical, short run, problems and reacted slowly. The business community responded much faster and, at the initiative of Svennilson, who quickly sensed the changing winds, the Industrial Institute for Economic and Social Research began to look into the issue. When Minister of Finance Ernst Wigforss in March 1943 launched plans for governmental inquiries into the transition to peace economy, the institute was invited to participate in the investigations that were concerned with industry.[47]

In January 1944, a conference on the theme 'The Economy Facing the Peace' [*Näringslivet inför freden*], with a thousand participants, including the Swedish political and industrial elite, was held in Stockholm with the Industrial Institute for Economic and Social Research as one of the main organizers.[48] One of the high points of the conference was the presentation of an investigation of industrial employment after the war carried out by Svennilson and two of his colleagues at the institute, Erik Dahmén and Axel Iveroth. Their findings[49] were delivered to Wigforss at the conference and received positive attention in the media; the only dissenting voice was that of a Communist newspaper.[50] Even more attention was, however, directed toward an exchange between Wigforss and Gustaf Söderlund, chairman of the Swedish Employers' Confederation. The exchange was triggered by two speakers, Gerhard Törnqvist, Professor of Business Administration at the Stockholm School of Economics, and Dag Hammarskjöld, at the time Secretary of State in the Ministry of Finance, who referred to what they called the governmental frame and the so far unpainted canvas. Söderlund expressed concern that the framer would set about to smudge the canvas. Wigforss retorted that the frame theory was new to him and according to media reports he even raised a cheer for Swedish business during the final banquet.

[47] Henriksson (1990).

[48] Industriens Utredningsinstitut (1944a).

[49] Industriens Utredningsinstitut (1944b).

[50] Norrskensflamman (1944).

In October 1944, the Commission on Postwar Planning [*Kommissionen för efterkrigsplanering*], popularly known as the Myrdal commission after its chairman Gunnar Myrdal, put forth a proposal by Myrdal and Svennilson for an investment council that would consist of representatives from government agencies and business organizations. The council would be assigned the task of coordinating business investments with government business cycle policy. According to Leif Lewin, the shift of focus from consumption to investment 'marks the difference between economic thinking in the 1930s and 1940s.'[51] The proposal was accompanied by a memorandum on employment policy after the war, written by Svennilson. This memorandum stated that the business cycle would go through three stages: first stagnation when economies made the transition from war to peace, thereafter a strong demand for exports due to neglected needs and reconstruction, and finally a downturn emanating from the United States. It would be beneficial if countermeasures could be 'directed toward different industries in a planned way.'[52]

Svennilson was thus arguing along the same lines as Myrdal, who in a famous book warned against a depression after the war, like the one after World War I. Myrdal's warning was alarmistic. He predicted a crisis originating in the United States that 'may include a cumulation of the deflationary crisis at the beginning of the twenties and the giant crisis from 1929 to 1932.'[53] As we have seen, already in 1942, Svennilson had envisioned a postwar crisis like the one after the previous war.

The investment council turned into a heated issue in the debate on economic planning. Some industrialists questioned whether the representatives of industry on the Myrdal commission had not been taken hostage. There was even an open rift in the government of national unity, when Minister of Trade Ohlin turned to Minister of Finance Wigforss and asked if those who had saved money and built enterprises should have no more to say about the use of their capital than any other citizen, and one newspaper went as far as to claim that the Myrdal commission was becoming 'a pure four-year planning commission; it only lacks a Göring.'[54] Economist Arthur Montgomery cautioned that the council would grow from an

[51] Lewin (1967, p. 247).

[52] Svennilson (1944, p. 93).

[53] Myrdal (1944, p. 167).

[54] *Göteborgs Tidning* (1944).

advisory body into a full-fledged 'central planning authority in a planned economy.'[55]

As it seems, the investment council worked satisfactorily from the perspective of both government and industry. In 1946, it was, however, once more thrown into the debate when the Communists in Parliament [*Riksdagen*] proposed to provide it with decision-making powers. The Social Democrats, however, challenged them and the Communist motion was rejected.

In the spring of 1945, Svennilson stated that 'a more or less complete regulation of all markets' had been implemented during the war without major controversies; the main principle had after all been 'not [to] use more force than what was necessary.'[56] The question of the day was in what direction the regulatory policy would develop after the war. Svennilson, who again sensed that times were changing, predicted that foreign trade would continue to be regulated for many years to come. The main difference between war and peace was rather that policies would have to change from negative to positive. During the war, the economic policy had been dominated by restrictions and prohibitions. With the arrival of peace, what was needed was a policy which aimed at taking advantage of individual initiatives. 'Its task to a large extent will be to construct a framework for individual activity, to stimulate development in a certain direction rather than imposing prohibitions.'[57] As examples of such policy initiatives Svennilson mentioned support for technical research and rationalization measures in construction and agriculture. He continued by contrasting the centralized planned economy with the kind of framework planning[58] and negotiated economy that he advocated himself. Centralized planning—'bureaucratic dictatorship'—had certain immediate advantages in terms of efficiency. It could achieve

[55] Montgomery (1944).

[56] Svennilson (1945, pp. 3, 9).

[57] Ibid., p. 16.

[58] The concept of framework planning had been developed in the Swedish setting by Bertil Ohlin, who wrote about such certainties as legislation or 'fixed rules, which everybody must obey' which would make '[t]he game [...] proceed more smoothly and with greater efficiency' (Ohlin, 1936, p. 111). He also offered some examples of framework planning: urban and regional planning, government assistance to corporations to form industry associations, tariffs and regulation of agricultural prices. The general idea was that government should control the rules of the game but not intervene directly in it.

consistency, it was straightforward and decisions could be made quickly, without protracted negotiations. The advantage of a decentralized system, on the other hand, was that it could assimilate all the experiences and views of those who were to implement the decisions.

When the problems of the controlled economy were discussed at the Swedish Economic Association, Svennilson stated that he had had obtained new insights himself with respect to the functioning of the economic system. It was 'far more complicated than it seemed initially'.[59] To be able to control the economy successfully, 'the fine structure of economic life' had to be carefully studied.[60] Somewhat surprisingly, Svennilson contended 'that in this country we all have an approximately similar view regarding how far this control is to be pursued.' He then came back to his idea of a negotiated economy in a statement pointing forward to the future phase of indicative long-term planning:

> There is a way of bridging the gap between far-reaching control and the need for decentralization [...] namely discussions and negotiations [...] to arrive at a clearing between all experiences and intentions [...] in various places, centrally and in the periphery. [...] After all, during the war, both within government agencies and in the business community people have become used to new ways of cooperation.[61]

Peacetime Planning

The arrival of the peace changed the framework of the planning debate. When the government of national unity in the summer of 1945 was replaced by a purely Social Democratic government, armed with the labor movement's postwar program (quoted in the introduction to this article), the political temperature soared and the so-called PHM saw the light.

[59] At this time (March 1945), Svennilson was certainly acquainted with Friedrich von Hayek's (1944) *The Road to Serfdom*, published in the spring of 1944 and translated into Swedish later the same year. In a later famous article Hayek (1945, p. 519) argued that 'knowledge of the circumstances of which we must make use never consist in concentrated or integrated form, but solely as the dispersed bits of incomplete and frequently contradictory knowledge which all the separate individuals possess. This article was, however, published half a year after Svennilson's declaration of 'new insights'.

[60] Nationalekonomiska föreningen (1945a, p. 30).

[61] Ibid., p. 31.

PHM was a Swedish acronym for 'resistance against the planned economy' [*planhushållningsmotståndet*] used by the planning advocates as a nickname of the campaign against economic planning launched by the business community. The term was coined in July 1945 by Prime Minister Per Albin Hansson, who pointed to Gustaf Söderlund, chairman of the Swedish Employers' Confederation, as the instigator of the campaign.[62] The PHM campaign was run by different organizations and journals and funded by industry (through a special business fund, Näringslivets fond).[63]

In the midst of this heat, Svennilson raised a series of issues which all had implications for the scope and content of economic planning: full employment, labor immigration, agricultural policy, regional planning, trade policy and structural rationalization. Let us take a look at some of them.

On several occasions, Svennilson dealt with regional planning. In an address at the Swedish Economic Association, he referred to British economic research on 'external economies'[64] resulting from the insertion of individual companies into a larger local context, where they could benefit from common arrangements for transportation and distribution of electrical power, a common labor market with certain professional traditions, and technical experts.[65] He furthermore came back to the concept of framework planning:

> In principle, it is self-evident that [...] [the plan] can only supply a framework for construction and business. At what speed and to what extent different parts of this framework will be filled, is a later question. The plan will prevent movements in certain undesirable directions and indicate the direction for development in general.[66]

This kind of plan, normally at the county level, should indicate where a new industry could be established, but not what it should produce.

[62] Lewin (1967, p. 321).

[63] Dahlqvist (2003, pp. 177, 185–195).

[64] Theories on economic externalities and agglomeration (a word not used by Svennilson) date far back, at least to von Thünen (1875) [1826] and, in the British context, Marshall (1890).

[65] Nationalekonomiska föreningen (1945b, p. 78).

[66] Ibid., p. 79.

It should allow for alternative developments and should be constantly renewed and revised. Svennilson doubted that the public administration could perform such a difficult task, but he concluded that this type of planning must be handled by an authority above the municipal level. He was convinced that entrepreneurs would appreciate regional planning—it would perhaps even make them 'drool.'[67] In the discussion that followed upon Svennilson's address, a business representative stated that the absence of government planning had been the very cornerstone of the development of the free economy. Svennilson dismissed this objection by saying that if there was a need for urban planning there was also a need for regional planning.

In a report on Swedish postwar trade policy Svennilson dealt with the need for government control over Sweden's foreign trade. He cautioned that regulatory interventions might trigger countermeasures from other countries, pointed out that Sweden was known to be an advocate of free trade and stressed that this represented a goodwill that should not be wasted. He predicted that 'a certain regulation of foreign trade for some time after the war will probably be necessary' but also that 'rather soon a tendency towards freer trade relations should manifest itself.'[68]

In late 1946, Minister of Trade Gunnar Myrdal used the term 'organized free trade' during a debate at the Swedish Economic Association. This term made Eli Heckscher speak of 'a kind of free trade which is immensely similar to international dictatorship.'[69] Svennilson had used the same term in a journal article and acknowledged that it could be interpreted in different ways. However, he claimed, the purpose of organized free trade was to remove trade barriers and open markets: 'the purpose is not national planning of foreign trade but international planning *for* multilateral free trade.'[70] What Svennilson had in mind was the Bretton Woods system (agreed upon in 1944) for regulating international monetary and trade relations, with its three components: the International Monetary Fund, the World Bank and the (never established) International Trade Organization.

[67] Ibid., p. 87.

[68] Industriens Utredningsinstitut (1945, pp. 41, 46).

[69] Nationalekonomiska föreningen (1946, p. 131). The debate did not end well for Myrdal. He warned that import controls might be needed, which turned out to be a self-fulfilling prophecy. This episode contributed to his resignation as Minister of Trade.

[70] Svennilson (1946a, p. 19).

According to Lewin, the issue of structural rationalization of business life was one of the most central issues of planning ideology raised by the Myrdal commission and the most contentious: 'the new ideological divide in the debate on economic planning.'[71] Structural rationalization occupied a central place in Svennilson's vocabulary. He stated that the term had entered the Swedish economic discussion during the preceding four years and that 'to a large extent [it] had been applied to the burning issue of the relation between state and business.'[72] Since the Industrial Institute for Economic and Social Research had issued regular reports on other countries during the war, not least on German economic policies, one would perhaps expect that the term was of German origin. Svennilson, however, referred to experience from the United States. He defined structural rationalization as having to do with issues concerning '*the construction of the production and distribution apparatus within an industry.*'[73] The main issue was how to achieve greater efficiency through economies of scale and production in long series.

Rationalization would, however, not be achieved automatically by competition. There were obstacles that had to be overcome. Svennilson presented two interesting cases. The first dealt with smaller companies paying low wages and offering scanty welfare benefits to their employees. This meant that the superiority of larger companies could not fully manifest itself through competition. Svennilson found it 'urgent that an equalization of wages and the general social standard at different companies within an industry is achieved. This will be a means to strengthen competition and put all companies on an equal basis.'[74] Here, Svennilson seems to anticipate the solidarity wage policy launched by Gösta Rehn and Rudolf Meidner a few years later.[75] The second case concerned an

[71] Lewin (1967, p. 249).

[72] Svennilson (1946b, p. 1).

[73] Svennilson (1946c, p. 350).

[74] Ibid., p. 355.

[75] The Rehn-Meidner program was launched in 1951 at the Swedish Trade Union Confederation [*Landsorganisationen*] Congress (LO, 1951). Svennilson's anticipation of the solidarity wage policy was noted by Lundberg (1972, p. 315). Gösta Rehn had been Svennilson's student at Stockholm University; see Erixon (2011) and Erixon and Wadensjö (2012). Lennart Erixon (2011, pp. 101–102) delves into the *differences* between Svennilson's and Rehn-Meidner's ideas and states that Svennilson's 'Verdoorn's Law' (high production growth leads to high productivity growth) is "the antithesis of the

industry in which the total capacity is too large. Svennilson describes a market failure like sunk costs and destructive competition without using those exact terms:

> In such an industry with a declining market, overcapacity can sometimes endure for a long time, especially if plants are relatively capital intensive, or when employees are relatively settled and therefore prepared to endure relatively low wages and short-time work. In such cases, protracted tough competition, where nobody wants to give in, may break out.[76]

In cases like these, Svennilson argued, a 'rough-handed rationalization' of industrial structures might be necessary. This could be achieved if an industry developed a plan for reconstruction which then was negotiated with and approved by the government, which then could help to liquidate excess capacity. When this operation had been performed, 'competition could once again be unleashed from sounder points of departure.' Some industries might fear such operations, but according to Svennilson, their fear was unfounded since the government simply wanted 'to give a hand to industry in order to achieve more normal free competition.'[77]

Long-Term Planning

After the war, the Swedish economy—especially the balance of payments—was in a state of crisis and Svennilson was of course involved in giving advice of how to cope with the imbalances. He argued that the Swedes had lived beyond their means for several years. A general reduction of the demand for goods would have to be carried out through increased savings and reduced investment. The government as well had to increase its savings and the best recommendation that Svennilson could make to that end was to introduce a powerful sales tax. He had his doubts, however: 'I fear that one will instead choose a road with ever more

Rehn-Meidner growth theory", according to which lower aggregate demand and profits eliminate weaker production units, resulting in higher productivity for the industry. Erixon (2011, p. 96) also notes that already Cassel (1902) and Gösta Bagge (1917) argued that solidarity wage policy would put pressure on inefficient firms and result in rationalization and increased overall productivity.

[76] Svennilson (1946c, p. 356).

[77] Ibid., pp. 356–357.

complex regulations, perhaps in the end also of the labor market, which means that initiatives and willingness to work will be slowly suffocated.'[78] Svennilson's colleague Erik Dahmén once again took a different stand. He agreed that the Swedes had lived beyond their means and wanted to reduce consumption but *increase* investment instead, in order to expand the production capacity in the longer run.[79]

At a meeting of the Swedish Economic Association in 1948, Svennilson explained that the Swedish crisis was of a structural kind and could not be overcome in the short run: 'Sweden, the country which came out of the war most intact among Western European countries, has paradoxically enough demonstrated the weakest ability, compared to the period before the war, to pay for its imports with its exports.'[80] The way out of this dilemma was to regulate imports more and exports less. Regulation of imports would, however, bias production toward the domestic market—a major problem according to Svennilson, who ended his speech with a sigh: 'The task seems hopelessly difficult.'[81]

The epilogue to the debate on the planned economy was enacted during the 1948 election campaign, when Ohlin and the non-Socialist parties almost conquered power. The Social Democratic harvest had been rather meager because of the massive PHM resistance. 'The battle of the harvest time did not lead to any substantially increased influence of the state authorities over the economy [...] The failure could not be concealed.'[82]

In August 1948, Karin Kock, Minister without Portfolio, announced that Ingvar Svennilson would form part of a committee, summoned to investigate questions posed by the OEEC on how countries involved in the Marshall Plan intended to undertake reconstruction after the war. Already in October, this committee delivered a Swedish survey for 1947–52/53.[83] The main target of this 'long-term program' was to attain an export level that would allow Sweden to have balance in its payments without having to borrow money. A prerequisite for this was increased

[78] Svennilson (1947a, p. 15).

[79] Dahmén (1947), (1948).

[80] Nationalekonomiska föreningen (1948, p. 83).

[81] Ibid., p. 95.

[82] Lewin (1967, p. 329).

[83] SOU (1948:45).

production particularly in the export industries, while imports had to be reduced. In the debate, the program was often referred to as a 'four-year plan.' However, in the document there was no mention of a plan but of 'an alternative,' based upon rather arbitrarily chosen preconditions and 'illustrating how a certain possible development of foreign trade might relate to the economic development in general.'[84] The program was immediately sent to the OEEC and its Economic Cooperation Administration (ECA) by the Swedish government.

The long-term program had thus been quickly delivered. In January 1948, Ingvar Svennilson had proposed an extensive investigation of 'Sweden's Needs and Resources – 1960' to the board of the Industrial Institute for Economic and Social Research [Industriens Utredningsinstitut].[85] He had visited the United States in the spring of 1947 and had then been inspired by a similar inquiry, 'America's Needs and Resources,' funded by the Twentieth Century Fund. Svennilson obtained green light for his own investigation. We may thus assume that he began preparing an investigation already at the beginning of 1948 and that this work constituted an input into the work on the long-term program as well. At a board meeting in November, he argued that this program, in turn, could form the basis for the 1960 investigation. Several board members then expressed doubts about a forecast going so far into the future. The chairman, Ernst Wehtje, however, put his weight behind Svennilson, arguing that if industry did not take the initiative, such an investigation might be initiated by the government.[86] The work on this 'ten-year program' eventually resulted in several volumes (in 1952) on population, labor supply, income distribution, distribution of goods and transportation.

The 'four-year plan' got considerable attention in the media. Representatives of the export and shipping industries argued that it was too optimistic; representatives of the food industry complained it was too pessimistic. The plan was also subject to an extensive discussion in Parliament and received a favorable verdict from most speakers. The Social Democratic Prime Minister, Tage Erlander, even used the occasion to invite business representatives to free discussions. Only the Communists

[84] Ibid., p. 37.

[85] Industriens Utredningsinstitut (1948a).

[86] Industriens Utredningsinstitut (1948b).

were negative. Their objections were that it was not a 'real' (Soviet style) plan, that stability can never be achieved under 'capitalist anarchic conditions,' and that the whole purpose of the Marshall Plan was to involve Sweden in preparations for World War III. Erlander countered these objections with a dose of humor: How would the Communists like to solve the problem of foreign trade deficits and investment needs without taking the available resources into account? 'It would be of interest not only to Swedish economists, but to economists all over the world, to learn about this.'[87]

On a couple of occasions, Svennilson responded to criticisms against the program for being too optimistic. He predicted a period of unparalleled expansion of European production, comparable to what had recently been achieved by the United States or the Soviet Union and called the Swedish program cautious in comparison to programs in other Marshall countries.[88] Svennilson also turned against those who chose to refer to the program as a regular plan. It was nothing but '*a relatively uncertain estimate of the future* and must in any case not be called a plan like the ones that may be presented by the outspoken planning countries.'[89] Still, he dismissed the objection that it was impossible to survey a period of four or five years. This was indeed 'a short period of economic development.'[90] Planning for the future was absolutely essential: 'Public economic policy cannot [...] focus solely on the immediate future without resulting in grave mistakes.'[91] Svennilson also attempted to disarm the critics who feared that the long-term program was a gateway to economic planning. Viewing economic development and planning in a longer perspective called for increased mobility in the economy and reduced the risk of permanent government regulations.

In early 1949, Svennilson and his co-workers presented a revision of their program.[92] The OEEC had published a report on European reconstruction efforts based on the preliminary programs prepared in countries included in the Marshall Plan. The Swedes, in turn, argued that their

[87] Riksdagen (1948, p. 80).

[88] *Dagens Nyheter* (1949), *Svenska Dagbladet* (1949).

[89] Svennilson (1949, p. 68).

[90] Ibid., p. 72.

[91] Ibid., p. 73.

[92] SOU (1949:15).

preliminary program had been cautious and that export developments in 1947 and 1948 suggested that it would be possible to exceed the plan target. However, the prospects for exports of forest products to the United States appeared gloomy and signaled reduced dollar payments.

In July 1949, it was announced that Svennilson would leave the Industrial Institute for Economic and Social Research and Sweden to conduct a historical study of economic trends in Europe for the United Nations. This study would eventually result in his most well-known book, *Growth and Stagnation in the European Economy*.[93] In an interview for *Industria*, Svennilson was asked about his (and the institute's) relations to the business community and the government. His message was that relations with both camps were characterized by cooperation and trust.[94]

When Svennilson returned to Sweden after his stay in Geneva he became chairman of the third, fourth and fifth long-term surveys in the 1950s and 1960s. This was of course quite logical since the 'ten-year program' initiated by Ingvar Svennilson in early 1948 had been the point of departure for the 'four-year plan,' which in turn paved the way for a number of long-term surveys.

Planning in Retrospect

Even though the immediate postwar 'harvest' was meager, Gunnar Myrdal, the leading Swedish planning advocate, was in no way discouraged. He envisioned, like Adolph Wagner in the late nineteenth century, a long-term irresistible development of the welfare state in tandem with economic planning (Wagner's law). Myrdal stated that in all countries 'architects are incessantly working to simplify, coordinate and streamline' and that no country had come farther than Sweden in the development of a welfare state. 'This coordination of interventions and their constant adaption to the development tendencies revealed in forecasts, does not take the shape of a rigid, all-embracing plan. Nevertheless it means a constant development toward planned economy [...]'.[95]

[93] Svennilson (1954).

[94] *Industria* (1949).

[95] Myrdal (1961, pp. 8, 68–69).

When Svennilson around the same time looked back on the Swedish experience of long-term planning, he characterized it as a broad cooperation involving government, business and research, and as a combination of forecasts and guidelines for economic policy, which reflected the 'middle way' of the Swedish economy, where one-track plans had been replaced by alternative plans or strategies. The purpose of these plans was to serve as a background to the public debate, private decisions and government policy. In this way, a shared perception of the future would emerge. 'It would need an enormous organization to integrate these planning activities into one unit. [...] It is also very doubtful if a higher degree of centralization would give better results.'[96]

A few years later, Svennilson declared that in the fifth long-term survey there was a shift toward increased emphasis upon price formation as an instrument to guide development. Immediately after the war, in a situation characterized by scarcity, it had been natural to focus on physical targets, especially with respect to housing, transportation and public services. In such a situation, free price formation would have created socially unacceptable results.[97] Interestingly enough, Svennilson acknowledged that an 'ideological-political shift' had also taken place in this survey:

> Price formation should be used as a steering instrument to replace rationing according to certain criteria or brought about through queueing. The implications of this view are that one accepts the consumer's perception of what is best for him and rejects the idea of government "guardianship" in respect to consumer's choice.[98]

Many years later, Carl-Johan Åberg, who was in charge of the Swedish long-term surveys in the 1970s, summarized Svennilson's ideas about planning in a market economy:

[96] Svennilson and Beckman (1962, p. 75). Another Swedish economist, Assar Lindbeck (1975, 165–166), characterized the Swedish long-term surveys as 'forecasts, with some discussions on economic policy initiatives, rather than plans. [...] The reports can perhaps be characterized as a moderate type of "indicative planning"'.

[97] Svennilson (1966, p. 39).

[98] Ibid., p. 38.

> His basic approach stems from his 1938 dissertation where he outlined how the course of the economy is guided by different actors' expectations and plans. These change all the time when they meet other actors' [...] views of the future. The state in no way has to take on the role of a superior body in this model and it becomes natural to try to map the planning of different actors in the economy and allow their scenarios of the future to face each other. This basic approach would characterize a long series of long-term surveys.[99]

Conclusions

During the 1940s, Ingvar Svennilson wrote and spoke continuously of issues related to economic planning. He outlined the need for central planning during the war and he emphasized the common interest of government and industry. Svennilson did his utmost to stay on 'the middle course' without taking a stand on either side when the Social Democrats outlined their postwar plans and the ideological battle over planning began. He was cautious and, through his position at the Industrial Institute for Economic and Social Research, he could mobilize an unparalleled body of knowledge about business life conditions. By and large, it seems, he was successful. Occasionally he met with opposition, but most of the time he was treated respectfully both by the politicians and by the media on both sides of the ideological divide.

At the end of the war and during the first postwar years, Ingvar Svennilson often spoke about planning as a framework for the economy and thus used a concept (framework planning) which had been developed in the Swedish setting by Bertil Ohlin in the 1930s. When Svennilson was in charge of the first long-term survey in 1948, he argued in favor of long-term planning, not in order to produce a regular plan, but rather a forecast which all the actors in the economy could relate to. Such a forecast would increase the mobility in the economy and reduce the need for government regulation. Svennilson's ideas at the end of the 1940s are a clear expression of what is usually called indicative planning, i.e. planning by providing the economic actors with information, projections, targets and opportunities to discuss, negotiate and coordinate their individual plans. As we have seen, elements of these ideas had been present in Svennilson's writings long before.

[99] Åberg (2009, p. 166).

To summarize: Ingvar Svennilson's ideas about economic planning in the 1940s shifted gradually in a Liberal direction, from central planning and government control during the war, via framework planning at the end of the war and, finally, to indicative planning and reduced need for government regulation after the war. These gradual shifts mirror a changing reality: an economy operating in world where a war is going on requires other means of government control than one operating in a world in peace. Ingvar Svennilson's approach to economic planning was a pragmatic one, dictated not by ideological considerations but by what the particular economic circumstances at each moment called for. The extraordinary circumstances produced by World War II required extraordinary measures, but once the wartime restrictions began to ease, the content of planning would have to change (To this came the increasing resistance to planning and commands by the Swedish business community after the war. After all, Svennilson was heading a private research institute funded by industry). Altogether, his voice was one of restraint and fact-based reasoning in a debate which was all too often characterized by preconceived notions and loud and shrill voices. Through his direct influence on the long-term surveys carried out during the first postwar decades he contributed to putting Sweden on a path that was more market-oriented than for example the one of its Scandinavian neighbor, Norway.[100]

Published in *History of Economic Ideas*, Vol. 25, 2017. Reprinted by permission from Fabrizio Serra editore.

References

Ingvar Svennilson's books, articles and addresses are available at http://www.ifn.se/publikationer, discussions at the Swedish Economic Association (*Nationalekonomiska föreningen*) at http://nationalekonomi.se and Swedish government official reports (SOU, *Statens Offentliga Utredningar*) at http://runeberg.org/sou/.

Åberg, Carl-Johan (2009), 'Långtidsutredningarna—en blandekonomins spegel', in: Magnus Henrekson (ed.), *IFN/IUI 1939–2009*. Stockholm: Ekerlids Förlag.

[100] The Norwegian predilection for economic planning is often attributed to economist Ragnar Frisch and his followers of the Oslo School; see Eriksen and Sæther (2010).

Appelqvist, Örjan (2000), *Bruten brygga: Gunnar Myrdal och Sveriges ekonomiska efterkrigspolitik 1943–1947*. Stockholm: Santérus Förlag.

Arbetarrörelsens efterkrigsprogram (1945), *De 27 punkterna med motivering*. Stockholm: AB Arbetarnes Tryckeri.

Bagge, Gösta (1917), *Arbetslönens reglering genom sammanslutningar*. Stockholm: AB Nordiska Bokhandeln.

Bagge, Gösta, Lundberg, Erik och Svennilson, Ingvar (1933), (1935), *Wages in Sweden, 1860–1930*, in two parts. London: P.S. King & Son, Ltd.

Barber, William J. (1988), *From New Era to New Deal: Herbert Hoover, the Economists, and American Economic Policy, 1921–1933*. Cambridge: Cambridge University Press.

Bergström, Villy (1977) 'Nationalekonomerna och arbetarrörelsen' in: Jan Herin and Lars Werin (eds), *Ekonomisk debatt och ekonomisk politik: Nationalekonomiska föreningen 100 år*. Stockholm: P A Norstedt & Söners Förlag.

Brunius, Axel (1942), 'Ett svenskt industriprogram', *Industria*, Vol. 38, No. 22, 903–906.

Carlson, Benny (1994), *The State as a Monster: Gustav Cassel and Eli Heckscher on the Role and Growth of the State*. Lanham, MD: University Press of America.

Carlson, Benny and Lundahl, Mats (2014), *Ett forskningsinstitut växer fram: IUI från grundandet till 1950*. Stockholm: Ekerlids Förlag.

Clark, John Maurice (1926) *Social Control of Business*. Chicago: University of Chicago Press.

Dagens Nyheter (1941), 'Förargelseväckande sätt att spara', 8 June.

Dagens Nyheter (1949), 'Framtidsutsikter på Hindersmässan', 30 January.

Dahlqvist, Hans (2003), *Fri att konkurrera, skyldig att producera: En ideologikritisk granskning av SAF 1902*–1948. Växjö: Acta Wexonensia 31

Dahmén, Erik (1942), 'Ekonomisk strukturanalys: Några synpunkter på den ekonomiska utvecklingen och konjunkturväxlingarnas problem', *Ekonomisk Tidskrift*, Vol. 44, No. 3, 177–194.

Dahmén, Erik (1947), 'Är investeringsbegränsning förnuftig?' *Industria*, Vol. 43, No. 11, 49, 68.

Dahmén, Erik (1948), 'Mera arbetskraft till exportindustrin?' *Industria*, Vol. 44, No. 12, 7.

Eriksen, Ib E. and Sæther, Arild (2010) 'Keynesian Economics and the Oslo School', *Nordic Journal of Political Economy*, Vol. 36, Article 3, 1–17.

Erixon, Lennart (2011), 'A Social Innovation or a Product of Its Time? The Rehn–Meidner Model's Relation to Contemporary Economics and the Stockholm School', *European Journal of the History of Economic Thought*, Vol. 18, No. 1, 85–123.

Erixon, Lennart and Wadensjö, Eskil (2012), 'Gösta Rehn (1913–96)—en otålig samhällsreformator', *Ekonomisk Debatt*, Vol. 40, No. 8, 71–82.

Från Palm till Palme: Den svenska socialdemokratins program 1882–1960 (1972) Stockholm: Rabén & Sjögren.

Göteborgs Tidning (1944), 'En generalstab', 9 November.

Hayek, Friedrich A. (1944), *The Road to Serfdom*. Chicago: Chicago University Press.

Hayek, Friedrich A. (1945), 'The Use of Knowledge in Society', *American Economic Review*, Vol. 35, No. 4, 519–530.

Henriksson, Rolf G. H. (1987), *Konjunkturinstitutet under Erik Lundbergs tid*. Stockholm: Konjunkturinstitutet.

Henriksson, Rolf G. H. (1990) *Som Edström ville—hur IUI blev till*. Stockholm: Industriens Utredningsinstitut.

Hoover, Herbert (1952), *The Memoirs of Herbert Hoover: The Cabinet and the Presidency 1920–1933*. New York: The Macmillan Company.

Industria (1949), 'Industriens Utredningsinstitut', Vol. 45, No. 6, 13–17, 29, 32.

Industriens Utredningsinstitut (1944a), *Näringslivet inför freden: anföranden vid konferens i Stockholm den 28 januari 1944*. Stockholm: IUI.

Industriens Utredningsinstitut (1944b), *Industriens sysselsättning under åren närmast efter kriget*. Stockholm: IUI.

Industriens Utredningsinstitut (1945), *Svensk handelspolitik efter kriget*. Stockholm: IUI.

Industriens Utredningsinstitut (1948a), Protokoll fört vid sammanträde med styrelsen för Industriens Utredningsinstitut, 15 January.

Industriens Utredningsinstitut (1948b), Protokoll fört vid sammanträde med styrelsen för Industriens Utredningsinstitut, 6 November.

Keynes, John Maynard (1936), *The General Theory of Employment, Interest and Money*. London: Macmillan.

Lewin, Leif (1967), *Planhushållningsdebatten*. Stockholm: Almqvist & Wiksells Tryckeri AB.

Lindbeck, Assar (1975), *Swedish Economic Policy*. London: Macmillan.

Lindbeck, Assar (1978), 'Förvanskningar om ekonomerna och arbetarrörelsen', *Ekonomisk Debatt*, Vol. 6, No. 1, 34–39.

LO (1951), *Fackföreningsrörelsen och den fulla sysselsättningen*. Stockholm: Landsorganisationen i Sverige.

Lundberg, Erik (1972), 'Ingvar Svennilson: A Note on his Scientific Achievements and a Bibliography of his Contributions to Economics', *Scandinavian Journal of Economics*, Vol. 74, No. 3, 313–328.

Marshall, Alfred (1890), *Principles of Economics*. London and New York: Macmillan and Co.

Montgomery, Arthur (1944), 'Industrien och efterkrigsplaneringen', *Svenska Dagbladet*, 15 November.

Myrdal, Gunnar (1944), *Varning för fredsoptimism*. Stockholm: Albert Bonniers förlag.

Myrdal, Gunnar (1961), *Planhushållning i välfärdsstaten*. Stockholm: Tiden.

Nationalekonomiska föreningen (1941), Budgeten och samhällsekonomin, 4 February.

Nationalekonomiska föreningen (1945a), Den dirigerade ekonomins problem, 19 March.

Nationalekonomiska föreningen (1945b), Behöva vi en regional planering för näringslivets utveckling?, 29 November.

Nationalekonomiska föreningen (1946), Världshandelns återuppbyggnad och svensk handelspolitik, 5 December.

Nationalekonomiska föreningen (1948), Kan vi komma ut ur krisen?, 13 October.

Norrskensflamman (1944), 'Märklig konferens', 7 February.

Ohlin, Bertil (1936), *Fri eller dirigerad ekonomi*, Uddevalla, A.-B. J.F. Hallmans Bokhandel, i distribution.

Ohlin, Bertil (1937), 'Some Notes on the Stockholm Theory of Savings and Investment I-II", *Economic Journal*, Vol. 37, No. 185, 53–69, No. 186, 221–240.

Ohlin, Bertil (1978), 'Nationalekonomernas hållning till samhällsproblemen', *Ekonomisk Debatt*, Vol. 6, No. 4, 253–258.

Persson, Mats and Siven, Claes-Henric (2009), 'Ingvar Svennilson 1908–1972', in: Magnus Henrekson (ed.), *IFN/IUI 1939–2009*. Stockholm: Ekerlids Förlag.

Persson, Mats and Siven, Claes-Henric (2010), 'Ingvar Svennilson', *Ekonomisk Debatt*, Vol. 38. No. 7, 28–34.

Petersson, Jan (1987), *Erik Lindahl och Stockholmsskolans dynamiska metod*. Lund: Lund Economic Studies 39.

Riksdagen (1948), Andra kammaren, no 34, Ang. regeringens ekonomiska politik. Stockholm: Kungl. Boktryckeriet, P.A. Norstedt & Söner.

SOU 1948:45, *Svenskt långtidsprogram 1947–1952/53*. Stockholm: K.L. Beckmans Boktryckeri.

SOU 1949:15, *P.M. med synpunkter på det svenska långtidsprogrammet i anslutning till OEEC:s interimsrapport*. Stockholm: K.L. Beckmans Boktryckeri.

Svennilson, Ingvar (1938), *Ekonomisk planering: Teoretiska studier*. Uppsala: Almqvist & Wiksells Tryckeri AB.

Svennilson, Ingvar (1940), 'Industriell planering i Sverige under den nuvarande krisen', *Föredrag för utländska pressmän*, 31 May.

Svennilson, Ingvar (1941a), 'Industriproduktionen i folkhushållningens tjänst', in: Torsten Hèrnod, Gunnar Hägglöf, Ivar Högbom, Vilhelm Lundvik,

Ragnar Sundén, Ingvar Svennilson and Gustaf Söderlund, *Vår folkförsörjning i avspärrningstider I*. Stockholm: Industriens Utredningsinstitut.

Svennilson, Ingvar (1941b), 'Industriellt ledarskap och social kontroll', *Föredrag i Malmö*, 21 April.

Svennilson, Ingvar (1941c), 'Industriell planhushållning: Några synpunkter på krigstidens svenska erfarenheter', *Ekonomisk Tidskrift*, Vol. 43, No. 4, 295–308.

Svennilson, I. (1943), 'Svenska industriella framtidsproblem', i: *Ingeniörsklubbens i Falun förhandlingar 1942*. Falun: Ingeniörsklubben.

Svennilson, Ingvar (1944), 'Avvägningsproblem inom sysselsättningen efter kriget, annex to Skrivelse ang. investeringspolitiken', in: SOU 1944:57, *Utredningar angående ekonomisk efterkrigsplanering VII. Framställningar och utlåtanden från kommissionen för ekonomisk efterkrigsplanering I*. Stockholm: Isaac Marcus Boktryckeri-Aktiebolag.

Svennilson, Ingvar (1945), 'Näringspolitiken under kriget—i fredsperspektiv', Föredrag Nationalekonomiska föreningen, 2 March.

Svennilson, Ingvar (1946a), 'Från krigs- till fredshandel', *Utrikespolitik*, Vol. 1, No. 1, 12–19.

Svennilson, Ingvar (1946b), 'Strukturrationalisering', *Föredrag vid Nordiska ingenjörsmötet i Stockholm*, 27 May.

Svennilson, Ingvar (1946c), 'Strukturrationalisering', in: *En samling uppsatser tillägnade Harald Nordenson på 60-årsdagen 10 augusti 1946*. Stockholm: Generalstabens Litografiska Anstalts Förlag.

Svennilson, Ingvar (1947), 'Sveriges ekonomiska kris och dess följder', Föredrag, Skånes nationalekonomiska förening, undated.

Svennilson, Ingvar (1949), 'Det svenska långtidsprogrammet', *Svensk Tidskrift*, Vol. 36, No. 1, 67–74.

Svennilson, Ingvar (1954), *Growth and Stagnation in the European Economy*. Geneva: United Nations Economic Commission for Europe.

Svennilson, Ingvar (1966), 'Swedish Long-Term Planning—The Fifth Round', *Skandinaviska Banken Quarterly Review*, Vol. 47, No. 2, 37–44.

Svennilson, Ingvar and Beckman, Rune (1962), 'Long-Term Planning in Sweden', *Skandinaviska Banken Quarterly Review*, Vol. 43, No. 3, 69–76.

Svennilson, Ingvar and Waldenström, Erland (1942), *Till frågan om det industriella framåtskridandet i Sverige*. Stockholm: Industriens Utredningsinstitut.

Svenska Dagbladet (1949), 'Ökade exportansträngningar på USA blir ofrånkomligt för Sverige', 30 January.

von Thünen, Johann Heinrich (1875) [1826], *Der isolierte Staat in Beziehung auf Landwirtschaft und Nationalökonomie*. Berlin, Verlag von Wirgandt, Hempel & Parry.

Wikipedia (2017), 'Hanns Johst'. https://de.wikipedia.org/wiki/Hanns_Johst. Downloaded 4 May 2017.

CHAPTER 5

From the Western Front: Axel Iveroth in Washington

(with Benny Carlson)

Industrial Attaché Iveroth

Go West, young man! (Horace Greeley)

One of those recruited to the Industrial Institute for Economic and Social Research [Industriens Utredningsinstitut—IUI] when the latter was founded in 1939 was Axel Carlsson. He was 25 years old. Carlsson had graduated from the Stockholm School of Economics the year before. During his study years there he had worked as a treasurer at the Anagra shirt factory and, from 1937 also an announcer at Radio Sweden [Radiotjänst], where he became the person who announced that World War II had broken out. Carlsson became an assistant [*amanuens*] at the IUI. He continued to work at the radio until June 1941, when he became the secretary of the IUI. The same year, he changed his last name to Iveroth.

Axel Iveroth was a dynamic person who left a strong imprint on the IUI. His specialty at the Stockholm School had been economic geography and during his time at the institute, during 1940 and 1941, he carried out an investigation with a clear geographic connotation, a study

M. Lundahl, *Twelve Figures in Swedish Economics*, Palgrave Studies in the History of Economic Thought, https://doi.org/10.1007/978-3-030-94327-1_5

of Swedish small-scale industry, published in 1943.[1] It was the first major study published by the IUI, a well-written work that enjoyed a large readership.[2]

In the summer of 1944, Axel Iveroth left the IUI in order to become an industrial attaché at the Swedish legation in Washington, DC. He disembarked in Philadelphia on Midsummer's Day. Iveroth, however, did not sever his contact with the Industrial Institute for Economic and Social Research, but wrote numerous letters back home to Ingvar Svennilson during his entire period in Washington.

The First Letter to Sweden[3]

The first extant letter by Iveroth is dated 18 July 1944. It is long: nine typewritten pages. He conveys the picture of a slightly bewildered young man who had problems trying to cope with all his chores:

> I had planned to use the summer and the heat, which after all dampens the work pace several degrees in civil service departments and institutions, [...] slowly suffering, reading basic, general knowledge works on the USA, little by little gaining solid ground underfoot, and thereafter taking up one thing after another. – A complete failure. Up to now, I have by and large only managed to read the daily newspapers, and it took only a few days before I began cutting, and now the boxes with clippings are growing and a new paste boy has to be hired. The only way to acquire some general education is that of traveling into the countryside, which I have now planned to do together with Per Persson from the SvD [the Swedish newspaper *Svenska Dagbladet*]. I intend to bring books with me and in addition we will only speak Swedish with each other one hour per day.

Much of the content of the letters that Iveroth sent to Ingvar Svennilson dealt with the literature that he shipped back home to the IUI. This had been prepared already before Iveroth's departure for the United States. On 27 April, the chairman of the board of the institute, Ernst

[1] Iveroth (1943).

[2] For a discussion of the small-scale industry report, see Carlson and Lundahl (2014, Chapter 5).

[3] The letters are found in the archive of the Research Institute for Industrial Economics [Institutet för Näringslivsforskning] at the Centre for Business History [Centrum för Näringslivshistoria], Serie E, Korrespondens, E 1 be.

Wehtje, from Skånska Cement, with the assistance of Iveroth himself, had written to the trade section of the Ministry for Foreign Affairs and inquired whether current literature on economic subjects could be purchased through the Swedish legations abroad and forwarded to the Industrial Institute for Economic and Social Research, whether reports from the legations to the Ministry could be regularly put at the disposal of the institute and whether they could be drafted in such a way as to shed light on circumstances of special interest to the industrial community. On 4 May, the Ministry for Foreign Affairs sent a letter with a positive answer to Wehtje's request.

The access to foreign economic literature was very scant in Sweden during the war. Hence, the idea of using the legations was not an original one. Gunnar Myrdal had been in the United States several times between 1938 and 1943, first in order to work on his monumental *An American Dilemma*,[4] until 1942, and the following year as a counselor at the Swedish legation with the task of studying the economic situation in the United States and its probable future development. This resulted in a completely mistaken forecast of an imminent depression, in the book *Varning för fredsoptimism* [Beware of Peace Optimism].[5] He had agreed with Bo Siegbahn, who at the time was an attaché at the legation, that the latter should regularly send back home such literature that Myrdal was interested in, but not much had come out of the agreement. 'S. has not done much more than storing what ... has arrived and I am under the impression that the flow has begun to dry up,' wrote Iveroth to Svennilson on 18 July.

In the same letter Iveroth states that he was busy collecting books and journals that were to be sent home with the diplomatic courier to Sweden at the end of the month, 'quite a lot, helter-skelter.' The normal transport routes did not function under the wartime conditions. He asks Svennilson whether he would not consider making the IUI a sort of a clearing center for the literature that he sent back home. It was important that the publications reached the right recipient.

> Could not the institute set up an America library or a 'library for industrial news from abroad or post-war program news from abroad'. Since you

[4] Myrdal (1944a).

[5] Myrdal (1944b).

> do not have any reception central at the Ministry for Foreign Affairs for incoming material of this kind, I think that it is better to send most of it to the IUI. Otherwise, you will have to draft accompanying letters, that is for each book. If not, it will remain at the ministry or end up at the wrong address. It ought to be easier to judge at home who are most interested in different questions.

Iveroth had realized the importance of making the latest economic findings available to the leading Swedish researchers and hence planned to collect as much material as possible, assemble a telegraphic report about the economic situation in the United States each month, write short surveys of controversial issues, gather material about long-run issues—a theme that the IUI would become more and more involved in during the coming years.

Iveroth in addition planned to organize the work on economic reports at the legation, 'run around and talk to people and pick up literature.' 'I buy liberally at the expense of the institute. If the purchases have to considered from the legation point of view, it will take a long time and limit the scope.'

Iveroth was not unduly impressed by the administrative efficiency in Washington. 'Of the legation, the people here, I will speak on another occasion.' This he did on 23 September, partly in earnest, partly teasing:

> It is rumored that [Under Secretary of State for Foreign Affairs Erik] Boheman is coming here. Shouldn't he think twice. This antisemitic country, I think he will have a hard time.
>
> Besides, thy send us all the counts and barons that exist, Ramel, Wachtmeister, Bonde, Aminoff, de … [Wästfelt], – in front of all the nobility you put a d. [Sven] Dahlman attempts to improve his bourgeoisie by a marked D'Ahlman.

It is obvious that Iveroth considered the Swedish representation in New York to be pretty hopeless. On 27 November, he confided to Svennilson what he thought of it:

> … otherwise, the stock here (with the exception of … some innocent attachés) is a poor sight. The heads of the consulate general and the cargo commission [*lastkommissionen*] are incompetent, perhaps a bit too much said about [Consul Victor Emanuel (Manne)] Lindholm in the cargo, because he possesses a certain dispatch energy of the sergeant major kind.

But, other than that, he is ignorant and messy ... and he smiles to those above him and oppresses those below him, those he thinks lack influence.

It was better in Chicago, which Iveroth visited in December. On the 15th, he wrote: 'The personnel at the consulate in Chicago is really high-class: [Consul General Gösta] Oldenburg, [First Vice Consul Eyvind] Bratt and [the attaché Kjell Nordenskiöld] all nice and wise, good spirit and working conditions and style. Differs sympathetically from the New York equivalence.'

On 1 November, Iveroth described a legation that stood out as rather inefficient. 'At the legation there is so much talk, everybody is used to talking and taking one's time, being at one's case, and I cannot break that habit. At 11–11.30, the entire personnel drinks coffee.' Iveroth himself had no problem filling his day. Reporting and gathering literature was time-consuming:

... I am sorry that there will be no more reports, that I am so bad honoring promises with respect to special subjects, etc. But the explanation is simple. There is not enough time. What cannot be explained by time. ... I rise at 8.30, am at the legation at 9.30; there are today's issues of Washington Post, New York Times, Herald Tribune, Journal of Commerce and Wall Street Journal etc. I have attempted to read them and put to gather an archive of clippings but am about to give up. In the first place, nobody except myself is interested, I mean: knowing that the matter cannot be organized on a long-run basis, organizing for further reporting, dampens your enthusiasm. Also, I have no desire to bury myself in current issues, if at all possible. At least a couple of more assistants are needed for the person who is to be in charge of the economic reporting. Therefore, I do not wish to handle the economic reporting, hitherto I have been my own assistant. It takes time, and still I do not have the time to read all the clippings.

To this, you had to add the reading of book catalogues and reviews in order to facilitate the shipping of literature, plus activities that Iveroth considered completely meaningless:

Then comes the task of meeting people, I have begun to run around and make interviews, that is, it is meaningless. The purpose is to seek out people who are in good positions and grab as many mimeos and printed documents as possible. But then you have to have lunch and dinner with some people – in addition to all the cocktails and suppers that characterize the purely diplomatic environment. – If I go to New York, it is impossible to get any time for work. There, you never go to bed before 2 at night. In Washington, it happens that you get home before 12 on some occasion during the week. To travel and look at industries is completely out of question.

Iveroth wanted the economic reporting to be systematic and he had strong views of how it should be organized, views that he conveyed to Svennilson on 27 November:

In a former letter I gave you some reasons why I had no real interest to bury myself in the production of reports in Washington. What I would like to have is firstly security with respect to the continuity of this work. I would like the task of organizing the report work about economic (and social) issues on a long-run basis. At least to make a suggestion. It is damn frustrating to read about what you accomplish at the American legation in Stockholm and of the importance attached to reports from Sweden. How you sent specialists on different questions. ... in Sweden. Here, what they do is to send [Bo] Siegbahn back home, the only economically educated official at the legation, except myself ... That America report was not particularly profound. Among other things, a trade attaché post was filled in San Francisco. I have met the man, Malméus, who contends that this trade he handles in a quarter of an hour per day. Here, you need at least a couple of people who can devote themselves to the writing of current reports. For the time being, when it is impossible to be here for extensive free studies, there would of course be a swarm of 'special assistants' at this legation in the same way as at the American legation in Stockholm.

Bo Siegbahn was one of the few people at the legation that Axel Iveroth appreciated. On 28 January 1945, when Siegbahn was about to leave Washington, he portrayed him:

I like him well, he is intelligent and a great searcher of the truth. He is, however, not a diplomat. He does not take into consideration how other people react to his inquisitiveness. He likes to put people in a quandary, he is intellectually brusque, rough in his actions and judgment. But basically, he is very kind, in spite of all his criticism, which tends to degenerate into grumbling and nitty-gritty. He, however, has a sharp mind, and writes fairly well too. Myrdal dislikes him. – He has talked about finding some task in relation to the LO [the Swedish Trade Union Confederation], Sterner's institute.[6] There is where he belongs, according to his political conviction, at least his former one. Sometimes I have managed to correct his economic views. Hence, he is not doctrinaire. At times, he has talked about, inquired about, the possibilities for a person like himself to make the transition into the business world, an industry or something. He has political ambitions. Of course, how far he can advance within the party I don't know. In any case, it won't hurt to consider the possibility that he will become some kind of economic advisor in the Social Democratic context. But he probably does not care too much about to which forces he will devote his ambition, as long as he has an analytical, interesting, decently paid, job. – It ended up being a long characteristic. It is, however, fun to talk to him.

The Mohn Affair

In his first letter to Svennilson, from 18 July 1944, Iveroth also brought up 'a question of more general interest,' about which he obviously had heard through the grapevine and was deeply indignant at. The issue was about the counselor of legation Paul Mohn, who had been the chairman of the international commission that had been created in 1942 in order to ensure grain deliveries from Canada to Greece in Swedish bottoms and fair distribution among the Greek population of cereals, vegetables, milk powder and medicines through the Red Cross. A disappointed Mohn had been removed from his office by the Swedish government in 1943, according to Iveroth under circumstances that left a lot to be desired. He had then ended up at the Swedish legation in Washington and had been given the task of keeping an eye on the conferences that the newly created United Nations Relief and Rehabilitation Administration (UNRRA)—an institution for the administration of aid to war victims—had begun to organize, under very peculiar circumstances:

... the case of P. Mohn, the former chairman of the commission for Greece, who does nothing around here. He was dismissed under murky circumstances (in a hardly acceptable way) from his position and was replaced by the justice of the Supreme Court [Emil] Sandström. The person who 'engineered' this probably is ... [the envoy Sven] Allard. Nobody has explained

[6] The'institute' was the research section of the Swedish Trade Union Confederation. It was headed by Richard Sterner, who had been the assistant and co-author of Gunnar Myrdal when the latter wrote *An American Dilemma* (Myrdal 1944a). He defended his doctoral dissertation *The Negro's Share* (Sterner 1943) in 1944.

the new arrangement to me, nobody has made complaints against his way of handling his position. On the contrary, everything seems to indicate that he has worked very skilfully. Sandström, however, has obviously made a complete mess of things and acquired a reputation for being impossible to cooperate with, etc. [Foreign Minister Christian] Günther asked Mohn, already on his arrival in Stockholm, for advice about how he should handle the difficulties which S. had managed to create during the short time of three months that had elapsed since he left! Mohn came to Stockholm after the ignominious retirement. He then received an offer from the U.N.R.R.A. to come to the U.S. as an expert. Here, the U.N.R.R.A. hasn't given a damn about him. He hardly has his travel money left. Since February, he lives at his own expense. His expertise is, however, used every day by different parts of the administration, the F.E.A. [Foreign Economic Administration], the U.N.R.R.A., etc. [The head of the Swedish legation, Envoy Wollmar] Boström has in a telegram requested to hire him as a special contact and report person in relief matters (half time). The Ministry for Foreign Affairs has refused and stated that it does not have any funds. He is hence without any fixed employment whatsoever now. And will probably have to make a lot of fuss to make the U.N.R.R.A. pay his return trip.

Iveroth was outright mad at the treatment that Mohn had received from the Swedish Ministry for Foreign Affairs:

Mohn is one of the most knowledgeable persons that I have met, speaks German, French, Dutch, English, and some Greek and Spanish. Well, he knows everything and, strangely enough, he possesses the same profound knowledge in almost all fields, especially the social one. He has the title of Counselor of Legation. He is obviously also in possession a practical, organizational, talent. [...] I think that this is a pretty pitiable story. Regardless of the moral side of the issue: shouldn't the man be utilized? ... our entire post-war aid activity, to make sense, has to get in touch with those in the belligerent countries who plan the work. If nothing else, you ought to observe what they are up to. Everybody should know that this is no easy matter, given the muddle that these institutions seem to be in. [...] That somebody should follow the relief effort seems pretty self-evident to me (and Mohn and Boström!!!). Who can do it better than Mohn? He can represent our serious willingness to take part in the humanitarian work excellently. – Well, now I am tired. But you understand what I mean.

Iveroth, could, however, not restrain himself, but in a 'Supplement' to his letter he came back to the issue:

> I have to say something more about Mohn, on a new sheet.
>
> The cooperation of [Bengt] Helger [chief registrar at the National Social Welfare Board] and Mohn in Greece has been excellent. Helger strongly opposes both Sandström and Allard (Allard later left Greece, I think). An example of what Mohn accomplishes or is capable of accomplishing is that he recently managed to organize a common approach to the English and American governments by the ambassadors of Norway, Holland, Belgium and France in London, and thereby to bring about rapid organizational and other action to help the children in the respective countries. The idea of a common approach is also due to Mohn. This kind of approach from fellow allies is not popular either in the State Department or in England. Then you cannot neglect the issue or play on several strings, but you have to get going. I mention this as an example of the kind of connections that Mohn has, and he does not lack possibilities to use them.

In February 1945, it was still not clear what would happen to Mohn. Once more, Iveroth was furious:

> It looks like Mohn will return home at the beginning of April. He has had a certain chance of becoming an adviser at the UNRRA delegation in Italy, but because of all the formalities that plague this country it appears to come to nothing as well. He is beginning to be pretty depressed now. [...] ... he has an evident feeling for economic policy. A more extensive experience in the cultural and linguistic field than what he possesses should be rare in Sweden. If a Swedish institute[7] is created – I know that it is underway and that a combination of Swedish heartwood is in charge – he should be the undisputed head of it.

Iveroth, however, contended that the Swedish business community should create its own institute, with a journal, in order to extend its information to foreign countries, and then again. Mohn was a given candidate, first as chief editor of the journal and then as head of the institute.

> Mohn by the way has written a book here, for which I may have provided son inspiration every now and then, the purpose of which is to tease the Swedes back home with their fairly large self-satisfaction and willingness to remain seated. There, he offers his views on a possible Swedish

[7] The Swedish Institute was created in 1945 in order to inform about Sweden and build relations to people in other countries.

> immigration policy, the need for more constructive – in many senses – contributions abroad by Swedish industry, etc. ... What he asks for above all is a more idealistic goal formulation, based on a combination of personal entrepreneurship and willingness to take risks in the cultural and economic fields. He says that we need this in order to compete with those who, due to the war circumstances, have been forced to sacrifice lives and matter in order to keep their countries alive. I also think that this is more true than the opposite opinion that they will be tired of everything.

Nothing came of Iveroth's plans for Mohn. The latter instead became an observer at a couple of more UNRRA conferences before he got to organize the Red Cross sections in Germany and Austria. In 1947, he became a member of the United Nations Special Committee for Palestine, before, the following year, he became the political counselor of Folke Bernadotte during the attempt of the latter to mediate in the conflict between Israel and the Arabs. His last mission was that of heading the Swedish representation on the Neutral Nations Supervisory Commission in Korea in 1953–1954.

Climate and Culture

On 4 August, Iveroth complained about the summer in Washington, DC:

> I am unfortunately not in the position this time either to write a carefully prepared letter. This is still due to the heat, which has put me in bed for a week with fever and cold symptoms. Probably I have got it from too many 'fans'. In order to stand the heat, you sit in a fan draught as much as possible. At times I have regularly taken baths during the night to be able to sleep. The climate is terrible. In mid-July, we had a cool week with a temperature around 30°. If it is not one way, it is the other way. The day before yesterday, some 250 mm of rain poured down, so in many parts of the city you had to row. During the rain, it is relatively cool. But afterwards, the humidity of the air ascends to what amounts almost to sauna concentration. It appears as if all things ugly flourish in this unhealthy greenhouse atmosphere.

Axel Iveroth did not feel at all at ease in the Washington summer climate and had taken measures to make life reasonably bearable. A little more than a week later, on 13 August, he wrote:

> I am not terribly fit for work, for two reasons: 1) The climate is terrible, I have described it in the other letters, so I will leave it out presently. 2) Partly as a result of the heat I have been sick and I have not recovered completely. But it will pass. To speed up the process, I have had to rent a flat, the cost of which I do not dare to mention. It is air-conditioned. I cannot sleep with a night temperature of 30°, let alone the day temperature. And then I need an apartment which allows me to receive people, in order not to fall by the roadside. I have discovered that it is more expensive here than what Myrdal suggested. But I will probably go on as long as the money lasts. I now think that the Ministry for Foreign Affairs could have given me a little more.

It was no wonder that Iveroth felt relieved when, at the end of September, he could tell Svennilson that he had been hiking in Vermont for a few days with Per Persson. 'It was a blessing to be able to leave the tropics of some time.'

One thing that was as bad as the climate in Washington was the American culture. Iveroth was not impressed at all. On 1 November 1944, he wrote:

> ... there is not much that is profound. The impression you get from a superficial confrontation is that everything is superficial. Of course, there is a lot of good culture as well but not much in a relative sense, and it does not make itself felt ... (Washington has a single theater, the capital of the country only has traveling theater companies, opera performances once a month, its only 'real' theater, i.e. where there are people on the stage without any movie is the Gaiethy Th. ... Its standard is about 10 categories below that of the Odeon revue in Stockholm, at its worst, I mean the Odeon revue. Not only do girls undress while prancing around, you can always watch that, but it is what people laugh at, chamber-pot humor is a far too appreciative label. – Then we have the so-called comics ... special supplements to every newspaper, which actually constitute the foremost cultural experience that the American people allows itself during wartime years, I mean non-wartime years, because it probably makes no difference. And then the movies, which on average are worse than at home, even if you include our own ones in the average. [...]
>
> Here, there is only one way to entertain yourself, to be cultural, enjoy life, it is Broadway – Gaiety – drinks, nightclubs, etc., and the ranking of the existing standard is completely dependent on money, how much and how often, in which quantities you can afford it.

In New York, the cultural problem was the opposite of that in Washington. 'In New York, it is no fun to go to the theater, when there are some 200, no delight at the experience, since it is distributed wholesale. The development lacks quality since it has had and still has such an enormous scope for expansion,' wrote Iveroth on 15 December.

American Organization

On 6 August 1944, Iveroth reviewed the lack of organization of the American planning for a return to a peacetime economy when the Germans had been defeated. A '*cut back in war production*' of 50 percent had to be reckoned with, which of course called for measures, but Iveroth was not impressed by what he saw:

> It is of course the risk of a fast peace that makes you eager, in the circles that understand economics and are responsible, to have prepared the transition in time. Then, it is deplorable that you cannot separate these preparations from the immediate armament effort. It is of course difficult. But it could have been done a lot better. Right now, everything is a great big mingle. All agencies talk at the same time and trespass into each other's territories. The best example of the organizational mess is that for a while you were playing with the thought of creating a new organization to supply the people needed in certain war industries. Right now!

On 12 April 1945, Iveroth concluded that still nothing had happened on the reorganization front. He had met the head of the Bureau of Foreign and Domestic Commerce at the Department of Commerce:

> He stated that an elaborate plan for the economic policy of the transition period was still lacking. Nothing has actually been done since all work on that front was stopped in the fall. Thereafter the army has come out completely against it. At present, the administration cannot begin until Congress has provided the framework, the lines of guidance for the policy. [...] Now, through preparatory negotiations with senators and congressmen, they intend to create a platform for bringing the issue into Congress. You have to be careful with the new Senate, which has turned out to be so reactionary, in the American sense. The initiative to these discussions must and will come from the president.

Swedish-American Relations

On 13 August 1944, Iveroth had drawn up a strategy for the organization of the gathering of literature. He wanted to assemble as many books, pamphlets, journals, etc., as he could find on current economic issues and send everything home as soon as the couriers departed. In addition, he planned to write reports on more important economic issues, gather material on long-run problems and send home. (He did not think that he would himself get the time or the peace needed to perform any profound analysis.) Iveroth also planned to travel around and meet people. Most important, he argued, was to send brief telegraphic economic reports on current issues, and he asked Svennilson to make comments on his proposal. He thought that the IUI should establish itself as the 'America institute.'

Axel Iveroth was eager to develop the relations between the United States and Sweden. In August, he had been in contact with a representative of the Research Institute of America, which produced a large number of newsletters. The institute, which had more than 1,000 employees, was interested in publishing such a newsletter also in Sweden, which could be edited in an office there, to be created as soon as the war came to an end. The contents should deal with information about markets, trade policy, etc., in the US, and possibly also South America—information of interest to Swedish industry and commerce. The idea was not only to focus on Sweden, but, according to Iveroth, the reasoning went as follows: 'We, the US, need some fixed point in Europe after the war, a point of departure for the long-run development of economic relations between America and Europe. They don't count on England, which supposedly will be inward-looking. What you have is Spain, Switzerland and Sweden, and they prefer Sweden.'

It could, however, not be taken for granted that the views of the institute would be shared by everyone. Sweden also had to take into account

> the opinion that we are riding far too high on the view that the Americans are viewing the post-war period in a business-like manner, that we do not have to fear any political and emotional resentment due to the war. I do not know how true it is that we are known to be too ... ['clever'] and that they would not at all be disinclined to squeeze us if it is possible.

Altogether, however, Iveroth thought that the initiative taken by the institute was worth supporting and he had promised to undertake a first investigation of the interest in an American newsletter in Sweden and he asked Svennilson to help him with this. In a letter written a week later, he also asked him to find out Gunnar Myrdal's views of the Research Institute of America. He had by then heard that its newsletters were expensive in relation to their content.

On 20 October, Tore Browaldh, Iveroth's successor as a secretary at the IUI, answered that the interest probably was not as great as Iveroth thought. 'As far as the possibility of establishing a Research Institute subsidiary here in Sweden is concerned, Ingvar and those we have spoken to tend to be very sceptical. The interest in American circumstances is limited to some 100 large corporations, so the reports of the subsidiary would not get too much circulation.'

The telegraphic reports as well came to nothing. Browaldh communicated that

> The idea of telegraphic reports must be written off. The cost is too high and the interest in receiving fresh information with respect to production, employment, etc., is rather limited among the industrialists. However, it would be great if you could focus on typewritten reports about long-run issues.

Swedish-American Industrial Contacts

Iveroth never dropped the idea of contacts between the American and Swedish industries. When he wrote home on 28 August 1944, he had visited the National Association of Manufacturers (NAM), the general interest organization of the American industries, especially the larger ones, and had then met the Swede Erik Kjellström, who was employed there. Iveroth summarized his impressions in a special report which he did not want to show to the Ministry for Foreign Affairs:

> I have written a kind of report-like letter with viewpoints that I consider important to present before the delegation to the 'Business' conference here in November have been appointed and sent off. I gathered them in a special letter in case you would like to show them to others or make copies. I must underline that its has not been read by the legation and that I do not want it to be read there.

In the report, Iveroth pointed out that contacts were insufficient in both directions. The American industry was ignorant about circumstances in Sweden but was interested in closer cooperation. He called for official contacts on a high level between the industrial associations of both countries.

Iveroth also brought up the international chamber of commerce conference that was scheduled for November 1944 and to which Swedish business representatives had been invited. It was to be run by the United States Chamber of Commerce, and Iveroth had been nagging Ingvar Svennilson that the latter ought to make an effort to join. 'Try to come and improve the impression, the bad impression that [Bertil] Ohlin has made on some people as a Swedish economist. It seems as he has been pretty high-brow,' wrote Iveroth on 18 June and in the accompanying letter to the report of 28 August he continued: 'Everybody is mad with Ohlin and his "lofty" behavior. There is one thing that is appreciated by Americans: a straightforward, not intellectual, behavior, a simple way of discussing and humble ways among those who come to see them, I do not mean creeping, but listening, for instance.'

On 13 August, Iveroth had hinted that the Federation of Swedish Industries ought to send a representative group that could make contact with its American counterpart. He was convinced that direct industrial contacts would be a great deal more efficient than official contacts through established diplomatic channels. From Erik Kjellström Iveroth had learned that his visit to the NAM had been considered important and that the organization wanted to make him meet a number of their leading men. He, therefore, wanted to be able to point to visits by important Swedish industrialists, preferably, the chairman of the Federation, Ernst Wehtje. 'The delegation in addition should consist of first-rank men, among them people who are well acquainted with business policy matters, state and industry, etc.' He mentioned the chairman of the Swedish Employers' Confederation, Gustaf Söderlund, Torsten Hèrnod from Svenska Cellulosa Aktiebolaget [the Swedish Cellulose Corporation], Harald Nordenson from Liljeholmens Stearinfabrik, Ruben Rausing from Åkerlund & Rausing and Per Egon Gummeson from Höganäs-Billesholm, as suitable names, and in addition possible buyers of American industrial products, like Axel Axelson Johnson from Rederiaktiebolaget Nordstjärnan (shipping) and Axel Bergengren from Borås Wäfveri (textiles).

There was one person who Iveroth under no circumstances wanted to see at the conference. In the accompanying letter, he writes:

> Is it inevitable that [Sigfrid] Edström[8] will come. I doubt that he is an asset, any great asset. He of course has his name, but he is old, and he does not stand out as an interesting discussion partner for the Americans. In addition, he may prevent others from joining, that is, may prevent the delegation from getting a really skilful leader.

In the end, the conference took place in Rye, New York, on the border of Connecticut, 10–18 November. Ingvar Svennilson never came (Iveroth instead planned a visit in the spring of 1945), but Iveroth took part himself—together with a very numerous Swedish delegation. In the book, based on interviews with him, that was published the year after his death, he enumerates them. To his chagrin it was led by Edström—which was probably inevitable, since at the time the latter was the chairman of the International Chamber of Commerce.

> In addition, the participants were Carl-August Wicander, Wicanders Korkfabrik, Sven Salén, Sr., the Salén shipping company, Karl-Fredrik Göransson, the Sandvik Steel Works Co., Einar Flygt, Svenska Cellulosa [SCA], and Olof Lamm [Stockholms Sjöförsäkrings AB, maritime insurance]. Advisors were Gunnar Engberg, Eriksbergs Mekaniska Verkstad [engineering], Göran Holmquist, Nordiska Kompaniet [department store], Thomas Ihre, Uddeholm [forestry], Einar Kördel, the Federation of Swedish Wholesalers and Importers, Tore Nilert, ABA [AB Aerotransport], Walter Wehtje, Atlas Diesel [engineering] and W. Gordon Stiernstedt, the Stockholm Chamber of Commerce. Technical assistants were: Dan Axel Broström, Svenska Ostasiatiska Kompaniet [the Swedish East Asiatic Company], E. Cedercrantz, the Stockholm Chamber of Commerce, Lars Ekelund, Holmens Bruk [paper], Sven G. Malmberg, the Swedish Government Cargo Clearance Committee, O.G. Marell, the Swedish Chamber of Commerce in New York, Lars-Erik Thunholm, at the time at Svenska Handelsbanken, and myself.[9]

Lars-Erik Thunholm's memory of the conference was positive:

[8] Sigfrid Edström, the chairman of the board of ASEA, had been the chairman of the board of IUI between 1939 and 1943.

[9] Iveroth (1994, p. 56).

> What conferred special timeliness and interest on the conference was the debate which went on in the fall about the post-war international currency system. A few months before our conference, the so-called Bretton Woods agreement had been signed and the foundation laid for a new order and regulation of the international currency relations. What you thereby strove to avoid was the chaotic and for the world trade disturbing circumstances that had prevailed in the 1930s. In Rye, with prominent representatives of the private business community of the world, an opportunity was provided for a presentation of views of these questions which are so vital for international trade. Not least for us Swedes, who for so long have been cut off from international contacts, the opening of international cooperation and exchange of information that was provided here was enormously valuable.
>
> The Rye conference was important also because it injected new life into the ICC, which since the beginning of the war has been almost completely frozen. The initiative and the massive attendance at the conference from all countries that had a possibility to participate under the difficult war circumstances was a sign that the war was coming to an end.[10]

But for Axel Iveroth the conference apparently was a disappointment. In a letter written in haste on 18 November, he states: 'I have been to a conference, and what a conference! I have never seen such a great mess in most respects. But I do not have the time to elaborate the text, since I only have twenty minutes to write this letter.' Iveroth sent a set of all the reports from the conference back home, which he thought that the IUI should distribute.

> You could have everything mimeographed and publish it as one of those brown cover things. But do it quickly, before [Gordon] Stjernstedt [sic] [managing director of the Stockholm Chamber of Commerce] comes home and starts to screw things up. Why the heck should Stjernstedt [sic] ... be present? S is the nicest zero that you can find. But that is not reason enough. In addition, in this capacity, he managed to mess up as many things as he could because he lacks organization capacity. All the rest of us had to take care of him,

wrote Iveroth on 27 November.

For lack of time, Iveroth on 18 November refrained from summarizing the conference. 'It would of course not have hurt anyone to have an

[10] Thunholm (2005, pp. 83–84).

introduction with impressions from the conference. But I have not had the time to put such a thing together. In addition, the comments that I will make on the conference are not of the kind that lends itself to wider distribution.'

On 27 November, Iveroth had more time to write letters and make comments about the Rye conference:

> On my part, one of the jerky things was the international business conference. From the experience point of view it was interesting. But possibly you could have the used the time more efficiently. Its main value was to be found in the impressions that you got of the representatives of different countries, their way of acting and reasoning. Secondly, it is not unimportant to manifest unity with respect to the demand for free world trade and fixed exchange rates. It did, however, not offer much exchange of views or discussion of problems. Most typical were the free enterprise discussions where people outbid each other with beautiful expressions of the excellence of free enterprise and of the conviction that it can solve all problems. The question of its relation to the state or other forces in society was hardly touched at all. Blinders.

The composition of the Swedish group was not the one that Iveroth had desired. Above all, Sigfrid Edström had been its chairman:

> Edström was precisely the calamity that was to be expected. He put his foot in it during two dinners … On the first occasion, he boasted about Sweden's benevolence and ability to pay. 'We can pay cash and there isn't [sic] many countries that are able to tell you that.' On the second occasion, he declared that he was ready to answer questions, and among other things answered that he thought that in fifty years Sweden would be Russian. He is so incredibly egocentric, but of course in his own way, somewhat condescending. And it would of course be difficult for anyone to miss the last occasion to appear in an international context and meet old playmates. But he could not act as the representative of the Swedish business community. The latter followed its own routes. Everybody did his own thing. I must say – without denying the importance of individual business transactions also in the present situation – that it might have been politically wiser to send people with a broad outlook, prepared and capable of general reasoning. With the aim of building a foundation for the post-war business exchange. That should have been the purpose when making the selection. Now, we have seen a few transactions here and there, well. […] But we missed the occasion to make direct contact with Americans – and

English, Canadians – during and after the conference. – It would have been a great deal better if Edström had stayed at home and [Fredrik] Göransson [chairman of the board of the Sandvik Steel Works] could have been the chairman. He is a bit tired and not too mobile, but wise, and he accepts advice and reason. He has been very depressed because of Edström's antics. Where he has been given the opportunity to act he has made up well.

In Iveroth's view, Edström was, however, not the only Swede that had made a fool of himself during the conference. The Swedish delegation contained two more charlatans. One was Göran Holmquist from NK:

Mr ... [Holmquist] proved to be excellently capable of making naïve 'statements'. He then walked around and prided himself that the report from ... [his] section 'built' on his views. He has made himself known an 'energetic and able' young man (Edström) and has looked as damn cocky as only he can do, abruptly able. I do not understand why I did not dislike him outright back home. Now I think that I have focused my eyes on his real format.

The second charlatan was Olof Lamm from Stockholms Sjöförsäkrings AB:

Lamm talks immensely: 'I certainly believe that according to my opinion every nation has the greatest interest in certain respects – to participate in an international agreement – if it comes to that point where that could be achieved, and Sweden recognises this fact too. Of course, I wouldn't say that this is our definite position but bla, bla, bla.' But it was effective. He was called upon to testify about currency matters and was seen as the great oracle in that section. This actually says that that you were not too much below the surface.

A third Swede who in Iveroth's view made a complete fool of himself was Gordon Stiernstedt from the Stockholm Chamber of Commerce, on the press conference held in New York before the Swedish delegation went home.

Among other things he was asked the following question: 'What is the Swedish view on the future of the gold standard?' The gold standard issue had been discussed, but Edström [who was the chairman at the press conference] had probably not been present then or had forgotten about it. In any case, he knew nothing about it. He looked around, a bit puzzled and in the end, he spotted Stiernstedt, the head of the Chamber of Commerce. 'You Gordon, you answer that question!' It probably dawned on Edström that he had heard Stiernstedt make statements about the free nations clause, and he somehow sensed that the two concepts were related to each other. The latter looked confused for a moment but began tentatively. 'The gold standard is considered ...' Edström then began to nod, and Gordon took this as a sign that he should continue. He therefore continued by saying: 'The idea of the gold standard has been accepted and many people now talk of it as a possible means for reestablishment ...' He now spoke in his typical Swenglish way, which I am unable to reproduce in writing. '... and many people begin to think it is becoming specially important ...' Edström nodded and Gordon contimued: 'Actually the Swedish delegation ...' Then Edström began to wrinkle his forehead. Then he said: 'Actually the Swedish delegation might come to the conclusion, that we should reintroduce the gold standard, and we will consider that further.' Then, [Einar] Flygt [from the SCA], who was sitting close by, and whispered: 'It's the other way round!' Whereupon Stiernstedt saved the situation by saying: 'But after having considered the matter further a few times, we have become doubtful and it is not so sure any longer, that we will have support for a decision to reintroduce the gold standard. There are too many problems attached to the matter.' Thereafter, the press conference came to an end without the final speech that Edström had planned.[11]

An Important Cooperation

Axel Iveroth stressed the importance for Swedish businessmen of penetrating in earnest the philosophy of the American industry and the environment in which it had to work. Central to this philosophy was the '*free enterprise*' notion. It 'cannot be more deeply rooted than what it is in this country.' But this freedom was about to be chipped away at the edges.

> The American entrepreneurial world is ... conscious of the fact that it must fight to keep its position, both inwardly and outwardly. Inside the country its is meeting ever more potent contrary forces. It is above all the radical tendencies within the two big parties, but above all the Democratic one, entertained partly by radical scientific advisors, partly by the increasing political interest within the labor movement.

[11] Iveroth (1994, pp. 59–60).

Swedish industrial firms had to pay attention to this tug of war in its efforts of building business relations with the US in anticipation of the postwar period. The economic influence of the state and society was of course not as important as in Sweden, but nevertheless you could take for granted that 'American entrepreneurship would be in opposition, and a very vivid one, to all kinds of governance that wants to increase the economic power of the state; with all means it opposes the present regime and its tendencies in this direction.' The conclusion was clear-cut: 'It appears self-evident that these simple truths should constitute the point of departure for Swedish overtures to the American entrepreneurship.'

Iveroth thought that it was essential to 'get to talk above the head of the administration, to speak directly to the industrial community and its organizations.' He, therefore, wanted an 'industrial legation' to be established in New York. 'Government trade representation in Washington would not have the same impact. In the first place, Washington is a purely administrative city, and secondly, collaboration with government agencies would be viewed with suspicion.' You had to understand and approach the freedom urge of the American industry, and Iveroth cautioned adamantly about emphasizing certain Swedish virtues:

> The worst thing you can do if you want to arouse the benevolence of the industrial community is of course to brag, rightly or wrongly, about state railways, state tobacco and liquor monopolies, municipal streetcars, the cooperative movement, 'mixed corporation' and other middle ways. This is practically the only news that you receive in this country about the Swedish economy. If you want to arouse the interest of the American entrepreneurs in Sweden and in doing Swedish business, it is of course much more efficient to describe the free enterprise that is left, and to clarify that the Swedish businessmen oppose socialism, that there are other business initiatives of Swedish origin than state monopolies and cooperation. The general information activities carried out by the Swedish American News Exchange play a lot on such strings and from the point of view of commercial relations probably do not make any positive contribution.

Norwegian-Swedish Cooperation

When Iveroth had been in Vermont in September 1944, he had met some Norwegians, among others 'an influential businessman,' named Osmund, a manager at International Harvester, and had discussed Norwegian-Swedish cooperation with him:

> I got a pretty different impression of the attitude of the Norwegians to Sweden than the one which had been considered the correct one in Washington … [Osmund] considered that the antagonism had been exaggerated. He spoke warmly of Swedish-Norwegian cooperation. Norway will essentially deal with the merchant fleet, the fisheries and the special industries for which it is suited, some forestry and waterfall industries. Otherwise, Sweden would have to take care of the industrialization, the one that requires at least a Nordic market. And then they of course wanted assistance with the merchant fleet – and assistance to exploit the waterfalls.

The Norwegian government in exile in London took for granted that after the conclusion of the peace the wartime control and regulation system will be liquidated.

> … yes furthermore: the trade and industry organization would themselves administer the distribution of raw materials during the transition period. The government in London was supportive of the business community and would not use the occasion, the favorable occasion, for social maneuvers. … [Osmund] did not think that the political climate in Norway would be at all in favor of this.

Other views with respect to this were, however, possible and Iveroth, therefore, favored a joint Scandinavian industrial offensive:

> Wouldn't it be a good idea for the Swedish industry to collaborate ostentatiously with Danish and Norwegian business. They will like it and it is not certain that they are more careful in those countries in their radicalization orgies and endeavors and that the entire political development will be more bourgeois-national, at least more than indicated by the pre-war development.

New York

Axel Iveroth had nothing against leaving the 'swamp' that was Washington. His first trip away from there went to New York, in mid-August. On the 20th, he enthusiastically reported from there to Ingvar Svennilson:

> My first trip to New York. The city is fantastic; there is nothing like it. You hardly believe that this is true. Still, I arrived by train and emerged from the underground and missed the skyline view from the sea. – This I did the first night: went to bed around half past five in the morning

> after nightlife with expert guidance. There is not much difference between day and night here. This I did the second day: went to Long Island to bathe, lost my newly acquired straw hat in the sea, returned half fainted by subway, went to bed with fever and shivers. – Then I had to lie down on the third day, a slight heatstroke. I have entered a period of bad luck, which I, however, hope has reached its climax with this. I am in New York to become acquainted with the Swedish institutions here: the Cargo Clearance Committee, the consulate, the news agency, the banking section, etc. Then I will go into the countryside for a week.

It is evident that Iveroth liked New York and took all chances to go there. 'I have begun to feel more at home with the circumstances—not least the traffic—I have noticed that it is important to feel that you are on solid ground. Now I go back and forth to New York like between Stockholm and Uppsala,' he reported on 23 September. On 1 November, he once more described an entry into the Big Apple in enamored language:

> Now the train has passed New Ark [sic] and is on its way across the swamps west of the Hudson toward New York. The flames from the garbage fires and burning reeds light the evening. An aeroplane with green and red lanterns follow us for a while. Now we go into the tunnel under Queens and the Hudson and thus I am in Gotham.
>
> The ticket collector passes through the wagon and says Better get off in New York, wake up now or you will find yourself in Boston. – There is plenty of cordiality, openness and friendliness and New York is a beautiful city, but cruel, flashy, terrible for those who have to live their lives there working for small pay.

Canada and Chicago

After the Rye conference, Iveroth in December went to Canada, and from there back to Washington via Chicago, together with Fredrik Göransson and Lars-Erik Thunholm from the economic secretariat at Handelsbanken. He accounted for the trip, which he considered as a preparation for a longer later trip, in a letter to Ingvar Svennilson on 15 December. The Swedes had lunch with the Canadian Minister for War Materials and Reconstruction in Ottawa and had then also made contact with the Minister of Trade and the Assistant Minister of Finance. They had visited the Bank of Canada, the Canadian Chamber of Commerce, the Canadian Exporters Association in Toronto, the University of Toronto

Press, the Canadian Manufacturers Association, an investigation agency in Bagg Street in Montreal as well as the ILO headquarters there (Since Switzerland was surrounded by German dominated nations, the ILO had relocated from Geneva to Montreal in 1940). The conclusion from his Canadian trip drawn by Iveroth was that it was important not to conceive of Canada as 'an appendix to the USA.' Direct attention would be 'favorable.'

On the way home, with train via Chicago, visits were paid to Jacob Viner at the University of Chicago, the Chicago University Press and the Association of Commerce and the Continental Bank and Trust there. In addition, an excursion was made to Northwestern University in Evanston, where the Swedes met some ten economists and got a list of American and English economic literature suitable for European universities. 'The list is of course what I have been looking for since I arrived.' Iveroth liked Evanston:

> The Evanston environment is nicely academic and the people that we met informally sympathetic. But you need time to digest such visits. You need to stay in place for at least a week. Otherwise, you don't get close enough to the people to get anything out of the talks. I hope that I can come back after these good contact visits.

At the beginning of 1945, Axel Iveroth received a compact letter from Tore Browaldh, dated 16 January, where the latter described the recent activities at the IUI and how the material that Iveroth had sent back home had been used. The real purpose of the letter, however, was different. Browaldh was an accomplished jazz pianist, with Teddy Wilson as his idol. He, therefore, wondered whether Iveroth

> … on my behalf could buy two gramophone record albums which have just been issued. I assume that they can hardly be sent home during the war, but since the albums have been issued in a very restricted edition, I would be grateful if you could ensure that you get them. The albums are *Mary Lou Williams*, piano solos, an album which among other things contains Lullaby of the Leaves and St Louis Blues, and *Art Tatum*, piano solos with guitar accompaniment, an album on the Comet label with 12-inch records containing among other things The Man I Love, Flying Home, Body and Soul. The place where these records will certainly be available is the Commodore Music Shop, 42nd Street, New York City.

The two Mary Lou Williams tunes formed part of a series of three 78ths recorded for the Ash label (*Lullaby of the Leaves* is a sextet recording, not a piano solo). Williams during the 1930s had played piano with and arranged for Andy Kirk's Twelve Clouds of Joy in Kansas City, before she became a solo artist.[12] Art Tatum is the musician who many consider to be the foremost jazz pianist of all times, a technical wizard who mainly played solo piano, but in 1944 he had a trio with Tiny Grimes on guitar and Slam Stewart on bass, which recorded three 78ths for Comet.[13] The record store that Browaldh refers to was owned by Milt Gabler who also owned the legendary Commodore Records label. (The location of the store was 136 East 42nd Street.) It was Gabler who in 1939 recorded Billie Holiday's *Strange Fruit*, the classic tune about lynching that the major labels did not dare to touch:

> Southern trees bear a strange fruit
> Blood on the leaves and blood at the root
> Black bodies swinging in the southern breeze
> Strange fruit hanging from the poplar trees ...[14]

It was also Gabler who contracted Bill Haley for Decca and in 1954 recorded *Rock around the Clock.*

Before Axel Iveroth returned to Sweden he had time for a visit to Boston combined with a week of skiing in New Hampshire. Both disappointed him. On 27 February, he wrote:

> Today, I have just returned from a week of combined vacation and study trip to Boston and surroundings. Skiing in this country consists in going in an aireal [sic] tramway to the top of a mountain and then you slide or fall down a geronticidal narrow forest trail. I at least escaped from it without broken legs, but it was pretty close, since we had an icy rain for the first two days, which, to make things worse, made a glass mountain of the whole thing. What a country, as I have said before. In addition, Boston disappointed me. That city has always been said to be very different, with something like a European atmosphere. It certainly exists, in certain quarters, but in the main the city is as dirty, as badly constructed, deplorably ugly as all other American cities.

[12] For Williams' biography, see Dahl (1999).

[13] Tatum's biography is found in Lester (1994).

[14] The *Strange Fruit* story is told in Margolick (2000).

Among the last things that Axel Iveroth experienced during his year in the United States was the death of President Roosevelt on 12 April, He had just left the Cosmos Club, where he had met Amos Taylor, the head of the Bureau of Foreign and Domestic Commerce in the Ministry for Trade:

> So I left, via the Lafayette Park, and saw a lot of people gathered in the streets around the White House. I went there and thought that it was strange that you had a reception when the flag was simultaneously flown at half-mast. The flag, I presumed, was for the South African minister, who was buried the same day. Since nothing happened, I continued my walk and after a few steps I saw half the front page of a newspaper. It said Roosev and I asked myself why I had not understood before. I actually saw that the people looked different, they were standing alone on the curbs, looking into the air. And there was an exceptional number of people wandering in the streets, looking for newspapers that were sold before anybody could see what happened. In the end, I managed to get a copy of the Washington Post and took a streetcar to the legation.

Axel Iveroth flew home from the United States on 31 May 1945. He had received a cryptic telegram from the chairman of the Swedish Employers' Confederation, Gustaf Söderlund and Ernst Wehtje at Skånska Cement: 'Axel, we need you at home. Try to find the first possible flight to Stockholm.'[15] On 14 January, he had expressed a certain satisfaction with life:

> After the first, six months – I don't understand what happened to them – I now feel pretty secure here. I imagine that this is the best evidence that six months have passed. I have never felt so footloose as when I left the boat in Philadelphia on Midsummer's Day 1944. All the way until I had been in New York for the first time, I walked in a quagmire. After the trip to Canada and Chicago I walk everywhere like in the streets of Stockholm. I imagine that this is what is called experience.

Nevertheless, he left Washington without regret. In his last two letters to Ingvar Svennilson, he felt that the abominable Washington summer was once more imminent. The first one is from 23 April, less than two weeks after the death of President Roosevelt:

[15] Iveroth (1994, p. 67).

> This is probably the last letter before returning home, written on an unusually cool and nice Sunday in Washington. There is nothing in this paradisiac afternoon thar betrays the offensive with fire and water that the climate may any day turn loose against the pretty defenseless human body. It is astonishing that the presidents live as long as they actually do in this swamp.

There was, however, one more letter. 'It is beginning to get hot and damp now, so I will be glad to leave,' he continued on 18 May.

* * *

Upon his return to Sweden, Axel Iveroth received the explanation of the cryptic telegram. He had to begin by modernizing the journal of the Swedish Employers' Confederation, *Industria*. At the same time, he became a manager at Cementa, 1945–1952, and thereafter chief executive and chairman of the cooperation agency of the European cement industry, Cembureau, 1949–1957. Together with Tore Browaldh and Lars-Erik Thunholm he took the initiative to the foundation of the Center for Business and Policy Studies [Studieförbundet Näringsliv och Samhälle, SNS], modeled on the American Committee for Economic Development.[16] Iveroth was its chairman 1948–60, and from 1957 to 1977 he was the managing director of the Federation of Swedish Industries.

Swedish version published in Benny Carlson and Mats Lundahl, *Från Värmland till Washington: Episoder ur IUI:s historia*. Stockholm: Samhällsförlaget, 2020.

References

Carlson, Benny and Lundahl, Mats (2014), *Ett forskningsinstitut växer fram: IUI från grundandet till 1950*. Stockholm: Ekerlids Förlag.

Dahl, Linda (1999), *Morning Glory: A Biography of Mary Lou Williams*. New York: Pantheon Books.

Iveroth, Axel (1943), *Småindustri och hantverk i Sverige*. Stockholm: Industriens Utredningsinstitut.

Iveroth, Axel (1994), *Det härliga livet: Minnen, skrönor och debattinlägg*. Stockholm: Industrilitteratur.

[16] Ibid., pp. 63–66, 74–75.

Lester, James (1994), *Too Marvellous for Words: The Life and Genius of Art Tatum*. New York and Oxford: Oxford University Press.
Margolick, David (2000), *Strange Fruit: Billie Holiday, Café Society, and an Early Cry for Civil Rights*. Philadelphia, PA and London: Running Press.
Myrdal, Gunnar, with the Assistance of Richard Sterner and Arnold Rose (1944a), *An American Dilemma: The Negro Problem and Modern Democracy*. New York and London: Harper & Brothers Publishers.
Myrdal, Gunnar (1944b), *Varning för Fredsoptimism*. Stockholm: Albert Bonniers Förlag.
Sterner, Richard (1943), *The Negro's Share: A Study of Income, Consumption, Housing and Public Assistance*. New York: Harper & Brothers.
Thunholm, Lars-Erik (2005), *Flydda tider*. Rimbo: Fischer & Co.

CHAPTER 6

From the New World: Ingvar Svennilson in the United States and Cuba

(with Benny Carlson)

During the year when Axel Iveroth was industrial attaché at the Swedish legation in Washington, DC, 1944–1945, he at various times suggested to Ingvar Svennilson that the latter ought to come to the United States, first as a natural participant in the Swedish delegation which was to take part in a business conference arranged by the United States Chamber of Commerce in the late fall of 1944. This, however, came to nothing. Iveroth then told Svennilson to come in the fall of 1945 instead so that they could travel around together and visit factories, universities and research institutes and perhaps even go to South America.

This, however, did not work out either. It was not until the winter and spring (February to May) of 1947 that Ingvar Svennilson made a three-month study trip to the United States. In a report to the board of the Industrial Institute for Economic and Social Research [Industriens Utredningsinstitut, IUI] in June 1947, he explained that the purpose of the tour had been 'to get a general orientation with respect to economic conditions and economic research in America.'[1]

Together with his wife Margit, Svennilson began his voyage on 31 January on M/S Gripsholm. After a few days in New York, he went to Boston and Harvard, where he gave a talk on Swedish investment policy

[1] *Protokoll* (1947, bilaga). The account of the journey is based on this supplement.

M. Lundahl, *Twelve Figures in Swedish Economics*,
Palgrave Studies in the History of Economic Thought,
https://doi.org/10.1007/978-3-030-94327-1_6

at Alvin Hansen's seminar and got an opportunity to meet a number of famous economics professors: Gottfried Haberler, Joseph Schumpeter, Edward S. Mason, John Henry Williams, Edward Chamberlin, Sidney Alexander and Paul Samuelson. He also participated in a seminar at the Harvard Business School, led by the human relations prophet Elton Mayo.

Industry Visits

In March and the beginning of April, Svennilson visited a number of American industries. The list is long—some 30 companies and organizations in 16 cities. Among the most well-known were Macy's in New York, Monsanto in Anniston, the Tennessee Valley Authority in Knoxville, Firestone in Memphis, Ford and Chrysler in Detroit, where Svennilson had dinner with the directors of the car companies and gave a talk together with Axel Iveroth, Carnegie and Westinghouse in Pittsburgh as well as the Swedish ball-bearing company SKF in Philadelphia.

The most important impression from the industry visits, according to Svennilson, was that the mass-producing industries, not least the car factories in Detroit, displayed 'an enormous efficiency, in terms of the number of unites produced per work hour.'

> Otherwise, the industrial sector from the Swedish point of view does not leave any particular impression. Possibly, mechanization is partly more advanced, but the factories and offices are often old-fashioned, the general hygienic and social standard is usually low, the factories are often dirty and do not always impress you as being well organized.

The work intensity was difficult to gauge, but according to Svennilson's 'ocular inspection,' it was high only in the South, where black laborers were used. The work pace of the industries of the Northeast had been reduced considerably as a result of the organization of trade unions. In the companies where efforts were made to keep the unions out attempts were made to strengthen the contacts between the employers and the employees.

> One of the main impressions from the industrial trip was thus that when it comes to technology and organization we do not have all that much to learn from America. The American advantage is almost entirely due to the

> possibility of mass production. [...] The insights that I got into American goods distribution, however, gave me a clear impression that in certain ways it is much more efficient than in this country.

Svennilson explained the high standard of living in the United States by four factors: (1) efficient mass production and mass distribution, (2) a favorable endowment of natural resources, (3) ruthless exploitation of these resources, (4) exploitation of the black labor force. The American economic growth was not sustainable. 'The bill for this will undoubtedly be presented during the coming decades.' The conclusion for Sweden was laconic: 'When it comes to our own efficiency problems, we thus do not have much to learn from America.'

University Visits

At the end of March, during the industry trip, Svennilson also visited Northwestern University in the Chicago suburb Evanston. In April, he went to Washington and met a number of people at the Swedish legation, among others were the ambassador, Herman Eriksson, the trade counselor Leif Belfrage, the financial secretary Bengt Metelius and Dag Hammarskjöld. He visited the American departments of commerce and labor and gave a talk on Swedish economic policy to the staff of economic advisors of the president. He thereafter flew to Los Angeles and visited UCLA.

At the beginning of May, Svennilson was at the University of California, Berkeley, where he studied, lectured to students on the development of the Swedish economy and met the economics professors Howard Sylvester Ellis and William Fellner. More professors followed: Corwin Edwards in Evanston, Illinios, and the mathematician William Feller at Cornell, Ithaca, New York. On 24 May, he went back home on M/S Queen Elizabeth.

The cost of the trip amounted to a total of 25,800 kronor, which corresponds to about half a million today. Svennilson himself paid 9,500 and the IUI 16,300 kr.

Enormous Investment Needs

In the June issue of *Ekonomisk Tidskrift* 1947, Svennilson published an article on the economic future of America, which dealt with an investigation by J. Frederic Dewhurst from the Twentieth Century Fund of 'America's Needs and Resources' (see below). There he came back to the theme that the high standard of living in many quarters in the United States built on an unsustainable foundation—'that the American so far has not paid what it costs to live in an urban way at this high standard.' At the same time, the investments had lagged behind after many years of crisis and war and Svennilson described 'the dominant impression on the contemporary visitor to America. You are mainly moving about in the America of 1929, you live and work in 1929 vintage houses, travel on 1929 vintage railroads, sit in 1929 vintage cinemas.' It was 'completely clear that the investment needs of America are enormous.'[2]

Overproduction?

In the summer of 1947, the chief editor of *Dagens Nyheter*, Herbert Tingsten, in a letter of 14 July reminded Svennilson that the latter had promised an article about his experiences in America. Svennilson did not reply until after two months (letter, 19 September) and deplored that he had been delayed due to illness, but that he then had begun a series of four articles. The first one was to deliver a critique of Gunnar Myrdal's forecast of an overproduction crisis after the war. Tingsten, who was himself on his way to America, answered promptly (letter, 20 September) and hoped that Svennilson would write relatively extensively about the American social legislation.

In the fall of 1947, Svennilson thus published four articles in *Dagens Nyheter*, which built on what he had learned during his trip, on the theme 'new characteristics of the economic structure of the United States.'[3] The first article dealt with the risk of overproduction. The point of departure of the reasoning was the following:

> Some people fear that a new crisis of the dimension of the 30s will shake the entire Western cultural area. Others seem happy when they speculate

[2] Svennilson (1947e, pp. 170–171).

[3] This was the main heading of all the articles.

that such a crisis would deprive the United States of its present position in world politics. Most at least seem to be of the opinion that the economic system in the United States is such that the country is predestined to get into violent fluctuations between booms and depressions.[4]

According to Svennilson, all these observers, however, had no idea about the crucial changes that the American economy had undergone since the 1920s and 1930s. Both the resilience of the structure of the economic system and the economic–political power of action had changed in a decisive way since the 1930s.

The forecasts of an imminent crisis in the United States were often based on 'a coarse overproduction theory.' It was, however, evident that the American consumer, in spite of his high standard of living, was far from having satisfied all his demands. The overriding issue was the purchasing power of the American public, and this 'the most excellent crisis mongers have as a rule not bothered to study closely.'

In Sweden, the overproduction case had been argued by Gunnar Myrdal in his book *Varning för fredsoptimism* [Beware of Peace Optimism], published in 1944.[5] He had emphasized the timing. The American consumer, after fifteen years of crisis and war, with cuts in non-military consumption, would not be able to keep up with the fast peacetime production increase. Svennilson, however, believed that, on the contrary, the long abstinence would facilitate the return to a higher standard because of all the pent-up demand of regular families. Millions of unemployed had returned to work and received higher incomes. 'In the face of this fact, as far as I understand, the entire lag theory is dissolved.' Myrdal had also predicted 'enormous difficulties' with the transition in the labor market. That prophesy as well had turned out to be erroneous, 'As a matter of fact, a restless transition took place which surprised not only Myrdal, but also the majority of the American economists.'

In this context, we may note that Svennilson in 1944 had been close to Myrdal in his views of the risk of a postwar depression. In a memorandum about employment policy after the war, he had predicted that the economies during the transition from war to peace would pass through three stages: first stagnation, then strong demand due to neglected needs

[4] Svennilson (1947a).

[5] Myrdal (1944).

and reconstruction and finally a contraction with its origin in the United States.[6]

The Advance of the Trade Unions

The second article in Svennilson's series dealt with the increased influence of the trade unions and began with the following sentence: 'A fundamental change in the American economy in comparison with the 30s is that the labor market has lost its previously unregulated features and that most of the industrial sector has been covered with a net of collective contracts.'[7]

When Franklin D. Roosevelt via the Wagner Act and the creation of the National Labor Relations Board in 1935 lent his support to the trade union movement, the number of organized workers was 5 million. In 1947, the number had tripled. The most important features of the new legislation were that the employer had to negotiate with the union organizing the largest number of workers and that the employer but not the union could be prosecuted for breaking the wage agreement. The trade unions hence could break signed agreements without any real risk of being sanctioned. At the same time, the anti-trust legislation together with the individualist attitudes of the employers put obstacles in the way of organization on the employer side. The trade unions therefore had 'the opportunity to choose and attack the weakest link' in the industry. In several cases they had managed to create strong monopolies because the employers had been forced to agree to 'closed shops,' to employ only union members, and 'check off,' to deduct union membership fees from the wage also in case of non-members. The power of the trade unions had grown substantially without any corresponding clarification of their responsibilities.

> It has been clear for a long time that certain duties and limitations which correspond to the support that they have received in the legislation and administration must be imposed on the trade unions. ... That this view was shared also by very radical circles is clear from the statements made by

[6] Svennilson (1944, p. 93).

[7] Svennilson (1947b).

Myrdal in 1943 in his 'Amerika mitt i världen [America at the Center of the World].'[8]

During the summer of 1947, this insight had resulted in the Taft-Hardly Act, which made agreements binding also for the unions, prohibited 'closed shops,' limited 'check off,' created certain guarantees of democratic work forms within the trade union movement and strengthened the mediation system. In certain circles, this law was portrayed as a mortal blow to the American labor movement, something which Svennilson considered exaggerated. 'In all these respects, the new legislation constitutes a step in the normalizing direction—seen from the Nordic point of view.' The new law, however, implies that the extent of political and administrative intervention in the labor market increased more and more. According to Svennilson, this was inevitable.

> The only possible alternative would have been a deregulation also of previous interventions undertaken to protect the unions and a transfer of the responsibility for the rules of the labor market game in some kind of Saltsjöbaden spirit, Such a deregulation, however, seems to be ruled out, both because the trade unions lack an equal counterpart on the employer side and because the hastily groomed trade union movement to a large extent lack the traditions of democratic sense and moderation that the Swedish one has assimilated during decades of hard fights and tedious organizational work.

A decisive question for Svennilson was how the collectivization and politicization of the wage formation process in America would affect the trade cycle. Monopolization and rigid wages could trigger crises or delay recovery. Thus, the 'strongly monopolistic construction unions' in many cases had deliberately reduced—sometimes halved—the work pace and prevented the introduction of new and labor-saving methods, which threatened to trigger a crisis. 'The high construction costs now block the resurrection of the construction of dwellings, in spite of the fact that the need for new and replacement construction is enormous. This constitutes the perhaps most important threat of a new, deep and long American depression.'

[8] Myrdal (1943).

On the other hand, 'a general, relatively strong opposition to wage reductions [offered] a more secure basis for a stable economic situation.' The increasing influence of the trade unions had also contributed to the reduction of wage differences that had taken place since the 1930s. In short, Svennilson followed the rule of thumb of the balanced economist in his considerations of the trade unions in the United States: on the one hand ... on the other hand.

Social Policy and Income Distribution

The third article discussed social care and income equalization. Svennilson came back to the observation that consumption had by then been brought to the forefront and that the time had arrived for a 'social harvest time.' The most important phases of the development were (1) the strengthening of the trade unions (which he had already dealt with), (2) a general social insurance plan and (3) increased progressive taxation. The foundation for the second phase was laid when Roosevelt, through the Social Security Act in 1935, began the march toward 'a modern social state where free enterprise goes hand in hand with a generous measure of social security and income equalization.'[9] The act incorporated unemployment insurance, a state system financed by fees from the corporations, insurance for the elderly and the survivors, a federal system financed by employee and employer fees as well as need-based contributions to unsupported elderly, blind and children, a mixed federal and state system. 'This information shows that the general minimum standard guaranteed by American social legislation by and large is on a relatively high level in comparison to Europe. The program still has holes, but intensive work is being carried out to fill them.'

Increased government spending and increased tax revenues had an automatically stabilizing effect. 'Public spending for these purposes increases automatically during a depression, while the corresponding public revenue decreases when unemployment rises.'

Taxes had increased to a level where they were of 'very considerable importance for the distribution of income' and this in turn meant that the risk of overproduction and stagnation had been reduced:

[9] Svennilson (1947c).

> The taxes for high-income earners have thus been brought up to a level completely comparable with the Swedish ones during the war. Due to the low initial level, the increase has, however, been substantially stronger; in fact, it constitutes a veritable revolution in the income distribution. ... It is probable that the income equalization has increased the share of the national income that is devoted to consumption—the propensity to consume and not save the incomes has by and large probably increased.

Economic Policy

In the fourth and final article, Svennilson accounted for his views on the economic policy environment. By the increased activities of the federal administration, the American states had been bound 'more tightly together through an economic and social policy led from Washington,' even though parts of the Mid-West, the South and the West Coast had made themselves less dependent on the influence of the East Coast.

> There is ... no doubt that the Congress and the American people nowadays have accepted completely that the administration in Washington is responsible for the general economic development. ... The business community has had to accept that in many cases the important discussions and decisions no longer take place in Manhattan but during consultations in the Washington administration.[10]

The enormous war effort of the United States had been made possible by the cooperation between the politicians in Washington and the large business corporations. The question was what this cooperation would be like during a future economic crisis. In leading circles at any rate 'the modern view about the importance of the balancing of the budget for the general economic situation had been accepted.'

> The American government has ... shown that even in a democratic society with competition between parties it is possible to carry out a budget policy which stabilizes the economy, a policy which implies that during a boom with inflationary pressure you keep the tax level up and cut down on expenditures.

[10] Svennilson (1947d).

There were, however, gaps in the preparation for a crisis. No extensive planning had been undertaken to support private construction activities with public works or to keep investments up, should they display a tendency to fall. On the other hand, public opinion appeared to be prepared for measures also in these areas.

> If a crisis materializes, such measures will presumably be pushed through forcefully, under the impact of the opinion that you meet everywhere in America, that you will not allow another crisis like the one in the 1930s to unfold and that in view of such a risk you are prepared to use measures as powerful as those employed during the war.

A Ten-Year Plan

During the IUI board meeting in January 1948, Svennilson presented a sketch of an investigation of Sweden's needs and resources.[11] He began his 'strictly confidential' document with the following words:

> Since my return from America, the undersigned has been thinking of suggesting that the institute should embark on a major investigation of the possibility of economic development in the somewhat longer run. ... Such a project would be a natural development of the program of the institute until now ... It goes without saying that no secure forecasts can be made for the long run. On the other hand, it would be very valuable to identify the different development alternatives ... A corresponding investigation, which has recently been carried out by the Twentieth Century Fund (America's needs and resources) demonstrates that such an investigation is possible.

To some extent, the investigation would consist of a summary of work previously carried out at the IUI, for example, of the labor force, forestry yields, investments and productivity. In addition, you could calculate the future national product and its distribution between exports and the domestic market, and between savings, consumption and investment. An essential element would deal with the income distribution.

Svennilson counted on having BA Jonas Nordenson as the leader of the project. As experts he hoped to be able to recruit outstanding economists like Torsten Gårdlund and Erik Lindahl. He also hoped that

[11] *Protokoll* (1948a, bilaga 2).

the IUI could cooperate with the research department of the Federation of Swedish Farmers and that thereby the project would appear as 'a manifestation from the entire business community.' The investigation ought to be undertaken during 1948 and 1949 and published in 1950. Svennilson calculated that the program would need extra funding of 40,000 kronor during three years.

Already during the next board meeting, in June 1948, Svennilson was able to tell that several sub-projects had already been started, and the board agreed to fees to Gårdlund och Lindahl.[12]

During the November board meeting, Svennilson accounted for the participation of the IUI in the long-term program 1947–1952/53 (the four-year program) that the Swedish government had sent to the OEEC. The work on this program had been very time-consuming during the fall, but it had also coincided with the ten-year 1960 project. The four-year program could be viewed as a starting point for the ten-year program.

Jonas Nordenson presented the plans with respect to the ten-year program which then required 75,000 kronor of additional funds. Various board members turned out to be skeptical against such a long planning horizon. Svennilson, however, explained that the 1960 project 'was not to be regarded as planning or a forecast but as a scientific study of connections and tendencies where the "forecast" should be regarded as a mere illustration.' Nordenson, in turn, contended that the different development alternatives that were to be identified 'should be regarded as numerical examples.' Ernst Wehtje, the managing director of Skånska Cement, backed Svennilson and Nordenson by stating that the long-term program 'would be of great value if you just avoided exaggerations' and that it was important for the business community to take the initiative 'since otherwise you would easily risk that it would be initiated elsewhere' (i.e. by the government). Svennilson in turn emphasized that it was important 'that the industry when it came to investigations did not have to obey orders from the state but, if possible, should act before they were issued.' He thereafter summarized the discussion by simply concluding 'that the board was positively interested in the completion of the work on "Sweden's needs and resources" according to the existing plans.'

[12] *Protokoll* (1948b).

In October 1949, Svennilson took leave of absence in order to work for the United Nations on what would become his *magnum opus*, *Growth and Stagnation in the European Economy*.[13]

At the IUI board meeting a month later, Nordenson presented an account of the progress of the work on Sweden's needs and resources and presented two alternatives: either the entire material would be presented at the same time as the investigation was finished or the results would be published little by little but with a concluding summary.[14] The board supported the latter alternative. The result of the grandiose ten-year plan was a number of IUI volumes in 1952 about population growth and labor supply, income distribution, the distribution of goods and transportation.[15]

Svennilson in Cuba

Ingvar Svennilson left the Industrial Institute for Economic and Social Research in October 1949. He had been granted a two-year leave of absence for his UN project. Svennilson would never return but would also in the future keep close contact with the institute. In 1960, he was back in the United States, at Yale University in New Haven, where he held the Irving Fisher chair in economics. From there he sent sporadic reports to the director of IUI, Jan Wallander, of how he and his family were doing and about the American political situation. At the same time, together with his family, he took the opportunity to visit Cuba. Then, exactly like Fredrika Bremer, who visited the island 109 years before,[16] he wrote letters back to Sweden, in his case to Jan Wallander. On 25 February, he reported:

> We have been in Cuba for a week. The girls accompanied us and we had a nice winter vacation in summer heat. I knew nothing about Cuba before I traveled there. But we ought to learn more about the world. And Cuba's problems are probably found in other parts of Latin America [as well]. I wrote the attached notes when I came home, and maybe they are of some interest. I don't want to have them published, however. Perhaps you can

[13] Svennilson (1954).

[14] *Protokoll* (1949).

[15] These volumes are presented in Carlson and Lundahl (2019).

[16] Bremer (1983).

let them have a limited circulation. You may want to call it a travelogue that I have sent to you personally.[17]

In Revolutionary Havana

The visit to Cuba had taken place between the 12th and the 25th of February. It had been permeated by the political situation. When Svennilson came to Havana not much more than a year had passed since Fidel Castro, on 8 January 1959, had arrived there at the head of his *barbudos* after the exit of the dictator Fulgencio Batista on New Year's Day. Svennilson's visit was not a pure pleasure trip. He had been invited by the Cuban Minister of Finance, Rufo López-Fresquet, to lecture on economic development together with a few American economists. He took advantage of the occasion to meet people from the Ministry of Finance and Economy, businessmen and Swedish commercial representatives and in addition had time for a couple of days in the countryside.

The Svennilson family stayed in the fancy twenty-five-storey hotel Habana Hilton, which had been inaugurated a mere two years before in the presence of Conrad Hilton. In June 1960, Catro nationalized the hotel and renamed it Habana Libre. He had lived there himself during the first three months after his entry in Havana. Thereafter, Svennilson stated, he had led an itinerant existence: 'Castro is a very bohemian character without any fixed abode, who sleeps where he happens to be; sometimes even in the super modern 25-storey hotel Hilton, where I stayed.' At the time, the hotel was mainly empty, since the American tourists had been scared away by the change of political regime. 'At times, when Castro stayed there, you could see a couple of bearded "barbados" [sic] wielding their guns run through the lobby at full speed.'

Ingvar Svennilson described Havana as 'pretty calm.' But one night he had been awakened by explosions. Batista supporters had flown in from Florida or Rafael Trujillo's Dominican Republic and had attempted to bomb the house where they believed Castro was staying but had been scared off and dropped their cargo elsewhere. Otherwise, the Cuban capital had left a favorable impression:

> The city is completely Americanized with a lively traffic of American cars. The people, dominated by Spaniards, but in addition with Negro blood in

[17] Svennilson (1960). The following builds on this letter.

different colors, is beautiful, well nourished and well dressed. The carnival was celebrated as always.

The beaches around the city are framed with simple and more elegant clubs with club houses, playas and marinas. Large modern residential neighborhoods spread out. The architecture is modern and very high-class. There are old picturesque neighborhoods. But it is cleaner than in an American city. By and large, Havana (around 1 million inhabitants) gives a more modern and opulent impression. Simply a wonderful city to live in under peaceful political conditions.

This was before Havana began to decay.

The Cuban Economy

Svennilson was impressed by the Cuban nature and the 'enormous' fertility of the soil. The climate was pleasant, and everything could be cultivated in Cuba. The precipitation was both abundant and well distributed, and fertilizer only had to be used in special cases. 'The sugar cane grows like weeds. [...] You think with shame on our own excellent cultivation of sugar beets, which we (as far as I recall) afford a higher protection than any other agricultural product.'

Ingvar Svennilson had arrived in a country where the new regime had the advantage of being able to take over assets built up by the former one. The Batista regime had been dictatorial and corrupt. It was not defended even by 'the businessmen who then had had great times.' Nevertheless, you could not escape the fact that Batista had accomplished quite a lot:

> [A]s usual you forget that in spite of everything, dictators often produce rapid development. Cuba now has an extensive railway network, super modern roads and ports, first-class hospitals, schools and universities, sports facilities which Stockholm cannot match in any way. Castro now has the advantage of not having to spend much on the 'infra-structure'. In addition, the country was open for foreign investment and the Americans have invested billions. The hotels and beach resorts are impressive. There you find all kinds of American-style service facilities. And an incipient modern industry is in place (Cement factories, chemical factories, etc.).

Svennilson, however, understood that also the new Cuba had income differences, between different categories of workers and between town and country. The heritage from Batista was still alive at the time. He had put his own people into the trade unions and conferred considerable power on the latter. Svennilson considered the gap between the privileged worker categories and the seasonal workers in the countryside excessive.

The Support for Castro

Ingvar Svennilson raised the question why the Cubans had rallied around Castro. He identified four causes. In the first place, they revolted against Batista's dictatorship and his suppression of human rights, Castro, on the other hand, had adhered to democracy and Western freedom values. They had also reacted against the widespread corruption in the old regime. Thirdly, Castro had promised a land reform. The large estates owned by Batista's cronies and by Americans were to be converted into family farms. Finally, Cuba had since long been specialized on sugar production. The United States had bought half the sugar harvest at a price above the world market price in exchange of tariff preferences on manufactured goods. Castro interpreted this as a colonial dependency which acted as a break on Cuban industrialization. He wanted to break this pattern, increase tariffs and export more to other countries than the United States.

Svennilson was not convinced that the path ahead would go in the right direction. 'There is a risk that Cuba—perhaps contrary to Castro's original intentions—will become a totalitarian political and economic society.' Much would depend on Castro himself. Svennilson wavered in his attitude toward him. At the beginning of 1960, there were still many who had hopes that he would not be radicalized. On the one hand, he cannot hide a certain admiration in his letter to Jan Wallander:

> His position among those who have not turned away from him is close to that of a saint or a god. His strength is that he has the masses, notably the peasants, behind him. He has studied law, he is the son of a wealthy farmer. There are no signs that ideologically he should be a Leninist Communist. On the contrary, I think—but this is simply a personal impression—that you may take his professed adherence to Western democracy seriously. His main interest appears to be an equalization of incomes and living conditions, what in Swedish terms would be considered social democratic. This is manifested in the large programs to construct good houses for the farm workers and to bridge the income gap between country and town.

Castro had not yet officially turned Communist, but Svennilson sensed in which direction he could go. 'What makes the island especially interesting at present is that it is situated close to Florida and that the United States risks having a hostile nation with a Communist orientation close to its coast.'

Svennilson's observations were sharp or else he had astute informers. He had arrived in Cuba after a year characterized by increasing tensions: on the one hand, between the different fractions supporting Fidel Castro, on the other hand, between Cuba and the United States. This becomes clear when you compare Svennilson's letter with the huge work of almost 1700 pages about Cuba published by the English historian Hugh Thomas, author of the classic study of the Spanish Civil War.[18] The similarity of opinion is striking.

The Critical Year 1959

Thomas deals with the first year after Castro's assumption of power in great detail.[19] In January 1959, Fidel did not quite know in which ideological direction he wanted to move. 'It is impossible to believe that in January 1959, his mind was made up to create, say, in Cuba a Communist state; impossible too not to believe that he was going to press far whatever he did.'[20] You could fear the worst from the United States. John Foster Dulles was still US secretary of state and his brother Allen head of the CIA. Both had a magnificent record from the McCarthy era, in Latin America not least through the US involvement in the coup that toppled the democratically elected, progressive president of Guatemala, Jacobo Árbenz, in 1954, and in Cuba, the Americans, not least the mafia,[21] had worked closely with the Batista regime. The value of the American investments there was higher than in any other Latin American country, with the exception of Venezuela. In per capita terms their value was three times that of any other Latin American country. The United States, however, had no clear idea of how to handle Cuba at the beginning of 1959.

[18] Thomas (1961).

[19] Thomas (1971, Chapters 86–101).

[20] Ibid, s. 1059.

[21] See Cirules (2004) and English (2008).

Thomas contended that Castro at the time had an 'undefined addiction to revolution for its own sake' and that 'his ambition was too great, his temperament too quixotic to enable him to submit to the discipline and higher authority such as Communism regards as necessary ...'[22] He was an ardent nationalist and had an almost Garibaldian-romantic view of the revolution, if we are to believe Thomas. In any case, his success built on his person, on the phenomenal ability that he would develop in 1959 to make the masses listen for hours to his improvised, glowing speeches, in direct contact without any need for a stiff, bureaucratic party organization to serve as intermediary.

Nevertheless, in 1959, Castro was facing a choice: in which direction should he let the revolution develop, in the bourgeois direction—a bourgeoisie which was strongly North Americanized and which could conceivably spoil or water down his ideas about economic and social transformation—or toward some kind of dictatorship of the proletariat?

Svennilson thought that Castro was losing the support he once had had among 'the educated middle class' and certain businessmen. These groups were getting cold feet, in a situation where free enterprise began to be curtailed and the newspapers did not dare to discuss the danger inherent in an embrace of Communism. The Cuban government contained both liberal and more Communist-oriented elements, but what the future would be like was far from clear. Svennilson held that the liberals were losing ground and he did not trust Castro. '... as I have already pointed out, he is a bohemian. His marathon speeches on the radio are no signs of psychic equilibrium.'

Possibly, Svennilson speculated, it could be the case that Castro was subject to influence that went beyond the democratic. He did not see any clearly formulated political program which rested on democratic foundations and his cabinet met more and more infrequently. This was not good. There was the one suspect in particular who stood out:

> This leaves room for advances from favorites, usually old front companions, and created an ideal environment for maneuvers from possible Communists. Who they are and to what extent is difficult to tell. Most deny it. So does the one who with the aid of Castro's general popularity has taken the lead in the economic field, [Ernesto 'Che'] Guevara (long hair across the shoulders, always dressed in uniform). He is an Argentinian physician,

[22] Thomas (1971, p. 1055).

> who during Castro's exile in Mexico joined him and became the military strategist of the revolutionary army.

Svennilson's conclusions are confirmed by Hugh Thomas. The main leftist influence on Fidel derived from his brother Raúl and from Che Guevara, who both were considerably closer to Communism, and their influence on him was strong. Fidel was skeptical against doctrinaire Communism, not least as manifested in the old Cuban Communist party, which had not played any role in his guerrilla war against Batista, but in 1959, the balance was changed. Castro made up his mind. The liberal elements who formed part of the Cuban government had to yield to the radicals and little by little the gap between the old and the new radicalism was bridged. Liberals were outmaneuvered, in spite of the fact that they tried to play along.

It was no longer possible to criticize Communists. The grotesque show trial against Huber Matos, Castro's former brother-in-arms, the military commander of Camagüey, who had resigned because he thought that the revolution had been infiltrated by Communists, took its beginning on 11 December. Matos was accused of anti-patriotic and anti-revolutionary behavior. Castro testified during the trial—rambling for many hours about irrelevant issues. On the 15th, Matos was sentenced to twenty years of prison. He barely escaped a death sentence but had to serve all his twenty years under extremely difficult conditions.

INRA

When Ingvar Svennilson was in Cuba, Che Guevara had obtained extensive powers to transform the economy. He had become the head of INRA (Instituto Nacional de Reforma Agraria), set up in 1959, in order to carry out a land reform. INRA, however, was growing into a combination of a hydra and an octopus:

> … a huge government institution which runs confiscated farms, factories, transportation (trucks and toll roads), builds up a retail network in the countryside and wants to run an import monopoly (suggested by Guevara). You cannot turn around in Cuba without meeting the letters INRA. This is a state within the state. Its activities made the situation impossible for the liberal head of the National Bank, [Banco Nacional de Cuba], Passos

[Felipe Pazos] who resigned and was replaced by Guevara. When I was in Cuba, one of the investment banks was added to the National Bank.

Felipe Pazos would fare considerably better than Che. While the latter in 1967 met his death in his unrealistic attempt to use a guerrilla movement initiated from outside to topple the Bolivian president, René Barrientos and his government, Pazos was allowed to leave Cuba at the end of 1959 and later work for the Alliance for Progress and the Inter-American Development Bank. He survived Che by more than thirty-three years.

In addition to INRA you had 'the bearded revolutionary army,' led by Fidel Castro's brother Raúl. Svennilson posed the question whether Castro had not become a prisoner of the system. He also asked himself whether INRA would ever distribute any land to the farmers, whether there would be free elections, a free press and room for private enterprise, The situation was one of the delicate balances when he was in Cuba and he apparently sensed what would happen. The trade unions were about to be dominated by Communists and when the demands of the latter on the employers were not met, the state 'intervened' and had the Ministry of Labor determine the wages, which often had grotesque consequences:

If the entrepreneurs then declare that the company cannot be run with those wages, the ministry appoints a company overseer who (on this point I received conflicting information) either controls or runs the company (the ownership does not change, although it turns into a chimera). According to one source, these overseers are recruited from the trade unions, according to another from the revolutionary army. Under such circumstances the companies cannot function. In order to escape controls, they are forced to accept even unreasonable wage demands.

INRA was not simply an organization that was to handle the land reform that was carved out in 1959:

[It] rapidly became the main agency of the new government, for its task was not simply to expropriate and distribute land, but to organize road-building, health, education and housing in the country. INRA was also given a credit department, and it absorbed the old Sugar, Rice and Coffee

> Stabilization Institutes. It became, indeed, a kind of shadow government of its own.[23]

Svennilson had understood the role of the institute correctly.

The Relations with the United States

Ingvar Svennilson argued that Cuba's relations with the United States were characterized by a 'big brother complex.' The Americans were accused by the government of having backed Batista and of having exploited Cuba economically. The economic dependency was unearthed as the Cuban land reform was put into action. The United States attempted to protect its companies and demanded immediate compensation when the nationalizations and expropriations began. Svennilson regretted that the United States' contacts with Cuba had been almost exclusively commercial and that technical assistance and culture had been neglected. This conferred an advantage on the Soviet Union. When Svennilson was in Havana, Anastas Mikoyan had just signed a treaty of technical assistance to Cuba, which among other things included delivery of complete factories and the Russians had in addition undertaken to buy one million tons of sugar per annum at the world market price.

Svennilson ascertained that Cuba was subject to a lively activity from the Communist world, 'openly and certainly also underground.' He, however, did not want to jump to conclusions and had not quite given up his hope about Castro:

> In spite of everything, the direction of future developments is still an open question. A completely Communist-inspired totalitarian system can be constructed successively even though … [it] actually has no resonance among the Catholic population of the country. The Communist-oriented forces may stage a coup backed by the army. On the other hand, Castro could begin to seek support from and support more liberal circles. There is also talk about the possibility of a counter-revolution supported from abroad, but this appears improbable to me. Much depends on how skilfully the United States will handle the political situation and thereby support more democratic forces, perhaps with the aid of other South American states.

[23] Thomas (1971, p. 1217).

Ingvar Svennilson could not have sensed that the relations between Cuba and the United States would undergo a drastic deterioration during the coming two, three years. Cuba was drawn into the cold war. On 17 April 1961, 1,500 US-trained and US-supported exile Cubans landed in the Bay of Pigs on Cuba's south coast. The invasion attempt ended in a complete fiasco. After three days, it was over. The survivors were captured by Castro's forces and were exchanged the following year for 53 million dollars' worth of child food, medicines and tractors. Politically, the operation backlashed completely. The day before the invasion, after a failed bombing of Cuban airplanes, Castro proclaimed the Cuman revolution to be socialist and Marxist.

Castro had definitely moved into the Communist camp, and during 1962, he signed an agreement with the Soviet Union which allowed the Russians to place missiles capable of carrying atomic weapons in Cuba. Nikita Khrushchev felt threatened because the Americans had placed middle distance robots in Italy and Turkey, close to Russian territory and wanted to retaliate. The United States, in turn, answered with a maritime blockade of Cuba. The world was on the brink of a third world war, but thank heavens, the incident ended with both sides dismounting their missiles.

* * *

Ingvar Svennilson's report from Cuba offers interesting reading. It is still good today. The modern reader is struck by how he, without any previous knowledge at all, managed to interpret the frequently ambiguous signs of in which direction things would turn. He saw through the rhetoric and offered well-thought-out and carefully argued reflections on a new political regime which had not yet achieved political stability.

Swedish version published in Benny Carlson and Mats Lundahl, *Från Värmland till Washington: Episoder ur IUI:s historia*. Stockholm: Samhällsförlaget, 2020.

References

Bremer, Fredrika (1983), *Hemmen i den nya världen, del III, A*. Kalix: K/B Sterno Coordinato.

Carlson, Benny and Lundahl, Mats (2019), *Ett forskningsinstitut expanderar: IUI från 1950 till 1966*. Stockholm: Ekerlids Förlag.

Cirules, Enrique (2004), *The Mafia in Havana: A Caribbean Mob Story*. Melbourne and New York: Ocean Press.

English, T. J. (2008), *Havana Nocturne: How the Mafia Owned Cuba—And Then Lost It to the Revolution*. New York: William Morrow.

Myrdal, Gunnar (1943), *Amerika mitt i världen*. Stockholm: Kooperativa förbundets bokförlag.

Myrdal, Gunnar (1944), *Varning för fredsoptimism*. Stockholm: Albert Bonniers Förlag.

Protokoll fört vid sammanträde med styrelsen i Industriens Utredningsinstitut, fredagen den 26 juni 1947; bilaga: Redogörelse för resa till Amerika februari-maj 1947 (1947). Stockholm: Industriens Utredningsinstitut.

Protokoll fört vid sammanträde med styrelsen för Industriens Utredningsinstitut torsdagen den 15 januari 1948; bilaga 2: Förslag till undersökning angående 'Sveriges behov och resurser – 1960' (1948a). Stockholm: Industriens Utredningsinstitut.

Protokoll fört vid sammanträde med styrelsen för Industriens Utredningsinstitut tisdagen den 1 juni 1948 (1948b). Stockholm: Industriens Utredningsinstitut.

Protokoll fört vid sammanträde med styrelsen för Industriens Utredningsinstitut lördagen den 19 november 1949 (1949). Stockholm: Industriens Utredningsinstitut.

Svennilson, Ingvar (1944), 'Avvägningsproblem inom sysselsättningen efter kriget'. Annex till Betänkande den 4 oktober 1944 angående investeringspolitiken, in: SOU 1944:57, *Utredningar angående ekonomisk efterkrigsplanering*. Stockholm: Finansdepartementet.

Svennilson, Ingvar (1947a), 'Nya drag i Förenta staternas ekonomiska struktur: Risken för överproduktion', *Dagens Nyheter*, 15 October.

Svennilson, Ingvar (1947b), 'Nya drag i Förenta staternas ekonomiska struktur: Fackföreningarnas ökade inflytande', *Dagens Nyheter*, 18 October.

Svennilson, Ingvar (1947c), 'Nya drag i Förenta staternas ekonomiska struktur: Socialvård och inkomstutjämning', *Dagens Nyheter*, 21 October.

Svennilson, Ingvar (1947d), 'Nya drag i Förenta staternas ekonomiska struktur: Konjunkturpolitiska förutsättningar', *Dagens Nyheter*, 22 October.

Svennilson, Ingvar (1947e), 'Amerikas ekonomiska framtid', *Ekonomisk Tidskrift*, Vol. 49, No. 2, 167–172.

Svennilson, Ingvar (1954), *Growth and Stagnation in the European Economy*. Genève: United Nations Economic Commission for Europe.

Svennilson, Ingvar (1960), Letter to Jan Wallander, 25 February, with an Appendix: 'Besök på Cuba 12–25 februari 1960'.

Thomas, Hugh (1961), *The Spanish Civil War*. London: Eyre & Spottiswoode.

Thomas, Hugh (1971), *Cuba: The Pursuit of Freedom*. New York: Harper & Row.

CHAPTER 7

'Well, But in Those Days, Booze Was Cheap': Jan Wallander in the Värmland Forests

(with Benny Carlson)

In our book *Ett forskningsinstitut växer fram* [The Creation of a Research Institute],[1] we devote one chapter to Jan Wallander's doctoral dissertation *Flykten från skogsbygden* [The Desertion of the Woodlands].[2] The dissertation analyzes the migration currents out of and into the forest regions of Värmland in the mid-1940s. It was commissioned by the Uddeholm corporation which at the time had problems keeping its work force in the forests.

> Apparently, people did not want to continue to live in the forests as they had done for centuries. Many of them were descendants of the population of Finns who had arrived there during the time of Karl IX. But now, apparently new winds were blowing, and the company was visualizing a situation where all youths had deserted the woodlands and only old women and men were left.[3]

The logging decreased and the industry could not obtain the wood that it needed.

[1] Carlson and Lundahl (2014).

[2] Wallander (1948).

[3] Wallander (1997, p. 187).

M. Lundahl, *Twelve Figures in Swedish Economics*, Palgrave Studies in the History of Economic Thought, https://doi.org/10.1007/978-3-030-94327-1_7

Our chapter is mainly devoted to the contents of Wallander's book and to some extent also to the circumstances surrounding its creation, which he describes himself in the first volume of his autobiography.[4] At the time, we had no possibility to provide a detailed account of the field study he carried out in 1945 and 1946. That would have been to go too far.

There, however, exists a fragmentary source material which together with Wallanders written reminiscences shed light on an experience which he preserved for the rest of his life. The material consists of field notes from the interviews Jan Wallander and his close collaborator Marja Hedström, who 'led about half of this work,'[5] together with Eva Holmström and Bert Hellberg, made, not only with the forestry workers but also with company representatives and other people in three Värmland parishes: 'In the north, Norra Ny, where farmer forestry dominated, in the east, Gustav Adolf, where the company and the Church were the completely dominant owners, and then in the south, Sunnemo which represented a mixture of company and farmer forests.'[6]

The following is an 'on-the-ground' account of what Wallander, who had grown up in Valhallavägen in Stockholm, as a fresh BA got to see and experience during his time in the Klarälven valley. Hopefully, it can contribute to the picture of the young Jan Wallander, who had just been employed at the Industrial Institute for Economic and Social Research [Industriens Utredningsinstitut, IUI] and who, headlong, had been thrown into an extensive research task, and of the field environment in which he had to work, and which gave him such strong impressions.

From Valhallavägen to Risberg

Wallander's first contact with Värmland and the social reality surrounding the Uddeholm corporation was when he, together with Ingvar Svennilson and the architect Jöran Curman, who had just been hired by the company to assist with the renovation of its dwellings, traveled by train from Stockholm to Karlstad sometime in the spring of 1945.

[4] Wallander (1997).

[5] Wallander (1948, p. 11).

[6] Wallander (1997, p. 188).

When we arrived in Karlstad late at night, we were met by Nils Danielsen, and since we were in his company, we were allowed to go in the special manager trolley from Karlstad up to Uddeholm one the narrow gauge Nordmark-Klarälven railroad. The trolley had been purchased by one of his predecessors as manager, Troili, and consisted of a large automobile which had been put on train wheels. Jammed into this we rolled along the Klarälven. It was dark and the message had been sent to all trains on that line that here comes the manager, so they had to keep away. They had been backed into different side tracks with their gleaming headlights. At the stations, the stationmasters came out and saluted, dressed in uniform and black bow tie. In one place, they came up and delivered eggs and sandwiches which we were to eat during the trip. They had forgotten the salt, but that arrived at the next station. We asked somewhat vaguely who owned the land on both sides of the line and found out that with the exception of some kilometers at the beginning of the trip, where the Mölnbacka Trysil forests closed in on us, we were traveling through the domains of the Uddeholm corporation, and I had a vision of what it was like to travel with the king through his realm. For Uddeholm really was a kingdom. I cannot believe that there is any other company which so completely dominated an entire valley with power mills, railroads, forests ... pulp mills, paper mills and a number of farms. This domination went back hundreds of years.[7]

Jan Wallander moved to Värmland together with his wife Ann Charlotte at the beginning of June 1945. They would stay there for a year—a year that Wallander would never forget. In his memoirs, he writes:

When I look through my notes, it almost appears unreal that I did not spend more than a year up there, in Uddeholm. It was in June 1945 that we moved there and lodged in a gardener's house near Risberg, which was the mansion where the manager lived. And it was a year later that we packed our stuff—we had borrowed most of the furniture and other things from the company—and moved back to Stockholm. Admittedly, the time was prolonged by the fact that I was back in Uddeholm quite a lot during the spring and then came back during the fall of 1946 for a few meetings, but a year of experiences that would shape me in many ways.[8]

[7] Ibid., p. 184.

[8] Ibid., p. 185.

Jan Wallander had calculated that it would take four people to carry out the interviews (in the end 255 households and 983 persons). He attempted to employ a number of students from Stockholm College, but it did not work out the way that he had fancied. Biking around in the Värmland forests, interrogating lumberjacks and other local people was not something that the students lined up for. Some of those who came rapidly made it back to the capital. 'I, however, was lucky to make contact with Marja Hedström, a young lady who became a real mainstay in the project.'[9] In practice, Jan and Marja had to share most of the work. Jan Wallander himself carried out a couple of hundred interviews. Marja was a model of support. Reading the preserved field notes, there remains no doubt whatsoever that she was a person with both acute observation skills and an ability to perceive both the humoristic and the serious details of the sites that she visited. 'She then assisted me for a long time with all the other work on the project.'[10]

We Down Here, You Up There: The Värmland Class Society

The Uddeholm company was worried about the results of the investigation. It was evident that there was tension between the management and the forestry workers. On a meeting at Uddeholm on 6 July 1945 with what was the Committee for the Forestry Investigation [Kommittén för Skogsbygdsundersökningen] the company forest manager, Gösta Wesslén, 'a choleric man, but at the same time a person who sensed what was going on,'[11] suggested that the investigation should be carried out completely under the auspices of the IUI. Wesslén's motivation was that 'it would be easier to get in touch with the population if it was the Institute and not the Company that appeared to take the lead.' Jan Wallander was given the task of writing an 'article presentation' about the investigation for the three most important Värmland newspapers: *Värmlands Folkblad*, *Nya Wermlands-Tidningen* and *Karlstads-Tidningen*.[12]

[9] Ibid., p. 189.

[10] Ibid.

[11] Wallander (1997, p. 185).

[12] *Protokoll, fört vid sammanträde med Kommittén för Skogsbygdsundersökningen*, Uddeholm 6 July 1945.

There was widespread doubt about the quality of the forestry workers. The company had carried out a workplace investigation of its own. The result was depressing. One of the company engineers described it: You 'found that the very human material is very heterogeneous. You get a strongly skewed curve, with a long tail of no-gooders. This is a sensitive issue and has not been published.'[13] One of the foresters testified about how the company made a distinction between people and people:

> We got ... to the treatment of the workers and he openly confessed that he was biased and when I asked him if somebody who had had a bad land tract one year could have a good one next year, he answered that if he was a decent and diligent worker he could, but if he was a troublemaker, they tried to get around him.[14]

The company managers considered the lumberjacks to be stubborn. 'There is Finnish blood in the people around there; if a thought has entered their minds, they won't drop it.'[15]

The workers held quite different views. 'In Gustav Adolf there was an abyss between the company and the rest of the population.'[16] In his memoirs, Jan Wallander tells a bizarre story about how deep-seated the hatred against the company could be:

> I remember how late one evening I was interviewing a lumberjack in the glow of what was left of a candle in his cold cottage, where we tried to get some heat out of a few soaking wet pieces of wood in the stove. I had waited for about half an hour for him to return after a long day in the forest. We talked about forestry work, and he told me how hard it was. Suddenly, it flashed, and his voice became full of hatred when he related how the forester had come to him in a clearing and declared that the charcoal pile that he had built did not have the full dimensions and then had kicked it down. It was almost eerie to see him when he let his hatred flow over the forester, and I felt a bit astonished since I knew the latter to be a modest man. I had severe problems imagining that he would go into the forest and alone with this man proceed to kick down his charcoal

[13] Samtal med civilingenjör L, undated, Jan Wallander.

[14] Samtal med skogvaktare H, 22 October 1945, Jan Wallander.

[15] Samtal med jägmastare F, in: Anteckningar från Gustav Adolf, undated, Jan Wallander.

[16] Wallander (1997, p. 198).

> pile. I therefore cautiously asked whether it was really forester A. It then turned out that it was not at all about this forester but that the experience dated back to a district administrator who had served there during the first world war. But for the man in the cottage, it was so vivid that it was like it had taken place yesterday.[17]

In the spring of 1946, Jan Wallander and his assistants had gathered more or less all the primary material for the investigation. Wallander was preparing to move back to Stockholm. Before that, however, in the afternoon of 27 May, he had to go with the omnipotent Nils Danielsen to the community house [Folkets hus] in Hagfors.[18] 'On the stairs were rebellious tenants with an ombudsman from the Forestry and Log-Driving Union in Gävle as well as [the forester Sven G.] Ekman and [Gösta] Wesslén.' The situation was tense. In his memoirs, Wallander writes:

> At the time, the Uddeholm corporation was endeavoring to set up regular contracts with its forest crofters. The purpose of the contracts was to secure that the latter would put some of their labor at the disposal [of the company]. It was hence the first step toward a fixed pool of forestry workers. This met with resistance in many quarters. People were accustomed to having complete liberty and to working only to the extent that they needed to get an income.[19]

New lease agreements were to be signed by the tenants of the Uddeholm corporation, and, unlike the previous contracts, they contained a paragraph about obligation to work. The Värmland press had got the news of this and written about it in a way that the company management did not like. Danielsen struck out hard:

> With my speech I want to correct a few things and clarify others, which have been distorted in the newspaper polemic. You are one of the few worker groups who have had complete liberty in your work, the others are the free entrepreneurs, and I understand very well that you have wanted to keep this liberty to the utmost. But the modern society requires specialization both by you and me. If you demand your liberty this does simply not fit our system, the way society is built. It is absolutely necessary for us

[17] Ibid., pp. 197–198.

[18] Anteckningar från besök på Hagfors Folkets hus, 27 May 1946, Jan Wallander.

[19] Wallander (1997, p. 202).

to be able to calculate how much work we can get from you. Otherwise, we cannot make any realistic plans.

As Wallander noted, Danielsen also pointed out that 'the forestry workers don't work nearly as much as they want to believe themselves.'

The problem of the company was that it could not persuade the workforce to remain in the forests. 'We have initiated an important program of construction of new dwellings in the forests, but it makes no sense for us to do it unless we know that we can get people who live persistently in the forests. The tenant farms are a bad deal for us.' Danielsen pointed to everything that the company had done for the workers—roads, railroads, electricity and better tools—and everything that it possibly planned to do—community centers, housing loans, pensions through the company, a forestry worker school in combination with a farm worker school, leisure facilities and information about the company (if there was demand for this). Finally, he mentioned the IUI investigation about the reasons for dissatisfaction in the forest areas and the reason for the out-migration from there and asked the workers to answer the questions that they would get from the researcher honestly and straightforwardly.

Danielsen immediately received an answer, a 'straightforward' one from a toothless lumberjack, 'Mr. E' (according to Wesslén a difficult character who 'had been told to take it easy'): 'You ask why the workers desert the forests; my answer is that payment is far too bad. That is my view.' Danielsen did not agree but insinuated that the reason why they were badly paid was that they worked less than the industrial workers. The positions had been clarified and Wallander could ascertain that '[w]hen the big shots had left, the real discussion began of which position to assume.'

Wallander also relates how he participated in a meeting in the Social Democrat youth club Gustav Adolf.[20] As usual he arrived there on bicycle, around eight in the evening, pitch dark and rain. 'The meeting was scheduled to take place in a small house a bit into the forest. When I made it up the slope toward the house, I could not see any lights in the window, so I began thinking of turning back. The meeting had probably been called off.'[21] However, there were a few bikes near the road

[20] Demokratiska ungdomsklubben Gustav Adolf, 25 October 1945 at 20.00, Jan Wallander.

[21] Wallander (1997, p. 196).

so Wallander went into the small room and shook hands with everybody. Four persons had shown up, all board members of the club.

> The floor was swept, and chairs were put in front of the table of the chairman, in two rows. Time elapsed and it became clear that no more members would arrive. A general discussion of this sad fact ensued ... Above all, people deplored that no girls came—you ought to have a car to drive 'em here—the company oughta get that. Giggle. No, if there is no dancing no chicks will come. [...] Everybody was wating, the chairman moved his papers around and it became more and more obvious that there would be no meeting.

The whole thing was about to go down the drain until the discussion of Wallander's investigation began. The meeting which had begun around 8 PM continued almost until midnight. '... it was obvious ... that people nourished a very intensive hatred toward the company and a well cemented mistrust toward all its undertakings. They talked and talked but nobody dared to approach the forester, [...] Everybody was full of stories about injustices.'[22]

The views of the company varied in the Klarälven valley. There was no apprehension, but people felt that they were treated honestly, contended the vicar at Norra Ny,[23] while the municipal treasurer in Sunnemo stated that 'Here, they apparently are of the opinion that of all the companies the Uddeholm corporation is the toughest one to deal with.'[24]

In Sunnemo, Wallander heard from another informant that all the skilled forestry workers had moved out and that those who remained constituted 'the bottom part.' Many cut for a mere hundred kronor per month. The elderly were allowed to remain in the cottages, with their children, against the orders of the former manager, Troilis, and Wesslén. They got firewood and pensions from the state. They were allowed to do what they could manage. They were not suffering. At times, the municipality had to step in. No domestic crafts existed. 'The people of Värmland are not up to this, they lack business acumen.'[25]

22 Demokratiska ungdomsklubben Gustav Adolf 25 October 1945 at 20.00, Jan Wallander.

23 Interview with the vicar John Finnson, 29 May 1946, Jan Wallander.

24 Interview with Gustav Ericsson in Lid, undated, Jan Wallander.

25 Anteckningar om Sunnemo undated, Jan Wallander.

The forestry workers were critical of the work management in the woods. 'The forester has such a bad temper.' 'The forester is so difficult that you can hardly imagine it. He is bad-tempered and he never has time.' 'The forest rangers never come to see us. They are busy with the moose hunt.' 'The work management is bad. It is impossible to complain—then they answer that you can go home. It is the way it is because they demand that you creep.' 'The regime is too hard. Just brutality and sacking.' 'The leadership is not the best. I do not think that the intentions of the forest ranger are always the best.'[26]

On the Ground

The field notes of Wallander and his collaborators testify about how the four biked around in the Klarälven valley, on sometimes close to inexistent roads, in parts that sometimes were hardly inhabited and where you could not see anything in the evening. The farms were often found in rough terrain: 'The road there is deplorable. The surroundings, however, are very beautiful.'[27] 'The road there was pretty bad ... Rather difficult to move around in the dark, slippery across the fields and not a trace of light.'[28] 'A fantastic slope that can at least not be negotiated by generator gas cars, frozen and hellish.'[29]

It was probably good that Jan Wallander was forced to make a large number of interviews himself. Thereby, he made direct contact with the people in the forest, contacts that he would hardly have got if his original plan, to use students, had worked:

> It meant that I sat down with a cross section of the inhabitants in the three parishes and met young and old, foresters, people receiving social assistance, confident big farmers and retarded jailbirds, caird women and blossoming farmer's daughters, vicars and truck drivers, Pelle in the kiosk and Kalle in the store. Had to sit there and slowly and gently tray to get out of them what their lives had been like. We also touched their relations

26 Yttranden om arbetsledningen i skogen, Gustav Adolf, undated, Jan Wallander.

27 Interview no. 261, 27 September1945, Bert Hellberg.

28 Interview no. 331, undated, Jan Wallander.

29 Interview no. 336, undated, Jan Wallander.

> to other family members, to the company, to the farmers, to the other paupers in the old folks' homes.[30]

In the preserved field notes considerable interest is devoted to descriptions of what it looked like outside and inside the homes where the interviews were made. The circumstances differed widely. Some people made the best of their situation with small means. Eva Holmström visited a blacksmith family:

> The house was nicely furnished and well kept [...] Nice and functional furniture. Nicely furnished kitchen with good workbenches and cupboards. Beautiful flowers, clean curtains and windows. Nice cloths [lysdukar] on the table and clean cooking utensils. [...] As far as I can understand, the family is living in small economic circumstances, but it gave the impression of being satisfied with its lot.[31]

Sometimes, it was almost idyllic, in spite of the fact that it was in September and that the best season was over:

> [The house] was a bit above the lake on the other side of the road with a surrounding view. Neighboring cottages were seen at some distance. We went up the grass slope, passing a patch with parsley and some cauliflowers left. A black cat with a big, bushy tail was sitting on top of a few stakes. The barn was found a bit before the dwelling house and the road in between was full of clay because of all the rain—unsuitable for low-heeled shoes. There was also an apple tree and some flowers, which had, however lost most of their splendor.[32]

The appearance was deceptive, however. Wallander and his company entered the cottage. 'A rather fat woman with a cloth around her head and the black hair sprawling in all directions under it was standing in the middle of the floor in a rather plucky position and with an uninviting expression. [...] She was not a grateful interviewee. Her life was as uneventful as that of a fish in an aquarium and her views were mainly characterized by "don't know".' The eighteen-year-old girl of the family was no better. 'A hump-backed, thin girl who rather looked down and

[30] Wallander (1997, p. 191).

[31] Interview no. 168, 26 September 1945, Eva Holmström.

[32] Inteview no. 204, 24 September 1945, Jan Wallander.

sat with her hands clasped between her legs. Sublime. It was even more difficult to get anything out of her than out of her mother—it was impossible to extract from her any view of what she wanted to be. Full stop. Her mother tried to push, but in vain.' In the end, however, Wallander managed to extract a clear view on one point. 'The main problem for ... [her mother] seemed to be the water issue. The spring, as she called it, was a helluva way from there and you just had to carry the water all the way,' at least 125 meters.

Sometimes, interiors that were probably quite a bit above the expectations emerged[33]:

> Everything was perfect in the home. The floors shiny and well entertained with varnish: the furniture neatly placed and well-polished with nice covers against sun and dust. In the windows there were plenty of beautiful flowers in shining pots. The curtains were bright, light and beautifully draped. The family had a well-endowed bookshelf with works by both domestic and foreign authors. These books were not so-called circle books or cheap editions. The family must have bought every book because of its interest in the contents. I was also invited to 'coffee with dip' [where you dip your cake in the coffee]. The coffee was served from a tray with a beautifully embroidered tray cloth and in real Rosenthal cups with a small napkin between the cup and the saucer. Very neat. The cake and the cookies as well bore testimony to imagination and ability to create a cozy atmosphere.

In spite of what you may think, the household was not a bourgeois household, but a farmer household, however probably a relatively wealthy one, with a genuine interest in social issues.

> I met both spouses and they were very interested in economic and political issues and everything indicated that they were well updated. Among other things they knew a lot about post-war planning in America and exports and imports. One issue that they also appeared to want to discuss was state monopolies, gasoline restrictions, oil monopolies and other economic questions.

Other situations were characterized by utter destitution, People who would have needed help from the social authorities were left to their own devices:

[33] Interview no. 170, 26 September 1945, Eva Holmström.

> Situated a bit into the forest /some 20 minutes' walk from the nearest neighbors/ Only a very small patch where potatoes were grown. [...] The dwelling was very dirty and ill kept. The barn was neglected, so the family did not even know whether the roof would make it through the winter. Inside the barn it was incredibly dirty, in spite of the fact that at present there was only a single pig. The walls certainly had never been whitewashed and the floor offered clear traces of cows. The kitchen floor was incredibly dirty, the dishes were found on a chair, and it smelled of dirty clothes, filth, dust and leftover food.
>
> Mrs P greeted me very meekly and then sat down on a chair and kicked off he shoes, whereupon a pair of torn stockings and dirty feet became visible. Awful. ... Mrs P wore a ragged skirt provisionally patched together with safety pins. On her head she wore a less than clean woolen scarf, which had been pulled down across the forehead. Everything was incredibly filthy and neglected. Did not see a single complete object.
>
> Mrs P was very confused. She did not even know when her children were born or what they were called ... One thing that she was, however, able to point out was how expensive everything was and what a bad job the municipality did taking care of its poor. [...] Mrs P just smiled foolishly when I asked something.[34]

In a radio talk during the summer after his visit to Värmland, Jan Wallander reflected about what was actually hidden behind the statistical poverty indicators:

> What first strikes you when you do a job like this is how immensely difficult it is to imagine how other people fare before you have seen it with your own eyes. My profession for example consists in keeping track of the calorie supply per head in Sweden and where the undernourishment limit is found and how many percent of the Värmland households have more than 5 person units per room unit. But it was not until I one evening arrived in a cottage and saw how the school children were given soup made on water and overcooked potatoes and how two adults and three children went to bed in a tiny, tiny kitchen that I understood what different figures may mean.[35]

Some dwellings were incredibly small.[36]

[34] Interview no. 143, 29 July 1945, Eva Holmström.

[35] Wallander (1997, p. 192).

[36] Interview no. 217, 5 October 1945, Marja Hedström.

> The cottage is no bigger than a playhouse, grey from wind and weather and patched with roof paper on the exterior walls. A couple of unstable wooden steps lead to the green front door which opens toward the outside, so that you almost fall of the stairs again. For there is no room for the door to swing! [...] I knocked ... and went into a kitchen that was no larger than 2 x 1½ [sic] at most. A stove, a table with food that had not been touched, 3 chairs, a bench for preparation under a cupboard, a shelf, an alarm clock and a few flower pots was more or less all there was. A rug on the floor too, the rest a board floor with masonite on top.

In this household, there were two adults and two small children, a boy of 4 or 5 and a baby. The cottage has a tiny bedroom. 'The room was no ... bigger than the kitchen, a table in the middle and two ... ottomans and a baby crib and a couple of chairs. *Where* did all the people sleep? There was no radio, nor any sewing machine—where would there be room for them anyway?' The housewife was a mere 21 years old and had a bad reputation in the neighborhood, as I had been told indirectly, since she was no more than 17, 'unmarried of course,' and the husband had been forced to marry her. 'That's the way things are and the neighborhood pities him. [...] He looked a bit like a fool (forgive me), I thought.' The place breathed loneliness and the man seemed to be longing to leave.

In other instances, the composition of the family was strange[37]:

> I stepped into the kitchen ... and there was the family, 6 men and 1 old woman (frump, I would say), eating. The space around the table was crowded, the old woman, Mrs L herself, actually was sitting at a table nearby [...] The men stared but continued to eat (the knives in their mouths) and when I went around greeting them, they rose one by one and said: L. The last time I almost said: I could have guessed that.

Higher Up

On a higher social echelon you found the bourgeoisie, in general, and the clergymen. The merchant C pointed to the destructive consequences of both modern dancing and rationalization. 'Look at me, take it easy

[37] Interview no. 219, 28 and 30 September 1945, Marja Hedström.

instead.' Wallander characterized him as 'bourgeois and conservative—not too bright.' Still, he was nice and well-meaning. He even offered a drink.[38]

The manager of the cooperative store lived, as often, on the second floor, in a two-room apartment which seemed 'very modern.'[39] 'It conveyed the appearance of opulence and coziness,' with a flower table with a trellis and an oil painting on the wall, books—'Vackra vita tänder [Beautiful White Teeth] among others,' conversation dictionaries, novel series and literature about cooperative stores, about sales techniques. 'Mrs G had gold rings in her ears and *somewhat* too short skirts.' The spouses 'looked so warmly at each other and laughed that nobody could believe that they had been married for 8 years!' Marja and Bert were made to sign their names in a guest book with green leather.

And then, Jan Wallander met the men of the Church. On one occasion he had coffee with the parson, 'a particularly unpleasant figure, boasting, dirty, greasy, the sweatband full of sweat. Fat and glutton.'[40] It was much better in the home of the non-conformist preacher.[41] Bert Hellberg and Marja went into the kitchen. Neat and clean, decorated with flowers, landscape photographs, a tapestry with a weeping birches and simple 'pictures' with religious motives and a crucifix, in the simple home which lacked water and drain, welcomed by an 'angelic appearance,' the twenty-four-year-old wife of the preacher. She had gone to junior secondary school, he—the son of a farmer from Jämtland—had attended folk high school and four years of preacher education, having skipped one year, 'probably gifted.' They were, 'in short sympathetic people who very diligently answered the questions without misunderstanding … The wife then offered coffee (3 cups).'

On 29 May, Wallander interviewed the vicar of Norra Ny, John Finnson.[42] He describes him as cheerful, nice and helpful, very vivacious—a man who was always in a hurry. He got the impression that the vicar had good contact with the population. He also had a well-thought-out view of the out-migration. According to the vicar, the latter was

[38] Talt with the merchant C, undated, Jan Wallander.

[39] Interview no. 226, 25 September 1945, Marja Hedström.

[40] Interview with the vicar John Finnson, 29 May 1946, Jan Wallander.

[41] Interview no. 220, 25 September 1945, Bert Hellberg.

[42] Interview with the vicar John Finnson, 29 May 1946, Jan Wallander.

no problem, but the number of inhabitants remained relatively constant. Those who left did not at all go to Hagfors, as you might believe, but to other rural areas in Värmland, to Malung or to Stockholm. They wanted to keep their freedom and therefore did not make the transfer to the industrial sector. It was not easy to make it into the latter unless you came from one of the company's 'own' parishes. The sons in general stayed at home, far too much according to the vicar. It resulted in too many subdivisions of the farms.

During bad years when there was no logging, the farmers cut back their expenditure and lived on the money they had put in the bank. Those who were only forestry workers, however, were in dire straits, but they were not many, mainly from Månäs and Ambjörnby. The daughters, often very well-to-do, however, left for Stockholm during the winter to work as housekeepers, 'in order to get around and get to know the world.' Often, they returned home in the summer. The parish displayed a female deficit, but there were a number of girls who you could marry and there were many oldish boys and girls who did not get around to marrying. They were perhaps engaged since many years. Often, they had extra-marital children. No fresh winds were blowing across the parish. The women were extremely important for the recruitment of forestry workers. 'The women are tired of slavery, and it really is slavery, and without women there will be no men.'[43]

A contributing factor to the out-migration of the girls, according to the interviewees, appeared to be the lack of amusement in the Klarälven valley. The communications with Hagfors were bad. In order to go to the cinema there, you had to take a taxi home. If you were from Uvanå and wanted to go to the cinema in Gustavsfors, the car (taxi) was also the solution. If you were a few people it was three kronor 'per head.'[44] 'Sometimes they dance in the Barn in Uvanå. Else, we have the religious zealots who keep all the youth away from the dance floor.'

Jan Wallander drew his own conclusions. 'All amusement events are under the control of the district police superintendent ... On another

[43] Forester F., in: Anteckningar från Gustav Adolf (1945).

[44] Intervju nr 303, undated, Jan Wallander.

occasion, I got the impression that the only purpose of the permission is to facilitate the proper collection of the amusement tax.'[45]

The middle group also contained small capitalists. Bert Hellberg got to meet a caramel maker.[46] Her home had a piano and armchairs, a mixture of old and new furniture, 'relatively expensive but boring.' The caramel maker was '24 years younger than her husband. She appeared to be pushy, bossy and somewhat grumbling. Complained about the injustice in this world. Had declared 3,000 kronor's income from making caramels but was taxed for 6,000. Pure theft. You lose your desire to work.' The husband was timider, naturally enough, since he did not earn so much money, but was dependent on his wife who had paid for the renovation of the house and the furniture.

At the Top

At the top of the social hierarchy was the Company. The stamp of the Uddeholm corporation was found everywhere. Uddeholm 'was a small community which was completely dominated by the main office of the company,' wrote Wallander.[47] 'The order was well established there.'[48]

> When I was there in the mid-40s there were only two people outside the company, even though these two also were dependent. One was the district physician who had his office and infirmary in a building close to the main office, and the other one a merchant who ran the store in the locality. For a sociologically curious person it was interesting to study the distinct social order which existed in this place and which rested on the position of the man in the company hierarchy.[49]

At times, the social hierarchy became virtually Byzantine—completely unintelligible for uninitiated:

[45] *Protokoll fört vid sammanträde med bygdekommittén för Gustav Adolfs socken, i Gustavsfors Folkets Hus, den 20 sept* [1945] *klockan 11.*

[46] Intervju nr 233, 29 september 1945, Bert Hellberg.

[47] Wallander (1997, p. 198).

[48] Ibid., p. 199.

[49] Ibid., p. 198.

When in the morning I went to the office with somebody from Uddeholm, the latter noted that the dinner jackets were hanging here and there in the gardens The manager had had a party last night. He had not been invited himself, but that was natural for obviously Karlsson had not been invited either. The line had been drawn higher up. That Fornander and Wikmark and Halle and Gustafsson had been there was self-evident. On the other hand, he asked himself, why had Klintemalm been invited? His dinner jacket was obviously hanging outside his house. This led to plenty of pondering and speculation. After a while, together we arrived at the solution. Wasn't it the case that one of Klintemalms' daughters had married a mining engineer from some company in Skåne and had the manager and his wife not been at the wedding? The reason for that was probably that Mrs Danielsen was a good friend of Mrs Klintemalm's. In their youth they had attended the same school. [...] After having found the key to the mystery we once more felt easy.[50]

At the very top of the social hierarchy the managing director of Uddeholm was found—Nils Danielsen.

The company charter at that time stipulated that the chief executive officer was entitled to be called bruksdisponent [managing director]. I only had a vague idea of what the title implied when I was sitting in the trolley, but later I found out that in the world order of the Swedish forestry industry of course God had the highest rank, but right below you had the real managing directors [bruksdisponenter]. Then it was quite jump until you came to the mining engineers and then—a great deal further down—[middle level] managers, foresters etc.[51]

Poor Marja in Sunnemo stumbled across a real prig of a lower-level forester [forstmästare].[52] She did not do anything to hide her antipathy:

I had already beforehand heard that this forester V was not a real forester, but I still thought that he would be a bit more educated than what he was. [...] Then, he finally arrived. Dark, shiny, not too skinny and with his gold teeth exposed in a greasy smile. I smiled back and introduced myself and

[50] Ibid., pp. 198–99. *Forstmästare* was the title of a person with a lower-level degree from the Forestry Institute [Skogsinstitutet] and its successor, The College of Forestry [Skogshögskolan].

[51] Ibid., p. 184.

[52] Interview no. 277, undated, Marja Hedström.

then nicely accompanied him into the upstairs hallway, where we sat down in armchairs. I preferred to sit decently but he threw himself delightfully into the chair so his head ended up at the bottom and the rest of the body described an upward curve all the way to his knees, where the curve was suddenly interrupted in a sharp angle and went directly into the floor.

I still smiled, looked around and was about to begin after a chilly breath when he began. 'He he, it was such a funny letter that I received the other day, it was formulated in such a strange way, he he …'— 'He he … he he…' 'So you received it?', I said to show my sympathy. 'Yes, wait …' /he fetched the letter/. 'Here you see, Miss … he he … it says: the undersigned members have formed a committee … you see, Miss?' Yes, I saw, but understood nothing, just continued to smile. […] In every conceivable way he tried to convey what an important person he was in the parish and how badly managed the latter was by Social Democrats and Communists. […] He also wanted to get out how well liked and influential his father had been and how large land tracts he had owned … he bragged and beamed of self-satisfaction from the depth of his chair for about 45 minutes, until all the superlatives about his and his family's contributions to the best of the parish began to thin. Worst of all, at any rate was the tax. He and his wife could not stay in the same place because then the tax became so high, but she had to register and live in Filipstad, where at present she was a teacher—but of course she did not have to, contended the miser.

On the whole he did not seem to be very trustworthy—everything he said was an attitude, designed to impress. When he sensed that the effect of it was rather minimal, he had to resort to another means to assert himself. This he did by saying that he did not want to answer most of the questions … to make himself great again he asked me want kind of education I had for this. I told him as much as I thought was his concern and almost asked him with what right he called himself a forester … I began feeling sick just looking at the man and hence wanted the whole thing to come to an end. He seemed to realize this so at last, he expressed a desire that if Mr Wallander wrote a dissertation about this it would be sent to him so he 'could erase a few things in the margin', as he expressed it. He he. And it was really interesting to discuss this with you, Miss—if he had not been so incredibly short of time he would have liked to write a statement himself expressing all his valuable points of view /which?/ but it was impossible to do so at present. And I was welcome back again if I wanted to talk more. But he was hardly ever at home.—It was never as nice to make it back into the fresh air again. Brr.

The interviewers at times had to accept to be regarded as ignorant. 'But you must understand why people move away from the countryside without having to ask.'[53] Often, however, the atmosphere became quite nice and cordial during the interviews.'Just above the ferry landing on the western side of the lake was the cottage of the blacksmith P O, by the road without any farms around.'[54] The blacksmith, who was a bit deaf, asked Marja to accompany him into the kitchen where dough was fermenting.

The old man was talkative and told a bit about times past, he had run the ferry alone then—now there were two who took turns, and you could cross at any time of the day. He was very vital for his age, but hardly made it beyond the strait. He had not biked for the past 11 years, has had got a telephone and did not have to go anywhere. A few people from the ferry came to talk and he had to be content with that. In order to make the long winter pass, he subscribed to Dagens Nyheter. Then his wife arrived. She was round and happy and had just fetched the mail. 'Vi' and 'Karlstadstidningen'. When asked about the forest, the old man thought that things were quite OK now, in comparison not before, and had no objections at all. He became eager when he talked and crept closer and closer to me across the table. [...] They wanted me to stay longer because it was so nice to have somebody visiting, but I had to go on.

Jan Wallander's own place in the Värmland pecking order was undefined, naturally enough, since he was an outsider and was doing something that differed very much from what the company people were doing. 'Such exotic animals as bachelors of arts were outside the world order.'[55] It, however, didn't work too long. The outsider had to be put in somewhere.

[53] Interview no. 258, 26 September 1945, Bert Hellberg.

[54] Interview no. 216, 28 september 1945, Marja Hedström.

[55] Wallander (1997, p. 184).

> When I arrived in Uddeholm, I must have been put somewhere between the foresters and the forest rangers. I had an academic degree. But it was way down the hierarchy. When the family had arrived and we had settled down near the Risberg mansion—where the managing director lived—it became known that Mrs Danielson had been seen in our kitchen on several occasions, and obviously had busied herself with drinking coffee and talking to Ann Charlotte. I was now rapidly moved up the scale and ended up somewhere between foresters and mining engineers. This had the valuable effect of making it easier for me to access paper and pens and other office material and get assistance to borrow typewriters.[56]

The Elderly

At the bottom of the Värmland social ladder were the old and the poor. In his memoirs, Wallander describes what it looked like in one of the old folks' homes in the community. The Swedish welfare society had quite a bit left:

> The visit to the old folks' home stuck. In those days, the inmates were still 'paupers' who lived on what the municipality provided, and they were a mixture of poor and feeble elderly who in some cases were heavily senile and confused. There were also some retarded children. To sit down and interview the people who constituted our sample and who could take part in an interview was a shocking experience, when at the same time, the elderly who were sitting nearby had problems taking care of themselves and spread filth around themselves.[57]

It was difficult for the elderly as well. Family ties often played a decisive role for whether they fared bad or not. 'When my daughter-in-law moves away from here, how will I fare? If I could get an opportunity to get to a town and sit by the roadside some day before I die. An old person like me cannot take care of herself.'[58] In his memoirs, Wallander related how in one household the four daughters time after time moved back and forth between Stockholm and their native parish. It appeared incomprehensible

[56] Ibid., p. 199.

[57] Ibid., pp. 191–192.

[58] Interview no. 315, undated, Jan Wallander.

until he got to know the reason. 'All the unmarried girls had to take turns, coming home to care for their parents, one year at the time.'[59]

Sometimes, everyday tragedies took place:

> The old man did not feel like slaughtering. The day when I was there, he had prepared himself and gone to the forest district office to cut up a moose, and this was obviously a great moment for him. He was the only one in the neighborhood who knew how to do it. But then he became so exhausted by the excitement and the bike trip that he couldn't do it. When push came to shove he was forced to return home, which he resented very much.[60]

Some managed without any help at all. Marja Hedström met three old people in Gustav Adolf[61]:

> I knocked and went into a very large kitchen, the largest one I think that I have ever seen. In this kitchen, there was a rather old and rather hump-backed old man in blue denim. He did not seem to be doing anything. At the large table by one of the windows sat a rather old woman, busy with something. I presented my business but had to scream a few times, because I discovered that they were pretty deaf: soon after me another old woman arrived with—if I am not mistaken—firewood in her arms. She seemed a bit strange and sat down in the far corner of the kitchen. [...]
>
> I began the interview and, in spite of everything, things went rather well. The old man was the one who had the best hearing, and it was also he who most of the time answered the questions. The woman who came in and sat down in the corner turned out to be blind, so you must say that it was a fairly typical household in the present situation: three elderly, one deaf, one blind and one a bit of each. In addition, the old man had broken his leg a while ago and had not quite recovered yet. But according to another source, he is supposed to have a poetic vocation which from time to time he has demonstrated in Husmodern, and he is known to know history both back and forth, in spite of his advanced age. Nobody beats him at that. [...] I remain surprised by the fact that these three, with one foot in the grave can keep this homestead going [with four cows and two heifers]. [...] But the people in Gustava appear to manage and stand quite a lot, as a matter of routine'. And that is good for them.

[59] Interview no. 335, undated, Jan Wallander.

[60] Ibid.

[61] Interview no. 3101 [sic!], 24 oktober 1945, Marja Hedström.

Marja Hedström also interviewed a single—a unique—woman in Gumhöjden in the parish of Gustav Adolf[62]:

What a charming woman! [...] Most of her dress was made from a mattress cover and on top of that she wore a much shorter black skirt that was mainly held up by safety pins. A checkered blouse with a short sleeve was worn under the sleeveless mattress cover dress and on her head, she had a loosely crocheted cap over her blond sprawling chunks of hair. Sublime. The elbows protruded like those of a Belsen woman, but in spite of that she seemed to be in good shape.

Inside the house, Marja was met by a cat colony.

When I entered the tabernacle, some ten ragged cats slid down from chairs, boxes and tables unto the floor and out the door, ... The floor was a common board floor with a couple of rug stumps—and a half-eaten rat. The cats obviously had been taken by surprise. E picked up the rest of the rat and went out to throw it away on the ground. ... This looked juicy. [...] On a window table there was a kind of strange-colored blanket, designed for the cats. E later told that she had made it from the wool of an American woolen cat that she had once had. But now she only had regular Swedish farm cats, and hardly that. One cat was even blind. But don't believe for a minute that she was willing to part with a single one even though she had been offered a piece of pork for one of them. [...]

And she spoke of the mountain people who lived here in Gustava when her ancestors arrived from Finland four generations ago and settled in Gustavsfors. Those mountain people were no real trolls, but they were certainly not easy to handle. You had to be very careful, so you didn't get into trouble. [...]

E knows and does everything herself. She had made a carriage from two wheels connected by a wire and two wood plugs and a tray on top of them—it didn't bother her that the wheels described more or less deformed eights when she pulled the carriage behind her. And she plows, hoes and sows and harvests all by herself—you have to forgive her that she does not always fid the time to clean inside, since she is working all day long, [...]

There is no way that she wants to the old folks' home—she was so happy with what she had and did not want to exchange with anybody even though she is probably worse off than anyone else in all of Gustava.

62 Interview no. 380, undated, Marja Hedström.

Possibly her stance was rational. A pensioner testified that at home you had to follow certain routines and turn out the light at a set hour. You were admonished for bad table manners, the cleanliness requirements were stern, the food was strange and there were no facilities for offering coffee to visiting relatives.[63]

Others were more than eager to make it to the pensioners' home. The solitude was heavy, especially for those who once upon a time had led an active life in the middle of a family. In his radio talk, Jan Wallander told of an elderly woman who lived completely alone, without and family and without any close neighbors.

> It was ... a small cottage, beautifully situated on a tip on a lake and when I walked across the meadow, I saw a bent little old woman who was on her way to the well to get water, [...] Her husband had been a forestry worker there all his life, but he was long since dead. The children had left the home and worked in the cities, but they sent her money, so she managed well. She was now eighty-four years old and healthy under the circumstances. It was of course difficult for somebody that old to fetch water and manage the household, but she had been used to doing that all her life. So she had never thought of the possibility that this might be something to complain about. Still, she led a rather boring life and had had to experience something that all experience when they get old but which you feel especially strongly when your life is so lonely as hers. After all, the nearest store and post office was five kilometers away and one kilometer to the nearest neighbor. She thought herself that it was a bit isolated, especially in the winter when the snow made it difficult for her to get around and maybe they did not always keep track of how she actually managed. Therefore, she wanted to make it into a pensioners' home that they were now building in the parish. She had talked to a local politician who was involved in this, and he had promised that he would put her on the admission list.[64]

As time went by, the dream of the pensioners' home had turned into an obsession and at the same time the old woman had become paralyzed:

> She had heard that there were only a few places left and that you should have filed a written application in order to have any chance at all. Maybe

[63] Samtal med M ang, pensionärshemmet m.m., undated, Jan Wallander.

[64] Wallander (1997, p. 194).

> that local politician had forgotten everything. She had not heard anything from him and now so much time had elapsed since she talked to him that he ought to have left a message. Besides, she had heard that the home would soon be ready and that some people had learned that they would move in. [...] Somebody had said that only married couples would be admitted there, but it must certainly be the case that such a lonely and old person as she would be admitted. [...] She had lost contact with reality. To talk to that local politician on the phone was almost inconceivable. [...] She had completely lost the ability to straighten out the issue. [...] She sat there pondering it forever and the possibility of doing anything about is became ever more remote.[65]

Thank God, it turned out that the old lady's worries were unfounded. The local politician had done his homework and turned in her application. She was admitted to the home.

Maybe some other people should have been there too. 'Regardless of what you asked about, the old man just said, well, but in those days, booze was cheap.'[66]

* * *

The Uddeholm corporation stressed that it provided both jobs and housing to the population. The forestry workers could rent small cottages from the company, cottages that needed maintenance. Electricity and water were installed and roads were built. The company considered that it provided enough. Some workers thought that they received too little and that they had to wait far too long to get anything done. (Others thought that the treatment was fair.) The situation was not simple. Nils Danielsen had realized that mere rationalization of the work was not enough if the Uddeholm corporation wanted to provide sufficient quantities of wood. The issue also concerned the living conditions. If the forestry workers did not feel happy, they and their families would leave the forest.[67]

This was exactly what they did. They left forestry for other professions. It was not strange that people turned their back on the forest. The interviews that Wallander and his collaborators carried out, and the circumstances they describe leave a lasting impression of tristesse. In

[65] Ibid., pp. 194–195.

[66] Interview no. 345, undated, Jan Wallander.

[67] Carlson and Lundahl (2014, p. 348).

Flykten från skogsbygden, he speaks of 'the frequently isolated situation, way into the forests, stores, schools, diversions far away, bad dwellings and barns, etc. especially for the women is certain to stimulate out-migration from the parish or movement to more favorably situated parts.'[68] It was mainly the young who left, women between 20 and 25 and men between 25 and 30. The women moved more frequently than the men, especially those that were not married.

The men moved mainly to change professions. 'The reason why you do not want to work in the forest is partly that you consider that it gives a too low and too uncertain income, partly that you don't like the work and the working conditions.'[69] Forestry work was hard, it did not provide full-time employment and the atmosphere in the workplace was not always the best, at times tense. What was regarded as a good performance varied according to where you were on the social ladder.

In the Klarälven valley, the young bachelor of arts Jan Wallander from Valhallavägen in Stockholm was thrown into a microcosmos, a world *sui generis*, controlled by the omnipotent Uddeholm corporation. It was a strictly hierarchic world, where everybody knew his place, a world where those up there looked down on those down there and those down there frequently held a grudge against those up there.

The Klarälven valley was a pronounced class society, permeated by old-fashioned patriarchalism—for better or for worse—where those up there demanded obedience from those down there, who they mainly regarded as labor.

Wallander was not completely unprepared. His family had mingled with Social Democrats—the Myrdals, Gustav Möller and Else Kleen, Alf Johansson—and Jan's father had built the cooperative housing movement. But these Social Democrats belonged to the top echelon. In the Klarälven valley, the young Jan got to meet the foot soldiers—the real working class—literally in their home environment, daily, for a year. This left traces for the rest of his life. Did it possibly contribute to the creation of Oktogonen, which gave the employees of Handelsbanken, where Jan was the managing director, a share in the profits, twenty-eight years later?

[68] Wallander (1948, p. 232).

[69] Ibid.

Swedish version published in Benny Carlson and Mats Lundahl, *Från Värmland till Washington: Episoder ur IUI:s historia*. Stockholm: Samhällsförlaget, 2020.

References

The field notes that we refer to are available at the Centre for Business History [Centrum för Näringslivshistoria] in Bromma, Arkiv 1:1, Institutet för Näringslivsforskning, Serie F1 ai:2, 'Intervjuer' and ai:6, 'Diverse anteckningar.' We refer to them more or less under the headings found on the different documents.

Carlson, Benny and Lundahl, Mats (2014), *Ett forskningsinstitut växer fram: IUI från grundläggandet till 1950*. Stockholm: Ekerlids Förlag.

Wallander, Jan (1948), *Flykten från skogsbygden: En undersökning i Klarälvsdalen*. Stockholm: Industriens Utredningsinstitut.

Wallander, Jan (1997), *Livet som det blev: En bankdirektör blir till*. Stockholm: Albert Bonniers Förlag.

CHAPTER 8

'Like Locusts on the Mississippi': A Pioneer Study of the Expansion of the Swedish Public Sector

(with Benny Carlson)

The 1962 doctoral dissertation of *Den offentliga sektorns expansion* [The Expansion the Public Sector], by the Swedish economist Erik Höök, triggered a lively debate both within academia and in the media in Sweden. The perspective employed in the thesis rested on consumption theory, which implied that the public sector was viewed as a large firm whose activities were governed by the needs (demand) of the citizens and not by the (supply) ambitions of politicians. The dissertation received praise from leading economists, such as Erik Lundberg and Ingvar Svennilson, and was often labeled a valuable standard work of financial statistics. Most observers and debaters, however, thought that Höök's demand perspective was too one-sided. It was almost fatalistic and could hence be compared to Wagner's law or even Marx' fated theory. Even if the demand for, e.g. health care and education increased inexorably with wealth, it was not in any way given that this demand must be satisfied exclusively by the public sector.

The purpose of the present essay is to shed some light on Höök's work because, even though it was widely debated in Sweden in its day, it hardly stirred the international attention that might have been expected given the strong interest in the rest of the world in 'the People's Home [folkhemmet],' 'the middle way' or 'the Swedish model.' Why was Höök's dissertation written? How was it received in the press and in the

M. Lundahl, *Twelve Figures in Swedish Economics*,
Palgrave Studies in the History of Economic Thought,
https://doi.org/10.1007/978-3-030-94327-1_8

academic community, during the defense of the thesis, in reviews and in expert statements? What role has it played in the longer run in the discussions about the expanding Swedish welfare state? And what on earth has the discussion of locusts adrift with currents in the Mississippi to do with it?

Background Facts

Erik Höök (1920–1997) studied political science, practical philosophy and economics at Uppsala University, worked between 1948 and 1962 at the Institute for Economic and Social Research [Industriens Utredningsinstitut—IUI] in Stockholm, a research institute financed by the Swedish Employers' Confederation and the Federation of Swedish Industries, and, in 1962, defended his thesis on the public sector—a result of a five-year research project at this institute. After his thesis defense, he became head of the planning section at the Ministry of Finance, with responsibility for the long-term planning, the roots of which were to be found in the long-term program, for the years 1947 to 1952/53,[1] which had been elaborated under the leadership of Ingvar Svennilson during his period as head of the IUI. Thereafter, during 1976–1985, he was the managing director of Jernkontoret.

At the beginning of the 1950s, Höök worked at the IUI with questions which to some extent ought to have served as a preparation for his thesis work, questions regarding the development of consumption and the service sector as well as the influence of the state on the private sector. During the latter half of the 1950s and the beginning of the 1960s, he raised problems of child allowances, taxes, pensions and the size of the public sector in a comparative perspective. In a number of articles, he sternly rebuked the politicians, while at the same time he was optimistic with respect to the possibilities of increasing the productivity of public service production,[2] a question we will soon return to.

Plans for an investigation about the expansion of the public sector are mentioned for the first time in the minutes of the IUI board in the fall of 1957.[3] In the annual report for 1957, the stated purpose is to provide

[1] SOU 1948: 45.

[2] See, e.g. Höök (1960a), (1960b).

[3] *Protokoll* (1957, p. 1).

a statistical account of the expansion during the inter- and postwar years, to clarify in which areas the expansion had been most pronounced and to analyze the factors behind it.[4] Special attention was to be paid to the question of to what extent the demand for public service was affected by price and income factors and to the study of productivity issues. In addition, the expansion of the public sector was to be studied with the aid of theories about the shift away from primary sectors toward service sectors.

During 1958, the investigation was carried out according to plan. In the spring, Höök went to the United States to study the subject.[5] He examined different theories about shifts in the division of labor between different sectors as real incomes increase.[6] During 1959, statistical information was assembled from public budgets.[7] The following year, different expenditure items were analyzed: the judiciary, health care, social care and education. The 1960 annual report provided a glimpse of expenditure on the elementary school and the report for 1961 a glance at expenditure on the road network.[8]

For a few days during the spring of 1960, Höök's name bounced around in the Swedish press. The journalist Åke Ortmark had begun a series of radio programs about power factors in society. On 16 May, the theme was 'the immense public sector,' with the participation of Prime Minister Tage Erlander, Finance Minister Gunnar Sträng and the leaders of the bourgeois parties. The Social Democrat newspaper *Ny Tid* reported from this debate.[9] Erlander had declared that the expansion also in the future had to take place at the pace demanded by the citizens. He received unexpected support from Höök, 'who least of all turned out to be a propagandist for the Right.'

> The rest of the program became a strange duet between ... Höök and Finance Minister Sträng, who, point by point, turned out to share the same views. For example, both declared that it was the development of

[4] IUI (1958, p. 22).

[5] *Protokoll* (1958), *Promemoria* (1959).

[6] IUI (1959, p. 26).

[7] IUI (1960, pp. 18–19).

[8] IUI (1961, pp. 26–28), IUI (1962a, pp. 29– 39).

[9] H.W. (1960)

events over time that had led to the heavy expansion of the public sector. [...] And then it ended with both Mr. Höök and the Finance Minister forecasting a continued expansion of the public sector.

Productivity and Cost Disease

Höök early on paid attention to the development of productivity in the service sector. An interesting question is hence how he related to the explanation of the expansion of the public sector known as Baumol's Cost Disease. This explanation argues that productivity in, for example, cultural activities and education cannot be increased the way it can be in the industrial sector (a piece of classical music does not become better if you play it twice as fast, a teacher does not become more intelligible if he talks twice as fast) but the wages in these sectors must increase *pari passu* with industrial wages if you want to recruit musicians and teachers. The share of these sectors in GDP thereby grows. Höök could of course not relate specifically to Baumol's Cost Disease, since the latter was not formulated until the mid-1960s.[10] He did, however, relate to—and played down—the importance of this phenomenon. In a 1956 debate about the rising cost of white-collar workers he explained:

> The experience hitherto has provided several examples of how capital has been substituted for white-collar work, of how rationalization and mechanization have cheapened services. Through the automatic telephone, the need for telephone operators has been reduced, through radio, television and movies, the services of actors and musicians have become cheaper per listener ... Also in the service domain we must envisage that in the future ever stronger efforts will be made to rationalize and cheapen the work ... Why could not education be made more efficient, why should not the work of development and time study engineers and others be more efficient?[11]

Another contribution was made by Höök in 1961, following a lecture by Ingvar Svennilson at the Swedish Economic Association [Nationalekonomiska Föreningen] on education and economic policy. Svennilson argued that the cost of education as a share of GDP would

[10] Baumol and Bowen (1966). For an introduction to Baumol's Disease, see, e.g. Heilbrun (2003).

[11] Höök (1956, pp. 336 –337).

increase and named this tendency the 'Iron Law of Costs' of education,[12] and wrote it as a formula on the blackboard.

> The foundation of this 'law' is that wages dominate the cost of education and that the possibilities of labor-saving rationalization in this area are probably relatively limited. [...] Something similar appears to be true for other service branches in the public sector, among others, health care [...] My forecast therefore is that in the future, in the same way as hitherto, we must reckon that 'public consumption' will increase faster than GDP, i.e. amount to an ever larger share of the latter.[13]

Svennilson's 'Iron Law of Costs' appears to be identical with (and formulated before) Baumol's 'Cost Disease.' Höök was not convinced:

> I am of the opinion that in this context you must take into account the problem of teacher productivity [increase]. You can probably not take it for granted that it will always be zero. Professor Svennilson's formula implies that—to push the thing to its extreme—when we have all become doctors of technology, we will get a considerable deterioration in productivity. The pace of progress according to this formula is to a large extent determined by the substitution of more educated for less educated labor. When we have reached the point where no more such substitution is possible, production gains will by and large cease. Drawing out the consequences of this, in the end you get a situation where the productivity increase tends towards zero.[14]

Höök continued by contending that productivity had increased in the educational system and that it could continue to do so. He found it incontrovertible that the scientific progress that was being made must facilitate the acquisition of knowledge.

> If you deny this, I don't know where you will end up. Such discoveries as the earth being round, why the apple falls and the behavior of sound waves must indeed have facilitated the understanding of the surrounding world

[12] In the first issue of the year of ***Ekonomisk Tidskrift***, Svennilson had published an article on the same theme: Svennilson (1961). He did not, however, introduce the notion of the 'Iron Law of Costs' in this article.

[13] Nationalekonomiska Föreningen (1961, pp. 37–38).

[14] Ibid., p. 54.

> and the learning of facts. I hence think that there is some kind of productivity in this area and that you should not envisage a productivity [increase] that is always equal to zero. I thus hold a somewhat more optimistic view than Professor Svennilson on this point. Then, when it comes to teacher productivity as such, I also think that progress within pedagogy etc. has made it easier for a teacher to convey a certain measure of knowledge than was the case in 1913. This is, however, simply a belief. As far as I have been able to find, no clear information is available on this point.[15]

Svennilson contended that his Iron Law was 'pure mathematics' and his only objection to Höök's argument about the rising level of knowledge and pedagogical progress was a general statement: 'But I don't think that what ... Höök has demonstrated contradicts the idea that there is something in this "law" as a long-run tendency.'[16]

Doctoral Dissertation

In 1962, Höök's work on the public sector was ready as a doctoral dissertation: *Den offentliga sektorns expansion: En studie av de offentliga civila utgifternas utveckling 1913–1958* [The Expansion of the Public Sector: A Study of the Development of Public Civilian Expenditure 1913–1958].[17] In his introduction, Höök stressed that he had wanted to shed light on a forecasting problem but that it was hardly possible to 'arrive at a determination of determinants and relations in such numerically precise form as is needed for a balanced forecast.' Hence, the study should be seen as a 'preliminary study of the forecasting problem.' Höök also underlined that his 'line of attack' was well anchored in mainstream economic theory. 'More concretely, the approach to the analysis of the development of national and municipal expenditure used in the present work implies that the same schema of explanation that is being applied to shifts between firms and branches may also be applied to a discussion of the growth of the public sector.'[18] Höök explained that his economic approach was inspired by

[15] Ibid., p. 55.

[16] Ibid., p. 62.

[17] A very concise summary of the dissertation is available in Höök (1962b). The following year, the IUI published a 50-page pamphlet that summarized Höök's thesis. See *Offentliga utgifter 1913–58* (1963).

[18] Höök (1962a, p. 15).

what he had learned from his colleagues during his IUI years: Ragnar Bentzel's consumption studies, Erik Dahmén's views of the problems of transformation and Erik Ruist's productivity studies. Höök had also had the opportunity to discuss his work with his teacher from Uppsala, Erik Lindahl, and at seminars led by Bent Hansen, where he had received comments from Kurt Eklöf, Ulrich Herz and Assar Lindbeck. In the final stage he had obtained good advice from Erik Lundberg.[19]

So the ambition was to apply 'a traditional consumption theoretical approach,' but for some expenditure categories this was not possible, because some items had 'a pretty pronounced ambition to direct the market.'[20] This was true, e.g. for subsidies of housing and agriculture. The expenditure of public utilities and the military had not been included.

Höök concluded that public consumption expenditure (as a percentage of total civilian consumption expenditure) had increased at an even pace in most areas during the period under investigation. However, consumption expenditure on education and health had increased faster during the 1940s and 1950s than during the earlier part of the period. Some social transfers had increased heavily between 1946 and 1948: old-age pensions and child allowance.

The elements of the growth of public expenditure discussed by Höök were the following: expenditure complementary to private demand, transfer of expenditure from the private to the public sector and expenditure dependent on income and price changes. The complementary expenditures were those of road services and public services linked to private demand for different consumption and production services. The transfer of expenditure had taken place above all in social care and to some extent education, e.g. school meals and health care. The increased expenditure on education and health care could, however, to a very large extent be related to income increases in society.

Höök did not rule out that a transfer of expenditure from the private to the public sector could be motivated by political and ideological factors, but his ambition was to study economic, and not political, explanations of the expansion of the public sector. In his thesis he made some international comparisons. He found that the expansion of the public sector in Sweden was in the middle range in a European context. In Sweden, social

[19] Ibid., p. 18.

[20] Ibid., p. 386.

transfers and investments in publicly owned companies were smaller than in most other countries but public consumption was larger than in any other country. Public expenditure had grown at an even pace in Sweden, whereas Great Britain and the United Stated displayed a stepwise increase. In his international outlook and in the concluding discussion of the dissertation, Höök therefore brought up the theory of displacement effects launched around this time by Alan Peacock and Jack Wiseman.[21] This theory states that the resistance toward taxation weakens during periods of war and crisis, and that taxes and expenditures, once the crises are over, do not fall back to their previous level. The increasing tax revenues are instead used for other kinds of expenditure than military spending or crisis management. Since Höök had found that public expenditure in Sweden had increased at an even pace, he argued that the displacement effect theory was not applicable there. He also argued that the resistance to taxation in Sweden had been weakened by the tax system itself. 'Through progressive taxation, the public sector has received increased tax revenues at given tax rates, through the ongoing income increases in society. Thereby, room had automatically been made for an even expansion of the public sector.'[22]

In his dissertation, Höök also demonstrated his optimistic view of the development of productivity in the public sector: 'It is not completely improbable that the typewriter and the telephone are the individual phenomena that have had the strongest influence on the development of productivity in the public sector.'[23]

The Thesis Defense

Höök's dissertation was discussed in public at Stockholm University on 1 December 1962. During the defense, PhD Göran Ohlin acted as faculty

[21] Peacock and Wiseman (1961).

[22] Höök (1962a, p. 405).

[23] Ibid., p. 129. When Höök left the IUI in 1962 he was given a *festschrift* with contributions from the friends at the institute. His colleague Lars Kritz made the following comment with respect to the quotation about typewriters and telephones: 'We now understand better why business executives have at least three telephones on their desks. It furthers the productivity of the firm. But why are they still always impossible to reach?' (IUI, 1962b, p. 46).

opponent[24] and Ulrich Hertz[25] and Insurance Director Bror-Johan Lindgren were the two opponents selected by the respondent. Among the audience were Gunnar Myrdal, Erik Lundberg and the head of the Swedish Employers' Confederation, Bertil Kugelberg. According to the newspaper reports, the discussion was lively. Ohlin attacked Höök's thesis that was the demand of the citizens for public services, and not politically driven supply, that governs the expansion of public expenditure, an attack that in *Dagens Nyheter* was reported as follows:

> Don't you as a rule do the complete opposite? wondered Dr. Ohlin. Would for example the subsidies to agriculture be an expression of the 'preferences' of the majority of the voters? By clinging to his 'consumption theory' the author ends up in the most bizarre and misleading ideas about harmony in society ... Surely the politicians change the 'preferences' of the citizens—steer their demand—through political decisions that are perhaps arrived at with a slight majority. By disregarding this, taking no notice of political factors, the author in fact reveals a hidden ideology.[26]

In order to drive home his point, Ohlin employed a fanciful metaphor. He argued that politicians according to the view propagated in Höök's thesis could be compared to kicking locusts drifting down the Mississippi, thinking that they are good swimmers. Höök, however, bit back. The actions of the politicians might perhaps be of short run, but not long run, importance. All you had to do was to look at how differently the health care system was organized in Sweden, Britain and the United States, while at the same time expenditure on health care had developed uniformly in the three countries.

The second opponent, Ulrich Hertz, seconded Ohlin and called Höök's theory 'the most ludicrous, not to say dilettantish hypothesis.' Carsten Welinder, professor of financial law and financial science, opposed *ex auditorio* and wondered whether the political battle that had been raging about social insurance was simply a misunderstanding. He pointed out that public expenditure remained constant in the 1920s,

[24] Ohlin had got his PhD at Harvard in 1956 and had thereafter worked at Stanford, Columbia and Yale before returning to Sweden in 1962, to the Institute for International Economic Studies at Stockholm University.

[25] Hertz was a hard-working author and debater, who in the 1930s had fled Nazism and arrived in Sweden.

[26] *Dagens Nyheter* (1962a).

when governments were weak, but began to grow in the 1930s, when governments grew stronger.

In spite of their sharp criticism of the fact that Höök had applied only a demand perspective, the opponents underlined that the dissertation constituted a valuable contribution in an essential field and that it was an 'extremely valuable standard work in financial statistics' and that in addition the author was one of the 'socially most educated persons in the country.'

The thesis committee consisted of the economics professors Erik Lundberg and Ingvar Svennilson and in addition of David Hannerberg and Åke Hultkrantz, professors of geography and history of religions, respectively. The evaluation of the thesis was authored by Lundberg and Svennilson. They found that Höök had solved a 'very qualified problem ... reliably and with good judgment.' 'In this sense, the dissertation has become a standard work which the researchers in the area will have occasion to return to.' They also noticed that Höök had worked with laudable caution but called for 'a somewhat greater audacity in the statistical analysis.'[27] Exactly like Ohlin, they directed their criticism against Höök's one-sided consumption theoretical point of departure:

> As his point of departure he has chosen the so-called interest principle, whose content has been interpreted to mean that the public consumption exactly like the private one is determined by the preferences of the citizens. [...] The decisions with respect to public expenditure, [however], are the result of a complicated political process where the connection between the demand of the citizens for public services and the actual development of the latter is not clear-cut. [...] The only point of reference that he uses is private consumption, instead of inserting the development into a general context of politics, economics and financial policy. The suffrage reform at the beginning of the period and the shifts between the political parties from Höök's point of view stand out as insignificant and have fallen out of the picture.[28]

In their final comparison of flaws and merits, Lundberg and Svennilson found that the thesis was a good scientific contribution that ought to be rewarded with *cum laude*, which it also was.

[27] *Protokoll* (1962, pp. 1–2).

[28] Ibid., pp. 2–3.

The Reception in the Press

The medial reaction to Höök's dissertation was extensive. Only a few days after the defense, a telegram from TT News Agency had already been published in twenty newspapers,[29] where the causes of increased public expenditure were concisely summarized in three points. First, the latter is complementary to private expenditure, like expenditure on roads linked to the expansion of motoring. Second, transfers have taken place from the private to the public sector, as in the case of the introduction of free school meals. The third explanation refers to price and income changes in society; when incomes increase or the price of public services declines, more health care, education, etc. is demanded.

In connection with the defense, Höök's message was debated on the editorial pages in several national dailies and some ten local provincial newspapers. The editorial in the evening newspaper *Expressen*, published on the day of the defense, was wholly positive.[30] The dissertation was seen as valuable both because of its thorough statistical account of public expenditure and because of its attempt to analyze their development. The editorial of the leading Liberal daily, *Dagens Nyheter*, dealt with Göran Ohlin's criticism:

> In the approach chosen by Höök, political factors remain almost completely outside the picture of the development of society. [...] The opposition offered during the act of defense circled around this theme from the beginning to the end and many examples were brought forward of the unreasonableness of viewing the expansion of the public sector simply as an expression of 'preferences' of the citizens.

After these remarks, the editorial writer turned in another direction and explained that the criticism did not at all mean that Höök was wrong. The dissertation was of practical and political interest. 'It lends support to politicians who attempt to get beyond the old cliché way of thinking that every increase of "the public sector" in general is a manifestation of socialism [...].'[31]

[29] See, e.g. *Svenska Dagbladet* (1962).

[30] *Expressen* (1962).

[31] *Dagens Nyheter* (1962b).

While Höök was well received in Liberal newspapers, the Social Democratic *Aftonbladet* sang a much more critical tune:

> The work is usually called a standard work in financial statistics [...] On the other hand, Höök's main thesis, that the expansion of the public sector can be regarded as completely 'apolitical' and that it can be explained in terms of consumption theory—buyer preferences, income changes and price sensitivity—is criticized. It also seems correct that Höök has pushed his effort at such a purely economic explanation, within the framework of some, perhaps unconscious, ideological harmony theory, across the border of the ludicrous.

The editorial writer pointed to the Swedish ATP (General Supplementary Pension) reform as an example of how the labor movement had managed to create an understanding of the needs which 'of course had existed earlier but had not been recognized in any "consumption theoretic action patterns".'[32]

Höök's dissertation was also dealt with by Carsten Welinder, who had acted as opponent *ex auditorio*, in *Stockholms-Tidningen*. He pointed out that the dissertation constituted 'our first standard work of financial statistics' but raised certain objections. He contended that the world wars had been more important than Höök had admitted, since the public then became accustomed to higher taxes (the displacement effect). He also thought that Höök 'aims too low' regarding the question of the importance of political developments. The democratic breakthrough had increased expenditure on purposes of importance for the vast majority, during the weak governments in the 1920s public civilian consumption expenditure did not increase its share of total consumption, but in the 1930s, things took a different turn.[33]

The dissertation was discussed in several Conservative and Social Democratic provincial newspapers. Let us begin with the former. An editorial published in several newspapers objected to the view that the expansion was based on an increased living standard, with arguments that resembled those that John Kenneth Galbraith used to employ against private company advertising:

[32] *Aftonbladet* (1962).

[33] Welinder (1962).

> Politically, a new idea is born which holds that the public sector should intervene in some way in some sector. The propaganda builds up the idea and creates a demand among the citizens. Thereafter, the project is carried out and a few years later it is contended that it was actually we ourselves who demanded more public services.[34]

Another editorial pointed out that if you uncritically accepted Höök's causal chain, 'less responsible politicians will all too easily be able to motivate new demands for expenditure in the future.' 'Let us shift this private expenditure item to the municipality or the state and pay collectively—for we will have to pay anyway, they will say.'[35]

In the Social Democratic *Kuriren*, it was suggested that Höök had seen the light: '... there is a lot to indicate that science will put ever more people onto tracks that old man Marx once upon a time pointed out. You will soon hardly be surprised at the fact that searching scientists become socialists without even reflecting over it.'[36] *Ny Tid* was more critical and argued that Höök had underrated the role of politics and other forces. 'But there is one thing about which there cannot be any division of opinion: that it was the Social Democratic policy that was attuned to the demands raised by the development [of society], whereas the bourgeois one endeavored to act as a brake for as long as it was possible.'[37] An editorial published in Social Democratic provincial newspapers interpreted Höök's conclusions as not leaving 'any support whatsoever to the conservative view that it would be possible to stop or even reduce the increase of public expenditure.'[38]

The Reception in Professional Journals

In the first 1963 issue of *Ekonomisk Tidskrift*, a long review article by Göran Ohlin was published, based on his opposition at Höök's defense. Ohlin found it

[34] See, e.g. Håpe (1962).

[35] See, e.g. *Norrbottens-Kuriren* (1962).

[36] E-n (1962).

[37] Howard (1962).

[38] See, e.g. *Värmlands Folkblad* (1962).

surprising that Höök had chosen to push the parallelism between the economic analysis of the private and public sectors [so] untenably far. His investigation is meant to be a companion piece to Bentzel's earlier studies of the development of private consumption, where it was, however, stated that public consumption had been left out precisely because it had to be studied with the aid of other methods, as a result of a political process and not of private market decisions. [...] Anybody who is wondering about the character of the public economy must soon realize that it is impossible to explain why you have a public sector at all if you don't realize how it differs from the private one.[39]

Ohlin also reacted against the fact that Höök had used the interest principle as a theoretical cornerstone of his investigation and 'even had been audacious enough to turn this normative theory into something that it was never meant to be, namely an explanation of reality.' Instead of pondering the questions that arose in this context, 'the author majestically brushes away the troubles that he inflicted on himself when he opened the Pandora's box which the interest principle amounts to in the present context.'[40] A central question was what happens when different individuals' demands are in conflict with each other:

About that question the author does not say a word, but rather expresses himself as if in our political life we had realized the consensus principle that Wicksell discussed on an abstract level or as if we made parliamentary decisions by common vote, as in a Quaker meeting or in the Asian village councils that anthropologists report about.[41]

Thereafter, Ohlin stated the metaphor about the locusts on the Mississippi whose acquaintance we have already made. There are, however, good reasons for quoting it *in extenso*. Ohlin contended that according to Höök,

the political activity, in spite of all the noise and din that it gives rise to, simply serves to discover and realize the demands that are already alive in the breasts of the citizens. Our politicians are hence the victims of an illusion if they believe that their initiatives and their willingness to change

[39] Ohlin (1963, p. 4).

[40] Ibid., p. 5.

[41] Ibid., p. 6.

> society mean anything at all. Henry Adams once described American presidents who through the power of circumstances had been driven to great and fateful decisions and likened them to locusts drifting down the Mississippi river and who through their lively kicking convince themselves that they are superior swimmers. This is how the political life appears to be in Höök's interpretation of the management of our public sector.[42]

Altogether, Ohlin argued that Höök would have been 'better able to judge the development of the public sector as an historical phenomenon' if he had not chosen to combine 'his massive documentary contribution with such a peculiar theoretical apparatus.'[43]

The reviewer of *Industriförbundets Tidskrift* dwelt mainly on the arguments that had been discussed during the defense. Ohlin had among other things stated that the interest principle of taxation (which means that the preferences of the individuals decide the level of public spending), represented above all by Erik Lindahl, 'had been hovering like a lost soul' over the dissertation. The reviewer, however, liked Höök's spirit: 'The cliché-ridden thinking which constitutes a patent risk when it comes to the public sector and its dependence on political decisions have been made to give way to a more nuanced description of this ever more important part of our economy.'[44]

The journal of the Taxpayers' Union [Skattebetalarnas förening], *Sunt Förnuft*, also took issue with Höök's use of the interest principle and the idea that the development of public expenditure is independent of how you choose to register people's wishes and of how this expenditure is financed. In a rich and democratic country like Switzerland, popular referendums were held about public spending policy. 'It appears likely that it is precisely this which to a large extent has decided that Switzerland has a relatively limited public sector and such low taxes.' The article was headed 'Fate Theory' and it opposed the view that the development of the public sector 'would be determined by a few factors which could not be influenced and that we must expect a continuation along the same path.'[45]

[42] Ibid., p. 7.

[43] Ibid., p. 11.

[44] Grafström (1963, p. 18).

[45] H.S. (1963, pp. 4–5).

An article in *Industria*, the journal of the Federation of Swedish Industries, began with a question: 'Is Gunnar Sträng of any use to humankind?' According to Höök, the answer was negative, since the Minister of Finance by and large did not influence anything. The author of the article finished by arguing that there was 'a certain relation not only between the preferences of the citizens and the development of the public sector but also between the preferences and the political constellation.'[46]

Finanstidningen found that Höök 'shuts his eyes for or conjures away the fundamental difference between "public" and "collective".'

> However, the fact that the need for, say, education or health care or means of communication, must be satisfied collectively does not mean that they must be satisfied by society. Höök does not say that, but he remarkably easily bypasses the crucial issue, namely the question: couldn't a great deal of these collective needs be satisfied equally well through other forms of cooperation than the public sector? And is it not politics that has decided the choice between the alternative forms?

In spite of this and other objections, the journal 'in no way wanted to hide that through this dissertation we have acquired an almost inexhaustible, exemplary reliable in its factual details and extremely useful summary of most of what is worth knowing about the development of the public sector in our country since the first world war.'[47]

The Social Democratic *Aktuellt i politik och samhälle*, on the other hand, had no quarrel with Höök's analysis. Increased economic resources ought to be used for improvements 'where the shoe pinches most [...] Then undoubtedly the public sector will increase.' That there were still politicians who wanted to shrink the sector was astonishing. But they would draw the shortest straw. 'Surely, in spite of them, the institutions of society will bring about the necessary increase in activity and effectivity. The opposite would imply stagnation, retrogression, lowered standards.'[48]

[46] *Industria* (1963, p. 16).

[47] *Finanstidningen* (1963, p. 33).

[48] Hallbeck (1963, p. 9).

When the statistician Olof Lindahl reviewed Höök's thesis, he noted that the public sector was treated as a giant corporation 'whose activities are governed by the same laws as private business.'[49] He paid special attention to Höök's demonstration that a substantial increase in productivity had occurred place in the public sector. 'Not least for those who regard the public administration as a petrified and sterile bureaucracy, the endeavors to tailor activities to contemporary demands makes useful reading.'[50]

Höök also received attention in some reviews in foreign journals. *Ekonomiska Samfundets Tidskrift* (Finland) stated that countries like West Germany, France and Great Britain, which during the 1950s had been ruled by bourgeois parties, had larger public sectors than Sweden. Hence there was no 'reliable correlation between thirty years of Social Democratic Government and an expanding sector' in Sweden.[51] The reviewer of *Nationaløkonomisk Tidsskrift* (Denmark) wanted an investigation which dealt not only with governmental and municipal expenditure but also with, e.g. health and unemployment insurance and generally speaking called for a less schematic investigation of the vast statistical material which 'would lay the foundations for a more nuanced view of the growth of the public sector than the one expressed in the book.'[52]

Last but not least, Höök's book was reviewed in the *American Economic Review*. The reviewer, Edward Marcus from Brooklyn College, was especially interested in the effects of differences in productivity development between the private and the public sector.[53]

Expert Statements

In 1972, a chair in labor market policy was advertised at the Swedish Institute for Social Research in Stockholm. Erik Höök was one of the applicants, competing with, among others, Gösta Rehn, Ingemar Ståhl, Bo Södersten and Lars Söderström. The position went to Rehn. The expert committee consisted of the Danish professor of labor market policy

[49] Lindahl (1963, p. 178).

[50] Ibid., p. 180.

[51] Melin (1963, p. 276).

[52] Korsbæk (1964, p. 211).

[53] Marcus (1963).

Bent Rold Andersen and the Swedish economists Erik Lundberg and Lars Werin. Their statements give an idea about how Höök's dissertation was regarded at the time.

Andersen describes Höök up to the doctoral dissertation as 'an investigator as busy as an ant' who had produced both empirical results and theoretical reflections.[54] Höök's work was solid, of the type that tidied up the public debate. It was theroretically well-founded but not terribly original or scientifically innovative: a very extensive, cautious and sometimes astute analysis of the existing empirical data. Andersen, however, objected that Höök had pointed only to economic explanations. When he, for example, explained the transfer of social security solutions from the private to the public sector by increased mobility, which made it necessary to move tasks from smaller (e.g. the family) to larger units, it was not clear why it was precisely the public sector that had to shoulder the burden. Andersen concluded that Höök was a very productive researcher with great knowledge of the Swedish society, business community and labor market but that his work lacked scientific stringency and penetrating analytical ability. Andersen concluded that Höök was hardly qualified for a chair in economics, but that he was, though not wholly unequivocally, qualified for the advertised chair in labor market policy.

Lundberg called Höök's dissertation 'a very impressive work':

> This work very clearly shows Höök's critical mind and good judgment when it comes to the processing of statistical sources with varied content [that run] over long periods and presenting the material in a clear and pedagogical way. […] It should be stressed that Höök is in no way a 'simple' empiricist who collects and processes statistical material for the use of other researchers. Actually, his text abounds with hypotheses of all kinds about possible relations, frequently with imaginative speculations.[55]

According to Lundberg, Höök's way of working called to mind no less a person than Simon Kuznets. Lundberg thought, however, that he had pushed his consumption theoretical approach too far. Höök had overlooked factors such as the role of politicians as intermediaries, conflicts between different interests and the fact that taxes cannot be perceived only as prices in demand functions.

[54] Andersen (1972, p. 4).

[55] Lundberg (1972, pp. 5–6).

In his conclusion, Lundberg declared that Höök was not a theoretician who used refined analytical methods or produced contributions to economic theory. He did, however, possess 'a balanced judgment, a well-developed talent for critical scrutiny of statistical material, a good feeling for rewarding problems and adequate analytical methods, an interest in historical development and institutional change.'[56] Lundberg hence deemed Höök qualified for a chair in both economics and labor market policy.

Werin emphasized that he was less critical of Höök's consumption theoretical approach than many other observers. He provided an exegesis about Erik Lindahl's ideas about the interest principle of taxation and concluded that if Höök had only used a somewhat different terminology his reasoning would have stood up relatively well; 'it should be possible largely to eliminate its blemishes from the theoretical point of view, simply by changing the wording.' Werin's verdict about the dissertation was that it had some flaws when it came to the theoretical approach and that it was sometimes characterized by excessive caution, but that the merits—'a broad, knowledgeable and stimulating mapping and explanation of the trends in the development of the public sector'—clearly outweighed the flaws.[57] Werin declared Höök qualified both for the chair in labor market policy and for a chair in economics.

The Long-Run Impact

In Henrik Jordahl's words, Höök's dissertation implied 'that the IUI for a while was leading in Sweden in research on the public sector.'[58] Höök's colleagues at the institute have subsequently defended his demand-based explanation. Thus, Jan Wallander, the former (1953–1965) head of the institute, states:

> In his extensive investigation of the expansion of the public sector ... Erik Höök demonstrated that the expansion was essentially connected with the demands that derive from an increased standard of living. The increase leads to a greater need for such things as education, health care, social

56 Ibid., p. 9.

57 Werin (1972, pp. 9–10).

58 Jordahl (2009, p. 485).

care etc. In our country this in most cases was handled by public institutions. The difference between developments in Sweden and, for example, America was actually very small, even though private institutions dominated in the US. This was a bitter pill to swallow, so much the more, since the investigation attracted great attention and the author was linked to Gunnar Sträng's Ministry of Finance.[59]

Lars Lidén argues along similar lines:

Contrary to what some people may have thought—and the political debaters maybe had hoped for—it [the dissertation] did not become a polemical pamphlet. Instead, Erik Höök calmly and matter-of-factly demonstrated how he viewed the connections. An important part of the growth of the public sector, he claimed, was due to the fact that the government, the county councils [landsting] and the municipalities provided the kind of services—e.g. health care and education—the demand for which increased when incomes increased.[60]

In 1974, a group of economic historians in Uppsala began a large project about the causes of the expansion of the public sector in Sweden. The project was led by Bo Gustafsson and resulted in four doctoral dissertations.[61] When Gustafsson summarized the project, he began by referring on the one hand to Peacock and Wiseman and on the other hand to Höök's 'massive investigation': 'With his detailed and systematic description of the growth of different kinds of public expenditure, this study is probably still unsurpassed in the international literature.'[62]

One of the dissertations that sprang from the project was Anders Forsman's *En teori om staten och de offentliga utgifterna* [A Theory of the State and Public Expenditure], which argued that the function of the state is to preserve capitalist society.[63] When the economist Lars Söderström reviewed this dissertation, he compared Forsman's Marxist and

59 Wallander (2009, p. 86).

60 Lidén (2009, pp. 254–255).

61 Forsman (1980) wrote about public expenditure, Rodriguez (1980) about public revenue, Waara (1980) about public enterprise and Wickman (1980) about macroeconomic planning.

62 Gustafsson (1983, p. 11).

63 Forsman (1980).

Höök's consumption theoretical analyses, and got to within a step or two of Ohlin's locust metaphor:

> What characterizes Forsman's theory is that it does not attach any decisive importance to the political game for the expansion of the public sector. In this theory, the citizens/politicians are puppets under the direction of some 'invisible hand' that governs the development. This is an interesting idea, but it is not completely new. The same idea is in fact found in Erik Höök's dissertation of 1962, which is the only important Swedish work in the area. However, in Höök's theory, the invisible hand performs a different task. [...] In his view, the public sector is a conglomerate of companies that grow in competition with the firms in the private sector and the household units. Ultimately, the issue is how to produce goods and services in order to satisfy the demand of the public for comfort, safety and other things that yield satisfaction [...] This is a consumption theoretical approach. Exactly like Forsman, Höök provides no room for purely political considerations. He does not even provide any space for the traditional market forces (profit maximization, etc.), but the 'companies' in the public sector in some inexplicable way are made always to accommodate supply to current demand.[64]

In his book *Den offentliga revolutionen* [The Public Revolution], the political scientist Daniel Tarschys accordingly placed Höök's dissertation in the demand-oriented tradition:

> Toward the end of the nineteenth century, the German economist Adolph Wagner launched the thesis that the public sector would increase successively in all developed societies. 'Wagner's Law' became the point of departure for an extensive debate about this growth. Expansion patterns in different countries began to be studied. The leading Swedish contribution to this research is Erik Höök's study of the development of civil public consumption from 1913 to 1958.[65]

Which role did Höök's dissertation play in the longer run? The general impression you get while browsing the literature on the public sector from

[64] Söderström (1981, p. 248).

[65] Tarschys (1983, p. 38).

the late twentieth century is that Höök's figures were occasionally used—but not that he was used as a battering ram in the ideological battles over the welfare state.[66]

Concluding Remarks

Erik Höök's dissertation about the expansion of the public sector originated as a project at the Institute for Economic and Social Research (IUI) and it bore the imprint of the 'consumption theoretical' approach that had been employed there in a number of previous studies. The dissertation triggered a lively discussion in the Swedish press. Bourgeois newspapers took exception to Höök's main idea: that the expansion of the public sector was a more or less inevitable consequence of the general development of society. Social Democratic newspapers, in turn, found that Höök's thesis pulled the rug out from under the feet of the bourgeois politicians but did not want to view the development of the public sector as automatic, since Social Democratic politicians would then not be able to credit themselves for a number of reforms.

Höök's dissertation was a pioneering work in a field that would become ideologically ever more infected, and hence eagerly researched, during the following decades. The criticism that he had to contend with during the defense and in subsequent reviews and academic expert statements—that he almost exclusively viewed the expansion of public expenditure from the demand side and that the politicians therefore stood out as helplessly kicking locusts in an irresistible current—probably would have appeared as even more warranted if he had carried out his work one or two decades later. During the 1960s and the 1970s, a number of explanations of the expansion of the public sector were advanced by the public choice school which viewed the phenomenon from the supply side and concentrated on the vested interests of politicians and bureaucrats and the political orientation of governments. James Buchanan divided the explanations of the expansion of the public sector into responsive (demand-driven) and excessive (supply-driven) government.[67] In the

[66] See, e.g. Henrekson (1990, 1992, 1994), Herlitz (1989), Ringqvist (1996) and Uddhammar (1993). In some other works about the public sector, Höök is not mentioned at all. See, e.g. Fölster (1990), who does not goes no further back in time than to 1960, and Krantz (1987).

[67] Buchanan (1977).

words of Söderström, Buchanans point of view stands 'in bright contrast to Höök's assumption of a mainly harmonic relation between the citizens and the representatives of the public sector.'[68] When Höök carried out his work, Sweden was only at the beginning of the strong expansion of the public sector that would characterize the 1960s and 1970s and which meant that Sweden would differ from most other Western countries. As things turned out, his dissertation attracted much attention in the short run but was largely forgotten in the long run.

Published in *Statsvetenskaplig Tidskrift/Scandinavian Political Studies*, Vol. 122, No. 2, 161– 182, 2020. Reprinted by permission.

References

Aftonbladet (1962), 'Har politikerna inget att betyda?', 4 December.

Andersen, Bent Rold (1972), Yttrande vid tillsättning av professur i arbetsmarknadspolitik vid Institutet för social forskning (Archive of Stockholm University).

Baumol, William J. and Bowen, William G. (1966), *Performing Arts: The Economic Dilemma*. New York: Twentieth Century Fund.

Buchanan, James (1977), 'Why Does Government Grow?', in: Thomas Borcherding (ed), *Budgets and Bureaucrats*. Durham, NC: Duke University Press.

Dagens Nyheter (1962a), 'Doktorsdisputation: Politikerna gräshoppor som tror de kan simma', 2 December.

Dagens Nyheter (1962b), 'Ofantlig sektor?', 3 December.

E-n, F. (1962), 'Så sakteligt', *Kuriren*, 3 December.

Expressen (1962), 'Den offentliga sektorn', 1 December.

Finanstidningen (1963), 'Den offentliga sektorn', Vol. 41, No. 3, 30, 32–33.

Forsman, Anders (1980), *En teori om staten och de offentliga utgifterna*. Uppsala: Uppsala Studies in Economic History.

Fölster, Stefan (1990), *Den offentliga sektorn*. Bilaga 26 till Långtidsutredningen 1990. Stockholm: Allmänna Förlaget.

Grafström, Lennart (1963), 'Höök och den offentliga sektorn', *Industriförbundets Tidskrift*, Vol. 1, No.1, 16–18.

Gustafsson, Bo (1983), 'The Causes of the Expansion of the Public Sector in Sweden during the 20th Century', *Uppsala Papers in Economic History*. Uppsala: Department of Economic History.

[68] Söderström (1981, p. 250).

Hallbeck, Oscar (1963), 'Den offentliga sektorn synas', *Aktuellt i politik och samhälle*, No. 10, 8–9.
Håpe (1962), 'I kanten', *Smålands Allehanda*, 28 December.
Heilbrun, James (2003), 'Baumol's Cost Disease', in: Ruth Towse (ed.), *A Handbook of Cultural Economics*. Cheltenham and Northampton, MA: Edward Elgar.
Henrekson, Magnus (1990), *An Economic Analysis of Swedish Government Expenditure*. Stockholm: Fackföreningsrörelsens Institut för Ekonomisk Forskning.
Henrekson, Magnus (1992), 'Vad förklarar den offentliga sektorns utveckling', in: Bo Södersten, Bo (ed.), *Den offentliga sektorn*. Stockholm: SNS Förlag.
Henrekson, Magnus (1994) *Offentlig sektor och ekonomisk tillväxt*. Stockholm: FIEF Working Paper. Stockholm: Fackföreningsrörelsens Institut för Ekonomisk Forskning.
Herlitz, Urban (1989), *Om den offentliga sektorns framväxt*. Lund: Studentlitteratur.
Höök, Erik (1956), 'Arbetsstudier på kontor: Tjänstemannakostnadernas stegring – framtidsperspektiv', *Affärsekonomi*, Vol. 29, No. 6, 325, 336–337.
Höök, Erik (1960a), 'Är vår offentliga sektor ofantlig? De offentliga utgifterna i internationell belysning', *Industriförbundets Meddelanden*, Vol. 33, No. 8, 349–352.
Höök, Erik (1960b), 'Välfärdsstat eller välståndsstat', in: IUI, *Industriproblem 1960*. Stockholm: Industriens Utredningsinstitut.
Höök, Erik (1962a), *Den offentliga sektorns expansion: En studie av de offentliga civila utgifternas utveckling 1913–1958*. Uppsala: Almqvist & Wiksell.
Höök, Erik (1962b), 'Den offentliga sektorns expansion', *Ekonomisk Revy*, Vol, 19, No. 10, 710–715.
Howard (1962), 'Man lär om', *Ny Tid*, 4 December.
H.S. (1963), 'Ödesteorin', *Sunt Förnuft*, Vol. 43, No. 1, 4–5.
H.W. (1960), 'Oundviklig expansion för offentlig sektor', *Ny Tid*, 17 May.
Industria (1963), 'Den ofantliga offentliga sektorn', Vol. 59, No. 2, 16.
IUI (Industriens Utredningsinstitut) (1958) *Verksamhetsåret 1957*. Stockholm: Industriens Utredningsinstitut.
IUI (Industriens Utredningsinstitut) (1959), *Verksamhetsåret 1958*. Stockholm: Industriens Utredningsinstitut.
IUI (Industriens Utredningsinstitut) (1960), *Verksamhetsåret 1959*. Stockholm: Industriens Utredningsinstitut.
IUI (Industriens Utredningsinstitut), 1961. *Verksamhetsåret 1960*. Stockholm: IUI.
IUI (Industriens Utredningsinstitut) (1962a), *Verksamhetsåret 1961*. Stockholm: Industriens Utredningsinstitut.
IUI (Industriens Utredningsinstitut) (1962b), *Festskrift till Erik Höök*. Stockholm: Industriens Utredningsinstitut.

Jordahl, Henrik (2009), 'Forskningsprogrammet tjänstesektorns ekonomi', in: Magnus Henrekson (ed.), *IFN/IUI 1939–2009: Sju decennier av forskning om ett näringsliv i utveckling*. Stockholm: Ekerlids Förlag.

Korsbæk, Helge (1964), Review of Erik Höök: *Den offentliga sektorns expansion*, *Nationaløkonomisk Tidsskrift*, Vol. 102, No. 3–4, 208–211.

Krantz, Olle (1987), *Historiska nationalräkenskaper för Sverige: Offentlig verksamhet 1800–1980*. Lund: Skrifter utgivna av Ekonomisk-historiska föreningen.

Lidén, Lars (2009), 'IUI under senare hälften av 1950-talet', in: Magnus Henrekson (ed.), *IFN/IUI 1939–2009: Sju decennier av forskning om ett näringsliv i utveckling*. Stockholm: Ekerlids Förlag.

Lindahl, Olof (1963), Review of Erik Höök, *Den offentliga sektorns expansion*, *Statistisk Tidskrift*, Third Series, Vol. 18, No. 2, 178–180.

Lundberg, Erik (1972), Yttrande vid tillsättning av professur i arbetsmarknadspolitik vid Institutet för social forskning (Archive of Stockholm University).

Marcus, Edward (1963), Review of *Den offentliga sektorns expansion*, *American Economic Review*, Vol. 53, No. 5, 1140–1142.

Melin, Ingvar S. (1963), 'Den offentliga sektorn i Sveriges ekonomi', *Ekonomiska Samfundets Tidskrift*, Vol. 16. No. 4, 273–276.

Nationalekonomiska Föreningen (1961), *Nationalekonomiska Föreningens sammanträde den 23 mars 1961. Utbildning och ekonomisk politik*. https://www.nationalekonomi.se/NEF-forhandlingar. Downloaded 23 October 2019.

Norrbottens-Kuriren (1962), 'Varför ökar statens utgifter?', 5 December.

Offentliga utgifter 1913–1958: En sammanfattning av: Den offentliga sektorns expansion, 1963. Stockholm, Göteborg, Uppsala: Almqvist & Wiksell and Industriens Utredningsinstitut.

Ohlin, Göran (1963), 'Teori och empiri i studiet av den offentliga hushållningen', *Ekonomisk Tidskrift*, Vol. 65, No. 1, 1–12.

Peacock Alan T. and Wiseman, Jack (1961) *The Growth of Public Expenditure in the United Kingdom*. Princeton, NJ and London: Princeton University Press.

Promemoria rörande institutets verksamhet den 30 maj 1958 (1959). Stockholm: Industriens Utredningsinstitut.

Protokoll fört vid sammanträde med styrelsen för Industriens utredningsinstitut på Täcka Udden fredagen den 15 november 1957 (1957). Stockholm: Industriens Utredningsinstitut.

Protokoll fört vid sammanträde med styrelsen för Industriens utredningsinstitut i Falun onsdagen den 4 juni 1958 kl. 09.30 (1958). Stockholm: Industriens Utredningsinstitut.

Protokoll hållet vid sammanträde med Stockholms universitets historisk-filosofiska sektion den 4 december 1962 (1962). Ärende 6, bilaga 61. Archive of Stockholm University.

Ringqvist, Margareta (1996), *Om den offentliga sektorn: Vad den ger och vad den tar*. Stockholm: Fritzes.

Rodriguez, Enrique (1980), *Offentlig inkomstexpansion: en analys av drivkrafterna bakom de offentliga utgifternas utveckling i Sverige under 1900-talet*. Lund: Liber Läromedel.

SOU 1948:45, *Svenskt långtidsprogram 1947–1952/53*. Stockholm: K.L. Beckmans Boktryckeri.

Svenska Dagbladet (1962), 'Samhällets utgifter bara ökar: Forskare söker en förklaring', 29 November.

Söderström, Lars (1981), Review of Anders Forsman, *En teori om staten och de offentliga utgifterna*, *Historisk Tidskrift*, Vol. 101, No. 2, 246–252.

Tarschys, Daniel (1983), *Den offentliga revolutionen*. Stockholm: Liber Förlag.

Uddhammar, Emil (1993), *Partierna och den stora staten: En analys av statsteorier och svensk politik under 1900-talet*. Stockholm: City University Press.

Värmlands Folkblad (1962), 'Den offentliga sektorn', 11 December.

Waara, Lennart (1980), *Den statliga företagssektorns expansion – orsaker tillförstatliganden i ett historiskt och internationellt perspektiv*. Stockholm: Liber Förlag.

Wallander, Jan (2009), 'Mina år vid IUI', in: Magus Henrekson (ed.), *IFN/IUI 1939–2009: Sju decennier av forskning om ett näringsliv i utveckling*. Stockholm: Ekerlids Förlag.

Welinder, Carsten (1962), 'Varför stiger våra skatter?', *Stockholms-Tidningen*, 2 December.

Werin, Lars (1972), Yttrande vid tillsättning av professur i arbetsmarknadspolitik vid Institutet för social forskning. Archive of Stockholm University.

Wickman, Kurt (1980), *Makro-ekonomisk planering—orsaker och utveckling*. Uppsala: Uppsala Studies in Economic History.

CHAPTER 9

The Political Economy of Bo Södersten

Bo Södersten was born in Grängesberg in Dalarna in 1931, as the youngest of eight brothers and sisters. His father worked in the iron mine there. He was a trade union leader and a convinced Social Democrat. Bo was lucky, because unlike the other children he was given an opportunity to study. He graduated from high school in Ludvika in 1951, with top marks.

Bo got a bachelor's degree at Uppsala University in 1955 and a Politices Magister degree the following year: political science, sociology, statistics and economics. He became a member of the Social Democratic student club Laboremus and served as its president in 1956. Thereafter he continued his studies in economics for the licentiate degree, which he finished in 1959, with Erik Lindahl and Ragnar Bentzel as his supervisors.

The Licentiate Thesis

Bo Södersten's licentiate thesis dealt with the development of Sweden's foreign trade in a long-term perspective.[1] It first surveys the development of trade from 1870 until the beginning of the 1950s, the changes in the composition of exports and imports. The second chapter deals with

[1] Södersten (1959a).

M. Lundahl, *Twelve Figures in Swedish Economics*,
Palgrave Studies in the History of Economic Thought,
https://doi.org/10.1007/978-3-030-94327-1_9

the development of Sweden's terms-of-trade between 1870 and 1955. Bo constructs a model, with two completely specialized economies, of what determines the terms-of-trade: the growth rate of GDP, the income elasticities of imports and the demand elasticities of the countries' exports and imports, respectively, with respect to the terms-of-trade. The model is tested on Swedish data.[2]

The third chapter deals with the Swedish import capacity and balance of payments. The import capacity (the income terms-of-trade) is defined as the value of exports divided by an index of the import prices. Bo opposed the idea that deteriorating terms-of-trade caused the balance of payments problems. It was not possible to disregard the influence of the export volume, which he could verify with Swedish data. In the last chapter, Bo discusses the relative importance of the development of prices and productivity for the development of export shares in five export industries. In the expanding branches, productivity had increased continuously while contracting branches displayed stagnating or decreasing productivity.

The examiner of Bo's licentiate thesis was Ragnar Bentzel. He awarded him a *magna cum laude* both on the thesis and on the final examination.

Literary Interlude

Bo Södersten had a literary vein, which he let flow during his Uppsala years in two contexts, both of which to a great extent appear to be autobiographic. The novel *Kandidaterna* [The Students] was never published.[3] It was probably refused. No wonder. Both the intrigue and the portraits of the people feel stereotyped. The women bulge in front and the skirts are inevitably tight on the rear end. 'Have you ever met a woman who has been intellectually stimulating?' asks the protagonist.[4]

In 1962, Bo published a collection of short stories, *Övertygelser* [Convictions],[5] a title inspired by the English collection of essays, *Conviction*, written by a number of young Socialists.[6] It did not turn out too

[2] The model was published in Södersten (1959b).

[3] Södersten (n.d.).

[4] Ibid., p. 50.

[5] Södersten (1962a).

[6] MacKenzie (1958).

well, he writes, in an unpublished and unfinished draft of memoirs.[7] You cannot but agree with the author. The book is not good. The seven stories, with a single exception, deal with some kind of love. The blurb of the book summarizes:

> Love – and its company – jealousy, betrayal and the secret, perhaps unconscious reservations – is the constant theme of the collection of short stories that marks the debut of Bo Södersten. In different ways and phases this love is portrayed: as young love and deep devotion but also as somewhat shabbily practiced sex.

Doctor

After his licentiate thesis, Bo continued toward his doctoral degree, at Stockholm University, with Ingvar Svennilson as his supervisor. He was an assistant teacher there 1960–1961 and 1963–1964. From September 1961 to December 1962, he was in the United States, at MIT and the University of California, Berkeley. Bo continued on the track from the licentiate thesis: international trade and economic growth, but the doctoral dissertation was completely theoretical and mathematical.

Before that, he extended the theoretical analysis of his licentiate thesis in an article in *Ekonomisk Tidskrift*, in 1961.[8] There, he works with two countries that are both producing and consuming two goods. Production is determined by a time trend and by the relative price of the two goods (the terms-of-trade) and consumption by national incomes and relative prices. Using this model, he determines the change in the terms-of-trade.

Bo's analysis of the balance of trade and the terms-of-trade also constitutes the background to an article from 1962, on 'the new dollar crisis.'[9] At the end of the 1940s and the beginning of the 1950s, Europe had experienced a shortage of dollars, due to a large surplus on the American current account of the balance of payments. It was only because of the large contributions of the US to other Western countries that the latter had access to dollars, through the resulting deficit of the American balance of payments. At the end of the 1950s, this had reached the highest level of the decade. Bo's attempted to find out which the reasons

[7] Södersten (2001a).

[8] Södersten (1961), English translation, Södersten (1962b).

[9] Södersten (1962c).

for the increasing deficit might be, but he failed to come up with any conclusive results.

The Doctoral Dissertation: Growth and Trade

Bo Södersten's doctoral dissertation forms part of the neoclassical tradition of foreign trade which by John Hicks and Harry Johnson had been extended to the comparative static investigation of how economic growth (of GDP) affected the terms-of-trade, production and the national income.[10] Bo works within the standard 2 × 2 × 2 framework of two countries, two production factors and two goods.[11]

In the basic model, the sources of growth are not specified. The production capacity of the two countries simply increases. Bo demonstrates that which sector growth takes place is of fundamental importance for the development of relative prices and the national income. If growth is concentrated to the import-competing sector in Country 1, improvement of the terms-of-trade will reinforce the effect of growth on the national income. (So will growth in the export sector of Country 2.) Strong growth of the demand for the export good of Country 1 works in the same direction. Growth in the export sector of Country 1 (and in the import sector of country 2) may on the other hand lead to deteriorating terms-of-trade which will counteract the direct growth effect. The ability to adjust production when prices change will play an important role in the end result. This is formally expressed through the demand and supply elasticities in the denominator of the expression for the change of the terms-of-trade.

Next, growth is specified as factor accumulation. The Rybczynski theorem states that, with linearly homogeneous production functions, when one factor grows while the other one remains constant, the production of the good using the growing factor intensively will increase, and that of the other good decrease.[12] Bo demonstrates mathematically which factors on the production and consumption side determine the result and shows what happens to the national income. He also deals with the case

[10] Hicks (1953) and Johnson (1955).

[11] Södersten (1964a).

[12] Rybczynski (1955).

where growth is caused by technical progress.[13] What happens depends on the one hand on whether technical change is neutral—increasing the marginal productivities of the production factors in the same proportion—or they increase that of one of the factors more than that of the other, and on the other hand on in which sector it occurs. To this, you have to add the effects of the changes on the demand side induced by growth.

Bo also examines the special case when the factor proportions used in the production of the two goods cannot be varied and what happens when growth occurs in an economy where labor is available at a given wage rate.[14] The last chapter contains a discussion of how growth and the terms-of-trade have been discussed in some of the economic literature. The discussion focuses on two distinct 'schools.' The 'English' one goes back to Robert Torrens and the early 1820s.[15] Its main message was that the terms-of-trade of countries exporting industrial products were deteriorating because of diminishing returns in countries exporting agricultural products pushed up the price of agricultural goods. The second approach, associated with Hans Singer and Raúl Prebisch, contends that there is a tendency for the terms-of-trade of raw material producing developing countries to deteriorate over time.[16]

Bo Södersten defended his thesis on 15 May 1964, with Tore Thonstad from Oslo as his first opponent and Erling Olsen from Copenhagen as his second opponent. His defense was one of the longest on record. In order to understand why, it is necessary to make a detour.

Housing Policy: The Three Rents

In 1963, Bo began a polemic which led to a very long animosity between him and Assar Lindbeck. In an essay with the title 'Bostadsbristen och de tre räntorna [The Housing Shortage and the Three Rents]' he reviewed Ragnar Bentzel's, Lindbeck's and Ingemar Ståhl's *Bostadsbristen: En studie av prisbildningen på bostadsmarknaden* [The Housing Shortage: A

[13] His analysis develops that of Findlay and Grubert (1959).

[14] Cf. Lewis (1954).

[15] Torrens (1821).

[16] Singer (1950) and Prebisch (1950).

Study of Price Formation in the Housing Market],[17] where the authors advocated deregulation and market pricing.[18] Bo insinuated that they had not been motivated simply by scientific devotion but that political value judgments were behind their work. Also, they had overlooked that housing yielded three 'rents' which accrued to the homeowners. The first one was a Ricardian rent. As construction expanded outwards, from the city centers, prices in the more attractive locations increased. The second rent was due to inflation. The rents paid by the tenants increased in terms of current prices while the cost of the capital that the owners had borrowed remained fixed. This led to a transfer of income and wealth to the latter. The third rent stemmed from the slower productivity development in the construction industry than elsewhere which made the price of dwellings increase in relation to other prices.

The Thesis Defense

Assar Lindbeck never forgot the review and took revenge on a number of occasions. The first was Bo's thesis defense. He attempted to persuade Bo's supervisor, Ingvar Svennilson, not to allow the dissertation to be defended. Svennilson, however, refused and told Lindbeck that he would have to state his case in public. The defense dragged on for several hours. After the two official opponents came, the opponents *ex auditorio*. Gunnar Myrdal, who was in the middle of his most institutional period ever, complained about the use of formal models in general. He was followed by an extremely harsh and furious Assar Lindbeck and by Karl Jungenfelt and Östen Johansson. In the end, time ran so late that the defense almost interfered with the traditional post-defense dinner.

The thesis committee consisted of five economists: professors Gunnar Myrdal, Erik Lundberg, Ingvar Svennilson and Anders Östlind and the acting professor Assar Lindbeck, plus the professor of geography David Hannerberg and Anders Wedberg, professor of theoretical philosophy. Tore Thonstad had sent a summary of his opposition. Bo had used asymmetrical definitions of the shifts in the production possibility curves for the two goods in the model. His interpretation of the derived formulas left a lot to be desired. Partly they were erroneous and some of the

[17] Bentzel et al. (1963).

[18] Södersten (1963), reprinted in Södersten (1968b).

results which appeared to be novel had been derived from false premises. According to Thonstad, the most original part of the dissertation was the one dealing with technical progress. Bo was awarded a *cum laude* but without qualifying for the degree of *docent* [the equivalent of associate professor], the degree which would open the door to a future academic career.

Östen Johansson och Karl Jungenfelt published their opposition in *Ekonomisk Tidskrift*.[19] They took issue with the failure to include savings in the model. The use of comparative statics was a weakness. The conclusions were trivial but simultaneously complicated and obscure. The economic interpretation of the results was incorrect in some instances. It was not possible to draw dynamic conclusions from a comparative static model. The account of the derivation of the formulas was incomplete and sometimes outright erroneous. The model could not be used for the analysis of trade between developed and developing countries.[20]

After the Disssertation

When Bo Södersten had defended his dissertation, he substituted for Torsten Gårdlund as acting professor of international economics at Lund University in 1964–1965. During 1965–1966 and 1966–1967, he was visiting lecturer at the University of California, Berkeley. There, he began working on a modern textbook in international economics. In March 1966, Bo was finally awarded the title of *docent* of international economics in Lund. In April, he got a lectureship in economics and the following year an associate professorship in international economics.

At the same time as he worked on his textbook, Bo followed up his dissertation with a couple of technical articles. The first was written with Karl-Göran Mäler.[21] It compares John Hicks' and Murray Kemp's definitions of non-neutral technical progress, i.e. technical progress that does not increase the marginal productivities of the production factors in the same proportion. The definitions are not equivalent and the impact of technical progress on the marginal rate of substitution between the production factors hence differs as well.

[19] Johansson and Jungenfelt (1964).

[20] Bo answered his critics (Södersten, 1964b).

[21] Mäler and Södersten (1967).

The second article, written together with Karl Vind, was published in the *American Economic Review*.[22] It deals with the effects of a tariff on the national income and the terms-of-trade in two countries that trade with each other. The article contained a controversial result. Lloyd Metzler had in two papers questioned a result from the classic Stolper-Samuelson analysis: that a tariff increases the price on the imported good in the importing country.[23] His argument was that a tariff could induce an improvement of the terms-of-trade which was large enough to swamp the price-increasing effect of the tariff. Södersten and Vind, however, argued that Metzler's result was due to the assumption that tariff revenues were spent in a way that differed from that of other incomes and that hence the Stolper-Samuelson analysis was valid.

Bo's and Vind's result was, however, questioned by one of the leading international trade theorists of the time, Ronald Jones,[24] who demonstrated that it was critically dependent on the assumption that the two goods were gross substitutes, i.e., that if the price of one of the goods increases, the demand for the other good will always increase. A price increase, however, has two effects: a substitution effect—the demand for the goods whose price does not increase tends to increase—and an income effect—an increase of the price of the good represents a decrease of the income of the consumer—which tends to reduce the demand for both goods. The income effect is negative and may be stronger than the substitution effect for the good in question. Södersten and Vind had, however, simply assumed that this case could not arise, a fatal error, in the view of Jones. Bo and Vind defended themselves. An assumption can never be right or wrong. To argue otherwise was nonsense.[25]

Bo came back to international economic themes also in later years, but not in any systematic fashion. They figured among his many newspaper articles (see below), often topics related to the contemporary political and economic situation, and also in anthologies that he edited, including the EEC-EC-EU, notably the issue of Swedish entry and the effects on the Swedish economy, the EMU, exchange rate issues (fixed vs flexible

[22] Södersten and Vind (1968).

[23] Stolper and Samuelson (1941) and Metzler (1949a, 1949b).

[24] Jones (1969).

[25] Södersten and Vind (1969).

exchange rates), protectionism, developments in international economics during the postwar period, immigration (to Sweden).

Bo's last journal article on an international subject, from 2002, is co-authored with Karolina Ekholm.[26] There he goes back to the theme of economic growth and international trade, but the causal order is reversed. Which is the effect of international trade on economic growth? The point of departure was the income terms-of-trade: the export prices divided by the import prices, i. e. the commodity terms-of-trade, multiplied by the export volume: the import capacity of a country. The hypothesis was that fast-growing countries displayed rapidly increasing income terms-of-trade. It was tested on five fast-growing Asian countries—Hong Kong, Japan, South Korea, Malaysia and Singapore—and five old industrial countries—Austria, France, Sweden, Great Britain and the United States.

The Guy with the Book

In 1969 it was ready: the Book—the one that Bo had begun working on in Berkeley in 1965–1966 and which he himself regarded as his best work. In international circles, Bo became known as 'the Guy with the Book.' The book was *International Economics*, the first textbook in international economics which built on consistent application of general equilibrium theory. It was published in Swedish in 1969[27] and the following year in English.[28]

The book consists of five sections. This first one presents the static theory of international trade: Ricardo and the gains from trade, comparative advantage in the Heckscher-Ohlin formulation, factor price equalization, the effects of trade on the income distribution, and the Leontief paradox: the United States, a country abundantly endowed with capital, was found to export labor-intensive commodities.

The second part begins with a pedagogical account of international trade and economic growth during the nineteenth and twentieth centuries, before Bo presents the different chapters of his dissertation: the effects of unspecified growth, the Rybczynski theorem and the effects of different kinds of technical progress as well as the effects of growth

[26] Ekholm and Södersten (2002).

[27] Södersten (1969a).

[28] Södersten (1970a).

on the terms-of-trade according to the classical English school and Singer-Prebisch.

The third part of the book deals with macroeconomic aspects of international economics: the balance of payments, national accounting and the composition of the national income in an open economy, the connection between the national income and the balance of payments, the international propagation of business cycles, the functioning of the international currency market and the advantages and disadvantages of fixed and flexible exchange rates. Finally, Bo discusses how external and internal equilibrium can be achieved simultaneously: equilibrium in the balance of payments and full employment.

The fourth part of *International Economics* analyzes international trade policy: tariffs under optimal market conditions, the optimal tariff for a large country, quantitative import restrictions, tariffs and subsidies when distortions are present in the commodity or factor markets, effective or implicit tariffs (tariffs on value added). Two chapters are more empirical. The first one deals with the GATT, the EEC and the tariff reduction proposals within the so-called Kennedy Round, and the second one with UNCTAD and trade preferences for less developed countries and with stabilization of international raw material prices. The theory of customs unions is presented as well as the classical transfer problem: the effects on the balance of payments of a capital transfer from one country to another. Finally, the theory of direct investment and the effects of the latter on the investing and host counties are discussed.

The last section of *International Economics* examines the international payments system. It begins with a presentation of the problem of international liquidity, taking the US balance of payments and the balance between gold and dollar holdings in the currency reserve as its point of departure. The role of the IMF is highlighted. The next chapter discusses the adequacy of international liquidity, the price of liquidity, the American seigniorage from providing dollars and the adjustment mechanism of the international payment system when a country runs into a deficit in its balance of payments. The last chapter of the book presents the different plans for reform of the international payments system that was discussed around 1970.

International Economics was a commercial success. It was translated into Italian, Portuguese and Hungarian.[29] For a number of years, it was alone of its kind in the international textbook market. A second Swedish edition was published[30] and two more English ones,[31] updated as the institutions of the international economy changed, and new theories saw the daylight. The updates were necessary, not only because of the theoretical developments. The first edition of Richard Caves' and Ronald Jones' *World Trade and Payments* was published in 1973[32] and Paul Krugman's and Maurice Obstfeld's *International Economics: Theory and Policy* in 1987,[33] books that with time would become too powerful competitors. Bo's book, however, however, tagged along for more than twenty-five years: no mean feat.[34]

Essays

Between 1959 and 1961, Bo was a member of the editorial board of the Social Democratic journal *Tiden*. This provided an opportunity for him to cultivate a genre that attracted him a lot: the essay, including book reviews, a genre that did justice to his stylistic ability. In 1968, he published the first of four collections of essays: *Den hierarkiska välfärden* [The Hierarchic Welfare],[35] inspired—exactly like the collection of short stories—by the democratic, reformist, English Socialists in *Conviction*—essays which rest on a strong ideological foundation.

The first part deals with economics and politics. There, Bo reviews John Kenneth Galbraith's *The Affluent Society*.[36] This society was about

[29] Södersten (1976a, 1979a, 1985a).

[30] Södersten (1978a).

[31] Södersten (1980a) and Södersten and Reed (1994).

[32] Caves and Jones (1973).

[33] Krugman and Obstfeld (1987).

[34] In 1971, *International Economics* got a sequel: *Internationella resursfördelningsproblem* [Problems of International Resource Allocation], an elementary textbook which formed part of an experimental television and radio course in economics, in five parts, one of which was international economics. The book was written by Bo and his assistant at the time, Inga Persson (Persson and Södersten, 1971).

[35] Södersten (1968b).

[36] Galbraith (1958).

to be established, which called for a political distribution of consumption in a way which made society genuinely better. This could only be accomplished by the Social Democrats, but not within the framework of a capitalist economy A frontal attack was necessary. In 1967, Galbraith published *The New Industrial State*,[37] where he claimed that the modern industrial society required planning, however, not by the state but by the large corporations which were technically advanced and could dictate prices. Bo thought that the idea was superficial, and he opposed Galbraith's thesis that the managers had taken over the decision-making from the owners. A few families dominated the Swedish economy and the group of technocrats that was being constituted had interests that coincided with theirs.

A number of chapters in *Den hierarkiska välfärden* deal with planning and Socialism. The grip on the future of the Social Democrats was insufficient. Increasingly political appointments in the ministries were necessary to tackle the social and long-term issues. Bo doubted that it was possible to pursue rational planning in a capitalist economy. A choice had to be made between a Liberal and a Socialist system. Bo wanted structural planning which could guarantee long-run economic growth. The market system could not handle externalities, increasing returns to scale and indivisibilities, but the state had to step in and take control of the structural change.

In 1960, a commission was working on a new party program for the Social Democrats. The formulations employed suggested that the old demand for socialization was being watered down. Bo thought that the debate had ended on a side-track where thesis-chewing Marxists with ready-made solutions were facing revisionists whose only interest was efficiency. Socialization would not accomplish the latter, but it could contribute to equality and to the creation of a class-less society. The party program did not offer anything novel. It beat around the bush when it came to the fundamental organization of the economy. A powerful reform policy presupposed control of the income formation process.

Bo was interested in international Socialism, and in *Den hierarkiska välfärden* he writes about the Socialist International, a movement which in his view had not been overly successful. Bo argued that the international work on reform policies had to make goals like equality, an open

[37] Galbraith (1967).

society and a richer cultural life as its points of departure. The main tools of the reform policy should be a planned economy and socialization. The state had to assume the responsibility for full employment. The influence of the capitalists had to be eroded and fenced in, and you should never take any steps back from a position that you had secured.

The second part of *Den hierarkiska välfärden* deals with travels. We will come back to them below in the context of economic development. The third and last part consists of book reviews. The one which stands out deals with Herbert Tingsten's four-volume autobiography *Mitt liv* [My Life].[38] Tingsten was a legendary professor of political science in Stockholm, a Social Democrat who turned Liberal, the chief editor of *Dagens Nyheter*, the largest Swedish daily for a decade, a person always in the middle of the Swedish debate.

Bo deals with all four volumes of Tingsten's memoirs. He praises Tingsten because he was not self-righteous. He was, however, not in any way beyond reproach. Tingsten had been a Social Democrat until 1944, and Bo perceived that in later years he campaigned vehemently against his former party. Tingsten knew nothing about economics and thought that democracy was opposed to socialization and a planned economy. It was from this perspective that he attacked the Social Democracy. But his lack of interest in pragmatic policy also constituted a moral strength. 'Tingsten's greatness as a journalist was that he was there to preach the truth, not to achieve results.'[39] In spite of the weaknesses that he criticized, Bo was full of admiration for Tingsten. 'He is one of the few who cannot be imagined out of their time without it being changed.'[40]

Den hierarkiska välfärden clearly demonstrated that Bo was much better as an essayist than as a short story writer. While *Övertygelser* frequently feels artificial, the essay format allows him to develop the art of formulation which he abundantly possessed. The short stories offered few possibilties to display the irony, the erudition, the art of agitation and the allusions which characterize *Den hierarkiska välfärden*. The book can still be read with pleasure, even if you know that with time Bo would completely change his views with respect to which the forces were that created the wealth of the Swedish society.

[38] Tingsten (1961, 1962, 1963, 1964).

[39] Ibid., p. 223.

[40] Ibid., p. 225.

Per Albin and the Brotherhood

In 1970, Bo again displayed his essay talents, in a small book about Per Albin Hansson, the Swedish Prime Minister 1932–1936 and 1936–1946, *Per Albinlinjen* [The Per Albin Way].[41] Bo's chapter is called 'Per Albin och den socialistiska reformismen' [Per Albin and Socialist Reformism], one of Bo's most sympathetic and empathic essays.

Per Albin (as the Swedes knew him) has traditionally been considered a pragmatic tactician who kept the Socialist ideology in the background. Bo, however, argues that this is wrong. Per Albin had his own political message. The central idea was that of the People's Home [folkhemmet], a home which should house all Swedes, an idea which has often been regarded as conservative. Bo contends that this interpretation is erroneous. The idea was much deeper, and it was based on Per Albin's dream of brotherhood. It was his most genuine and original political thought. The Socialist society had to rest on brotherhood—equality, concern, cooperation and help. It was this attitude toward life that Per Albin wanted to turn into reality and which was behind the idea of the People's Home. It made him turn away from both the elite and the bureaucracy. He wanted to enjoy the company of common people.

Bo also deals with Per Albin's views of democracy: the thought that political democracy must have an economic counterpart and the highly original—somewhat strange—idea of a permanent government of national unity, where cooperation was the rule and where opposition would not take place only along party lines. The idea was difficult to explain, but Bo contended that it was based on the view of society as an organism. As economic democracy was realized, the class struggle would gradually recede. The means of production would gradually be socialized, a development which would relegate the bourgeois to a position of perennial opposition. But here, the brotherhood idea entered the picture, cooperation, consensus. Per Albin thought it was possible to create a new spirit of community, one where everybody accepted a Socialist order of society. The idea of a permanent government of national unity formed part of this vision.

In a newly written essay on reformist Socialism for his collection *Ut ur krisen* [Out of the Crisis] from 1981, Bo came back to Per Albin and

[41] Södersten (1970c).

the brotherhood theme.[42] Reformism had made its breakthrough in the 1930s and Bo predicted that it would again be brought to the forefront in the 1980s. The Social Democratic defeat in the 1976 elections had increased the polarization in Swedish politics. Bo conceived of this situation as an opening for reformist Socialism, but this could not be built from the top. It required decentralization and brotherhood, 'consideration, nearness, the will to understand and to encompass what is different, the individual.'[43] The party had to see to it that the open discussion was kept alive within it and that it remained open to anybody, in order to break the bourgeois hegemony.

The Hunt for a Chair

In 1968, two chairs in economics were advertised at Stockholm University. Bo applied for both but was declared not qualified by all the three appointed experts, Ragnar Bentzel from Uppsala, Leif Johansen from Oslo and Björn Thalberg from Lund. The following year, a chair in economics in Uppsala fell vacant after Tord Palander. The expert committee consisted of Harald Dickson from Gothenburg, Jørgen Gelting from Aarhus, Assar Lindbeck and Tord Palander, the retiring professor, a custom that was unfortunately common at the time. Again, Bo failed to meet the requirements as the committee saw it.

Lindbeck was mean.[44] He came back to Bo's dissertation. Neither the derivation of the results nor the presentation and interpretation of the results was satisfactory, and they could not be used for anything. Palander was even worse. His judgment of Bo bordered on the defamatory.[45] He began by portraying Bo's production as dominated by an exceedingly simplified special case, the one with two countries, two commodities and two factors, without mentioning that this was the dominant approach in the theory of international trade. The licentiate thesis he called primitive and impossible to apply to the Swedish economy and the doctoral dissertation had received too high a grade. Bo did not understand what he was doing. Palander insinuated that the mathematical deductions were not his

[42] 'Reformistiskt 80-tal [The Reformist 80s]', in Södersten (1981).

[43] Ibid., p. 18.

[44] Lindbeck (1969).

[45] Palander (1969).

own. Bo had demonstrated a weakly developed ability to plan and carry out a theoretical scientific investigation. His mathematical and economic education was deficient and his production very one-sided.

The next position that Bo applied for was an associate professorship in Lund, where the expert committee consisted of three professors who had already passed judgment on him: Ragnar Bentzel, Björn Thalberg och Assar Lindbeck. This time he qualified, but he did not get the position. Bo appealed and called Lindbeck biased, after what had taken place in connection with his thesis defense in 1964, but to no avail.[46] During 1968, two chairs in economics had also fallen vacant at the University of Copenhagen, Bo applied for both. The committee which collectively—the Danish system differed from the Swedish one—evaluated the applicants consisted of professors Jørgen Gelting, Aarhus, Trygve Haavelmo, Oslo, Anders Ølgaard, Copenhagen, and Poul Nørregaard Rasmussen, also Copenhagen, as well as the chairman of the board of the Danish National Bank, Erik Hoffmeyer. Bo received a mixed evaluation. His thesis was seen as a valuable attempt of exact treatment of some central parts of the theory of international trade and to a certain extent also of some new problems, although the mathematical treatment was not successful, and the textbook pointed to good knowledge about the new literature in the field, but it also had some defects.[47] It was not enough, however. Bo did not get any of the Copenhagen chairs.

It would take a fifth attempt to become a professor. In 1969, the August Röhss chair in economics in Gothenburg was advertised, with a committee consisting of Guy Arvidsson from Lund Ragnar Bentzel and Anders Ølgaard. Bentzel still refused to declare Bo qualified, although he came pretty close, mainly because he did not think that Bo dominated his analytical apparatus. The other two committee members, Arvidsson and Ølgaard, on the other hand, argued that Bo had been far too harshly judged by the former experts. Arvidsson contended that his dissertation had enough merits to warrant the grade of *docent*. He also praised the textbook manuscript, and in the end declared Bo qualified, with some hesitation.[48]

[46] Södersten (1969b).

[47] Gelting et al. (1969).

[48] Arvidsson (1970).

Anders Ølgaard was positive as well. In spite of its flaws, Bo's dissertation was a valuable contribution—the earlier evaluations had concentrated too much on formal defects—and he predicted that *International Economics* would get a wide international readership. Exactly like Arvidsson, Ølgaard considered that Bo qualified, with some hesitation.[49] Both Arvidsson and Ølgaard ranked Bo ahead of his competitor, Karl Jungenfelt, which meant that he got the Gothenburg chair.

* * *

Fifty years afterward, the choice of expert committee members for the chairs that Bo applied for stands out as odd. Ragnar Bentzel served no less than there out of four times in connection with the Swedish positions, Assar Lindbeck and Björn Thalberg twice each and Jørgen Gelting and Anders Ølgaard each once in Sweden and once in Denmark. It must certainly have been possible to find other experts within the Nordic countries so as to avoid completely predictable evaluations. This is the case not least with Bentzel and Lindbeck. It is difficult to get away from the suspicion that Bo's critical review of *Bostadsbristen* may have influenced their view of him. Drafting them in such a situation, not only once but several times, points to a good deal of bad judgment among the faculties which appointed them, an impression which is confirmed by Guy Arvidsson's and Anders Ølgaard's conclusion in connection with the Gothenburg chair, that Bo had been far too harshly treated by the previous committees.

The Swedish Institute for Social Research

From 1 January 1971, Bo Södersten was professor of economics in Gothenburg. He immediately took leave of absence, however. The reason was that the Institute for Labour Market Research at Stockholm University would be reorganized. Bo was appointed expert and secretary of the committee which worked with the issue. The Swedish Institute for Social Research [Institutet för social forskning—SOFI] began its activities on 1 January 1972 with Bo Södersten as acting director until a professor of labor market policy could be appointed.

[49] Ølgaard (1970).

Labor market policy was not Bo's field, but during his time at SOFI and shortly thereafter, he wrote a couple of essays on this theme.[50] The first one, 'Socialpolitik och ekonomisk politik [Social Policy and Economic Policy],' discusses the delimitation and function of social policy and its relation to the general economic policy. Bo focuses on the intervention with the market income formation in order to change the distribution of incomes and consumption and he discusses the impotence of traditional social policy measures during periods of mass unemployment. He defines the core of social policy as 'problems of social insurance and loss of income, revalidation, social allowance, welfare, mechanisms of social exclusion, etc.'[51] The task was to build methods to tackle these problems against the background of a more general economic and sociological context.

The second article, 'Modern inflations- och arbetslöshetsteori [Modern Inflation and Unemployment Theory],' contrasts the Keynesian recipe for full employment with the natural unemployment approach and the role of expectations in the latter. Economic policy measures to reduce unemployment would simply result in the adaptation of the expectations of the economic actors and the economy would revert to the natural rate of unemployment.

When the focus of the new institute for social research had been defined, a chair in social policy was advertised. Since Bo had been acting director of the institute, it was obvious that he would apply. Seven serious candidates were scrutinized by an expert committee consisting of Erik Lundberg, Lars Werin and Bent Rold Andersen. Lundberg declared Bo not qualified, arguing that his production was highly uneven, and he had not published anything in the field of social policy.[52] Lars Werin also pointed out that Bo had few publications in social policy. His overall competence in economics might qualify him, but this was not enough.[53] Bent Rold Andersen, finally, found Bo qualified, but only with considerable doubt. Again, the problem was Bo's lack of publications in the

[50] Reprinted in Södersten (1975).

[51] Ibid., p. 133.

[52] Lundberg (1972, p. 26).

[53] Werin (1972).

relevant field.[54] The chair instead went to Gösta Rehn, a person with a solid background in labor market and social policy issues.[55]

In the next few years, Bo published a couple of articles related to social policy. In the first, from 1975, written together with Nancy Barrett, which compared unemployment patterns in the United States and Sweden,[56] unemployment is split into two components: the average number of times that a person has been unemployed in a year and the average duration of the unemployment. The welfare implications differed between the two components. In the former case, it was possible that the unemployed person wanted to get a new job while in the second case there was a risk that he or she had problems finding a job. The unemployment pattern differed between the two countries. Americans were unemployed more often, but Swedes were unemployed for longer periods. In the United States, new jobs were found faster than in Sweden. Nancy and Bo did, however, not conclude that things were better in the United States. The statistics did not allow for a clear-cut division into voluntary and unvoluntary unemployment.

Three years later, Bo published an article about the situation of Swedish women in the labor market.[57] Their labor market participation had increased from 32% in 1960 to 50% in 1975. In order to explain this development, Bo resorted to the 'new household economics,' developed above all by Gary Becker, which claims that the decisions about participation in the labor market are made by the household, and not by the individuals. When real incomes and education increase, so does the income loss that you make by not working, which tends to increase the extent of female participation in the labor market. Bo was, however, skeptical. Attitudes toward work had changed as well: security, equality and independence as well as demonstration effects: other women worked.

54 Andersen (1972).

55 For a biography of Rehn, see Erixon and Wadensjö (2013).

56 Barrett and Södersten (1975).

57 Södersten (1978b). The same paper was presented in English at a meeting of the International Economic Association and was published in Södersten (1980c).

Gothenburg and Lund

After failing to get the chair in social policy in Stockholm, Bo had to return to Gothenburg. He taught there in 1973–1974. In 1974–1975, he again was on leave, serving as visiting professor at the American University in Washington, DC and as a visiting researcher at Harvard, before returning to Gothenburg, in the fall of 1975.

Bo came back to a deeply divided department. It had gathered a large number of Marxist teachers and students. Since Bo had never liked Marxists and made no secret of his feelings, it was inevitable that sooner or later it would come to serious clashes. At the time, a series of experiments with the democratization of the university departments was going on in Sweden, and Gothenburg had one of the more extreme forms, with a heavy representation of students and administrative personnel and frequent elections to the department board. Every time, a number of Marxists registered for studies at the economics department, and the mudslinging began. The worst moments were when positions were up for grabs in the department. This inevitably led to confrontation and letters to the university administration.[58] In a 1977 interview, Bo stated his views on Marxism, at a time when the department was again involved in a bitter struggle about a lecturership. Marxism was nothing but a religious salvation doctrine, a political ideology.[59]

In 1977, Bo left Gothenburg without regret. In 1976, Torsten Gårdlund, who had been a professor of international economics in Lund since 1965, retired and his position was advertised. Bo applied. The expert committee consisted of Gårdlund and the two Norwegians Jan Serck-Hanssen and Tore Thonstad. This time, nobody could threaten him. The chair was in his special branch of economics: international economics. Bo had worked mainly with international trade but also, to some extent, with development economics, another of the core areas included in the definition of the chair. The overall picture of him was mixed, but overwhelmingly positive.[60] The expert committee unanimously declared Bo qualified for the chair and put him first. He was appointed professor of international economics from 1 July 1977.

[58] For a thoughtful account, from the Marxist camp, of Bo's time in the Gothenburg department, see Lönnroth (2011).

[59] Franck (1977).

[60] Notat (1977, p. 6).

The Housing Market

Bo's third scientific monograph deals with the housing market in Sweden. The book—*Betalt för att bo* [Paid for Dwelling]—published in 1978, is co-authored with Bo Sandelin,[61] who the year before had defended his doctoral dissertation, *Prisutveckling och kapitalvinster på bostadsfastigheter* [Price Developments and Capital Gains in the Housing Market], at the University of Gothenburg.[62]

In *Betalt för att bo*, Bo and Bo provide times series from the 1950s to the 1970s which demonstrate that the average homeowner had made a good profit on his house. This they compared with the costs that the tenants in the housing market had incurred during the same period. The prices of single-family houses had increased by 13 percent 1973–1976, faster than the general price level. The population had grown and home construction had been concentrated on multi-family houses, while that of one-family houses had been lagging. Building costs and rent levels had increased rapidly, which had made people turn to the market for one-family houses. The increased building costs were the result of relatively slow development of productivity in the construction sector. The price increases on small houses had a wealth effect: both implicit (unrealized) gains) and realized profits.

The account of the situation in the market for small houses ends with a discussion of the taxation of the gains on one-family houses. The latter were either not taxed at all or taxed at a lower rate than other incomes. Such gains should be taxed in the same way as other incomes, or harder, since they were work-free incomes. Bo and Bo suggested that the taxation of housing should be founded on the principle that the dwellers should pay the cost per unit of time for the services rendered by their dwellings. They advocated a 40 percent tax on realized profits, and the current services rendered by the dwellings had to be taxed. The standard assessed revenue should be increased in order to ensure parity with the bank rate of interest (the alternative investment).

It was inevitable that the Sandelin-Södersten book would arouse the sentiments of the homeowners. It ended up on top of the placard of the largest daily newspaper in Sweden. The book was also criticized for confusing realized and unrealized profits, for not taking the importance

[61] Sandelin and Södersten (1978).

[62] Sandelin (1977).

of location into account and for taxing low-income earners out of the market for one-family houses. Besides, the book did not deal with the condominium market at all—a market where the same kind of profits were made as in the small house market.[63]

Bo continued to write about the housing market after the publication of *Betalt för att bo*. He then extended his perspective to the determination of rental levels in the regulated housing market.[64] These did not take location into account, and rent control created an excess demand. Contacts, nepotism and favoritism determined the distribution of the available apartments. It was impossible to achieve equality in each individual market in the economy. People's preferences for housing and consumption of other goods differed and there was no unequivocally 'fair' way of distributing apartments.

A book chapter from 1990, written with Arne Karyd, analyzes the effects of subsidization of housing.[65] Tax and interest subsidies distorted the housing market and led to unwanted redistribution of incomes and wealth. The house owners could deduct interest payments in their income declarations. The interest subsidies, in turn, went directly from the state to the real estate owners. Their purpose was to keep the cost of newly produced apartments down, but Arne and Bo argued that it would be preferable to let higher rents for more attractive apartments finance the construction of new houses. It was impossible not to take location into account. Regulation of the market would simply lead to the absurd situation where two apartments which differed with respect to the attraction of the neighborhood would have the same price. Of course, a deregulated housing market would have consequences for the distribution of incomes, but it would lead to the production of houses preferred by the consumers, and it would free resources for other useful projects in society.

[63] Lindgren (1978).

[64] Södersten (1989c). Bo had turned 180 degrees since his criticism of the Bentzel-Lindbeck-Ståhl book.

[65] Karyd and Södersten (1990).

The Dream of the Labor-Managed Economy

In 1970, Jaroslav Vanek published a book on the theory of the labor-managed firm.[66] Bo read it and become sold on the idea of decentralized Socialism. During the 1970s, he wrote a number of articles where he presented the main features of the theory and discussed its applicability to the Swedish economy. The first ones were short newspaper chronicles in *Aftonbladet*.[67] Bo discerned two main roads along which the advancement toward the labor-managed economy ought to proceed. One was that of increased influence of the employees in their companies. The second went via control of the capital formation, for example by the purchase of shares through collective funds. 'Capitalism has performed its duty. Capitalism can go.'[68]

The short articles in *Aftonbladet* were followed by a few longer ones. The first one presents the theory.[69] The labor-managed firm should maximize the net income per worker (the gross income minus the cost of capital) instead of profits. This, however, will provoke a 'perverse' reaction to product price increases. This backward-bending supply curve builds on two conflicting tendencies. You want as many workers as possible in the company in order to minimize the capital cost per worker, but you also want as few workers as possible, since this increases the production value per worker. An increase in the product price reinforces the latter tendency at the expense of the former. Those already working in the company attempt to reduce their numbers or at least not let any newcomers in, so production may decrease. To solve the problem, new companies must be created, but this will not occur spontaneously. A certain degree of central direction may be necessary. Bo, however, doubted that the tendency to shed labor was very strong in practice. He confided in worker solidarity.

In the labor-managed economy, capital would be collectively owned. The workers of the particular company would decide how the investments within the latter were made, but the money should be borrowed from a 'social fund.' The incentive structure would improve. The workers in the capitalist company minimize their effort, given the wage, since the result

[66] Vanek (1970).

[67] Reprinted in *Den svenska sköldpaddan* (Södersten, 1975).

[68] Ibid., p. 193.

[69] Södersten (1973).

of an increased effort will accrue to the capitalist owners. In the labor-managed firm, they would maximize their effort, since the increases will result in higher labor incomes. Bo romanticized work within the labor-managed firm. The employees would work together for the common good, assume collective responsibility for the company they all owned and support each other.

The reasoning is not convincing. As Mancur Olson had demonstrated in a classic book, the result will probably rather be the opposite one.[70] Since everybody gets a share in the result of the increased effort of the individual worker, everybody will wait for everybody else to do something. The net income of the company is a collective good for the employees, which nobody can be excluded from. Hence, the production of the company tends to be lower than the optimum, and the larger the company, the larger this problem will be.

When Bo published his book of essays *Den svenska sköldpaddan* [The Swedish Turtle] in 1975, he included a newly written essay where he linked the need for industrial finance with the need for a transition from a capitalist economic system to a system which rested on public control but without undue centralization.[71] This essay is arguably the most ideological one that he ever wrote. He paints the future society that he wanted to see, a society where the humans controlled their existence, were satisfied with what they did and felt well in general.

The Swedish Social Democrats had neglected the need for a coherent industrial policy that controlled industrial investment. The remedy was found in labor-managed firms combining worker influence and equality with efficiency. The group most interested in and most dependent on the success of the companies was the workers. The overwhelming part of the investment in the industrial sector was financed by profits, but it was not simply the management and the capital owners who created the profits. The influence of the employees had to increase, via increased representation on the company boards—a majority representation.

The criteria that should govern the activities of the labor-managed companies should be payment of the agreed wages and an investment rate satisfactory from the point of view of society. The labor-managed firms must cooperate with the state and take socioeconomic criteria into

[70] Olson (1965).

[71] Södersten (1975).

account when making investment decisions. Economic progress rests on structural change since society is subject to change all the time. This would come easier in the labor-manged economy, since the solidarity principle governing the activities of the individual firms could be extended to solidarity also *between* firms. An efficient industrial structure was in the interest of all employees. However, the establishment of new companies required an active policy. It implied risk-taking, it had to be coordinated by a central organization it had to be financed by a credit institute which could mobilize the necessary funds.

However, the strongest arguments for a transition to labor management were found on a different level, harder to grasp. 'There are large groups in our society, mainly blue- and white-collar workers within the large wage-earning collectives who at present do not get a reasonable chance to realize their creative power and their energy. The labor-managed economy could free large quantities of energy, creative power and organizational talent.'[72] The workers would feel that they themselves, and no outsiders, controlled the companies.

Bo's final words breathe both humanism and Socialism:

> A transition to labor management does not solve all problems. But it should solve several and above all do away with the fundamental opposition that exists between the economic organization of capitalism and all aspirations towards equality, brotherhood and humanity.
>
> A labor-managed economy will restore the value and dignity of work, It constitutes the form of economic organization which may constitute the foundation of the fully developed Socialist society.[73]

Bo Södersten returned to the labor-managed economy in an article that dealt with micro aspects.[74] He compared labor-managed and traditionally organized firms. The capitalist Scientific Management school aimed at standardized work routines, easy to measure and monitor, while the Human Relations literature strongly indicated that influence over the own work situation had a positive influence on both production and well-being. This spoke in favor of labor management. It made work meaningful and increased the solidarity with the company.

[72] Ibid., p. 56.

[73] Ibid., p. 57.

[74] Södersten (1976b).

In capitalist companies, on-the-job training tended to be underdimensioned since it was impossible to prevent the employees from moving. All the returns on this training did not accrue to the company. In the labor-managed firm, the propensity to move would be lower, since the extent of solidarity of the workers with the company would be higher. The character of technical progress also differed. The capitalist economy aimed for improvements that made it easier to monitor work and increase profits, while labor-managed firms would opt for changes that increased productivity by a better organization of the steering process characterized by worker influence.

Finally, Bo raised the issue of why we had not yet arrived at labor management if the latter was a superior form of organization. A possible answer was that there was no open competition between different organization principles. The institutions in society had been designed for cooperation with the already existing organization forms. The introduction of labor management would hence hardly be possible unless society underwent fundamental changes.

The issue of labor management was intimately related to the need for industrial investment, since the latter was what determined the rate of growth and thus also employment.[75] It did not make sense to concentrate the ambitions of the labor movement just on wage bargaining, but for the workers to assume their responsibility toward society and reduce their demands, they had to be offered something else instead: influence over the investment policy of the companies. Here, the much-debated wage-earners' funds came into the picture. They were based on arguments of equality and justice.[76] A tiny minority of people controlled the Swedish economy. A redistribution of incomes was necessary. It was of course not possible to rule out income differences in the labor-managed economy either. Profitability would differ between companies, but incomes would be directly related to the labor effort.

In 1977, Bo presented a practical proposal of how the wage earners could get more influence over investments: investment committees.[77] These should consist of both owner employee representatives, with the latter in the majority. The money would come from the future wage

[75] Södersten (1976c).

[76] Södersten (1976d).

[77] Södersten (1977a, 1977b).

increases—one-third—to be managed by the committees over periods of five years at the time.[78]

Two years later, in one of his last essays on the subject, Bo asked whether Sweden was on its way toward the labor-managed economy.[79] He linked the issue to the debate about the wage-earners' funds that was raging at the time. Those whose attitude toward the latter was positive should also embrace the idea of labor management. He found it strange that in a situation where the security of employment had increased and employee representatives had been introduced on the company boards, labor management had attracted so little interest. The capitalists had to be phased out, but Bo did not accept direct state representation either. The introduction of bureaucratic controls would simply reduce the efficiency of the firms. In the end, it was difficult to conceive of the wage-earners' funds without labor management.

Bo was not particularly optimistic when it came to the possibility of introducing labor-managed firms in Sweden. The fundamental principles were not well enough known and the international experience, for example from Mondragón in the Basque Country and Yugoslavia, had not received enough publicity. In the Swedish debate, labor management had been depicted as a threat to the pluralistic society. Bo considered this nothing but scare tactics. It was difficult to conceive of a more decentralized decision method than labor-managed enterprises. Bo was, however, not certain that Sweden was ready for the transition in the 1980s. The risk was high that the politicians would dump the responsibility for the economy on bureaucrats, company managers and public authorities.

Criticism

The labor-managed economy was Bo Södersten's principal contribution to the political debate in Sweden. He took great care to build an argument which rested both on economic analysis and on his—somewhat romantic—perception of the political realities of the 1970s—a perception which he had to modify over the years when he realized that the public opinion in Sweden might not share his views.

78 Bege (1977).

79 Södersten (1979b), English version in Södersten (1982b).

The idea of labor management, however, stood out as utopian.[80] If labor-manged enterprises were superior to the traditional capitalistic ones, they should not only have been established but should also have out-competed the latter. Also, it was not at all certain that there would be any fundamental organizational differences between the two systems. Labor-managed enterprises could also be forced to resort to more or less hierarchic forms of organization. There was no evidence that shirking would not occur in labor-managed companies. It is hard to detect and measure when the company operations rest on team production. It may also be difficult to establish new firms. It was hardly credible that existing companies would help competitors to enter the market or share their research and development results with them.

The dream of the labor-managed economy was a beautiful dream of a Socialist society with a more human face than the centralized command economy which rested exclusively on coercion or the capitalist economy with its inherent inequalities of income and wealth. But it was no more than a dream—a piece of wishful thinking, if you like. It is clear that Bo assumed the existence of a number of mechanisms and attitudes that are not likely to exist in real life. Gradually he realized this and gradually he chose to drop the idea. As we will see below, later in his life he would be converted into a staunch supporter of the capitalist economy.

More Textbooks

Spurred by good royalty incomes from his book in international economics, Bo embarked on more textbook projects. The first one was an anthology of the Swedish economy, *Svensk ekonomi* [The Swedish Economy]. The perspective was wide: one hundred years of Swedish development, the credit market, growth and structural change during the postwar period, stabilization policy, resource allocation in the public sector, industrial policy and the regional structural problems, environmental policy, and, finally, Sweden in the international economy and our position vis-à-vis the developing countries. *Svensk ekonomi* was published in three editions between 1970 and 1982.[81] In the later editions, chapters

[80] Eidem and Viotti (1974).

[81] Södersten (1970b, 1974a, 1982a).

were added on monetary policy and the place of women in the Swedish economy. The book was used in several Swedish universities.

In 1974, Bo and I edited a two-volume anthology on economic development, *Utvecklingsekonomi* [Development Economics], *Underutvecklingens mekanismer* [The Mechanisms of Underdevelopment] and *Planering och resursmobilisering* [Planning and Resource mobilization],[82] with a second, revised, one-volume, edition in 1979.[83] They remained on the university course lists for a few years.

In the fall of 1981, when giving a first-year course in macroeconomics, Bo realized that American textbooks were unsatisfactory from the Swedish point of view. Almost without exception, they dealt with a closed economy, a reasonable simplification as far as the American economy was concerned, but not for Sweden, with its large foreign trade in relation to GDP, and, of course, American textbooks had nothing to say about Swedish economic policy.

Bo drew the conclusion that a Swedish textbook was needed. In 1983, *Makroekonomi och stabiliseringspolitik* [Macroeconomics and Stabilization Policy] was finished.[84] The book is mainly traditional Keynesian with IS-LM analysis, the accelerator-multiplicator model and the effects of fiscal and monetary policy. The open economy and the problem of equilibrating the balance of payments is introduced as well as the foreign currency market and theories of devaluation. The longest chapter of the book deals with the labor market and inflation, the Phillips curve and the stagflation problem as well as the specific Swedish analysis of wage formation and inflation in disaggregated terms—one sector subject to competition and one protected sector—rational expectations and fixed versus flexible exchange rates. Another central chapter is devoted to the relation between means and ends in economic policy, internal and external balance in the Swedish context.

Makroekonomi och stabiliseringspolitik mainly builds on the Keynesian approach to macroeconomics, but a couple of alternative approaches are also dealt with. One is monetarism, with its emphasis on the influence of the money supply on economic fluctuations and its questioning of the Phillips curve. The second one stands out as somewhat odd in

[82] Lundahl and Södersten (1974b, 1974c).

[83] Lundahl and Södersten (1979).

[84] Södersten (1983).

the context: growth accounting. Bo's book deals mainly with short-run stabilization problems, but growth accounting is concerned with the separation of the long-term effects on the economic growth of population growth, capital accumulation and disembodied technical progress.

In 1987, five years had passed since the last edition of *Svensk ekonomi* had been published. That year, Bo replaced this anthology by a new one: *Marknad och politik* [Markets and Politics]. The new anthology saw six editions, the last one in 2004, before Bo passed the editorship on.[85] The purpose of the book was to highlight the changes that had taken place in the Swedish economy in recent years, to show how the most important markets worked, to highlight the functioning of the public sector and the tax system and how these interacted with the private sector of the economy. To this was added growth and stabilization problems and, in later editions, environmental policy, the health sector, the place of Sweden in the international economy, trade and direct investment, the welfare state and entrepreneurship. Bo himself wrote about the Swedish policy toward developing countries, in the first three editions, and thereafter about Sweden, the EU and the EMU. With time, a book was created that covered most aspects of the Swedish economy and its problems. The concept was sustainable. The book kept its place on the course reading lists.[86]

Economic Development

Bo Södersten's specialty was international economics. The step from there to Development economics was a small one. In Lund, the chair in international economics was defined in such a way as to explicitly incorporate development as well. Bo never produced any major work in development economics, only a number of articles and book chapters, and on two occasions he worked as a consultant for SIDA on development issues.

How should the development problem be tackled? The year before Bo and I published our economic development anthology, a government committee presented a report which proposed to earmark some of the

[85] Södersten (1987a, 1990a, 1996a, 1997a, 2000a) and Södersten and Söderström (2004).

[86] The latest edition so far, the twelfth one, was published in 2017 (Hultkrantz and Österholm, 2017).

Swedish aid money for research on developing countries.[87] We found that it left a few things to be desired, above all when it came to the identification and presentation of the main development problems and therefore wrote a critical article.[88] The report dealt too much with underdevelopment as a multidimensional problem and missed that in the end it was a matter of mass poverty, the mechanisms behind this poverty and finding ways of reducing it and increasing the standard of living for broad population segments. The development problem was mainly economic, which the report had missed, presumably because no economist had been involved in its writing.

Bo was impressed by the neoinstitutional approach to economic history represented by people like Douglass North and Nathan Rosenberg which he came back to in several newspaper articles.[89] At the beginning of the sixteenth century, the West was not economically ahead of other civilizations like China and Islam, but thereafter it managed to build institutions that facilitated growth-inducing international trade and exchange. Most important of all was that the rulers could be tamed so that they could no longer deprive the productive forces of the fruits of their labor. It took the West 300 years to build good institutions. Other nations failed to adopt the new institutions, on the other hand, and hence remained poor.

In two publications from 1993 and 1994, Bo surveys the relation between education, institutions and growth.[90] The growth-generation factors were endogenous.[91] Knowledge is produced, and it is used by firms. The knowledge of an individual depends not only on his own education but also on that of his colleagues, and it can be used by many people simultaneously. This tends to have strong growth effects, especially if it produces increasing returns to scale. Bo tied the effects of education to the Swedish industrialization process: a process driven by capital accumulation and by a modernization of the universities in the direction of natural sciences. Improved education interacted with good institutions which facilitated international trade.

[87] SOU 1973:41.

[88] Lundahl and Södersten (1974a).

[89] The approach is presented in Södersten (1991e, 1999a).

[90] Södersten (1993a, 1994a).

[91] Bo makes reference to Romer (1986, 1990a, 1990b) and Lucas (1988, 1990).

Income distribution was a theme that had engaged Bo for a long time. Inequalities were often wider in poor countries than in rich ones and had a strong impact on the living conditions of the poor.[92] Bo was not particularly optimistic with respect to the future. Positive effects of capital accumulation could easily be swamped by labor-saving technical progress. An innovation like the Green Revolution seemed to have dubious distribution effects. Only large farmers could afford the irrigation and mechanization that was often required to make the miracle seeds profitable. It was difficult to get a more equal distribution of incomes without changing the entire political and economic system in poor countries, and not even then was it certain that the living standard would increase.

At the other end of the income scale there was Sweden. In 1990, after participating in a symposium that compared the development of the Nordic and Latin American countries over a century,[93] Bo published a piece of the Swedish *siglo de oro*, the period 1870–1970. He tells the story of the industrialization of Sweden up to the First World War, the application of Keynesian stabilization policies between the two wars and the high growth after the Second World War up to 1970. Strangely enough, his account omits the construction of the welfare state. This is weird. Economic development is usually not defined simply in terms of growth, but the definition usually contains something about more equal income distribution and the abolition of poverty. Secondly, the welfare state was Sweden's claim to international economic and social fame. Finally, Bo had always emphasized distributional aspects. It becomes close to impossible to understand why he—with his Social Democratic heritage—would not emphasize how the fruits of growth had accrued to broad population segments in an account of the construction of modern Sweden.

In an article in Portuguese, on more or less the same theme, the account is more balanced.[94] There, Bo discusses the political role of the Social Democracy during the same period, the rise of the trade union movement and the Swedish labor market model, the solidarity wage policy and the struggle for income equalization via the tax system.

[92] Södersten (1974e).

[93] Södersten (1991a), Spanish version, Södersten (1990d).

[94] Södersten (1990e).

Cuba and Chile

Bo's main experience of developing economies stemmed from Latin America and Africa. Two countries that he kept coming back to were Cuba and Chile. Bo visited Cuba in 1967 and 1968. When he returned home, he reported his findings: the problems connected with the over-ambitious sugar production target, 10 million tons, employment, wages and the lack of consumer goods, the revolutionary enthusiasm and the government control of the citizens.[95]

Bo was back in Cuba at the beginning of 2000. I was there as well, trying to teach economics to Cuban bureaucrats. He and I wrote an article together about the Cuban economy forty years after the revolution.[96] The country was in dire straits. When the Communist regimes collapsed in Eastern Europe, the Cuban GDP took a record dive: between 30 and 50 percent 1989–1995. Castro was forced to permit a limited liberalization of the planned economy, but he learned nothing from the experience of China and Vietnam. Cuba was still a centrally controlled planned economy which displayed the usual signs of failure, not least the humiliating presence of ration books for goods that were nowhere to be seen. Castro hated the market economy and the changes had been rolled back as soon as he had a chance. The everyday life of the ordinary Cuban was dominated by the hunt for daily necessities.

Another Latin American country that Bo visited on a few occasions was Chile. The first time was in January 1974, only a few months after the military coup against Salvador Allende. Bo wrote three articles in *Aftonbladet*, where he analyzed Allende's economic policy. He also described the military terror. Bo got the same eerie feeling as when he visited Papa Doc's Haiti in 1968.[97] These articles were the starting point for a longer essay, 'Socialismen på prov: fallet Chile [Socialism on Trial: The Case of Chile],' written with Nancy Barrett from the American University in Washington, DC.[98] Nancy and Bo argued that the Allende regime failed to understand the economic situation during his presidency and that it was not familiar with the reform methods of reformist Socialism. Allende's

[95] Södersten (1968a).

[96] Lundahl and Södersten (2000).

[97] Södersten (1974b, 1974c, 1974d).

[98] Published in Södersten (1975).

economic policy was ideological and completely unrealistic. The government failed to devise efficient methods for dealing with the economy. The rate of inflation accelerated. Socialization and nationalization did nothing to improve the situation and the price controls that were introduced led to queues of the Soviet types and black markets. In the end, the policies of the Allende government paved the way for the military coup.

Ten years later, Bo wrote three more articles on Chile, after another visit to the country.[99] There was no question about the fact that Chile in 1984 was a dictatorship where terror and repression was still present, albeit not on the same scale as during the first years of junta rule. The Chilean economy was in deep trouble. The junta had implemented a neoliberal economic policy: privatization, a minimum of intervention, monetarism and free trade. Inflation had been brought down, production had increased and fruit and forestry products had begun to be exported. The economy seemed to be recovering. In 1979, however, the Chilean government committed the mistake of tying the peso to the US dollar. When the value of the dollar subsequently increased, Chile experienced export difficulties, while imports increased strongly. The current account of the balance of payments displayed persistent deficits and Chile became one of the most indebted countries in the world. At the same time, open unemployment soared to 25 percent. The gap between the rich and the poor increased.

In 1984, the government was hoping for an international upswing. The question was how long it would continue in power. Bo saw some hopeful signs among the opposition: the Christian Democrats and the Socialists. The best economists were found among the former and the Socialist party seemed to be overcoming inner tensions and was seeking inspiration not in Cuba anymore but in sister parties in democratic European countries like France, Spain and Greece. This was hopeful in a situation where a sudden collapse of the military regime could not be discarded.

After Bo's 1984 visit, the Chilean economy, which had hit bottom in 1982–1983, entered a growth phase. In 1989, the political situation changed as well. The Pinochet regime lost the elections and would be replaced by a democratic coalition. The following year, Bo visited Chile for the third time and wrote two more newspaper articles that did not

[99] Södersten (1984b, 1984c, 1984d).

endear him to the Swedish left.[100] The Swedish debate about Chile had been ideologically infected. It was time to wake up to reality. Whatever you might think about the Pinochet regime, it had managed to break the dependence on copper, diversify exports and put the economy on a growth path driven by free trade. With the democratic coalition, the economic policy would not be changed but the new government intended to do something about the large income gaps.

Ten more years would pass before Bo visited Chile for the last time, together with Kristian Nyberg, whose specialty was pension systems. This resulted in a journal article about the Chilean economy 1970–2000. Chile's free trade policy was a long-run success story. The large balance of payments deficits at the beginning of the 1980s were curbed when Chile abandoned the linking of the peso to the dollar. The peso depreciated and Chile began to pay off its foreign debt. The positive economic development of the 1980s continued under the democratic regimes of the 1990s and growth began to be translated into the construction of a welfare state. One of the most important components of the latter was a fully funded pension system which had been so successful that it began to serve as a model for other Latin American countries. Altogether, Chile was a country that could look to the future with confidence.[101]

The Chilean experience was vastly superior to the Cuban one.[102] The Swedish press had treated Cuba favorably, while Chile had been portrayed as a country governed by mass murderers. The public opinion was one-eyed. You could, however, not get away from the fact that since Castro had assumed power, 100,000 Cubans had been put in camps or in other institutions and between 15,000 and 17,000 had been shot. This had been downplayed in Sweden. The same was true with respect to the incontrovertible economic progress made in Chile, while the Cuban economy had broken down after the fall of Communism in Eastern Europe and the Cubans had not understood that they had to redirect their economic policy along Chilean lines.

A Latin American nation that appealed to Bo was Costa Rica, which he visited in 1967 and 1987. Bo described it as a country that differed favorably from the other Central American countries. It had avoided

[100] Södersten (1990f, 1990g).

[101] Södersten and Nyberg (2001).

[102] Södersten (2001c).

right-wing dictatorships and had a democratic left.[103] Bo thought that it was strange that neighboring Sandinist Nicaragua received Swedish foreign aid, but not Costa Rica.

Africa and Asia

In 1970, Bo got a SIDA assignment to analyze the economies of Botswana and Swaziland and their dependence on South Africa. He spent four weeks in these two countries and produced a report, most of which was reprinted in one of his books of essays.[104] There, he discusses the customs and currency unions with South Africa, which limited the possibility of trading with outside countries and made it difficult to pursue an independent economic policy. Also, workers in the two small countries were dependent on jobs in the South African mining sector. Most people, however, made their living from livestock raising and agriculture, a sector subject to overgrazing. Most Swedish assistance had been concentrated on education and Bo suggested that this should be continued and expanded.

The second time that Bo did a development consultancy he went to Ethiopia as part of a review of the health sector in connection with the country's fourth five-year plan. He participated in the analysis of the costs of the sector. It was clear that the planned expansion of health care could not be financed with the funds allocated in the budget. Either more money would have to be provided or patient fees would have to be introduced.[105]

Bo would later deal with the third country in Southern Africa: Namibia, in 1983, a decade after the Ethiopian study, in a paper presented in a symposium on the economics of the primary sector.[106] At the time, Namibia was administered by South Africa. The country had rich natural resources. Almost 50 percent of its GDP is derived from mineral production. Bo analyzed the Namibian economy in Ricardian terms: more productive (low-cost) mines are exploited before less productive ones. He trusted that the country would become independent in the near future and speculated about how the mineral rents would then be distributed

[103] Södersten (1984a).

[104] Södersten (1975).

[105] Imperial Ethiopian Government (1973).

[106] Södersten (1985b).

between the state, the capital owners and the workers. He saw a risk that in the process the rents would be squandered at the expense of future development. Also, Namibia ought to leave the customs union with South Africa in order to speed up the country's industrialization.

About Asia Bo only wrote a few newspaper articles. I drafted him for a seminar in Hanoi in 1989 around the theme of *Doi moi*—fence breaking—the Vietnamese term for liberalization of the economy. The Vietnamese had understood that central planning did not work and had introduced the market economy.[107] Bo saw the results in the streets of Hanoi: goods everywhere—the results of a process that Sweden ought to support. Another Asian country that had managed the transition from plan to market was India.[108] After forty years of Soviet-style planning, in 1991, the country had changed its course completely and cleaned out the mess of protection and regulations and put India on a growth path fueled by foreign investment and an excellent education system. The future of Hong Kong, which Bo visited in 1991, was far gloomier. It had had an amazing growth rate since the 1950s, but what would happen after the transfer from British to Chinese sovereignty in 1997 was far from clear. 200,000 people had emigrated from Hong Kong and it was in no way certain that the Communist regime would respect property rights in Hong Kong there, let alone political freedom. As we know, it didn't.[109]

In Parliament

In the fall of 1979, Bo began a nine-year period in the Swedish parliament, for the Dalarna constituency. As it seems, he had been aiming for a political career for quite some time. He had a political heritage from home, he had been the chairman of the Social Democratic club Laboremus during his Uppsala years, during the 1960s, he had written a number of excellent, ideologically colored essays, in the 1970s. During 1971–1972, he was a regular columnist in *Aftonbladet*.[110] Bo had also lectured, participated in meetings and spoken on May Day back home in

[107] Södersten (1989j).

[108] Södersten (2006c).

[109] Södersten (1991d).

[110] He collected most of his columns in Södersten (1975).

Dalarna and he had seen to it that he was visible in the newspapers by writing on a wide range of subjects.

Bo was elected, but his years in Parliament did not turn out as he had expected. Being an economics professor, it would have been natural for the party to put him directly into the Standing Committee on Finance, but he had to fight hard to make it there. Bo remained on this committee between 1982 and 1988. In 1983, he became the chairman of the Government Committee on Capital Gains, whose task it was to propose new rules for taxation of shares, bonds and options. Its work resulted in some minor changes, but the final proposal presented in 1986 was rejected by the Ministry of Finance, a fact which hurt Bo a lot. In 1984, he also became member of the Committee on Reformed Income Taxation [Kommittén för reformerad inkomstbeskattning—RINK].

At the beginning of his years in Parliament, Bo made a serious effort to fall in line with his party. Employment was high on the list of its priorities, and it was important for a new, ambitious MP to defend it. To that end, Bo even went so far as to advocate restrictions on foreign trade.[111] His suggestion resulted in a newspaper article by the economist Harry Flam, who lampooned his arguments by quoting his arguments in favor of free trade as he had presented them in *International Economics*.[112]

Bo's economist background made him frequently clash with those of his party colleagues who were more intent on rapid political gains. During a routine Tuesday meeting with all the Social Democratic MPs at the beginning of December 1984, the Minister for Social Affairs, Sten Andersson, argued that the Swedish economy was in such good shape that it was time to give back to the pensioners what they had lost on the 1982 devaluation. Bo was shocked and said that it was the most stupid thing he had ever heard. When finally, the economy was beginning to be under control, you could not just start squandering the gains.[113]

Bo's effort did not take him anywhere, so after a while, he gave up and began to push his own ideas. One of these, of course, dealt with the housing market. During the 1980s, large subsidies had gone into construction, largely for macroeconomic stabilization reasons. Bo thought that this was a waste of money. The subsidies mainly went to the big cities

[111] Södersten (1980b).

[112] Flam (1980).

[113] Södersten (2006b, p. 47).

and not for example to his own Dalarna. He got in touch with his fellow Social Democrat Dalecarlians for a common motion. The party leadership, however, was completely against it so he had to withdraw the motion.[114]

The story does not end there. Bo returned with another motion that stated that the subsidies were far too generous, that they tended to contribute to the overheating of the economy and that the regional focus was mistaken.[115] The housing motion was dealt with in Parliament on 28 April 1988.[116] When many of the MPs, including the Minister of Housing, Hans Gustafsson, were listening from their rooms, but when they understood how hot the topic was, they hurried to the session hall, which was quickly filled, to listen to how Bo did his best to discredit the Social Democratic housing policy. But nothing came out of Bo's motion, since it was not anchored with the top brass of the party.[117]

Perhaps the most important person in the Social Democratic establishment, as far as Bo was concerned, was Kjell-Olof Feldt, Minister of Finance 1983–1990. Bo and Feldt had met each other during their Uppsala years, but had never become close friends, and had had a few controversies. Bo had told Feldt that he was never going to be anybody. 'Bo aspired to become a minister,' says Feldt. 'When I became Secretary of State in the Ministry of Finance … he began to show some interest and inquired whether I had any assignment for him, but I didn't find any … I did not think that Södersten would be a good decision maker. Bo could drive people nuts by his comments.'[118]

According to Feldt, Bo made life in Parliament difficult for himself. He always spoke when economic topics were under discussion. In the beginning, many thought that it was great to have a professor of economics in the group, but he had a tendency to assume extreme positions. 'He went very far with his visions, illusions and aggressions. He easily worked himself up, which was a bit unnecessary in the group discussions, and the more disappointed he got, the more aggressive he turned.' Bo did not realize that in order to make it in politics you must be able to compromise. He was too egocentric, too stubborn and resisted compromises. Bo

[114] Ibid., pp. 46–47.

[115] Motion 1987/88.

[116] Riksdagens protokoll 1987/88:110.

[117] Södersten (2006b, p. 48).

[118] Interview with Kjell-Olof Feldt, 21 April 2021.

never managed to anchor his pet project—labor-managed firms—in the party top hierarchy. 'Olof Palme was against the idea. He thought that when the Codetermination in Industry Act had been passed, this was the most important democratic reform since that of universal suffrage. This was what would give the workers influence, not the takeover of firms. It was not possible to go any further. Two philosophies collided, and it was Palme who had the power.'[119]

Bo wanted to make a political career, but he had a way of bringing out his own person in a way which made decision-makers who were to assign people political tasks hesitate. He became aggressive against the party group and blew his top without any apparent reason. The result was that he never got the positions that he aspired to. If we are to believe Feldt, this was what made Bo turn around politically. He discovered that Social Democracy and Parliament offered no career prospects for him. He went from being a radical Social Democrat to become a Liberal, in very many respects.

The Debater

When Bo Södersten left Parliament in 1988, he returned to his chair in Lund, where he remained until his retirement in 1996. Two years later, he moved to Jönköping, where his wife, Birgit Friggebo, former Minister of Housing and Culture (including immigration and equality), had become County Governor. Bo and Birgit remained there until 2004, when Birgit ended her term. In Jönköping, Bo was affiliated with the Jönköping International Business School.

Bo continued writing scientific articles and book chapters and editing books. However, during the rest of his active life, his main activity consisted in writing newspaper articles on (mostly) controversial themes. Bo was a magnificent egocentric, a fact that he was aware of, and which was directly related to his desire to write newspaper articles. 'I know that my words will reach many people,' he writes in his memoir draft. 'Of course, this is nice, since I am an egocentric, but at the same time I want to fight that side by reaching outside myself.'[120] He felt an inner urge to state his view and became obsessed by his theses when he

[119] Ibid.

[120] Södersten (2001a).

wrote. From 1988, Bo contributed regularly to *Dagens Nyheter*, *Svenska Dagbladet*, *Sydsvenskan* and *Privata Affärer*, and in Jönköping, also *Jönköpings-Posten*.

Some of his articles were republished in collections of essays, but far from all. To *Den hierarkiska välfärden* [The Hierarchical Welfare] (1968), which I have already dealt with, have to be added *Den svenska sköldpaddan* [The Swedish Turtle] (1975), *Ut ur krisen* [Out of the Crisis] (1981) and *Kapitalismen byggde landet* [Capitalism Built the Country] (1991).[121] The latter collection, however, only contains articles written between 1984 and 1990, and nothing written between 1991 and 2006 exists in book form. In the following, I will make an attempt to deal with Bo's vast article output, roughly arranged by theme.

The first time that Bo became seriously involved in writing newspaper articles was when he wrote chronicles for *Aftonbladet* in 1971–1972. These dealt mainly with Socialist themes. The Swedish Social Democracy had weathered the crisis of the 1930*s* and contributed to the survival of capitalism. Wasn't it the time, then, for society to get an influence over how the firms were managed? Wasn't it fair that the municipalities should expropriate land without having to pay the owners compensation for value increases that were the result of public measures? Was it reasonable to attempt to realize Socialist goals within a system dominated by capitalism and private property? Did the stock market really contribute to capital formation or should it be compared with betting on the ponies? Bo wrote in *Aftonbladet* about the distribution of income between labor and capital, he criticized the political parties—right and left—he reviewed books, not least the memoirs of Bertil Ohlin, and in a comment on the new edition of Myrdal's classic *Vetenskap och politik i nationalekonomin* [*The Political Element in the Development of Economic Theory*] from 1972,[122] he criticized Myrdal for not including his teacher Gustav Cassel among the economists that posed as scientists when they acted as politicians.

121 Södersten (1968b, 1975, 1981, 1991i).

122 Myrdal (1972). The English translation is from 1953 (Myrdal, 1953).

Economic Policy

Bo Södersten participated in the debate on Swedish economic policy during his entire professional career. His views changed over time, as a result of his movement from the left to the right on the political scale when he left Parliament in 1988. In his youth, he was a Socialist who advocated extensive intervention in the market mechanism and a large public sector. During his Parliament years, however, he gradually became convinced that excessive tampering with the market might result in various types of government failure and reduced welfare.

In 1971, Bo scrutinized the budget of the Social Democrats. It stressed industrial investment. The private companies had been granted a 10 percent deduction on their investments, but Bo argued that these investments should be controlled by the state as part of the creation of a planned economy.[123] Five years later, Sweden got its first non-Socialist government since the 1930s. Bo reviewed its first year.[124] The krona had been devalued twice. Devaluation, however, was a short-run measure that mainly served to give the economy breathing space and its efficiency was dependent on the restriction of total demand, something that the new government had not managed. To ensure a long-run expansion of the economy, completely different measures were called for. The solution—as always for Bo at that time—was found in a combination of labor-managed firms and wage-earners' funds.

In 1981, Bo Södersten published his third collection of essays, *Ut ur krisen* [Out of the Crisis].'[125] The title essay analyzes the 1970s crisis and the crisis policy of the Liberal-Center-Conservative government. Bo argued that it had failed. The stimulation measures employed in 1978 and 1979 had led to an increase in the size of the public sector, while the effects on the private sector had been small, and the income distribution had become more unequal. Bo sketched an alternative economic policy. The current account of the balance of payments was negative so he wanted to switch the demand from imported to domestic goods by supply stimulation: selective measures directed at specific branches, like import substitution in the energy sector. The nuclear power issue was locked after the 1980 referendum (see below), but Bo wanted to de-ideologize

[123] Södersten (1971a).

[124] Södersten (1977c).

[125] Södersten (1981).

it and let the economic arguments speak. Another such measure was the subsidization of the construction of dwellings.

In 1982, the Social Democrats were back in power. An OECD forecast for 1986 indicated that the Swedish growth rate might deviate negatively from that of the rest of the Western world. A growth-oriented economic policy was needed.[126] Bo saw three threats to the Swedish long-run standard of living.[127] Unless Sweden was at the front of technical development, factor prices would be equalized, and wages would be reduced. The foreign debt had increased from 70 billion kronor in 1976 to 350 billion in 1982, and it was possible that all the fruits of growth, and more, might have to be spent on servicing this. Finally, the trade unions had developed into special interest groups which made demands that were not compatible with the growth rate.

In this situation, surprisingly, Bo argued that the Swedish Social Democracy would benefit from a Conservative slave on the triumphal chariot.[128] Conservative ideas had played an important role in the Swedish industrialization process—hard work, altruism and imagination. The Conservatives, however, had not developed their positive heritage but had degenerated to the defense of privileges, grumbling and flight from reality. The heritage had to be resurrected.

1988 was Bo Södersten's last year in Parliament. Toward the end of it, he concluded that the Social Democrats had managed the economic policy relatively well. Above all, they had managed to reduce both the public expenditures and the budget deficits. Bo called for further expenditure reductions, but the parliamentary situation, with the Greens tipping the scales, made this difficult. Bo wanted agreements across party lines. It was time to say goodbye to bloc politics and be pragmatic.[129]

Saulus Falls off the Horse

In 1990, Bo launched a frontal attack on the Social Democrats. In an article with the provocative title 'Kapitalismen byggde landet [Capitalism

[126] Södersten (1985d).

[127] Södersten (1985c).

[128] Södersten (1986).

[129] Södersten (1988b).

Built the Country],'[130] an article which also provided the title of his last book of essays,[131] he contended that they had played a very small role in the process that created Sweden's wealth. Without the capitalist market economy, the Social Democracy would not have had any role to play. The high and even growth between 1870 and 1970 was due exclusively to private capitalism. Not even during the 1930s had the Social Democracy played any decisive role. What put a brake on the depression in Sweden was the abandonment of the gold standard, but that took place in 1931 before the Social Democrats formed their government, and the rate of unemployment stayed at the 10 percent level throughout the decade. The 'miracle years' of the 1950s and 1960s, in turn, were due to the international boom. The role of the Social Democrats had simply been to redistribute the wealth generated by the capitalist growth process.[132]

The year before the parliamentary elections in 1991, Bo wrote an article where he criticized the Social Democratic crisis package.[133] Too many remained outside the labor market and it was too easy to manipulate the system of social insurance. The Swedish krona was under pressure, the package was not focused, and nothing was done to address the structural problems. The Social Democrats risked losing the elections, which was precisely what happened. In another article, after the elections, Bo reflected about what could happen after this 'historical' defeat when the long leftist trend in Swedish politics was broken. The Social Democrats and the Left received less than 43 percent of the votes, the Greens were outside Parliament and two new parties, both on the right, entered. It was not certain that the Social Democrats were prepared to undertake any self-examination.[134]

Bo was not particularly impressed by the new government. The new Prime Minister, Carl Bildt, had managed to put the wrong people in the wrong positions. The government consisted of too many weak links.[135] Each party concentrated on its pet questions and failed to see the overall picture. The public sector was too large and too unproductive. It had to

[130] Södersten (1990j).

[131] Södersten (1991i).

[132] Södersten (1990j).

[133] Södersten (1990l).

[134] Södersten (1991g).

[135] Södersten (1992f).

be trimmed and the costly ATP pension system (see below) had to be phased out in favor of a fully funded system. The new government lacked reform ideas. What was needed was an unprejudiced retreat from exaggerated and unrealistic welfare ambitions. Marginal adjustments would not do. The government could not continue to focus on the traditional recipients and favor its own voters.[136]

1994 was both an election year and the year when the Swedish people was to vote about the possible entry into the EG. The best thing would be if after the elections the Social Democrats and the Moderates could cooperate. The smaller parties had demonstrated their negative impact on the economic policy. If the Greens made it back into Parliament they were likely to collaborate with the Left and turn the Social Democrats into a populist direction, with uncontrolled budget deficits and possibly a no to the EG.[137] The elections resulted in a safe leftist majority. Bo thought that a majority of the Swedish people wanted a government with both Social Democrats and Conservatives, but that was impossible. The gap between the Social Democrats and the Moderates was unbridgeable. The only alternative was a Social Democratic government, an alternative that did not appeal to Bo.[138]

A fortnight later, Bo sharpened his tone against the Left. How much was its triumph in the elections worth? Its analysis of the causes of the economic crisis was erroneous—that the 1990 tax reform and the deregulations of the credit and currency markets had created a speculation economy and a bank crisis, and that unemployment was due to the low total demand. The parties on the left had problems making it beyond the traditional Keynesisan recipe. But the situation required control of the budget deficit, not expansion. The Greens and the Left probably wanted to go back to the old regulations but that was impossible.[139]

Among the political left, the skepticism of the market was cemented. The market economy made leftist policies impossible, it was undemocratic and it made it impossible to arrive at a reasonable income distribution. Bo thought that the position was hilarious.[140] There was no 'right' income

[136] Södersten (1992g, 1992h).

[137] Södersten (1994d).

[138] Södersten (1994f).

[139] Södersten (1994g).

[140] Södersten (1995d).

distribution. Voting on it would simply lead to majority exploitation of the minority. The opulence of the Western world rested on the fact that arbitrary political interventions in the economy had been ruled out. The Swedish problem was not that markets had been given free rein. The political system had to take a step back and let the market work on its own premises. Bo saw a flight from reality among the Swedish politicians. The media were chasing sensations and entertainment and the politicians loved to sit down in the TV sofas. Neither the politicians nor the media had the stamina to focus long on the problems, even when they had long-term implications. Pseudo problems were invented that were substituted for the real ones.[141]

In 1997, the Social Democrats had one year left in office. Bo did not think that they had managed the economic policy particularly well. Unemployment was high, which was due not least to the mistrust of the market in the party which preferred state monopolies and expansion of the public sector. This had resulted in a high tax burden and low growth and employment.[142] During the next elections, in 1998, the Social Democrats lost 30 seats while the Left won 21. This did not bode well. The former would have to lean on the latter, with all that this implied in terms of hostility against the market and populism. More monopolies and subsidies of the public sector were sure to come.[143]

In 1999, Bo pointed out that Sweden was sensitive to changes in the international economy because of its large public sector and its high tax burden. The country had failed to put the economy in order during the upswing in the 1980s, in bright contrast to countries like Holland and Denmark. The necessary measures had to be implemented during good times, not bad. If not, the situation would simply grow worse. The contrast between Holland and Denmark on the one hand and Sweden on the other were bright. Sweden had ended up in a situation of political passivity, high unemployment and dependency on social insurance, while Holland and Denmark had addressed the problem and cut the unemployment rate in half. The rate of growth of the economies of the latter two countries had been twice as high as the Swedish one.[144]

[141] Södersten (1994h).

[142] Södersten (1997c).

[143] Södersten (1998d).

[144] Södersten (1999d).

In 2005, Erik Jonasson, Lars Pettersson and Bo criticized the Swedish employment policy.[145] At the beginning of the 1990s, half a million jobs had disappeared. Between 1994 and 1998, the economy was'cleaned up,' but in the wrong way: by increasing the tax burden. No less than 85 percent of the GDP increase 1994–2000 was taxed away. In 2005, unemployment remained high so the government put together a work group to find out how the labor supply could be increased. Erik, Lars and Bo argued that this amounted to putting the cart before the horse. Never in modern times had so many been outside the labor market. The demand for labor must be stimulated in the private, competitive sector, through tax reductions.

The growth rate of the Swedish economy was decent: 2.3 percent per annum, but employment did not expand. Far too many were outside the labor force and far too many were reported sick, for reasons that were not exclusively medical.[146] Why were there no new jobs? In economies at the level of development of Sweden, most new employment opportunities were created in the service sectors: childcare and care of the elderly, education, travel and entertainment. Sweden had opted for producing many of these services in the bloated and low-productive public sector. The competitive sectors, in turn, were capital-intensive and their growth did not create many jobs. The employment opportunities were found in the service sectors, but these had to be exposed to competition and their production had to be determined by the market.

The Overgrown Public Sector

It was inevitable that Bo would deal with the public sector. During his Socialist period, he defended it, like when in 1971, he began a polemic about how SACO (the Swedish Confederation of Professional Associations) calculated real wages. SACO had concentrated exclusively on private consumption by calculating the after-tax wage. The taxes paid by its members were wasted and increases of the contributions to social insurance only led to a reduced living standard. Bo thought it sensational that an organization whose members were mainly producing public services

145 Jonasson et al. (2005).

146 Södersten (2005e).

completely disregarded the utility of its own work.[147] Lars Tobisson, the SACO head of investigations, answered that Bo's accusation was blatantly wrong. The organization had never denied the welfare value of public services, but its members as a rule paid more in taxes that what they got back, and the after-tax wage was more interesting than the pre-tax wage as far as the private consumption standard was concerned.[148]

In connection with his participation in the committees on capital gains and reformed income taxation in the 1980s, Bo edited a book on the new tax system that was being forged, *Skattereform och skatteplanering* [Tax Reform and Tax Planning].[149] His own chapter dealt with the probable effects of a broadened tax base and changes in capital taxation.[150] He discussed not only the technical aspects but also the political factors that influenced the work. One of the most important proposals was a reduction of the tax on labor incomes, a measure applauded by the center-right parties but booed by the Left and the Greens. The Social Democrats had supported the committee work but all their members might not agree.

The year after the publication of *Skattereform och skatteplanering*, Bo edited a second volume on the same theme, *Den stora reformen* [The Great Reform].[151] By then, the proposal had been worked out. It implied that 90 percent of all Swedish taxpayers would pay only local taxes and not state income tax. The lower limit for the latter in the end was fixed at 180,000 kronor, an agreement which would become known as 'the tax reform of the century.' Bo's own introductory chapter is basically a variation on the theme he presented in the first book. He accounts for how the reform was conceived and presents its probable economic effects.

Taxes were but one component of the public sector. Another important aspect of the latter was its size, the largest among the industrialized market economies. Bo thought that it had grown *too* large, and its productivity was low, which was reflected in the wage level. The remedy was obvious. The productivity of the public sector could only be increased through incentives for the employees and a reduction of their number. This should not be too difficult. Labor was scarce in Sweden at the end

[147] Södersten (1971b).

[148] Tobisson (1971).

[149] Södersten (1989a).

[150] Södersten (1989b).

[151] Södersten (1990b).

of the 1980s, so people would not become unemployed.[152] This would, however, soon change. At the beginning of the 1990s, Sweden entered a period of economic stagnation. By then, it was difficult to find ways to move people out of an ever more inefficient public sector into the more productive parts of the economy.[153]

Nourishing and Draining

In 1992, Bo Södersten assumed a more and more aggressive position vis-à-vis the public sector. He did not hesitate to call it 'draining [tärande]' as opposed to the 'nourishing' private sector. In two articles, he contended that those who were looking for the roots of Sweden's economic problems were looking in the wrong place. He presented a table showing how the balance between the 'nourishing' and 'draining' sectors had changed between 1970 and 1992. The latter numbered those in the public sector, the pensioners, those reported sick and on parental leave, those seeking asylum, those in the programs of the National Labour Market Board and the openly unemployed. The 'nourishing' were those employed in the private sector. The ratio of'draining' to'nourishing' had increased from 0.9 in 1970 to 2.3 in 1992. The former were paid through taxes and contributions. The number of 'nourishing' had been reduced while the number of employees in the public sector had increased. This was no sound development, since the productivity in the latter had deceased. Many had opted out of the labor market. The real age of retirement had decreased from 67 to 61–62 thanks to generous rules and high compensation levels.[154] The 'central Swedish problem' was to restore the balance between the two groups.

In common parlance, the shit hit the fan. The politically correct and the employees depicted Bo as a vulgar agitator, who called the employees in the public sector parasites, a humbug and a categoric economic guru, who by his writings hardly contributed anything 'nourishing.'[155] However, Bo maintained that he was right. The consumption of the public employees and their clients was paid with taxes on the private

[152] Södersten (1988c).

[153] Södersten (1991h).

[154] Södersten (1992d, 1992e).

[155] Sundell (1993) and Bergqvist (1993). See also Rothstein and Boëthius (1993).

sector.[156] The welfare state was a thing of the past. Jobs were lost in the industrial sector and people on welfare payments had been substituted for workers. Those in the public sector did not have to contribute to their wages, The taxpayers saw to it that they got paid.[157] Bo thought that the policy built on the 'After us the deluge' principle.[158]

The attacks on Bo's vocabulary continued. In 1994, Bengt Furåker, professor of sociology in Gothenburg contended that his statistics were shaky. The dependency ratio must be calculated on the basis of the entire population. Those paid for by the private sector amounted to no more than 32 percent in 1992, a picture that differed radically from the one presented by Bo.[159] The latter, however, continued his criticism in 1994. Sweden had 600,000 openly unemployed or in public employment programs and a budget deficit that was matched only by that of Greece.[160] It could be reduced only through public sector reforms: pensions, family policy and a reduction of the exaggerated payments via the social security system.[161] The reform of the public sector was not simply a matter of cutting back, but also of reprioritization: in the industrial sector and in education, to ensure that people would work in high-productivity branches.[162] But the politicians stood out as powerless and did nothing.

Pensions: Reform of the ATP System

One of the most important components of the public sector is the pension system. At the beginning of the 1990s, the public sector was handling more than 60 percent of Sweden's resources. In spite of this stunning fact, no textbooks existed that dealt with it. Bo therefore edited an anthology where he contributed a chapter on pensions himself.[163] The chapter is mainly a historical account of how Sweden got a pay-as-you-go system

[156] Södersten (1993b).

[157] Södersten (1993c).

[158] Södersten (1993d).

[159] Furåker (1994).

[160] Södersten (1994b).

[161] Södersten (1994c).

[162] Södersten (1994e).

[163] Södersten (1992b).

where current payments financed the expenditures during the same year, a fact which Bo attributed to the strong economic growth 1870–1960.[164] He then discussed the differences between this and a fully funded system, where the individuals' pensions are based on their previous payments. In the Swedish ATP supplementary pensions system, this link was missing. Bo thought that the Swedish pension system had defects, but a transition to a fully funded system was not without problems either. The members of the generation which had to pay for the phase-out of the pay-as-you-go system without getting any pensions within this system themselves would in principle pay their pensions twice, both in the old system and in the new, fully funded, one.

Changes to the ATP system were on their way. In 1993, a work group in the Ministry for Social Affairs was working on a reform to establish a link between lifetime incomes and pensions. Bo saw this as an indication of a 'limited sobering up' and pointed to the absurdities of the actual system, where pension levels were based only on the income of the fifteen best years and you had to work for a mere thirty years for full pension: a system where low-wage earners who had worked their entire adult lives subsidized high-income earners with short careers.[165] In 1994, the pension system was changed into a system based on payments. Bo was worried about the financial aspects. The tax burden was so high that it was doubtful whether the taxpayers could stand any more taxes and fees. Half the pension fees would be paid by the employers and the other half by the employees themselves, which would increase the average tax rate to 60 percent and the marginal one to 75–80 percent.[166]

The work on the pension reform continued after 1994. The reform was not sanctioned until 1998. One feature of the reformed system was that the individuals themselves could determine how 2.5 percent of the payments would be placed, However, in 1999, this was being sabotaged by the state, argued Bo, by confiscation of up to 90 percent of the fee agreed between the individual and the institution contracted to handle his funds, which would make the transaction unprofitable for the private

[164] Södersten (1992c).

[165] Södersten (1993e).

[166] Södersten (1995f). For an evaluation of the 1994 pension reform, see Kruse and Ståhlberg (2020).

agents.[167] Bo wanted to see a fully funded system where the size of the pensions was determined exclusively by what the individuals had paid and how well their funds were administered. Good institutions had an important role to play. The pension system had to be removed from the political sphere and transferred to the exclusively economic one.[168]

Nuclear Power

In 1980, the future of nuclear power was subjected to a referendum in Sweden. Bo was in favor of a gradual phase-out determined by how much electricity the country needed to preserve employment and welfare. When, at the end of the 1980s, the question of an early phase-out was put on the political agenda, he argued that this amounted to madness. Nuclear power was cheap and efficient, and a premature phase-out would lead to large economic losses. No realistic possibility existed that alternative, sustainable, energy sources could be substituted for it in the short run. Sweden needed nuclear power for its future development.[169]

In 1990, when it had been decided that the twelve existing Swedish nuclear reactors, on grounds that Bo thought completely erroneous, he edited an anthology where he and eight other authors defended the use of nuclear power.[170] It dealt with the relative costs of nuclear and other forms of power, the economic implications of a phase-out and the issue of pricing and consumption of electricity. Sweden had a strong comparative advantage in electricity production, not only hydroelectric but also nuclear power. The Swedish politicians, however, wanted to destroy the latter, an attitude that indicated not only lack of contact with reality but also fishing for votes.[171] When, in 1997, it was decided that the Barsebäck power station would be closed, Bo reacted immediately and called the decision irrational.[172]

In 1999, twenty years had passed since the referendum. Bo thought that the Swedish energy policy still was as bizarre as then. It was not

[167] Södersten (1999b).

[168] Södersten (1991h).

[169] Södersten (1989f, 1989g, 1990k).

[170] Södersten (1990c).

[171] Södersten (1996g).

[172] Södersten (1997b).

possible to scrap nuclear power and simultaneously cut down on fossil fuels. If you did not want the former, the natural thing was to import electricity and increase the use of natural gas.[173] Bo could never let go of the idea that the Swedish attitude to nuclear power was irrational. In 2004, he thought that it was time to wake up and reconsider the nuclear power decision. Why not use the fact that Sweden had one of the most efficient power systems in the world, hydroelectric and nuclear. The latter had contributed to the success of Swedish industry, but the Social Democrats were undecided.[174]

Daycare Centers or Preschools?

Somewhat unexpectedly, Bo Södersten entered the debate about family policy and public childcare which had been initiated by Alva and Gunnar Myrdal in their book *Kris i befolkningsfrågan* [Crisis in the Population Question] from 1934, where they advocated collective childcare and daycare centers in order to make it possible for women to enter the labor market.[175] Bo did not agree. He thought that the Swedish family policy had derailed.[176] In 1981, he had been a member of a group from the Swedish parliament which had made a study trip to Leipzig and Paris to study childcare methods there. The conclusion of the trip was that the Swedish system was inefficient and costly, had far more personnel than needed and lacked an elaborate pedagogic structure.[177]

Instead of daycare centers, Bo advocated a voluntary preschool, with a pedagogy that made it possible for a single teacher to handle 12–15 children. Bo had brought the issue up regularly in Parliament.[178] In Lund, an experiment was going on, which showed that the preschool concept worked. Bo wanted the experiment to be extended, but the local 'daycare center Stalinists,' the politicians from the local governing coalition, the Social Democrats, the Left Party—the Communists, and the Green Party,

[173] Södersten (1999c).

[174] Södersten (2004e).

[175] Myrdal and Myrdal (1934).

[176] Södersten (1988a).

[177] Fransson et al. (1981).

[178] Södersten (2006b, pp. 36–37).

together with the daycare personnel, did their best to kill it.[179] Nothing happened. Bo thought that the Swedish childcare system was hopeless. Sweden was a high-tax country, but the Swedes were not free to choose. Couples who wanted to raise their children at home received no contributions whatsoever. Bo thought it immoral to deprive the citizens of 65 percent of their incomes and then not let them choose themselves.[180]

University Politics

Between 1990 and 1996, Bo Södersten was the chairman of the Swedish Association of University Teachers—SULF. When he began, the universities were administered by the state, centrally administered. However, the view of central control had begun to change. Decentralization, autonomy and foundation colleges began to be prestige words in academic circles. Bo was worried about the quality of the universities.[181] They could not be centrally managed, but the departments had to have a high degree of autonomy. The recruitment to university positions had to be based on scientific merits, on the tenure track system, but too many saw university positions simply as a way of making a living and had been appointed on obscure criteria. The bureaucratic garbage had to be removed. 'The universities are not there for all kinds of administration. Research and teaching are their only central tasks.'[182]

The universities had been mistreated for twenty years, and the definition of what was a university education was very generous indeed. The idea seemed to be to keep the Swedish youths away from the universities and give them a more 'practical' education, an idea that had met with success. The universities were underdimensioned, and half the teaching staff lacked a PhD. This was fatal.[183] In 1991, Bo presented a proposal for reform of the Swedish university system.[184] It needed more resources but also increased efficiency. Central control had to go. The universities could handle the admission system themselves, based on marks and tests.

179 Södersten (1989h, 1989i).

180 Södersten (1996f).

181 Södersten (1987b).

182 Ibid.

183 Södersten (1990m).

184 Södersten (1991f).

It was not reasonable that first-year students with no overview of the university system and administrative and technical personnel should be on boards that made decisions about scientific issues. Those possessing factual knowledge should govern the universities.

In 1992, Bo edited a debate anthology, *Pendeln svänger—röster i högskoledebatten* [The Pendulum Swings—Voices in the University Debate], with contributions from politicians, administrators and academics.[185] The pendulum had begun to swing back from the centralized extreme. Bo stressed that Sweden's opulence is built on knowledge and education. Positions with no opportunity for research should be abolished. Another problem was the lack of female representation in higher academic positions. When in 1994, the Minister of Education, Carl Tham, declared that this had to be changed, SULF produced an action program. Women who applied and qualified for a professorship but were not ranked first should be given their own chairs. Special support should be provided on the road toward a possible professorship.[186]

Bo did not drop the university issues after stepping down as chairman of SULF. In 2004, he pointed out that the quality of the Swedish universities was being undermined. The requirements on doctoral dissertations had been lowered and chairs were manned through internal promotion instead of through open competition. Outside customers should not determine the contents of research. That would turn the universities into consultancy firms. The universities had to be led by academic researchers and teachers. The university world had to be viewed in a wider perspective. Sweden's economic success had built on the principle of meritocracy, but in certain contexts, this principle had been discarded, like when at Uppsala University admission to law school had been based on ethnic criteria instead of high-school grades.[187]

Immigration

One of the most controversial questions within the EU was immigration. Sweden's policy had deviated considerably from that of more

[185] Södersten (1992a).

[186] Jalakas (1994).

[187] Södersten (2004f).

restrictive countries, like Finland.[188] It worked until 1970: labor immigration which yielded a net contribution to GDP. Thereafter, however, the picture had changed, with the immigration of refugees. The immigrants were heavily overrepresented among those living on welfare. They had problems making it into the Swedish labor market. The integration was miserable. Bo posed the question of whether the immigration policy should not be changed so as to favor well-educated groups from Eastern Europe.

The Swedish share of immigrants in the total population was twice the Danish one. In Denmark, seven years of residence was required for a permanent residence permit, persons who had committed crimes were deported immediately, the immigration of family members was limited and the immigrants had to prove that they could support themselves. In Sweden, where requirements were less stringent, the simple, manual jobs had disappeared, and in certain groups, open unemployment was as high as 40–50 percent.[189] The Swedish immigration policy had been a failure during twenty years.[190] The net cost of immigration amounted to 2–3 percent of GDP. Among African and Arab males, the rate of employment was below 50 percent, and among women a great deal less. Around 80 percent of those applying for asylum lacked identification papers, an indication that they wanted to hide something from the authorities.

The Swedish Prime Minister, Göran Persson, appeared not to share Bo's views on labor immigration. He had cautioned against 'social tourism' from the new EU countries, which Bo interpreted as resistance to labor immigration from the Baltic states and Poland.[191] Sweden had signed the Maastricht treaty, with its four liberties, one of which was labor mobility, and hence could not pursue the opposite policy. It was absurd if the only immigrants arriving in Sweden would be people who would live on welfare.[192]

A city which had been hit particularly hard by the inability of the immigrants to support themselves was Malmö, where the employment situation was much worse than in other comparable cities. One reason

[188] Södersten (2001b).

[189] Ekberg et al. (2002).

[190] Södersten (2003).

[191] Ibid.

[192] Ibid. For a critique of Bo's statement, see Ekdal (2003).

for this was the high share of immigrants in the population, 24 percent, and their high dependence on welfare. However, the government had simply offered more welfare contributions.[193] Bo indefatigably continued his campaign. Certain immigrant groups systematically abused the welfare system.[194] It was obvious that the Swedish social policy must be redirected toward more self-support and less welfare. Early retirement alone cost 50 billion kronor per year, which Bo thought was an absurdly high figure, and nobody knew on what grounds it was granted.

'The Catching Culture': More Welfare Abuse

The Swedish employment policy contributed to job creation until the beginning of the 1990s. Then, however, the level of employment was reduced both for men and women. Sweden had failed to reform the economy and, according to Bo, had become a 'workfare state' that increased employment through generous financial contributions and by an equally generous social policy made it possible to retire early. At the same time, the solidarity wage policy in combination with the feminist ideology which demanded special wage increases for women obstructed the transfer of labor from the low-productive public sector to the high-productive private sector. All this led to the creation of negative attitudes in the labor market. To Bo, it was obvious that the Swedish welfare state had been allowed to grow in an uncontrolled manner.[195]

Between 1994 and 2004, Sweden's GDP had increased by 30 percent, but no new jobs had been created and no less than 25 percent of the adult population between 20 and 65 years of age remained outside the regular labor market.[196] Early retirement and sickness absence had become regular features of it. The construction of the welfare system encouraged this. Sweden was becoming a 'soft' state that did not impose any requirements on the citizens and which required the world's highest tax burden to muddle through.[197]

[193] Södersten (2004c).

[194] Södersten (2004d). For a retrospective view, see Widmalm (2019).

[195] Södersten (2005a).

[196] Södersten (2005b).

[197] Södersten (2005c).

The root of the evil, as Bo saw it, was the law on social services from 1980. In 1994, he launched a frontal attack on it. The individual had the right to assistance from the social welfare board for his maintenance and life in general. Bo took this to mean that here was the guarantee that the individual would never have to worry about his maintenance and went on to argue that an ample system of social insurance, early retirement and social service had been built up supported by an administrative bureaucracy and a legal system.[198] The system was impossible.

Bo received sharp criticism from the professor of social work in Lund, Ulla Pettersson, who pointed out that the right to social assistance was not unconditional. Assistance required that needs could not be satisfied in any other way, meaning that houses, cars, etc., would have to be sold before a person would qualify. In addition, the creation of the institutions that Bo referred to preceded the law.[199]

Bo, however, persisted in his criticism of the social welfare system. If nothing was done about the structural problems of the welfare state, our welfare would be threatened.[200] The social insurance system did not work. The state of the economy determined how many people were away from work. During boom years with plenty of work opportunities, it was easy to stay home. When jobs were scarce, people went to work. Why had Sweden not followed the Dutch example and seen to it that people returned to the labor market?[201]

In Bo's world, there was no place for child and health care personnel who regularly stayed away from work. Productivity was low in health care. Of the 85,000 employees in the Stockholm region, every day of the year, 27,000 never showed up: an absurd situation.[202] It was not only among nurses and auxiliaries that you could make efficiency gains. In 1996, Bo and his nephew, the physician Anders Milton, the managing director of the Swedish Medical Association, published an article that contended that Sweden had too many physicians.[203] The number of physicians had

198 Södersten (1994e).

199 Pettersson (1994). Bo's article also invited criticism from four economist colleagues. See Björklund et al. (1994). Thus, when a job was available, it had to be accepted.

200 Södersten (2000c).

201 Södersten (2002a).

202 Södersten (1992g).

203 Milton and Södersten (1996).

trebled since 1970 but the number of doctor appointments was only half of the Western European average. However, the politicians were not particularly interested in increasing efficiency.

Early retirement and sickness absence were not equally distributed across the country. Certain regions, especially the Norrland counties, were conspicuous. In Småland, the figures were much lower. There you did not live on local insurance office payments. Norrland, on the other hand, was dominated by a 'catching culture.' 'It begins with picking berries and fishing in the fall and then comes one of the great events of the year, the moose hunt. It continues with small-game hunting and winter fishing and culminates with fishing in the sun during Easter.'[204]

Concentration of Power

During his years in Parliament, Bo Södersten did not make it within a party which he conceived of as too centralized. He presented his argument in an article in *Aktuellt i Politiken*, the Social Democratic weekly.[205] Parliament was an institution that rubberstamped decisions made elsewhere. The individual MPs did not have much of a say. The Swedish Social Democracy was characterized by an extreme concentration of power to the executive committee and a small group of ministers. Bo warned that democracy was a frail plant. In order to make it flower, it was necessary to listen to what the common people had to say. The party could not become an ombudsman party governed by professional party leadership. The basis of the recruitment to the party had to be broadened.

In a talk given a few years later, Bo developed the theme. He described how decisions were made in his own party:

> The Social Democratic group in Parliament meets every Tuesday afternoon when Parliament is in session. A Social Democratic government has to have the support of its own group if it is to get its proposals through Parliament. It is therefore the custom that all proposals are presented to the parliamentary group before they are introduced in Parliament. Usually, the minister in question makes a presentation to the group on Tuesday and the proposal is introduced the following Thursday. It is in the nature of

[204] Södersten (2005d).

[205] Södersten (1988d).

> things that it is hardly possible to stage any real discussion ... under such circumstances.[206]

The parliamentary group was large, more than 150 people. Already that made detailed discussions difficult, but it was not part of Social Democratic good manners either to speak too often or make lengthy statements within the group. The latter was as a clearance central, completely subordinate to the party leadership.[207] Bo did not hesitate to call his party 'Leninist.' When it came to the election of party chairmen, beginning with that of Per Albin, there had never been more than a single candidate, and in 1995 it was time again. Ingvar Carlsson wanted Mona Sahlin to succeed him.[208] Bo. However, Sahlin made the ridiculous mistake of using a government credit card for personal expenses and had to refrain from running. She had to wait until 2007—when she was the sole candidate.

The other side of centralization was that only few persons were responsible for the contents of politics. Bo did not hesitate to charge them. In 1996, he attacked Prime Minister Ingvar Carlsson, as responsible for the Swedish crisis.[209] As Minister of Housing during the 1970s, he had contributed to weakening government finances by exaggerated subsidization of construction. In 1996, he wanted to increase taxes for high-income earners, which Bo argued would reduce the efficiency of the Swedish economy and undermine the recent tax reform. He was a weak party leader who wanted to please the Left in order to remain in power.

The political centralization within the Social Democratic party went hand in hand with the increasing symbiosis between the party and the trade union movement. The person to be blamed for his was Olof Palme, who had not been able to keep the vested interest represented by the LO at bay.[210] Palme and his generation were prisoners of collectivistic thought.[211] The earlier compromises in labor market matters were gone and the trade unions could resort to legislation to make sure that their

206 Södersten (1993?).

207 Södersten (2000b).

208 Södersten (1995e).

209 Södersten (1996b).

210 Södersten (1996c).

211 See also Södersten (1997e).

demands were met. Palme could not resist but accepted to run union errands in exchange for votes.[212]

The Swedish Social Democracy was weak: a party with a systematic incompetence cult. It was intellectually and morally bankrupt and in addition backward-looking.[213] The recruitment to the party left a lot to be desired. The Social Democratic group in Parliament had long been feeble and new members were recruited in a way which bred incompetence: one of two below forty and one of two a woman, instead of using the self-evident democratic principle: free elections. Ignorant and inexperienced politicians did not rock the boat but followed the unwritten laws of the party, above all that of complete loyalty.

The Limits of Democracy

The centralization and the cult of silence led to the question of how democracy was faring in Sweden. Bo did not think it worked particularly well.[214] For a political regime to be considered democratic, four requirements had to be met: free elections, changes of power, constitutional freedoms and rights and efficient exercise of power. Sweden was deficient with respect to the second and fourth criteria. The power hegemony of the Social Democrats had never really been challenged in spite of the fact that other parties had been in government for a few periods.

The Social Democrats remained in power after the 2002 elections. This was not good since it cemented the impression that Sweden was a one-party regime,[215] something that would guarantee that nothing changed. This hegemony influenced how power was wielded. It was difficult to oppose the party. The public administration was dominated by the Social Democrats, and those intent on a career virtually always ended up on the side of those in power.[216] Bo argued that exercise of power had to be tamed, limited and controlled so that it did not degenerate into oppression. Power had to be exercised in a competent and efficient way. As Bo saw it, this was the case only with monetary policy, an area handled by the

[212] See also Södersten (1998b).

[213] Södersten (1996e).

[214] Södersten (1997f).

[215] Södersten (2002c).

[216] Södersten (1997f).

Riksbank and not by Parliament, i.e. by competent specialists. This kind of solution could be implemented also in other areas: tax policy, health care, housing policy, energy policy and transport policy.

As could be expected, Bo was criticized from all quarters. Democracy was in danger and had to be defended at any cost. Bo was a totalitarian and a representative of shady interests. It was impossible to leave decisions with respect to the political *goals* to experts. Those decisions were collective and had to be taken in Parliament. Technocracy and bureaucracy would easily breed corruption, especially if allowed to build their own, closed worlds.[217] The Västerås bishop, Claes-Bertil Ytterberg, compared Bo's ideas to those of Adolf Hitler,[218] and an entire university department, that of journalism, media and communication, at Stockholm University, jumped him. Bo's recipe would lead to despotism. Bo did not even pretend to adhere to the principles of democracy.[219]

In 1995, Bo took his argument about politics one step further. He accused the politicians of corruption.[220] Again, his point of departure was the swollen public sector and the mistaken prioritization within it. It was OK to switch between the Labour Market Board programs for unemployed and unemployment benefits as long as you were 'at the disposal of the labor market.' It was enough to have had a paid job for 75 days to live on benefits and unemployment programs for the rest of your life. Bo asked why Sweden had ended in a situation where the senseless public expenditures skyrocketed, and the tax burden was all too high. His answer was phrased in terms of corruption. He defined two types: the one where you are after personal gains and the one where you try to conquer power by buying votes and distributing advantages. The former was absent from Swedish politics but not the latter. This was what had produced the overdimensioned public sector, the monstrous tax burden and the public debt swamp.

217 Bergström (1997).

218 Ytterberg (1997).

219 Fornäs et al. (1998).

220 Södersten (1995a). The article was translated into French (Södersten, 1995b).

Systemic Defects

After leaving Parliament in 1988, Bo began to argue that the Swedish economy was plagued by severe systemic defects. Sweden was sliding downwards in international comparisons. The high marginal tax rates discouraged people from working and making money. The economic systemic defects, like the low productivity of the public sector, were well known, but not the political ones. The Social Democracy was far too much governed from the top. Sweden had become a society where ownership of houses and shares mattered more than the ability to work. The concentration of power had led to a populist policy.[221]

Bo identified those responsible for the systemic defects: the high priests of the Social Democratic party, Olof Palme and Ingvar Carlsson.[222] The efficiency that the Social Democratic power apparatus had displayed from the beginning of the 1930s to the end of the 1960s had been replaced by populism: symbol issues and hope for a fast answer from the voters. The party was characterized by reserve and discipline. The leaders seldom had problems getting acceptance for their views and a good ear made for a place at the fleshpots. Bo wanted perestroika within the party. The Social Democrats were led by the nose by the trade unions.[223] The 1980s had been a decade of wage increases completely incompatible with the development of the economy. The trade unions could demand and get away with anything. Given the 1990 tax reform, curbing wage demands ought not to be a problem, but Ingvar Carlsson had to show some real leadership with respect to economic policy.

Time after time, Bo pointed to the systemic errors in childcare, housing and health care.[224] He had little hope that things would change since the Social Democrats lacked a firm stance on reforms. They had been able to set the political agenda for sixty years, but instead of using market-related incentives, it had resorted to a requisition mentality where the burden of the expansion of the public sector was put on the taxpayers.[225]

[221] Södersten (1989d).

[222] Södersten (1989e).

[223] Södersten (1990h).

[224] Södersten (1990i).

[225] Södersten (1991b).

If nothing was done to change this, it risked being reduced to a party without relevance for the future Swedish development.[226]

Reforming the Welfare State

The worst systemic defect of all was the degeneration of the welfare state. One of Bo's articles was given the provocative title 'Kvinnor har för höga löner [Female Wages Are Too High].'[227] The wage increases for industrial workers were lower than the productivity increases. The difference was taxed away by the state through the payroll tax. In the public sector, the situation was the opposite. Productivity had declined for a long time and resources had to be added continuously. Nurses and auxiliaries were subsidized by the industrial workers. Their marginal productivity did not differ significantly from zero. Structural reforms were needed. Wages had to match productivity. The principle of equal pay for all work was unsound.[228]

Other deficiencies were exposed in the geriatric care.[229] This was managed by the municipalities which were free to determine the charges. Bo contended that many of them had lost their sense of proportions and had converted themselves into robber institutions that confiscated the incomes and wealth of the elderly. The municipalities lacked the ability to save and often had a large budget deficit. The financing of geriatric care had to be reformed and some kind of insurance system should be introduced.

In 1996, Bo suggested a way to increase female wages—a way which was related to their productivity: a transfer of activities from the public to the private sector.[230] It was a sexist myth that women could only work in the public sector. Privatization would lead to competition, safe jobs for women and market-determined wages. Production would become efficient since only those firms that met the expectations of consumers would survive. That the welfare state could be reformed was proved by the

226 Södersten (1991e).

227 Södersten (1995c).

228 Södersten (1998c). Bo's provocation met heavy criticism. See e.g. Hedwall (1995), Janson (1995) and Nordh and Pettersson (1995).

229 Södersten (1998a).

230 Södersten (1996d).

Dutch experience. In the same way as Sweden, Holland had had an overdimensioned public sector. However, the Dutch had pulled themselves together and reduced public spending. The wage increases were held back through voluntary agreements between employers and employees. Employment increased and it even proved possible to get many people who had chosen early retirement back into the labor market. The Dutch success was due to coalition governments between center-right parties and Social Democrats. This provided a model for Sweden to follow.[231]

Bo Södersten's appreciation of the market mechanism underwent a drastic change over time. When Assar Lindbeck in 1972 praised the qualities of the market, Bo immediately attacked him. He thought that it was no use discussing how the Swedish industrial sector should be financed by the banks unless you discussed the need for technical change in the industrial sector at the same time. This called for concentrated, planned action and finance via public funds.[232] In the late 1990s, Bo's views of the market mechanism had changed radically. The stagnation of the Swedish economy was a result of the Social Democratic reluctance to accept the market economy. Sweden had a structural problem: high taxes, high public expenditures and a non-functioning labor market, but the Social Democrats refused to realize this. The market economy had to be extended to the public sector, providing signals of how resources should be allocated, of what should expand and what should contract.[233]

When Bo Södersten came to the Jönköping International Business School in 1998, he initiated a project called 'Globalization and the Welfare State.' This resulted, among other things, in two books that he edited himself, *Globalization and the Welfare State*[234] and *Den problematiska tryggheten—välfärdsstaten under tre decennier* [The Problematic Security—The Welfare State During Three Decades].[235] In an article in 2002, Bo reported some of the most important findings.[236] Sweden had an open unemployment rate of 4 percent, but if instead, you calculated how many people that did not work, you arrived at much higher figures.

231 Södersten (1998e).

232 Södersten (1972).

233 Södersten (1997d).

234 Södersten (2004a).

235 Södersten (2006a).

236 Södersten (2002b).

No less than 23 percent of the population of working age did not work. If you wanted a correct idea of the situation in the Swedish labor market it was not enough to count the openly unemployed and those in vocational training courses. You had to add those on the long-term sick list, those in early retirement, those studying (often because they did not get any job) and those who had left the labor market for other reasons, and that left all those who had reported sick, but who formally belonged to the 'working' category. Sweden was no longer a welfare state. The health insurance system sent the wrong kind of signals. The norms related to work and the use of the privileges of the welfare state had changed. The social insurance system had to change too.

In his chapter in *Globalization and the Welfare State*, Bo described the welfare society as a general equilibrium system, a system where changes in the private sector, the public sector and the welfare system all affect each other.[237] The reduced growth since the beginning of the 1970s had increased the rate of unemployment and the generous construction of the social welfare system had reduced the willingness to work.

In the second book from the welfare state project, the point of departure was the early 1970s, the period when Sweden began its journey from high to low growth, and the expansion of the welfare state thereafter. The purpose of the book was to sketch some of the major problems likely to be on the future agenda. Bo's chapter is an extended version of the chapter in the English volume, a somewhat curious mixture of the Swedish economic development 1970–2000 and his own experience in Parliament.[238]

People

One of Bo Södersten's best genres was book reviews. He had the ability to find interesting works and most of the time he treated them in a personal way. Bo was interested in history and the interpretation of it, he could not resist using the publication of some politician's memoirs to share his views of the author and, of course, he wrote about great economists. This is not the place to go into details. Let me just point to three somewhat 'different' pieces.

[237] Södersten (2004b).

[238] Södersten (2006b).

The first is the comparison that Bo made between the scientific contributions of Bertil Ohlin and Gunnar Myrdal.[239] There was a fundamental difference between the two. There was not a single theoretical achievement connected with Myrdal's name. That he had received the Prize in Economic Sciences in Memory of Alfred Nobel amounted to pure provincialism. He was obsolete. The case of Ohlin was different. The Heckscher–Ohlin and factor-price equalization theorems were here to stay. Ohlin's approach was still vigorous and had inspired many later economists.

The second piece deals with the Sveriges Riksbank Prize in Economic Sciences in Memory of Alfred Nobel. The prize was a matter of concern for Bo.[240] In spite of the fact that Myrdal had received it, that Milton Friedman had been met by political demonstrations and that Joan Robinson had been sidestepped, the process had worked decently well in the 1970s and 1980s. There were plenty of capable people to reward, people with strong roots in the social sciences. Thereafter, however, inspired by the natural sciences, theorems and econometric and mathematical methods had been favored and the links to the social sciences had been weakened. Bo was worried that this trend would continue and that hence the prize would lose its interest.

The third article dealt with a literary theme. It praised the authorship of Björn Larsson, professor of French in Lund,[241] who at the time had published a book of short stories and four novels,[242] and who in 1998 had received the prestigious French *Prix Médicis étranger* för *Le capitaine et les rêves*, the translation of his third novel in Swedish.[243] Bo was angry—rightly so—because these books had hardly received any attention at all from the Swedish cultural establishment.

Torsten Gårdlund

In 2003, Torsten Gårdlund, Bo's predecessor as professor of international economics in Lund, passed away. Lars Jonung, Bo and I wrote

[239] Södersten (1999e).

[240] Södersten (2001d).

[241] Södersten (2000/2001).

[242] Larsson (1980, 1992, 1995, 1997, 1999a).

[243] Larsson (1999b).

an obituary. Somewhat later, Bo called and asked me whether I wanted to collaborate with him on an article about Gårdlund for the series of portraits of economists regularly featured by *Ekonomisk Debatt*. I accepted, and we began to write. In the end, we produced two different versions of the article, a biographical book and an introductory essay on Gårdlund the essayist for a posthumously published book of essays of his that we edited.[244]

The writing process was not easy, for Bo's health had begun to deteriorate. A few years later, he would be formally diagnosed with Alzheimer's disease, but his illness had begun to make itself noticed already around this time. This made it difficult for him to concentrate and above all to write, so we developed a method whereby I read Gårdlund's works and we discussed them together before our thoughts were put on paper.

Torsten Gårdlund had his education from the Stockholm School of Economics where he graduated at the end of 1932. Thereafter, he chose an academic career, but at the time you could not pursue PhD studies at the SSE, so Gårdlund moved to Stockholm College, where he first got a licentiate degree on a book on economics and social policy in France between 1918 and 1938,[245] and in 1942 defended his doctoral dissertation on the Swedish industrialization process, *Industrialismens samhälle* [Industrial Society].[246]

In 1947, Torsten Gårdlund became professor of economics at the Stockholm School of Economics, where he remained until 1963. During his time there, he published collections of essays and wrote monographs about Swedish companies and industrial finance and, above all, his masterly biography of Knut Wicksell: *Knut Wicksell. Rebell i det nya riket*, translated as *The Life of Knut Wicksell*.[247] After spending some time in Morocco and Tunisia as an economic advisor, Gårdlund in 1965 moved to Lund, to a newly created chair in international economics. His years there were productive, with three books on economic development issues,[248] an impressing biography of the banker Marcus Wallenberg, Sr., one of

[244] Lundahl and Södersten (2004, 2009b), English translation of the latter: Lundahl and Södersten (2015), Lundahl and Södersten (2009a, 2010).

[245] Gårdlund (1939).

[246] Gårdlund (1942).

[247] Gårdlund (1956, 1958), respectively.

[248] Gårdlund (1965, 1967, 1968).

the most important figures in the Swedish industrial development during the interwar years,[249] followed by more biographic works and company monographs.

Bo and I labeled Torsten Gårdlund Sweden's only 'literary' economist. No one came close to him when it came to constructing elegant phrases, which he often thought out during his morning rides. (Gårdlund bred Anglo-Arab horses on his stud farm outside Lund.) He demonstrated his ability in all his works, but mainly in his biographies and essays. The latter was a genre especially favored by him. He had an unusual ability to find unexpected and intriguing themes which he developed in cultural articles in *Svenska Dagbladet* and later republished in his collections of essays. Gårdlund also had a well-developed philosophy about how to write a biography. He cultivated a style that never turned extravagant. The text should flow gently but you could permit yourself occasional bursts of linguistic lightning.

Torsten Gårdlund was a man who enjoyed the good life. One of his most memorable essays has precisely this title. It dealt with the kind of society which was found in the writings of the utopian Socialists: a society which they had endowed with everything that they had been forced to forsake in their own lifetime. It is impossible to escape from the feeling that Torsten Gårdlund shared most of their preferences.

Who Was Bo Södersten?

All who knew Bo Södersten realized that he was a complex person. He could be utterly charming, but he could also turn people off with brusque manners. When I was his student in Lund and we had undergraduate seminars in international economics, all too often the seminar began with a scolding of the opponent on the paper that was to be discussed. The opponent was incapable of asking a single intelligent question. Then, he took over the opposition himself and proceeded to deliver a harsh critique, frequently ridiculing the victim in the process.

Bo was not mean, however. He was intelligent and possibly this was why he did not tolerate fools. But he also needed resistance. If you stood up and argued your case, you stood a better chance, unless he had a bad day and chose to mock what you had written. It was easy to get into an

[249] Gårdlund (1976).

argument with him. Bo was hot-tempered but he easily forgave. If you wanted to hang out with him, there were certain things that you simply had to take in order to get to the better part of him. You had to learn to shrug your shoulders, not pay attention to everything he said, and try to change the topic of the conversation.

Those who Bo liked, he supported, one hundred percent. If he believed in you, you knew that he was behind you, come rain or come shine, should you need his support, and he went out of his way in critical situations to ensure that things worked out. He took all chances to point out the excellence of his students to the people he met. He saw to it that you got travel money when needed, persuaded publishers to accept your manuscripts and he got you consultancy jobs. It was no coincidence that he was given three festschrifts: one at his fiftieth birthday, one at his sixtieth and one at his eightieth.[250]

Bo was a good lecturer who easily inspired the students with his enthusiasm. He always contended that pedagogy was a non-issue in the university setting. If you knew your subject, you went into the classroom and explained it. That was precisely what he did. He was not an active supervisor in the sense that he provided topics that the students could write about. We had to come up with our own suggestions, and he never questioned them. Once they had been decided, however, he read, commented and followed up with a view to the next chapter.

Bo had a solid reputation for being a ladies' man, a fact that did not make life easier for him, but he somehow managed to keep his family life together. Those of us who were his students were invited to his home with our own families, which led to a stable social network that met regularly for dinners together with him and other faculty members. We were socialized little by little into the academic community until we became full-fledged members of it.

Bo came from a working-class family. He was the only one in the family who had been allowed to study. This was probably what accounted for his ambitions. When I first met him in 1968, he was one hundred percent intent on becoming a professor. Once this was achieved, he gave vent to his political ambitions, probably inherited from home. He made sure that he made it into Parliament, and once he had been elected his next aim was to become a minister, which, however, as we have seen, did not work

[250] Lundahl (1981, 2011) and Hansson (1993).

out. His personal characteristics got in the way. If we are to believe his own words, independent thinking was not a hard currency in his party, but his way of throwing out derogatory remarks did not help either. He never managed to subordinate to the party discipline and did not cherish the fact that his own pet ideas were not accepted by those who called the shots within the party.

Often, Bo had problems refraining from emptying his poison glands when he wrote. He had an outspoken penchant for extravagant formulations—formulations which frequently hurt. Bo was a popular educator—very pedagogical—in his writings. He was a debater, but even more a provocateur. He made systematic use of provocations to bring his message across. As the amount of criticism he received for his articles proved, the method was efficient. During his career, he first attacked the Social Democrats from the left, and then from the right. An article about him in *Dagens Nyheter* got the title 'Kritiker som alltid gått i otakt [A Critic Always Out of Step].'[251]

As I have pointed out various times, Bo all his life was an avid fiction reader: essays, novels, short stories and biographies, but also poetry. Since he came from Dalarna, Erik Axel Karlfeldt was a favorite. He would occasionally quote him. Bo's number one idol, however, was of a much later date: Gunnar Ekelöf, of the generation of the 'forties.' And he read Americans like Ezra Pound and Edgar Lee Masters. Bo had the collected works of Bertolt Brecht, presumably mainly because Brecht was a radical, but he never spoke much about German culture. He was essentially a Francophile and often spiced his conversation with phrases in French: 'Les Français parlent trop.' 'Les Français réagissent lentement.'

Bo's academic production is not very large. It is limited to the unpublished licentiate thesis, his doctoral dissertation, the book on housing, some articles and chapters in scientific books and the Gårdlund biography. To this, you have to add his contributions in the textbook genre, mainly *International Economics*, which was the first modern textbook in international economics, the macro book and the anthologies that he edited. However, his textbook production to a large extent amounted to 'writing for money.' *International Economics* was a success and of course stimulated Bo to seek other lucrative markets.

[251] Söderberg (1991).

The only times that Bo penetrated the world of theoretical economics dominated by models was when he wrote his dissertation and the articles that followed it. It is evident that he was not quite comfortable with that. He had studied humanities in high school—Latin and Greek—so his mathematical schooling was limited. He had to learn, course by course, and in the end on his own when he was about to write his dissertation. It shows. His approach is not elegant. Mathematics was not his bag, and his critics were right when they pointed out that he had problems interpreting his algebra. It was applying economic theory that was Bo's forte. He had a knack for converting theory into practical economic policy.

Bo did not quite have the stamina required for continued academic writing. Once you have received your chair you don't have to produce anymore. The informal Swedish history of economic doctrines is full of examples. Bo obtained his professorship at a time when the trick was to just clear the bar. It did not matter if it quivered. Then you could retire and enjoy your otium. But Bo was not lazy in any way. On the contrary. Lying on the sofa did not appeal to him, but he directed his energy toward other things. Maybe it was rather a matter of lack of academic concentration. As is well known, the picture of the academic/genius is completely false. Of course, you don't make a career without inspiration, but the latter does not have to be divine. You can make it anyway, but seldom without a large measure of transpiration and wearing out some pants. In the end, it leads to some kind of publications, but hardly to sensational publicity.

Bo Södersten was a pronounced intellectual. That always showed when you spoke with him. He was widely read, in many genres, and he willingly shared his *Lesefrüchte*, wherever he published them. His four books of essays present a *mélange* of economic, political and literary themes. The best of them is *Den hierarkiska välfärden*. It is a'real' book of essays where the ideas are in focus and Bo demonstrates his ability to find topics that matter, economic, political or literary. It is also the book where you feel that you are getting closest to the person Bo Södersten. He changed his political views later in life, but that is not the thing. *Den hierarkiska välfärden* is conceived by a man of flesh and blood. It was the first book that he gave to me and when I opened it, I immediately felt it: this was a book written by a man with a burning conviction which he managed to convey to the reader. The essay genre was ideally suited to his way of thinking: often an ideologically inspired idea that was applied to an author or some phenomenon in society. This side of Bo unfortunately receded over time, as political themes and economic policy took over, with one exception: the essay about Björn Larsson. Unfortunately, Bo did not quite deliver on his early promise. The following collections essays are more ephemeral, with the exception of *Ut ur krisen*, where he collected some of his more important contributions. Wholesale writing in daily newspapers has its price.

Which were Bo's goals in life? Was he a man who sought power? Once he said to me that the finest Harvard chair was worth nothing in comparison with the most insignificant ministerial portfolio. Or did he want to become a celebrity? He was a bit of lens louse. Sometimes he argued that it didn't matter what you were doing. 'The main thing is to keep your name in vogue.' But why? What did he want to achieve? It felt a bit like when the popular Swedish actor Edvard Persson entered the film studio: 'All the lights on me!' Was it therefore that he wrote all those newspaper articles? The headlines about him were far from always merciful and seldom laudatory. When the journalists found something about him that they thought smelled scandal—house deals, tax planning—they put wartime headings on the placards. However, you cannot get away from the fact that Bo had a phenomenal nose for controversial issues—issues that he used to put himself into the limelight.

How did Bo perceive himself? There were moments when you easily could feel that he was an egocentric suffering from a monumental overestimation of himself, a trait which surfaced not least when he had lost some race for a chair and appealed. He had been an A student and must when he arrived in Uppsala have been equipped with a cemented self-confidence, which he continued to document during the rest of his life. Bo was never weak in his faith. He had successfully done his bit of social climbing and could even speak about people as 'real working class.' He knew that he had left it himself.

How deep-seated was Bo's ideology? There remains no doubt that the roots were deep. He had been born into the labor movement and the Social Democracy. During his youth and way into his manhood he stood out as a radical hardcore Socialist—never in the revolutionary phrasemonger camp, that was below his dignity—but with time he made an about-turn and began his persistent criticism of the Social Democrats and their policies. In one respect, however, Bo remained a convinced ideologue for a rather long period. When the idea of the labor-managed firm appeared he immediately swallowed the bait. This was his great revelation in life and he did all that he could to launch the idea in Sweden. It did not go well. The trade unions never thought of the idea as valuable. It was possible to launch the wage-earners' funds without labor management. Maybe it was not so strange. The idea had sprung from abstract economic theory, not from the experience of the labor movement.

* * *

Bo's last years were not good. After having been diagnosed with Alzheimer's disease, he spent four years in a nursing home in Stockholm before he died on 5 September 2017. Perhaps the best summary of Bo Södersten was made by his longtime friend Villy Bergström, a man who never went around in circles but always spoke his mind. 'Bo can be absolutely devilish' he said, 'but it is impossible not to like him.'

References

Andersen, Bent Rold (1972), Sakkunnigutlåtande vid tillsättningen av professuren i arbetsmarknadspolitik vid Institutet för social forskning vid Stockholms universitet. 23 October.

Arvidsson, Guy (1970), Sakkunnigutlåtande rörande ledigförklarad professur i nationalekonomi vid Göteborgs universitet (Aug Röhss' professur). 29 October.

Barrett, Nancy and Södersten, Bo (1975), 'Unemployment Flows, Welfare and Labor Market Efficiency in Sweden and the United States', *Swedish Journal of Economics*, Vol. 77, No. 3, 199–302.

Bege (1977), 'Löntagarpengar i företaget säkrar ökat medinflytande', *Sundsvalls Tidning*, 2 May.

Bentzel, Ragnar; Lindbeck, Assar and Ståhl, Ingemar (1963), *Bostadsbristen: En studie av prisbildningen på bostadsmarknaden*. Stockholm: Almqvist & Wiksell.

Bergqvist, Anita (1993), 'Är professorns nonsensord närande men vård av sjuka och gamla tärande?', *Västerbottens Folkblad*, 13 February.

Bergström, Hans (1997), 'Stärk demokratin och medborgerligheten!', *Dagens Nyheter*, 21 December.

Björklund, Anders; Edin, Per Anders; Holmlund, Bertil and Wadensjö, Eskil (1994), 'Ekonomikollegor vilseleder', *Dagens Nyheter*, 14 October.

Caves, Richard E. and Jones, Ronald W. (1973), *World Trade and Payments: An Introduction*. Boston: Little, Brown and Company.

Eidem, Rolf and Viotti, Staffan (1974), 'Arbetarstyrda företag i en marknadsstyrd ekonomi', *Ekonomisk Debatt*, Vol. 2, No. 3, 166–172.

Ekberg, Jan; Södersten, Bo; Hammarstedt, Mats and Rooth, Dan-Olof (2002), 'Hårdare tag mot invandrare att vänta', *Dagens Nyheter*, 22 April.

Ekdal, Niklas (2003), 'Apropå snyltgäster', *Dagens Nyheter*, 30 December.

Ekholm, Karolina and Södersten, Bo (2002), 'Growth and Trade vs. Trade and Growth', *Small Business Economics*, Vol. 19, No. 2, 147–162.

Erixon, Lennaert and Wadensjö, Eskil (2013), 'Gösta Rehn (1913–96) – en otålig reformator', *Ekonomisk Debatt*, Vol. 40. No. 8, 71–82.

Findlay, Ronald and Grubert, Harry (1959), 'Factor Intensities, Technological Progress, and the Terms of Trade', *Oxford Economic Papers*, Vol. 11, No. 1, 111–121.

Flam, Harry (1980), 'En proklamation om handelskrig', *Dagens Nyheter*, 8 November.

Fornäs, Johan; Hultén, Britt; Hvitfelt, Håkan; Kleberg, Madeleine; Lindhoff, Håkan; Mårtenson, Bo; Nowak, Kjell; Pollack, Ester and Thurén, Torsten (1998), 'Expertstyret slutar i despoti', *Dagens Nyheter*, 8 January.

Franck, Anders (1977), 'Frälsningsläror hotar forskningen', *Göteborgs-Posten*, 11 February.

Fransson, Jan; Johansson, Anita; Persson, Anita; Silfverstrand, Bengt and Södersten, Bo (1981), *Rapport från studieresa i Östtyskland och Frankrike 21–27 juli 1981*. October. Mimeo.

Furåker, Bengt (1994), 'Försörjning och marknad', *Ekonomisk Debatt*, Vol. 22, No. 4, 433–439.

Galbraith, John Kenneth (1958), *The Affluent Society*. New York: Mentor.

Galbraith, John Kenneth (1967), *The New Industrial State*. Boston: Houghton Mifflin.

Gårdlund, Torsten (1939), *Frankrikes väg: ekonomi och socialpolitik 1918–1939*. Stockholm: Tidens Förlag.

Gårdlund, Torsten (1942), *Industrialismens samhälle*. Stockholm: Tidens Förlag.

Gårdlund, Torsten (1956), *Knut Wicksell. Rebell i det nya riket*. Stockholm: Bonniers.

Gårdlund, Torsten (1958), *The Life of Knut Wicksell*. Stockholm: Almqvist & Wiksell.

Gårdlund, Torsten (1965), *Att arbeta i u-land*. Stockholm: Wahlström & Widstrand.

Gårdlund, Torsten (1967), *Lamco i Liberia*. Stockholm: Almqvist & Wiksell.

Gårdlund, Torsten (1968), *Främmande investeringar i u-land*. Stockholm: Almqvist & Wiksell.

Gårdlund, Torsten (1976), *Marcus Wallenberg 1864–1943: hans liv och gärning*. Stockholm: P.A. Norstedt & Söners Förlag.

Gelting Jørgen; Haavelmo, Trygve; Hoffmeyer, Erik; Ølgaard, Anders and Nørregaard Rasmussen, P. (1969), Til det rets- och statsvidenskabelige fakultet ved Københavns Universitet. 19 June.

Hansson, Göte (ed.) (1993), *Trade, Growth and Development: The Role of Politics and Institutions. Proceedings of the 12th Arne Ryde Symposium, 13–14 June 1991, in Honour of Bo Södersten*. London and New York: Routledge.
Hedwall, Barbro (1995), 'Produktivitet, sa professorn', *Expressen*, 3 May.
Hicks, John R. (1953), 'An Inaugural Lecture', *Oxford Economic Papers*, Vol. 5, No. 2, 117–135.
Hultkrantz, Lars och and Österholm, Pär (eds) (2017), *Marknad och politik*. Tolfte upplagan. Lund: Studentlitteratur.
Imperial Ethiopian Government, Ministry of Public Health (1973), *Health Sector Review (Draft), Fourth Five-Year Plan*. Addis Ababa: Ministry of Public Health, 17 April.
Jalakas, Anne (1994), 'Södersten tänker om', *Arbetet*, 31 October.
Janson, Svante (1995), 'Bo Södersten måste avgå', *Dagens Nyheter*, 4 May.
Johansson, Östen and Jungenfelt, Karl G. (1964), 'Review of *A Study of Economic Growth and International Trade* by Bo Södersten', *Ekonomisk Tidskrift*, Vol. 66, No. 3, 222–230.
Johnson, Harry G. (1955), 'Economic Expansion and International Trade', *Manchester School of Economic and Social Studies*, Vol. 23, No. 2, 95–112.
Jonasson, Erik; Pettersson, Lars and Södersten, Bo (2005), 'Spåren av amatörernas framfart är förskräckande', *Dagens Nyheter*, 9 August.
Jones, Ronald W. (1969), 'Tariffs and Trade in General Equilibrium: Comment', *American Economic Review*, Vol. 59, No. 3, 418–424.
Karyd, Arne and Södersten, Bo (1990), 'The Swedish Housing Market from a Distributional Perspective: Market and Policy Interactions', in: Inga Persson (ed.), *Generating Equality in the Welfare State: The Swedish Experience*. Oslo: Norwegian University Press.
Krugman, Paul R. and Obstfeld, Maurice (1987), *International Economics: Theory and Policy*. Glenview, IL: Little, Brown.
Kruse, Agneta and Ståhlberg, Ann-Charlotte (2020), 'Pensionsreformen 1994 – ett kvarts sekel senare', *Ekonomisk Debatt*, Vol. 49, No. 7, 19–27.
Larsson, Björn (1980), *Splitter*. Stockholm: Wahlström & Widstrand.
Larsson, Björn (1992), *Den keltiska ringen*. Stockholm: Bonniers.
Larsson, Björn (1995), *Long John Silver*. Stockholm: Norstedts.
Larsson, Björn (1997), *Drömmar vid havet*. Stockholm: Norstedts.
Larsson, Björn (1999a), *Det onda ögat*. Stockholm: Norstedts.
Larsson, Björn (1999b), *Le capitaine et les rêves*. Paris: Éditions Grasset.
Lewis, W. Arthur (1954), 'Economic Development with Unlimited Supplies of Labour', *The Manchester School*, Vol. 22, No. 2, 139–191.
Lindbeck, Assar (1969), Sakkunnigutlåtande vid tillsättningen av professur i nationalekonomi vid juridiska fakulteten vid Uppsala universitet. 29 March.
Lindgren, Anne-Marie (1978), 'Fel lösningar på fel problem', *Tiden*, Vol. 70, No. 5, 245–249.

Lönnroth, Johan (2011), 'Han var trots allt nog ganska nyttig för oss', in: Mats Lundahl (ed.), *Den orädde debattören: En vänbok till Bo Södersten på 80-årsdagen den 5 juni 2011*. Stockholm: Ekerlids Förlag.

Lucas, Robert E. (1988), 'On the Mechanics of Economic Development', *Journal of Monetary Economics*, Vol. 22, No. 1, 3–42.

Lucas, Robert E. (1990), 'Why Doesn't Capital Flow from Rich to Poor Countries?', *American Economic Review*, Vol. 80, No. 2, 92–96.

Lundahl, Mats (ed.) (1981), *Ideologi, ekonomi och politik: Tankar i tiden*. Stockholm: Rabén & Sjögren.

Lundahl, Mats (ed.) (2011), *Den orädde debattören: En vänbok till Bo Södersten på 80-årsdagen den 5 juni 2011*. Stockholm: Ekerlids Förlag.

Lundahl, Mats and Södersten, Bo (1974a), 'Forskning för utveckling', *Ekonomisk Debatt*, Vol. 2, No. 2, 115–122.

Lundahl, Mats and Södersten, Bo (eds) (1974b), *Utvecklingsekonomi 1: Underutvecklingens mekanismer*. Stockholm: Aldus.

Lundahl, Mats and Södersten, Bo (eds) (1974c), *Utvecklingsekonomi 2: Planering och resursmobilisering*. Stockholm: Aldus.

Lundahl, Mats and Södersten Bo (eds) (1979), *Utvecklingsekonomi*. Andra, reviderade upplagan. Stockholm: Aldus.

Lundahl, Mats and Södersten, Bo (2000), 'Cuba i den halvhjärtade marknadsekonomins år', *Ekonomisk Debatt*, Vol. 28, No. 7, 669–680.

Lundahl, Mats and Södersten, Bo (2004), 'Ekonomporträtt: Torsten Gårdlund – en *grandseigneur*', *Ekonomisk Debatt*, Vol. 32, No. 8, 47–60.

Lundahl, Mats and Södersten, Bo (2009a), *Torsten Gårdlund: Det goda livets ekonom*. Stockholm: Timbro.

Lundahl, Mats and Södersten, Bo (2009b), 'Torsten Gårdlund – ett porträtt', in: Mats Lundahl, *Fem svenska ekonomer: Knut Wicksell, Eli Heckscher, Bertil Ohlin, Torsten Gårdlund, Staffan Burenstam Linder. Vad skev de egentligen?* Stockholm: Timbro.

Lundahl, Mats and Södersten, Bo (2010), 'Essäisten Torsten Gårdlund', in: *Vid kapitalismens sjukbädd och andra essäer. Texter av Torsten Gårdlund i urval av Mats Lundahl och Bo Södersten*. Stockholm: Timbro.

Lundahl, Mats and Södersten, Bo (2015), 'Torsten Gårdlund: A Portrait', in: Mats Lundahl, *Seven Figures in the History of Swedish Economic Thought: Knut Wicksell, Eli Heckscher, Bertil Ohlin, Torsten Gårdlund, Sven Rydenfelt, Staffan Burenstam Linder and Jaime Behar*. Houndmills, Basingstoke: Palgrave Macmillan.

Lundberg, Erik (1972), Sakkunnigutlåtande vid tillsättningen av professuren i arbetsmarknadspolitik vid Institutet för social forskning vid Stockholms universitet. 31 October.

MacKenzie, Norman (ed.) (1958), *Conviction*. London: MacGibbon & Kee.

Mäler, Karl-Göran and Södersten, Bo (1967), 'Factor-Biased Technical Progress and the Elastcicity of Substitution', *Swedish Journal of Economics*, Vol. 69, No. 2, 154–160.

Metzler, Lloyd A. (1949a), 'Tariffs, the Terms of Trade, and the Distribution of National Income', *Journal of Political Economy*, Vol. 57, No. 1, 1–29.

Metzler, Lloyd A. (1949b), 'Tariffs, International Demand, and Domestic Prices', *Journal of Political Economy*, Vol. 57, No. 4, 345–351.

Milton, Anders and Södersten, Bo (1996), 'Sverige har för många läkare', *Dagens Nyheter*, 24 December.

Motion till riksdagen 1987/88: Bo 208, om stödet till bostadsbyggande. Bo Södersten and Roland Sundgren. https://data.riksdagen.se/fil/C9F849B0-3252-41FA-A8DC-528000367BB4. Downloaded 22 September 2021.

Myrdal, Alva and Myrdal, Gunnar (1934), *Kris i befolkningsfrågan*. Stockholm: Albert Bonniers förlag.

Myrdal, Gunnar (1953), *The Political Element in the Development of Economic Theory*. London: Routledge & Kegan Paul.

Myrdal, Gunnar (1972), *Vetenskap och politik i nationalekonomin*. Ny omarbetad upplaga. Stockholm: Rabén & Sjögren.

Nordh, Sture and Pettersson, Torbjörn (1995), 'En manlig krigsförklaring', *Dagens Nyheter*, 10 May.

Notat (1977), Notat til møte 31 januar 1977 i 'tjänsteförslagsnämnden för samhällsvetenskapliga fakulteten vid Lunds universitet'. January.

Ølgaard, Anders (1970), Sakkunnigutlåtande rörande ledigförklarad professur i nationalekonomi vid Göteborgs universitet (Aug Röhss' professur). 1 November.

Olson, Mancur (1965), *The Logic of Collective Action: Public Goods and the Theory of Groups*. Cambridge, MA and London: Harvard University Press.

Palander, Tord (1969), Sakkunnigutlåtande vid tillsättningen av professur i nationalekonomi vid juridiska fakulteten vid Uppsala universitet. 18 May.

Persson, Inga and Södersten, Bo (1971), *Internationella resusrsfördelningsproblem. Nationalekonomi 5*. Stockholm: Svenska Utbildningsförlaget Liber AB.

Pettersson, Ulla (1994), 'Varför ser ingen att Södersten är naken?', *Dagens Nyheter*, 25 August.

Prebisch, Raúl (1950), *The Economic Development of Latin America and Its Principal Problems*. New York: United Nations.

Riksdagens protokoll 1987/88:110, 28 April 1988. https://data.riksdagen.se/fil/612D884E-9D69-4EAD-AEE7-5E7429342937. Downloaded 22 September 2021.

Romer, Paul M. (1986), 'Increasing Returns and Long-Run Growth', *Journal of Political Economy*, Vol. 94, No. 5, 1002–1037.

Romer, Paul M. (1990a), 'Endogenous Technological Change', *Journal of Political Economy*, Vol. 98, No. 5, 70–102.

Romer, Paul M. (1990b), 'Are Nonconvexities Important for Understanding Growth?', *American Economic Review*, Vol. 80, No. 2, 97–103.

Rothstein, Bo and Boëthius, Maria-Pia (1993), 'Ekonomernas kåranda tystar kritiken', *Dagens Nyheter*, 1 March.

Rybczynski, T.M. (1955), 'Factor Endowments and Relative Commodity Prices', *Economica*, NS, Vol, 22, No. 88, 336–341.

Sandelin, Bo (1977), *Prisutveckling och kapitalvinster på bostadsfastigheter*. Göteborg: Nationalekonomiska institutionen vid Göteborgs universitet.

Sandelin, Bo and Södersten, Bo (1978), *Betalt för att bo: Värdestegring och kapitalvinster på bostadsmarknaden*. Stockholm: Rabén & Sjögren.

Singer, Hans (1950), 'The Distribution of Gains between Borrowing and Lending Countries', *American Economic Review*, Vol. 40, No. 11, 473–485.

Söderberg, Karen (1991), 'Kritiker som alltid gått i otakt', *Dagens Nyheter*, 5 January.

Södersten, Bo (n.d.), *Kandidaterna*. Unpublished novel manuscript.

Södersten, Bo (1959a), *Studier i den långsiktiga utvecklingen av svensk utrikeshandel*. Mimeo. Uppsala: Nationalekonomiska institutionen vid Uppsala universitet.

Södersten, Bo (1959b), 'Utrikeshandel och ekonomisk utveckling', *Ekonomiska Samfundets Tidskrift*, Vol. 12, 276–288.

Södersten, Bo (1961), 'Utrikeshandel och ekonomisk tillväxt: den marginella aspekten', *Ekonomisk Tidskrift*, Vol. 63, No. 2, 115–128.

Södersten, Bo (1962a), *Övertygelser*. Stockholm: Albert Bonniers Förlag.

Södersten, Bo (1962b), 'Foreign Trade and Economic Growth: The Marginal Aspect', *International Economic Papers*, No. 11, 185–195.

Södersten, Bo (1962c), 'Den nya dollarkrisen', *Ekonomisk Tidskrift*, Vol. 64, No. 1, 1–21.

Södersten, Bo (1963a), 'Bostadsbristen och de tre räntorna', *Tiden*, Vol. 55, No. 5, 292–301.

Södersten, Bo (1964a), *A Study of Economic Growth and International Trade*. Stockholm: Almqvist & Wiksell.

Södersten, Bo (1964b), 'Svar på Johansson-Jungenfelts recension', *Ekonomisk Tidskrift*, Vol. 66, No. 4, 299–303.

Södersten, Bo (1968a), 'Kuba i det heroiska Vietnams år', *Tiden*, Vol. 60, No. 9, 548–558.

Södersten, Bo (1968b), *Den hierarkiska välfärden och andra essäer*. Stockholm: Rabén & Sjögren.

Södersten, Bo (1969a), *Internationell ekonomi*. Stockholm: Rabén & Sjögren.

Södersten, Bo (1969b), Till den juridiska fakulteten vid Lunds universitet. 3 November.

Södersten, Bo (1970a), *International Economics*. London and Basingstoke: Macmillan.
Södersten Bo (ed.) (1970b), *Svensk ekonomi*. Stockholm: Rabén & Sjögren.
Södersten, Bo (1970c), 'Per Albin och den socialistiska reformismen', in: Gunnar Fredriksson, Dieter Strand and Bo Södersten, *Per Albinlinjen: Tre ställningstaganden till en socialdemokratisk tradition*. Stockholm: Bokförlaget PAN/Nordstedts.
Södersten, Bo (1971a), 'För lite politik', *Arbetet*, 13 January.
Södersten, Bo (1971b), 'Reallön som partsinlaga', *Dagens Nyheter*, 26 February.
Södersten, Bo (1972), 'Assar Lindbecks liberala teser', *Aftonbladet*, 21 March.
Södersten, Bo (1973), 'Arbetarstyrd ekonomi', *Ekonomisk Debatt*, Vol. 1, No. 8, 479–490.
Södersten Bo (ed.) (1974a), *Svensk ekonomi*. Andra omarbetade och utökade upplagan. Stockholm: Rabén & Sjögren.
Södersten, Bo (1974b), 'Rapport från juntans Chile', *Aftonbladet*, 23 February.
Södersten, Bo (1974c), 'Juntans väg till makten', *Aftonbladet*, 25 February.
Södersten, Bo (1974d), 'Allendes tragedi: Det går inte att utrota fattigdomen på några år', *Aftonbladet*, 3 March.
Södersten, Bo (1974e), 'Inkomstfördelningen som globalt problem', *Tiden*, Vol. 66, No. 1, 5–13.
Södersten, Bo (1975), *Den svenska sköldpaddan: Politiskt, ekonomiskt, personligt ur ett socialdemokratiskt perspektiv*. Stockholm: Rabén & Sjögren.
Södersten, Bo (1976a), *Economia internazionale*. Torino: Unione Tipografico-Editore Torinense.
Södersten, Bo (1976b), 'Mikroaspekter av löntagarstyre', *Ekonomisk Debatt*, Vol. 4, No. 1, 30–41.
Södersten, Bo (1976c), 'Manifest över svikna ambitioner', *Tiden*, Vol. 68, No. 2, 109–122.
Södersten, Bo (1976d), 'Den sanna pluralismen: Teser om löntagarstyre', *Tiden*, Vol. 68, No. 4–5, 197–209.
Södersten, Bo (1977a), 'Arbetarna får dra lasset', *Arbetet*, 16 April.
Södersten, Bo (1977b), Löntagarna måste få styra investeringar(na). 17 April.
Södersten, Bo (1977c), 'Det borgerliga krispaketet', *Tiden*, Vol. 69, No. 7, 431–441.
Södersten, Bo (1978a), *Internationell ekonomi*. Andra omarbetade upplagan. Stockholm: Rabén & Sjögren.
Södersten, Bo (1978b), 'Kvinnan på arbetsmarknaden', *Ekonomisk Debatt*, Vol. 6, No. 8, 598–606.
Södersten, Bo (1979a), *Economia internacional*. Rio de Janeiro: Editora Interciencia.

Södersten, Bo (1979b), 'Mot ett löntagarstyrt Sverige?', in: Villy Bergström and Bengt Rydén (eds), *Vägval i svensk politik. Ekonomi och samhälle på 80-talet*. Stockholm: SNS Förlag.
Södersten, Bo (1980a), *International Economics*. Second edition. London: Macmillan.
Södersten, Bo (1980b), 'Frihandeln bör begränsas', *Dagens Nyheter*, 22 October.
Södersten, Bo (1980c), 'New Attitudes to Work', in: Edmond Malinvaud and Jean-Paul Fitoussi (eds), *Unemployment in Western Countries: Proceedings of a Conference Held by the International Economic Association at Bischenberg, France*. London: Macmillan.
Södersten, Bo (1981), *Ut ur krisen: Kortsiktiga lösningar och långsiktiga mål i svensk politik*. Stockholm: Rabén & Sjögren.
Södersten, Bo (ed.) (1982a), *Svensk ekonomi*. Tredje omarbetade upplagan. Stockholm: Rabén & Sjögren.
Södersten, Bo (1982b), 'Towards a Labour-Managed Sweden?', in: Bengt Rydén and Villy Bergström (eds), *Sweden: Choices for Economic and Social Policy in the 1980s*. London: George Allen & Unwin.
Södersten, Bo, under medverkan av Lennart Berg, Sten Magnusson och Bo Sandelin (1983), *Makroekonomi och stabiliseringspolitik*. Lund: Liber Förlag.
Södersten, Bo (1984a), 'Vi skall inte förblindas av revolutionsromantik', *Svenska Dagbladet*, 21 January.
Södersten, Bo (1984b), 'Ogrundad myt om kuppen 1973', *Svenska Dagbladet*, 4 March.
Södersten, Bo (1984c), 'Absurd ekonomisk situation', *Svenska Dagbladet*, 7 March.
Södersten, Bo (1984d), 'Palatset eller kyrkogården', *Svenska Dagbladet*, 15 March.
Södersten, Bo (1985a), *A külgazdaság hatásmechanizmusa*. Budapest: Közgazdasági és Jogi Könyvkiadó.
Södersten, Bo (1985b), 'Mineral-Led Development: The Political Economiy of Namibia', in: Mats Lundahl (ed.), *The Primary Sector in Economic Development: Proceedings of the Seventh Arne Ryde Symposium, Frostavallen, August 29–30 1983*. London and Sydney: Croom Helm.
Södersten, Bo (1985c), 'Bevarad standard?', *Göteborgs-Posten*, 13 May.
Södersten, Bo (1985d), 'Sverige sämst i klassen 1986', *Dagens Industri*, 6 November.
Södersten, Bo (1986), 'Socialdemokratin behöver en slav på vagnen', *Svenska Dagbladet*, 26 July.
Södersten, Bo (ed.) (1987a), *Marknad och politik: Strukturer och problem i svensk ekonomi*. Lund: Dialogos.
Södersten, Bo (1987b), 'Ryck upp universiteten!', *SACO-Tidningen*, No. 4, 30–31.

Södersten, Bo (1988a), 'Tänk om i familjepolitiken!', *Dagens Nyheter*, 24 January.
Södersten, Bo (1988b), 'Vi behöver mer pragmatism i mitten', *Dagens Industri*, 30 May.
Södersten, Bo (1988c), 'Ta chansen att dra in på folk', *Dagens Industri*, 20 October.
Södersten, Bo (1988d), 'Makten är något som gärna döljs', *Aktuellt i politiken*, No. 2, 30–31.
Södersten, Bo (ed.) (1989a), *Skattereform och skatteplanering: Vårt nya skattesystem i funktion*. Lund: Dialogos.
Södersten, Bo (1989b), 'Skattereformens politiska ekonomi', in: Bo Södersten (ed.), *Skattereform och skatteplanering: Vårt nya skattesystem i funktion*. Lund: Dialogos.
Södersten, Bo (1989c), 'Systemfel i bostadspolitiken', in: Ds 1989:47, *Bostadsstödet – alternativ och konsekvenser. Bidrag till ett seminarium anordnat av Expertgruppen för Studier i offentlig ekonomi*. Stockholm: Allmänna Förlaget.
Södersten, Bo (1989d), 'Populister skapar privilegier', *Dagens Nyheter*, 2 July.
Södersten, Bo (1989e), 'Systemfelens överstepräster', *Dagens Nyheter*, 13 August.
Södersten, Bo (1989f), 'Senarelägg avvecklingen', *Dagens Nyheter*, 17 August.
Södersten, Bo (1989g), 'Inga utfästelser om förtida avveckling', *Dagens Nyheter*, 8 September.
Södersten, Bo (1989h), 'Skandalen i Lund', *Sydsvenska Dagbladet Snällposten*, 13 November.
Södersten, Bo (1989i), 'Låt Arken leva', *Sydsvenska Dagbladet Snällposten*, 30 November.
Södersten, Bo (1989j), 'Stöd Vietnams väg mot marknadsekonomi', *Svenska Dagbladet*, 27 December.
Södersten, Bo (ed.) (1990a), *Marknad och politik*. 2:a reviderade upplagan. Lund: Dialogos.
Södersten, Bo (ed.) (1990b), *Den stora reformen: Handbok om de nya skatterna*. Stockholm: SNS Förlag.
Södersten Bo (ed.) (1990c), *Framtid med kärnkraft*. Stockholm: SNS Förlag.
Södersten, Bo (1990d), 'Cien años de desarrollo económico sueco (1870–1970)', in: Magnus Blomström and Patricio Meller (eds), *Trayectorias divergentes. Comparación de un siglo de desarrollo económico latinoamericano y escandinavio*. Santiago de Chile: CIEPLAN-Hachette.
Södersten, Bo (1990e), 'Estado, sociedade e mercado: Um estudio sobre experiências suecas', *Finisterra – Revista de Reflexáo e Crítica*, No. 6, 111–123.
Södersten, Bo (1990f), 'Ljus framtid för Chile', *Svenska Dagbladet*, 29 januari. Omtryckt i *Kapitalismen byggde landet*.

Södersten, Bo (1990g), 'Orimligt ge Chile bistånd', *Dagens Nyheter*, 30 January.
Södersten, Bo (1990h), 'Carlsson i LO:s ledband', *Expressen*, 7 February.
Södersten, Bo (1990i), 'Ett parti utan ledning', *Dagens Nyheter*, 5 May.
Södersten, Bo (1990j), 'Kapitalismen byggde landet', *Dagens Nyheter*, 2 August.
Södersten, Bo (1990k), 'Ni har lovat att ta ner månen', *Dagens Nyheter*, 22 August.
Södersten, Bo (1990l), 'Krispaketet håller inte', *Dagens Nyheter*, 27 October.
Södersten, Bo (1990m), 'Gör högskolan konsumentstyrd', *Sydsvenska Dagbladet Snällposten*, 13 December.
Södersten, Bo (1991a), 'One Hundred Years of Swedish Economic Development', in: Magnus Blomström and Patricio Meller (eds), *Diverging Paths; Comparing a Century of Scandinavian and Latin American Economic Development*. Washington, DC: Inter-American Development Bank.
Södersten, Bo (1991b), 'Sverige – dårarnas paradis', *Dagens Nyheter*, 27 January.
Södersten, Bo (1991c), 'S skapade ett klassamhälle', *Dagens Nyheter*, 28 January.
Södersten, Bo (1991d), 'Skugga över Hongkong', *Sydsvenska Dagbladet Snällposten*, 31 januari.
Södersten, Bo (1991e), 'Därför är vi så rika', *Dagens Nyheter*, 28 April.
Södersten, Bo (1991f), 'Groteskt högskolesystem', *Dagens Nyheter*, 8 July.
Södersten, Bo (1991g), 'Var hamnar makten?', *Sydsvenska Dagbladet Snällposten*, 23 September.
Södersten, Bo (1991h), 'Sparande, tillväxt och internationellt beroende', in: *Bankmöte 91. Anföranden och diskussion vid Bankmötet den 6 november 1991*. Stockholm: Svenska Bankföreningen.
Södersten, Bo (1991i), *Kapitalismen byggde landet*. Stockholm: SNS Förlag.
Södersten, Bo (ed.) (1992a), *Pendeln svänger – röster i högskoledebatten*. Stockholm: SNS Förlag.
Södersten, Bo (ed.) (1992b), *Den offentliga sektorn*. Stockholm: SNS Förlag.
Södersten, Bo (1992c), 'Det svenska pensionssystemet', in: Bo Södersten (ed.), *Den offentliga sektorn*. Stockholm: SNS Förlag.
Södersten, Bo (1992d), 'Därför går det så illa', *Dagens Nyheter*, 3 January.
Södersten, Bo (1992e), 'Yrkesgrupper utan berättigande', *Dagens Nyheter*, 4 January.
Södersten, Bo (1992f), 'Regeringen faller sönder', *Dagens Nyheter*, 17 May.
Södersten, Bo (1992g), 'De svaga länkarnas regering', *Dagens Nyheter*, 18 May.
Södersten, Bo (1992h), 'Möblera om bland ministrarna', *Dagens Nyheter*, 21 December.
Södersten, Bo (1993a), 'Institutions, Knowledge, Trade and Growth: A Personal Address', in: Göte Hansson (ed.), *Trade, Growth and Development: The Role of Politics and Institutions*. Proceedings of the 12th Arne Ryde Symposium. 13–14 June 1991, in Honour of Bo Södersten. London and New York: Routledge.

Södersten, Bo (1993b), 'Bromsklossen Westerberg', *Dagens Nyheter*, 7 March.
Södersten, Bo (1993c), 'Välfärdsstatens tid är förbi', *Dagens Nyheter*, 20 June.
Södersten, Bo (1993d), 'Efter oss syndafloden', *Sydsvenska Dagbladet Snällposten*, 12 October.
Södersten. Bo (1993e), 'Hur går det med ATP?', *Sydsvenska Dagbladet Snällposten*, 29 November.
Södersten, Bo (1993?), *Riksdagens minskade makt – myt eller verklighet?* Unpublished address.
Södersten, Bo (1994a), *Knowledge, Economic Progress and the State. Anförande av professor Bo Södersten vid Utbildningsdepartementets internationella symposium 'Science and the Powers' den 16–17 mars på Hässelby slott.* Stockholm: SULF.
Södersten, Bo (1994b), 'Män mest missgynnade', *Dagens Nyheter*, 4 January.
Södersten, Bo (1994c), 'M och s måste samarbeta', *Dagens Nyheter*, 5 January.
Södersten, Bo (1994d), 'I väntan på IMF', *Sydsvenska Dagbladet Snällposten*, 20 June.
Södersten, Bo (1994e), 'Hur kunde det gå så snett?', *Dagens Nyheter*, 9 August.
Södersten, Bo (1994f), 'Sverige idag i djupare beråd än någonsin', *Svenska Dagbladet*, 20 September.
Södersten, Bo (1994g), 'Kris och förnöjsamhet', *Sydsvenska Dagbladet Snällposten*, 3 October.
Södersten, Bo (1994h), 'Flykt från verkligheten', *Sydsvenska Dagbladet Snällposten*, 12 December.
Södersten, Bo (1995a), 'Politisk korruption förstör landet', *Dagen Nyheter*, 28 January.
Södersten, Bo (1995b), 'Esclavage fiscal. Gaspillage et corruption politique détruisent la Suède', *Courrier International*, No. 224.
Södersten, Bo (1995c), 'Kvinnor har för höga löner', *Dagens Nyheter*, 30 April.
Södersten, Bo (1995d), 'Ner i godtyckets träsk', *Svenska Dagbladet*, 26 May.
Södersten, Bo (1995e), 'Från Lenin till Sahlin', *Sydsvenska Dagbladet Snällposten*, 25 September.
Södersten, Bo (1995f), 'Pensionssystem i fara', *Dagens Nyheter*, 22 November.
Södersten, Bo (ed.) (1996a), *Marknad och politik*. Tredje upplagan. Stockholm: SNS Förlag.
Södersten, Bo (1996b), 'Carlsson huvudansvarig för krisen', *Dagens Nyheter*, 3 January.
Södersten, Bo (1996c), 'Palme var en svag ledare', *Dagens Nyheter*, 3 March.
Södersten, Bo (1996d), 'Nedskärningar bra för kvinnor', *Dagens Nyheter*, 13 July.
Södersten, Bo (1996e), 'Inkompetenskult inom s', *Dagens Nyheter*, 11 August.
Södersten, Bo (1996f), 'Dömda till misär', *Sydsvenska Dagbladet Snällposten*, 25 November.

Södersten, Bo (1996g), 'Fattiga kusiner', *Sydsvenska Dagbladet Snällposten*, 30 December.
Södersten, Bo (ed.) (1997a), *Marknad och politik*. Fjärde upplagan. Stockholm: SNS Förlag.
Södersten, Bo (1997b), 'S-gruppen svag och undfallande', *Dagens Nyheter*, 18 February.
Södersten, Bo (1997c), 'Lär av Tony Blair', *Sydsvenska Dagbladet Snällposten*, 16 June.
Södersten, Bo (1997d), 'S måste låta marknaden styra', *Dagens Nyheter*, 12 August.
Södersten, Bo (1997e), 'Kollektivet före individen', *Sydsvenska Dagbladet Snällposten*, 17 September.
Södersten, Bo (1997f), 'Begränsa demokratin!', *Dagens Nyheter*, 14 December.
Södersten, Bo (1998a), 'Röveri mot gamla och sjuka', *Dagens Nyheter*, 1 April.
Södersten, Bo (1998b), 'Facket i vågskålen', *Sydsvenska Dagbladet Snällposten*, 6 April.
Södersten, Bo (1998c), 'Metallbasen LO:s svagaste ledare', *Dagens Nyheter*, 7 August.
Södersten, Bo (1998d), 'Göran Persson ett problem för s', *Dagens Nyheter*, 24 September.
Södersten, Bo (1998e), 'Låt förtidspensionärer återgå i arbete', *Dagens Nyheter*, 28 November.
Södersten, Bo (1999a), 'Goda institutioner bakom västs framgång', *Svenska Dagbladet*, 6 May.
Södersten, Bo (1999b), 'Statligt översitteri saboterar pensionen', *Dagens Nyheter*, 22 May.
Södersten, Bo (1999c), 'Särintresset kräver företräde', *Svenska Dagbladet*, 28 June.
Södersten, Bo (1999d), 'Slarva inte bort även denna högkonjunktur', *Svenska Dagbladet*, 11 August.
Södersten, Bo (1999e), 'Ohlin framför Myrdal', *Sydsvenska Dagbladet Snällposten*, 18 October.
Södersten, Bo (ed.) (2000a), *Marknad och politik*. Femte upplagan. Stockholm: SNS Förlag.
Södersten, Bo (2000b), 'Många politiker är inte vana vid kritik', *Avisen*, 29 July.
Södersten, Bo (2000c), 'Folkhemmets trygghetssystem hotar välfärden', *Svenska Dagbladet*, 3 November.
Södersten, Bo (2000/2001), 'Björn Larsson djuplodar de sju haven', *Moderna Tider*, No. 122/123, 68–69.
Södersten, Bo (2001a), Unpublished draft of memoirs. Manuscript.
Södersten, Bo (2001b), 'Usel integration', *Sydsvenska Dagbladet Snällposten*, 26 februari.

Södersten, Bo (2001c), 'Attacs recept har gett armod på Kuba', *Dagens Nyheter*, 14 April.
Södersten, Bo (2001d), 'Ekonomipriset tappar sin betydelse', *Dagens Nyheter*, 10 December.
Södersten, Bo (2002a), 'Fram med sakfrågorna', *Sydsvenska Dagbladet Snällposten*, 8 April.
Södersten, Bo (2002b), 'Svenska modellen fungerar inte', *Dagens Nyheter*, 24 July.
Södersten, Bo (2002c), 'Mindre avund, tack', *Sydsvenska Dagbladet Snällposten*, 12 November.
Södersten, Bo (2003), 'Hymla inte om invandrare', *Dagens Nyheter*, 28 December.
Södersten, Bo (ed.) (2004a), *Globalization and the Welfare State*. Houndmills, Basingstoke and New York: Palgrave Macmillan.
Södersten, Bo (2004b), 'The Welfare State as a General Equilibrium System', in: Bo Södersten, (ed.), *Globalization and the Welfare State*. Houndmills, Basingstoke and New York: Palgrave Macmillan.
Södersten, Bo (2004c), 'Malmö på efterkälken', *Sydsvenska Dagbladet Snällposten*, 29 January.
Södersten, Bo (2004d), 'Chockerande siffror om förtidspension', *Dagens Nyheter*, 12 February.
Södersten, Bo (2004e), 'Grön återvändsgränd', *Sydsvenska Dagbladet Snällposten*, 2 October.
Södersten, Bo (2004f), 'Förutfattad bild av USA', *Sydsvenska Dagbladet Snällposten*, 30 October.
Södersten, Bo (2005a), 'Reform Failure and Poor Economic Performance: The Case of Sweden', in: Mats Lundahl and Michael L Wyzan (eds), *The Political Economy of Reform Failure*. London and New York: Routledge.
Södersten, Bo (2005b), 'En ohållbar ordning', *Sydsvenska Dagbladet Snällposten*, 9 April.
Södersten, Bo (2005c), 'Svårt att bevara välfärdsstaten', *Sydsvenska Dagbladet Snällposten*, 11 May.
Södersten, Bo (2005d), 'En fråga om attityd', *Sydsvenska Dagbladet Snällposten*, 17 June.
Södersten, Bo (2005e), 'Tillväxt utan jobb', *Sydsvenska Dagbladet Snällposten*, 3 November.
Södersten, Bo (ed.) (2006a), *Den problematiska tryggheten – välfärdsstaten under tre decennier*. Stockholm: SNS Förlag.
Södersten, Bo (2006b), 'Tre decennier med den svenska välfärdsstaten', in: Bo Södersten (ed.), *Den problematiska tryggheten – välfärdsstaten under tre decennier*. Stockholm: SNS Förlag.

Södersten, Bo (2006c), 'Det goda exemplet Indien', *Sydsvenska Dagbladet Snällposten*, 19 July.
Södersten, Bo and Nyberg, Kristian (2001), 'Trettio år av chilensk ekonomi', *Ekonomisk Debatt*, Vol, 29, No. 5, 347–358.
Södersten, Bo and Reed, Geoffrey (1994), *International Economics*. Third edition. Houndmills, Basingstoke and London: Macmillan.
Södersten, Bo and Söderström, Hans Tson (eds) (2004), *Marknad och politik*. Sjätte upplagan. Stockholm: SNS Förlag.
Södersten, Bo and Vind, Karl (1968), 'Tariffs and Trade in General Equilibrium', *American Economic Review*, Vol. 58, No. 3, 394–408.
Södersten, Bo and Vind, Karl (1969), 'Tariffs and Trade in General Equilibrium: Reply', *American Economic Review*, Vol. 59, No. 3, 424–426.
SOU 1973:41, *Forskning för utveckling. Betänkande avgivet av U-landsforskningsberedningen*. Stockholm: Utbildningsdepartementet. Göteborgs Offsetttryckeri.
Stolper, Wolfgang and Samuelson, Paul A. (1941), 'Protection and Real Wages', *Review of Economic Studies*, Vol. 9, No. 1, 58–73.
Sundell, Ingegerd (1993), 'Närande och tärande', *Nya Norrland*, 12 February.
Tingsten, Herbert (1961), *Mitt liv: Ungdomsåren*. Stockholm: Wahlström & Widstrand.
Tingsten, Herbert (1962), *Mitt liv: Mellan trettio och femtio*. Stockholm: P.A. Norstedt & Söners förlag.
Tingsten, Herbert (1963), *Mitt liv: Tidningen 1946–1952*. Stockholm: P.A. Norstedt & Söners förlag.
Tingsten, Herbert (1964), *Mitt liv: Tio år 1953–1963*. Stockholm: P.A. Norstedt & Söners förlag.
Tobisson, Lars (1971), 'Söderstens nidbild', *Dagens Nyheter*, 1 March.
Torrens, Robert (1821), *An Essay on the Production of Wealth*. London: Longman, Hurst, Orme, Brown & Green.
Vanek, Jaroslav (1970), *The General Theory of Labor-Managed Economies*. Ithaca, NY and London: Cornell University Press.
Werin, Lars (1972), Sakkunnigutlåtande vid tillsättningen av professuren i arbetsmarknadspolitik vid Institutet för social forskning vid Stockholms universitet. 30 October.
Widmalm, Sten (2019), 'De integrationspolitiska utredningarna som kulturkrig', *Respons*, Vol. 8, No. 6, 19–25.
Ytterberg, Claes-Bertil (1997), 'Södersten legitimerar nazism', *Dagens Nyheter*, 22 December.

CHAPTER 10

Rolf G. H. Henriksson: Portrait of an Economist

(with Benny Carlson)

Rolf G. H. Henriksson (1937–2020) was one of Sweden's leading historians of economic doctrines. He grew up as one of three children in Mölnbo, near Gnesta. His father first worked as a livestock manager on a large farm and thereafter at Scania Vabis in Södertälje. His mother was a housewife. Rolf was encouraged to study by his elementary school teacher. He attended junior and senior high school in Södertälje and then studied at the Stockholm School of Economics. Rolf was the first one in his family to move on to higher education. At the SSE, his teachers were Bertil Ohlin, Arthur Montgomery and Erik Dahmén. One of his strongest memories was when Dahmén, who spoke about the history of economic doctrines as a neglected subject, singled him out as his best student. Rolf considered himself to be under the spell of Ohlin, but worked in a cooperative store, followed the writings of Ernst Wigforss closely and become 'kind of a Social Democrat.'

Rolf Henriksson applied for and received a scholarship from the Sweden-America Foundation. He left with a letter of recommendation from Ohlin in his pocket and landed at Northwestern University in Evanston, Illinois, in 1960. There, he became course mate with Axel Leijonhufvud and together with Robert Clower taught a course in mathematical economics. 'Knowledge from the Stockholm School of Economics was hard currency,' he concluded. He also worked as an assistant professor

M. Lundahl, *Twelve Figures in Swedish Economics*, Palgrave Studies in the History of Economic Thought, https://doi.org/10.1007/978-3-030-94327-1_10

in Austin, Texas, where he taught price theory. Rolf got to know celebrities like the institutionalist Clarence Ayres, the growth economist Walt Rostow, the economic historian Robert Fogel and the financial economist Franco Modigliani, the latter two future Nobel laureates. He wrote an essay about Erik Lundberg which was so highly appreciated by Modigliani that the latter visited Lundberg in Sweden. In 1969, Rolf got his PhD degree at Northwestern.

Rolf Henriksson, however, did not like Austin all that much and already before presenting his thesis, in the mid-1960s, he returned to Sweden and the Stockholm School of Economics where he worked for a year as Ohlin's assistant. He thereafter got in touch with Lars Werin at the economics department at Stockholm University and began teaching there and in the department of economic history. His teaching interest, which among other things included the history of economic doctrines and economic history, was influenced not least by Torsten Gårdlund. As we have already pointed out, from the beginning, Rolf was an 'Ohlin fan,' Ohlin, however, was no friend of structural research but, using an exclamation which sometimes is claimed to be due to Hermann Göring, used to say that 'when I hear the word structure, I cock my revolver.' Rolf, however, was driven by an increasing interest in the structural research represented by economists like Johan Åkerman, Ingvar Svennilson and Erik Dahmén. As we will demonstrate below, he wrote several histories of economic organizations and fora, as well as portraits of individual economists and economic historians.

The Dissertation

Rolf Henriksson defended a doctoral dissertation on Swedish emigration 1860–1910.[1] Inspired by the school represented not least by Robert Fogel, known as New Economic History or cliometrics, he made a counterfactual analysis: What would the development of the Swedish population have been without the emigration to the United States and which were the effects on Swedish welfare of the emigration? Between 1860 and the first world war, one million of 3.9 million Swedes left their home country. The vast majority, 80 percent, went to the United States.

[1] Henriksson (1969).

Rolf Henriksson was inspired by Knut Wicksell's analysis of the emigration,[2] but he had his own approach. In Rolf's model, emigration and welfare both affect each other and the birth rates within each period, while the birth rates in the same period affect birth rates, emigration and welfare in the following period. Rolf employs an explicit counterfactual approach. Het takes the composition of the Swedish population in 1860 as his point of departure and with the aid of the observed death and fertility rates he calculates the hypothetical population in 1900. The available data did not permit him to proceed further, but he presents an extrapolation for 1910.

Rolf investigates the effects of emigration on the supply, the demand and the wage rate in the Swedish labor market. The supply of course was reduced. The demand was also reduced when the population shrank. Possibly, this was counteracted by the fact that the capital-labor ratio increased and with that the wage rate. Rolf first presents different possible net outcomes in a simple partial diagram, before he constructs a model where the supply of labor is determined by the emigration and the capital stock by the labor force: the more laborers, the higher the savings and the larger the capital stock. With the aid of the model, he shows that an increase of the capital stock in relation to the number of workers does not guarantee that the wage will rise and, conversely, that a reduction does not necessarily entail a lowering of the wage rate.

Rolf, however, contended that the emigration contributed to wage increases in Sweden and hence to increased welfare. He, therefore, went on to analyze the different components of his model. Wage data for 1870–1915 were obtained from Karl Jungenfelt's dissertation about the wage share in the Swedish economy.[3] In Rolf's model, the wage is affected directly by the emigration, the changes in the capital-labor ratio caused by it and by an efficiency factor, defined as the ratio of the elasticity of the marginal product of labor when the labor use changes and the elasticity of the same marginal product when the capital use is changed.

Rolf shows how emigration affected the labor supply during the entire period under investigation—above all in the late 1860s and the 1880s. Thereafter, he analyzes how savings may have been affected by the income reduction caused by emigration, by the effect on the propensity to save,

[2] Wicksell (1882). For a summary of Wicksell's views on emigration see Lundahl (2005, Chapter 6).

[3] Jungenfelt (1966).

via changes in the dependency rate and the distribution of income. His conclusion is that the net effect on savings and investment was negative, but that the reduction of the labor supply was stronger than the effect on the capital stock, so that the capital-labor ratio of the economy increased.

When it comes to the efficiency parameter, Rolf makes a distinction between factors which directly induced more efficiency and factors which changed the propensity to increase efficiency. (The difference is far from crystal clear.) The former effects arose both from the demand and the supply side. Emigration reduced the demand for low-quality goods and, via higher wages, increased the demand for high-quality goods. Rolf guessed that this change also made producers improve their techniques, in the former case to counteract the contraction and in the latter in order to be able to compete with imported goods. On the supply side, the impulses for productivity-increasing changes stemmed from productivity-increasing changes emanating from the wage increases caused by the emigration.

Rolf distinguishes two factors affecting the propensity to increase efficiency; an entrepreneurial factor and a factor which affected the sluggishness of the labor supply. The former is divided into one direct and one indirect component. The direct effect is due to the fact that many young people, who could otherwise have become entrepreneurs, emigrated, but since the emigrants mainly came from the lower ranks in society, Rolf does not consider it to be of major importance. Returning emigrants, who could have returned home with entrepreneurial impulses, were generally fairly old. The indirect component consisted in impulses which changed the entrepreneurial environment: improved education as a result of higher incomes and an increased awareness that wage increases might require changes of production techniques. Both capital and labor could, in turn, resist the attempts of the employers to mobilize, reallocate and reshape them, Rolf argues that there was no evidence that emigration had affected savings and capital formation in this respect. Possibly, the small savers had become more important, and the growth of the savings banks had increased competition within the bank sector, but at the same time this could have had a negative effect on risk-taking.

The labor that emigrated was young, with a higher potential for learning than the average, which might have led to increased adaptation difficulties. On the other hand, the emigrants usually came from stagnating branches, so Rolf concluded that emigration contributed to reducing the sluggishness of the transformation of the economy. The returning emigrants in turn probably contributed to the creation of a more flexible attitude. Presumably the wage increases had made the workers more prone to move to branches and regions where earnings were higher and in addition to educate themselves. Rolf concluded that emigration had acted as a stimulus for entrepreneurship both among employers and employees and lowered the resistance to change. All in all, it had contributed to increasing the efficiency of the economy, as defined by Rolf.

As always, when it came to drawing conclusions, Rolf Henriksson was careful in his summary evaluation of the Swedish emigration. It had contributed 'with high likelihood' to an increase of 'potential welfare' and therefore 'a strong a priori case has been made for the presumption that the effect on actual welfare was also beneficial.'[4] Rolf underlined the 'probable' in his conclusions. They are highly hypothetical. He arrived at them mainly through the use of models where much hinges on how large certain effects may be in relation to others, but where no hard data exist. In the end, the reader is left with a number of qualified guesses, Himself, he viewed his contribution mainly as a methodological exercise—an appreciation which appears correct to latter-day readers.

The Heckscher Studies

In connection with the centenary of the birth of Eli Heckscher, in 1979 a portrait of Heckscher and Swedish economics signed Rolf Henriksson, appeared in *Ekonomisk Debatt*. This was his first published article—earlier he had only published book reviews—and it was the first outlet for his life-long interest in Heckscher, where the ambition was to write Heckscher's biography. In his last portrait of Heckscher, which we will come back to, Rolf wrote about an on-going work on 'an intellectual biography of Heckscher' which had been initiated in the 1970s with the support of Eli Heckscher's son Gunnar.[5] No such *magnum opus* ever saw the light of day, but during the next quarter century, Rolf painted a number of Heckscher portraits in more manageable formats.

But let us begin with the first article. Rolf took a serious approach toward his subject. In a footnote, he explains that the article presents

[4] Henriksson (1969, p. 138).

[5] Henriksson (2006, p. 79).

'preliminary results of many years of studies of Heckscher, in connection with teaching economic history to doctoral students,'[6] whereupon he proceeds to thank about twenty-five more or less well-known persons for support and comments. It is an informative and well-written article which, however, lacks references to the reminiscences earlier published by Heckscher's colleagues and students. The article is a triptych which deals with Heckscher as an academic teacher, researcher and debater of economic policy. The first part focuses on the so-called president incident, the second on Heckscher's contribution as initiator of The Political Economy Club [Nationalekonomiska klubben] and the third on his contributions to the Swedish Economic Association [Nationalekonomiska föreningen], where he became the most frequent debater in its history. The article also sheds light on Heckscher the anti-Nazi and workaholic and on his way of dealing with science and politics.

The first Heckscher article became the point of departure for many of Rolf's later writings. There you find the Political Economy Club, the Swedish Economic Association, the Stockholm School of economists and names like Knut Wicksell, Arthur Montgomery, Bertil Ohlin, Erik Lundberg, Ingvar Svennilson and Erik Dahmén.

In his next essay on'Eli F. Heckscher: The Economic Historian as Economist', in an anthology edited by Bo Sandelin, *The History of Swedish Economic Thought*, Rolf used a different approach, although of course much of the content was the same. He notes that the most celebrated contribution by Heckscher to economic theory—the Heckscher-Ohlin theorem—at home was viewed almost as a 'bolt from the blue' that did not strike twice.[7] In Sweden, Heckscher was known and appreciated mainly as an economic historian. Rolf's account is chronological and picks up a few new threads, not least an article about economic history in *Ekonomisk Tidskrift* 1904 and his doctoral dissertation from 1907 about the importance of railways for the economic development of Sweden, which Rolf views as a predecessor to the American cliometric school. He then thinks of Robert Fogel's work on the importance of the railroads for the economic development of the United States, published almost sixty years later. Rolf also points to some decisive stages of Heckscher's road to becoming the godfather of economic history in Sweden, his 'declaration

[6] Henriksson (1979, p. 510).

[7] Henriksson (1991a, p. 141).

of intent' in a letter at the beginning of the first world war and his insight in relation with his fiftieth birthday and the president incident in 1929, that it was 'now or never.'[8]

The third Heckscher portrait was unveiled in the book *Ekonomporträtt* [Portraits of Economists] from 1991,[9] and returned slightly retouched in *Svenska nationalekonomer under 400 år* [Swedish Economists during 400 Years].[10] Not surprisingly, it builds on the former two works, offers nothing new, but constitutes a well-rounded complete picture of Heckscher. After that, a decade would pass before he returned to Heckscher again. During the intermediate years, he instead dealt with Erik Lundberg, to which we will return below.

The next Heckscher portrait was written in 2003, together with Mats Lundahl, in the book *Janusansiktet Eli Heckscher* [Eli Heckscher, the Janus Face]. The book contains texts by Heckscher sorted under three headings: Heckscher's programmatic declarations, Heckscher as an economic theorist, and the development of Heckscher's methodological position. Rolf and Mats analyze Heckscher's texts on theory and method from his 'hints' in the 1904 article to his study guide in economic history from 1951. Halfway in between, in a plea for theory in economic history, 1929, Heckscher argued that economic history should deal with the causes of economic development, while economics should be devoted to the explanation of economic phenomena at a given point in time. 'Thus, Heckscher appears to think that economic history is about dynamic processes while economics is limited to the explanation of the static picture,' summarize Rolf and Mats.[11] They find the key to Heckscher's scientific production in his licentiate thesis, from 1903, about the Swedish Navigation Act of 1724 [Produktplakatet], which points forward to the great works on mercantilism and the economic history of Sweden, and in the doctoral dissertation from 1907, which by its counterfactual approach points forward to cliometrics. Other conclusions are that Heckscher was a precursor of public choice, that he used economic theory more in his early works than in his later ones and that there is little trace of trade theory in them.

[8] Ibid., pp. 148, 154.

[9] Henriksson (1991b).

[10] Henriksson (2014a).

[11] Henriksson and Lundahl (2003, p. 28).

Rolf's last Heckscher essay is labeled 'The Making of the Economic Historian' and was published in *Eli Heckscher, International Trade, and Economic History*, edited by Ronald Findlay, Rolf Henriksson, Håkan Lindgren and Mats Lundahl. It was based on contributions to a 2003 conference on the occasion of the fiftieth anniversary of Heckscher's death In this essay, Rold follows and analyzes in detail Heckscher's early development during his study years in Uppsala to the licentiate thesis in 1903 and the 'manifesto' in 2004. The reader is invited to follow Heckscher's studies of history, political science and economics in Uppsala around the turn of the century 1900, with the historian Harald Hjärne and the economist David Davidson as his main escorts, up to his own mature conclusion, which Rolf summarizes in a single sentence: 'Economics and economic history had entirely different objectives.'[12] Heckscher repeatedly called for economic theory in the study of economic history, but Rolf's concluding message, exactly like in the 2003 volume, is that 'the core position of the manifesto' was still valid:

> Heckscher's famous plea for theory in economic history only concerned the explanation of a repetitive state in the past. The manifesto, as well as all later restatements of the method of economic history, gave economic theory little role as a tool in the explanation of economic development.[13]

The essay is a good example of Rolf's approach. He penetrates his research object deeply and attempts to reconstruct and interpret its intellectual world, but his way of dealing with his references does not always make it easy for the reader to question his interpretations. The history of Heckscher's development before the 'manifesto' (which he indeed quotes abundantly), Rolf states, builds mainly on Heckscher's correspondence. But it is not clear from which letters the information comes.

Montgomery and Ohlin

Rolf Henriksson wrote about the economists who had been his teachers at the Stockholm School of Economics: Arthur Montgomery, Bertil Ohlin and Erik Dahmén. The former two were the subjects of single articles. Dahmén turned into a serial which we will come back to below.

[12] Henriksson (2006, p. 72).

[13] Ibid., p. 79.

Arthur Montgomery, who was related to Heckscher and like the latter balanced on the border between economics and economic history had his life and work summarized by Rolf in an article in *Svenskt Biografiskt Lexikon* [Swedish Biographical Dictionary].[14]

Berftil Ohlin would have turned a hundred years old in 1999. On this occasion, the Stockholm School of Economics arranged a major symposium instead of the annual Ohlin Lectures. The papers from this occasion were published in a book edited by Ronald Findlay, Lars Jonung and Mats Lundahl, with a contribution by Rolf on Ohlin's doctoral dissertation.[15] In his memoirs, Ohlin writes: '[I] began ... to write the foundations of a to a certain extent new approach on the theory of international trade for which I had got the inspiration during a walk on Unter den Linden in Berlin in 1920.'[16] The most common interpretation of Ohlin's recollection is that the idea that he got was that of combining Eli Heckscher's factor endowments approach[17] and Gustav Cassel's general equilibrium approach.[18] Rolf questioned this. He had examined the correspondence between Heckscher and Ohlin, where the latter emphatically states that Heckscher had not exerted any influence on him until he was well into his work. Rolf instead advances the thesis that what Ohlin was pondering during his work was exchange rates. He had published an essay on equilibrium exchange rates in *Ekonomisk Tidskrift*[19] and Rolf was of the opinion that the real side of foreign trade was a mere preamble to an approach that would also contain monetary variables. The thesis is, however, not sustainable. As Rolf himself admits, there was nothing about exchange rates in Ohlin's licentiate thesis[20]—Ohlin had played with the idea but discarded it—and in the doctoral dissertation, they are discussed only marginally.[21] Rather, it may have been the case that on Unter den Linden Ohlin had found out that he could let go of the exchange rates and concentrate on

[14] Henriksson (1987a).

[15] Henriksson (2002a).

[16] Ohlin (1972, p. 79).

[17] Heckscher (1919).

[18] Cassel (1918).

[19] Ohlin (1921).

[20] Ohlin (1922).

[21] Ohlin (1924).

the general equilibrium approach and on the real side.[22] Possibly Rolf himself had doubts about his idea. The original version of his symposium paper,[23] consisted of 40 single-spaced pages while the printed version at the proof stage had been shortened to twelve more cryptically formulated pages. He had got cold feet.

The National Institute of Economic Research

In 1987, on the occasion of the fiftieth anniversary of the National Institute of Economic Research [Konjunkturinstitutet, KI], a book edited by Rolf Henriksson was published: *Konjunkturinstitutet under Erik Lundbergs tid* [The National Institute of Economic Research under Erik Lundberg]. The book deals with the first two decades of the institute, from the start in 1937 until Erik Lundberg's resignation as its head in 1955. Rolf himself framed the volume with an introductory chapter about the idea behind the institute and its monitoring of the Swedish economy and a concluding chapter about the organizational development of the institute. Within this framework, eight key persons of the history of KI deal with various facets of its activities: Claes Berg, Gustav Cederwall, Lennart Fastbom, Börje Kragh, Lars Lindberger, Lundberg, Bengt Metelius and Ingvar Ohlsson. In the preface, Rolf relates how the work on the book was carried out as an on-going seminar. That, as usual, his own work had been very meticulous is testified by all the institutions and people that are thanked on almost three densely written pages.[24]

In his rather short introductory chapter,[25] Rolf takes as his point of departure a meeting in the Political Economy Club in 1931 and goes on to the proposal for economic monitoring that on the initiative of Dag Hammarskjöld was presented in the Committee on Unemployment in 1934. In the longer concluding chapter, Rolf continues his story of the creation of the institute and its reorganization after the second world war.[26]

[22] Lundahl (2018), reprinted as Chapter 1 in the present volume.

[23] Henriksson (2001a).

[24] Henriksson (1987b).

[25] Henriksson (1987c).

[26] Henriksson (1987e).

During the course of the work, the vitality of the protagonist of the story, Erik Lundberg, decreased. Rolf carried out two interviews with him, one with and one without a tape recorder. In the preface, he writes about the first one:

> The planning of and the work with the present publication was initiated in the summer of 1986, while Erik Lundberg was still in good health. During a day of intense spiritual intercourse, from ten in the morning until about five in the afternoon, he emptied a large bag of memories, good advice, hilarious anecdotes and wishes on my table. Erik was in full swing and radiated all the charm and brilliance he could master. Came evening, I sat down, slightly exhausted, and attempted to reconstruct and summarize everything he had said, but with a pretty bad result.[27]

A day or two later, it became clear that Lundberg had a cancer relapse. The recorded interview reproduced in the book was carried out in April 1987[28] and Lundberg passed away in September the same year. One of the more dramatic episodes from Lundberg's period as head of KI figures in the interview. It took place when a couple of members of the commission that had to scrutinize the KI publications, the head of the central bank, Mats Lemne, and the secretary of state of the Ministry of Finance, Gunnar Lange, refused to authorize a passage in a 1953 report on the business cycle which pointed to a certain risk of inflation, which made Lundberg call Minister of Finance Per Edvin Sköld and ask to resign. He was, however, persuaded to stay, but the episode left its traces and he left KI two years later. The conflict is dealt with in detail in Börje Kragh's chapter in the book.

The Lundberg Studies

The book about the National Institute of Economic Research was the beginning of another of Rolf's extensive and lengthy projects: Erik Lundberg. Already in 1986, when Lundberg was still alive and able to make a selection of his works, the work on a Lundberg anthology was begun. After Lundberg's death, the entire responsibility for the work rested on Rolf. Nine years later, the Center for Business and Policy Studies,

[27] Henriksson (1987b).

[28] Henriksson (1987d).

[Studieförbundet Näringsliv och Samhälle, SNS] could publish *Studies in Economic Instability and Change*,[29] with a preface and a postscript by Rolf. The book contains thirty-seven texts from the beginning of the 1930s to the end of the 1980s, sorted under five headings: Contributions to Business Cycle Theory, Long and Short Run Aspects of the Stabilization Problem, Book Reviews, Biographical Notes and Assessments, and Polemics and Retrospect. And, finally, a bibliography with Lundberg's works in English and Swedish. In his preface, Rolf notes that the work had drawn out because of Lundberg's death, the supervision of the translation of 'the sometimes less transparent language through which Lundberg conveyed his often subtle thoughts'[30] and the research on the'life and letters' behind Lundberg's production. In his postscript, Rolf delved into the translation problem, among other things the difficulty of making the 'Lundbergianisms' sound right in English, and he also came back to the difficulty of grasping Lundberg's lifetime contribution.

> What has been particularly difficult to capture is 'the personal equation' behind Lundberg's achievements. Much of the key to an understanding of his career and his works is to be sought in his personality. However, here Lundberg presents in the words of a close associate 'a moving target'.[31]

Thereupon followed a swift number of Lundberg portraits. In the so-called Mattioli book with texts by Lundberg, *The Development of Swedish and Keynesian Macroeconomic Theory and Its Impact on Economic Policy*, Rolf presents a biography and a bibliography of Lundberg. He divides Lundberg's life into four periods: his youth until his doctoral dissertation in 1937, his years as the head of KI, his years as a professor at Stockholm University and the Stockholm School of Economics 1955–1975 and his emeritus years. During the first phase, Lundberg received impulses from leading Swedish and—as a Rockefeller fellow in the US 1931–32—American, economists and his dissertation, *Studies in the Theory of*

[29] That it was the SNS which published the book was no coincidence. Lundberg had been involved in the institute from the beginning and was for many years a member of its economic policy council.

[30] Henriksson (1995a, p. 9).

[31] Henriksson (1995b, p. 511).

Economic Expansion, according to Rolf, became 'the cornerstone work of the Stockholm School.'[32]

According to Rolf, Lundberg anticipated both Samuelson's formalization of the interaction of the multiplier and the accelerator and Harrod's and Domar's growth analysis, but because of its growth perspective, the dissertation ended up in a backwater since the world's economists were weaned on Keynes. Lundberg's next major work, *Konjunkturer och ekonomisk politik* from 1953,[33] had a liberal twist which put him at ends with the Social Democratic ideologists, and after the incident referred to above, he left KI. After the next twenty years as a pure academic, Lundberg, in Rolf's words had established himself as 'almost a guru of economic wisdom and foresight,' in key positions at the SE Bank, the SNS, the Royal Academy of Sciences, the Nobel Prize Committee and the International Economic Association.[34]

Exactly like in the case of Heckscher, and as we will soon see, that of Dahmén as well, Rolf's next step consisted in digging deeply into the early development of Lundberg, more precisely his licentiate thesis from 1930. After a very technical presentation of its contents, Rolf concludes that the work is 'surprisingly modern and harbours many ideas and conceptions that have only recently become mainstream.'[35] Finally, he published a short article on Lundberg in a dictionary of the business cycle.[36]

The Industrial Institute for Economic and Social Research

Another project which probably derives from the book about the National Institute of Economic Research dealt with the Industrial Institute for Economic and Social Research [Industriens Utredningsinstitut—IUI] which had been established in 1939. In 1989, it was the fiftieth anniversary of the institute. Rolf Henriksson then was given the task of writing its history. This in the end became the only book he ever published

[32] Henriksson (1996a, p. 144).

[33] Lundberg (1953), English translation, Lundberg (1957).

[34] Henriksson (1996a, p. 162).

[35] Henriksson (1996b, p. 354).

[36] Henriksson (1997).

himself, *Som Edström ville—hur IUI blev till* [What Edström Wanted—How the IUI Was Created].[37] From the beginning, the purpose was to write the story of the creation of the IUI and follow its activities until Ingvar Svennilson left the institute in 1949. It did not quite turn out that way. Rolf took his time. He dug out all conceivable material and he wrote long drafts, as he always did, before he cut. This time, however, he did not quite get to the cutting stage. In the preface, Rolf complains about the lack of time, and the result confirms it. The project resulted in three publications, two working papers and the book. None of them is very elaborate. They all give the impression of being building blocks for something that never quite materialized. The task was not an easy one, because the archive of the institute at the time had not been put in systematic order. Simply finding the necessary documents required a substantial effort.

The first part of the trilogy presumably was a preliminary version[38] of what the following year would become a book.[39] The latter deals, in minute detail, with the prehistory of the creation of the IUI and its first years. Rolf tells the slightly apocryphal story of how Per Albin Hansson, the Prime Minister, at a meeting with the managing director of ASEA, in addition head of the Swedish Employers' Confederation, Sigfrid Edström, stated that the business community was not well enough represented in the political debate and of how Edström thereafter realized the idea of a research institute that provide the business community with arguments.

It took a while before the Industrial Institute for Economic and Social Research could begin its activities in February 1939. Rolf provides an account of Edström's problem of making the general public aware of the key issues of the Swedish industry. The managing director of the Federation of Swedish Industries, Vilhelm Lundvik, opposed what he saw as a politicization of the business community, and this, he claimed, was true of Edström's institute as well. Together with the managing director of the Swedish Employers' Confederation, Gustaf Söderlund, Edström and Lundvik formed a committee in order to arrive at a proposal of how the research issue should be handled. In the end, Söserlund managed to present a compromise that both the Employers' Confederation and the

[37] Henriksson (1990a).

[38] Henriksson (1989b).

[39] Heenriksson (1990a).

Federation of Swedish Industries could accept: an institute which was to do research but stay out of party politics.

Rolf Henriksson's book about the IUI goes as far as 1943, the year that Edström resigned as the chairman of the board of the institute. At that time, the IUI had got its third director. The first one was the political scientist and newspaper man Ivar Anderson. He was relieved by Ragnar Sundén in 1940, who in 1941 passed on the baton to the economist Ingvar Svennilson. Rolf writes about the activities during the first two years, years marked by the war and the necessity of cooperation between the state and the business community, but above all he stresses the change that took place when Svennilson arrived, when the IUI was converted into a pure research institute. By then, a Norrland study and an investigation of the problems of small-scale industries carried out by Axel Iveroth and published in 1943 had already been initiated.

At the same time as he wrote the history of the creation of the IUI and its first years, Rolf worked on an account of what would become the most ambitious endeavor on the IUI of all times: the Norrland study.[40] The plan was that the book should extend so far in time that the latter could be incorporated. That proved, impossible, however, naturally enough. The Norrland project consisted of far too many parts. It was initiated in 1939 and went on, more or less intensely, for ten years before it petered out. No coherent final report was ever published. Rolf did not manage to present any overall picture either. He describes the course of the investigation in some detail until 1943, while the period thereafter, up to 1948, when the Norrland study was buried, is dealt with more cursorily.

The Dahmén Studies

Another economist subject to Rolf's profound interest was Erik Dahmén, who on his seventy-fifth birthday was honored with the book *Development Blocks and Industrial Transformation*, published by the IUI and edited by Bo Carlsson and Rolf Henriksson.[41] The two editors point to transformation and development blocks as the unique ingredients in the Dahménian approach, elements that extend what he had absorbed from his masters Joseph Schumpeter and Johan Åkerman. The book consists

[40] Henriksson (1990b).

[41] Carlsson and Henriksson (1991a).

of four sections: a summary of Dahméns licentiate thesis from 1942, an English translation of the summary in Dahmén's doctoral dissertation from 1950, the discussion of this thesis in the Political Economy Club, a few reviews and finally a selection of Dahmén's writings from the 1980s. Each part features an introduction. In the introduction to the licentiate thesis, Rolf focuses on the idea of malinvestment, transmitted to Dahmén from Hayek via Åkerman,[42] Dahmén's reaction to Schumpeter's *Business Cycles*,[43] and the theory that he developed in his licentiate thesis.[44] In the next introduction[45] the reader is invited to follow the further adventures of Dahmén at the IUI, under the influence of Svennilson, and his tour de force doctoral dissertation *Svensk industriell företagarverksamhet* [Entrepreneurial Activity and the Development of Swedish Industry].[46]

Five years later, Rolf published another paper on Dahmén's early development, this time on the occasion of the latter's eightieth birthday. The story is the same as that of the introduction to the licentiate thesis in 1991, but it is told in more detail. Among other things, Rolf contends that Dahmén by combining Schumpeter's theory of innovation and Hayek's malinvestment processes 'arrived at a more complete or generalized notion of the transformation than Schumpeter,'[47] and even anticipated the latter's creative destruction in *Capitalism, Socialism and Democracy* from 1942.[48] Since both Dahmén's thesis and Schumpeter's book are dated 1942 and since it takes longer to write a book than a licentiate thesis it is, however, difficult to determine who was first.

Once more, in a book published by the Ratio Institute, *Den svenska tillväxtskolan* [The Swedish Growth School], Rolf came back to Dahmén's early years. This time, he scrutinized in detail Dahmén's development before the licentiate thesis, above all his report on an undergraduate paper of his presented at a conference in Copenhagen in 1939. Rolf's conclusion was that already in 1939, Dahmén had 'arrived at a theory about the process which Schumpeter with a formulation which

[42] Henriksson (1991c).

[43] Schumpeter (1939), Dahmén (1941a).

[44] Dahmén (1941b).

[45] Carlsson and Henriksson (1991b).

[46] Dahmén (1950), English translation, Dahmén (1970).

[47] Henriksson (1996c, p. 14).

[48] Schumpeter (1942).

would become a classical household word precisely in 1942 called *creative destruction*' and that Dahmén had always considered himself a Schumpeterian, but that this was true only 'in a deeper sense': 'For it might be said that he did what the master attempted but failed, since he developed an excellent tool for historic casual analysis.'[49] One reviewer of the Ratio volume suggested that the editors of the book 'should have cautioned the readers of the considerably higher degree of difficulty' which characterized Rolf's contribution as compared with the rest.[50]

After the death of Dahmén, Ratio published a symposium volume in order to point to Dahmén's importance in a forward-looking perspective. Rolf reviewed it and protested against the fact that Dahmén was seen as a front figure of 'the Swedish growth school.' The Dahménian approach ought to have been presented as 'the Swedish school of structural transformation.'[51]

The Political Economy Club

In March 1986, Rolf Henriksson gave a talk about the Political Economy Club at a meeting of that club, seventy years after Heckscher's initiative to create this forum for discussion around Knut Wicksell, when the latter retired. A year later, his speech had been turned into an article, 'Nationalekonomiska klubben 1917–1951 [The Political Economy Club 1917–1951],' in *Ekonomisk Debatt*.[52] The article mainly builds on the not particularly detailed book of records of the club (which runs up to 1951) and on conversations with older economists who were around at the time: Leif Björk, Gustav Cederwall, Erik Lundberg, Bengt Metelius. The club was dominated, in turn, by Heckscher, Ohlin and Lundberg, but personal animosity saw to it that not all economists participated; Gustav Cassel and Gösta Bagge stayed away.

Rolf begins with an account of the all-time high in the history of the club, the visit by Keynes in 1936. Ohlin had greeted Keynes with 'the joy of recognition,' possibly alleging that the Stockholm economists on

[49] Henriksson (2002b, p. 97).

[50] Meyerson (2003, p. 78).

[51] Henriksson (2010, p. 94). Originally, Rolf had been thinking of writing a longer article and not a book review. In his collection of unpublished manuscripts there is a'preliminary draft' of 25 pages.

[52] Henriksson (1987f).

their own had arrived at insights similar to his, and the debate continued until midnight. The second 'peak' was when the younger economists in 1928, possibly excited by Keynes' *The End of Laissez Faire*, led by Gunnar Myrdal, attacked the older generation, primarily Heckscher. Not only Keynes, but also many other invited foreign lecturers appeared at the club in the 1930s, and after the Second World War the foreign guests again arrived. The central question when Rolf wrote his article was which role the club had played for the rise of the Stockholm School of economists—in 1987, it was fifty years since Ohlin had proclaimed the existence of this school. Rolf's answer was that the club had played an important role, not least by creating an '"oral" link in the transmission of the Wicksell heritage to the next generation.'[53]

Rolf developed his paper in a longer English version, or rather, two versions, for the conference held to celebrate the fiftieth anniversary of Ohlin's proclamation, the former slightly longer than the latter.[54] There, he played out his entire encyclopedic register of knowledge about Swedish economics, mainly during the 1920s and 1930s. Using the Political Economy Club as his hub, he scrutinizes the other elements of the institutional foundation on which the Stockholm School of economists rested—Bagge's Rockefeller project, the 1927 Committee on Unemployment, the licentiate seminar at Stockholm College—and the web of connections and antagonisms that characterized the Swedish economics profession. In his conclusions he stressed the importance of the club for the rise of the Stockholm School (the oral link to Wicksell, the revolt of the younger economists) as well as during its heyday. The articles about the Political Economy Club constituted an extremely successful research effort—a rich and exciting material, revealed in the right moment,

The Swedish Economic Association

The fact that Rolf had written about the Political Economy Club made him the obvious choice as Swedish representative at the 1999 Pisa conference on professional economics associations during the nineteenth century. The conference yielded an anthology, where Rolf wrote about the Swedish Economic Association [Nationalekonomiska Föreningen]

[53] Henriksson (1987f, p. 316).

[54] Henriksson (1989a) and (1991d).

until 1900, the institution which most of all contributed to the establishment of a qualified debate on economic policy in Sweden.[55] Rolf portrays the founding fathers of the association: Per Murén, businessman, chairman of the board of Sandvik, former Member of Parliament, and Carl Fredrik Waern, businessman, ironworks proprietor and former Minister of Finance. He speculates about the possible influence of existing Danish and English associations on the foundation in 1877, he provides an account of the most important statutes and members, the rapid expansion of the number of members, and presents, in some detail, the secretary, the banker and the founder of the villa town of Djursholm, Henrik Palme (1877–1881), the economist Claes Westman (1882–1890), The Member of Parliament and Liberal defender of free trade, Hugo Hamilton (1890–1896) as well as the banker Marcus Wallenberg, Sr (1897–1898).

Rolf also writes about the most important presentations and debates in the association. An important theme during the first ten years was tariffs and tariff policy. There were plenty of free traders in the association who did what they could to oppose the tendencies of increasing protectionism that had made themselves felt after its foundation, until the reintroduction of grain tariffs in 1888. Other themes that provoked a lively debate were social policy and the suffrage issue. A third, inflammable, theme was the conversion of the Riksbank into a full-fledged central bank with a monopoly on the issue of bank notes, something that the banker A. O. Wallenberg vehemently opposed and argued against during the meetings of the association. As Rolf demonstrates, more academic and theoretical themes were seldom touched during the meetings and did not arouse much interest. The link of the society to academic economics was weak during the entire period that he portrays.

Politics and History of Economic Doctrines

One of Rolf's early book reviews was devoted to Villy Bergström's *Den ekonomiska politiken i Sverige och dess verkningar* [Economic Policy in Sweden and Its Effects], from 1969.[56] The review is a mirror image of the book, relatively technical, but in any case, Rolf brought one good and one

[55] Henriksson (2001b).

[56] Bergström (1969).

bad piece of news. It was good that Bergström had analyzed economic policy in a historical perspective, but the study as a whole was 'very unsatisfactory.'[57] In a review of a book edited by Johan Lönnroth, *Den svenska politikens rötter* [The Roots of Swedish Politics],[58] his verdict was that from the point of view of the history of ideas, it made 'pretty poor reading,' but 'as a contribution to the ideological debate' it was stimulating.'[59] The politicians who wrote about the different political traditions of the parties in Parliament had mainly pointed to foreign inspiration sources. Lönnroth had attempted to compensate for that by focusing on older domestic thinkers, but Rolf thought that he had gone too far: 'In some cases, the suggestions are so anachronistic that you simply have to consider them an expression of his sense of humor.'[60] Among other things, he thought it 'too pompous to make Wicksell the foremost source of ideas of the Social Democratic ideological heritage.' Rolf thought that the politicians altogether were too prone to bring out 'distant fixed stars on the international firmament,' like Smith, Burke and Marx instead of people much closer in time and space, like Bertil Ohlin, Jarl Hjalmarsson and Tage Erlander. He finished with the following words: 'Clio is unfortunately often a harlot who for money brings out the narcissistic mirror for all people and institutions that need a grandiose or uplifting past.'[61]

When Rolf, together with the doctoral student Ingemar Eckerlund (1996) reviewed Bo Sandelin's, Hans-Michael Trautweins and Richard Wundraks *Det ekonomiska tänkandets historia* [The History of Economic Thought],[62] they began by pointing out that Swedish university education in economic took place in a vacuum as far as of the history of economic doctrines was concerned. This is not the place to examine the blame and praise doled out—praise for example for how Smith was dealt with but blame for the treatment of the rest of the classics ('veritable clear-cut areas'),[63] but there is no doubt whatsoever that Rolf thrived like a fish in the water of economic doctrines. And in spite of often critical

[57] Henriksson (1971, p. 362).

[58] Lönnroth (1986).

[59] Henriksson (1987g, p. 147).

[60] Ibid., p. 149.

[61] Ibid., p. 150.

[62] Sandelin et al. (1995).

[63] Henriksson and Eckerlund (1996, p. 76).

viewpoints, the summary verdict is good—the book had an obvious place in courses about the history of economic doctrines. Two decades later, Rolf reviewed *De ekonomiska idéernas historia* [The History of Economic Ideas] by Martin Kragh from 2012.[64] His verdict was generally positive, but it is close to impossible to present his views on just a few lines. This was Rolf's last, but also the most intricate and difficult, of his published texts.

A Meticulous Lone Wolfer

Rolf Henriksson's publications are characterized by extremely thorough preparation and an ambition to dig deep and sometimes interpret his research subjects beyond their own self-insight. He often begins with a panoramic view, as in the cases of Heckscher, Lundberg and Dahmén, and then goes on to a detailed analysis of the early development of his subjects, the formative years. His meticulousness meant that his works dragged on and that his total output did not become very large. On the occasion of the centenary of the department of economics of Stockholm University, Rolf was given the task of writing its history. He worked on this for several years, but no drafts were produced. Time elapsed and in the end something drastic had to be done. The seasoned journalist Svante Nycander had to save the project with the aid of Jonas Agell, Eskil Wadensjö and Hans Wijkander.[65]

The authors of the present essay were exposed to Rolf's meticulousness when during the winter of 2018 we had to go through his enormous collection of books, journal articles and documents, kept in eight basement storage rooms in Bergshamra. Take, for example, his collections of material about Eli Heckscher and Erik Lundberg. These avoided destruction by being moved to the Stockholm School of Economics in 37 moving boxes. They contained virtually everything written about and by these very celebrated and productive economists, and everything—all the way down to the tiniest review and note—had been penetrated, underlined and annotated in the margin. Also his own published works were full of such marks, which indicated that he could never really let go of what he had written. Research is indeed, like everything else, a process with no

64 Henriksson (2014b).

65 Nycander (2005).

end, but Rolf Henriksson obviously found it difficult even to come to a preliminary end. He was a bit of a lone wolfer, who had co-authors only in few instances (Carlsson, Eckerlund, Lundahl).

Swedish version published in Benny Carlson and Mats Lundahl, *Från Värmland till Washington: Episoder ur IUI:s historia*. Stockholm: Samhällsförlaget, 2020.

References

Bergström, Villy (1969), *Den ekonomiska politiken i Sverige och dess verkningar*. Stockholm: Industriens Utredningsinstitut and Almqvist & Wiksell.

Carlsson, Bo and Henriksson, Rolf G.H. (1991a), 'Editorial Preface', in: Bo Carlsson and Rolf G.H. Henriksson (eds), *Development Blocks and Industrial Transformation: The Dahménian Approach to Economic Development*. Stockholm: Industriens Utredningsinstitut.

Carlsson, Bo and Henriksson, Rolf G.H. (1991b), 'Editorial Introduction', in: Bo Carlsson and Rolf G.H. Henriksson (eds), *Development Blocks and Industrial Transformation: The Dahménian Approach to Economic Development*. Stockholm: Industriens Utredningsinstitut.

Cassel, Gustav (1918), *Theoretische Sozialökonomie*. Leipzig: C.F. Winter.

Dahmén, Erik (1941a), Review of Joseph Schumpeter; *Business Cycles. Statsvetenspalig Tidskrift*, Vol. 44, No. 2, 198–200.

Dahmén, Erik (1941b), Analys av några konjunkturteoretiska problemlösningar hos J. Schumpeter: Business Cycles. Lund: Licentiatseminariet i nationalekonomi, Lund VT 1941.

Dahmén, Erik (1950), *Svensk industriell företagarverksamhet: Kausalanalys av den industriella utvecklingen 1919–1939*. 2 Volumes. Stockholm: Industriens Utredningsinstitut.

Dahmén, Erik (1970), *Entrepreneurial Activity and the Development of Swedish Industry 1919–1939*. Homewood, IL: Richard D. Irwin, Inc.

Heckscher, Eli F. (1919), 'Utrikeshandelns inverkan på inkomstfördelningen. Några teoretiska grundlinjer', *Ekonomisk Tidskrift*, Vol. 21, No. 2, 1–32.

Henriksson, Rolf G.H. (1969), *An Interpretation of the Significance of Emigration for the Growth of Economic Welfare in Sweden, 1860–1910*. PhD thesis. Evanston, IL: Northwestern University.

Henriksson, Rolf G.H. (1971), Review of V Bergström, Den ekonomiska politiken i Sverige och dess verkningar, *Swedish Journal of Economics*, Vol. 73, No. 3, 359–362.

Henriksson Rolf G.H. (1979), 'Eli F. Heckscher och svensk nationalekonomi', *Ekonomisk Debatt*, Vol. 73, No. 8, 510–520.

Henriksson, Rolf G.H. (1987a), 'Arthur Montgomery', *Svenskt Biografiskt Lexikon*, Vol. 125, 709–714.

Henriksson, Rolf G.H. (1987b), 'Förord', in: Rolf G.H. Henriksson (ed.), *Konjunkturinstitutet under Erik Lundbergs tid*. Stockholm: Konjunkturinstitutet.

Henriksson, Rolf G.H. (1987c), 'Konjunkturinstitutsidén och konjunkturbevakning före konjunkturinstitutet', in: Rolf G.H. Henriksson (ed.), *Konjunkturinstitutet under Erik Lundbergs tid*. Stockholm: Konjunkturinstitutet

Henriksson, Rolf G.H. (1987d), 'Intervju med Erik Lundberg 25/4 1987', in: Rolf G.H. Henriksson (ed.), *Konjunkturinstitutet under Erik Lundbergs tid*. Stockholm: Konjunkturinstitutet.

Henriksson, Rolf G.H. (1987e), 'Organisatorisk utveckling och anomalier', in: Rolf G.H. Henriksson (ed.), *Konjunkturinstitutet under Erik Lundbergs tid*. Stockholm: Konjunkturinstitutet.

Henriksson, Rolf G.H. (1987f), 'Nationalekonomiska klubben 1917–1951', *Ekonomisk Debatt*, Vol. 15, No. 4, 305–317.

Henriksson, Rolf G.H . (1987g), Review of Johan Lönnroth (ed.), Den svenska politikens rötter, *Ekonomisk Debatt*, Vol. 15, No. 2, 147–150.

Henriksson, Rolf G.H. (1989a), 'The Institutional Base of the Stockholm School: The Political Economy Club (1917–1951)', *History of Economics Society Bulletin*, Vol. 11, No. 1, 59–97.

Henriksson, Rolf G.H. (1989b), *Under Edströms egid: Bakgrunden till IUIs start 1939 och de första verksamhetsårens utveckling*. Stockholm: Industriens Utredningsinstitut.

Henriksson, Rolf G.H. (1990a), *Som Edström ville – hur IUI blev till*. Stockholm: Industriens Utredningsinstitut.

Henriksson, Rolf G.H. (1990b), *Den stora Norrlandsutredningen vid IUI 1939–1948*. Stockholm: Industriens Utredningsinstitut.

Henriksson, Rolf G.H. (1991a), 'Eli F. Heckscher: The Economic Historian as Economist", in: Bo Sandelin (ed,), *The History of Swedish Economic Thought*. London: Routledge.

Henriksson, Rolf G.H. (1991b), 'Eli Heckscher', in: Christina Jonung and Ann-Charlotte Ståhlberg (eds), *Ekonomporträtt: Svenska ekonomer under 300 år*. Stockholm: SNS Förlag.

Henriksson Rolf G.H. (1991c), 'Editorial Introduction', in: Bo Carlsson and Rolf G.H. Henriksson (eds), *Development Blocks and Industrial Transformation: The Dahménian Approach to Economic Development*. Stockholm: Industriens Utredningsinstitut.

Henriksson, Rolf G.H. (1991d), 'The Political Economy Club and the Stockholm School, 1917–1951', in: Lars Jonung (ed.), *The Stockholm School Revisited*. Cambridge: Cambridge University Press.

Henriksson, Rolf G.H. (1995a), 'Editor's Foreword', in: Erik Lundberg, *Studies in Economic Instability and Change*. Stockholm: Studieförbundet Näringsliv och Samhälle.

Henriksson, Rolf G.H. (1995b), 'Editor's Postscript', in: Erik Lundberg, *Studies in Economic Instability and Change*. Stockholm: Studieförbundet Näringsliv och Samhälle.

Henriksson, Rolf G.H. (1996a), 'Biography and Bibliography of Erik Filip Lundberg', in: Erik Lundberg, *The Development of Swedish and Keynesian Macroeconomic Theory and its Impact on Economic Policy*. Cambridge: The Raffaele Mattioli Foundation/Cambridge University Press.

Henriksson, Rolf G.H. (1996b), 'The Early Contribution of Erik Lundberg: A Commentary to his Licentiate Thesis "On the Concept of Economic Equilibrium" (1930)', *Structural Change and Economic Dynamics*, Vol. 7, No. 3, 348–360.

Henriksson, Rolf G.H. (1996c), 'Towards the Dahménian Approach: A Review of the Early Contributions of Erik Dahmén', in: Håkan Lindgren (ed.), *Economic Dynamism: In Honour of Erik Dahmén*. Stockholm: Institutet för ekonomisk-historisk forskning.

Henriksson, Rolf G.H. (1997), 'Lundberg, Erik Filip (1907–1897)', in: David Glasner (ed.), *Business Cycles and Depressions: An Encyclopedia*. New York and London: Garland Publishing, Inc.

Henriksson, Rolf G.H. (2001a), Eureka Unter den Linden: A Reinterpretation of Ohlin's Early Contributions to the Heckscher-Ohlin Theme. Unpublished manuscript. Department of Economics, Stockholm University.

Henrikssson, Rolf G.H. (2001b), 'The Swedish Economic Association from Its Foundation (1877) to the Turn of the Century', in: Massimo M. Augello and Marco E. L. Guidi (eds), *The Spread of Political Economy and the Professionalisation of Economists: Economic Societies in Europe, America and Japan in the Nineteenth Century*. London and New York: Routledge.

Henriksson, Rolf G.H. (2002a),'Eureka Unter den Linden: A Reinterpretation of Ohlin's Early Contributions to the Heckscher-Ohlin Theme', in: Ronald Findlay, Lars Jonung and Mats Lundahl (eds), *Bertil Ohlin: A Centennial Celebration (1899–1999)*. Cambridge, MA and London: MIT Press.

Henriksson, Rolf G.H. (2002b), 'Den dahménska ansatsens tillkomst och dess ställning i den schumpeterianska tanketraditionen', in: Dan Johansson och Nils Karlson (eds), *Den svenska tillväxtskolan: Om den ekonomiska utvecklingens kreativa förstörelse*. Stockholm: Ratio.

Henriksson, Rolf G.H. (2006), 'The Making of the Economic Historian: Eli F. Heckscher, 1897–1904', in: Ronald Findlay, Rolf G.H. Henriksson, Håkan Lindgren and Mats Lundahl (eds), *Eli Heckscher, International Trade, and Economic History*. Cambridge, MA and London: MIT Press.

Henriksson, Rolf G.H. (2010), 'Den dahménska ansatsens framtid'. Review of Nils Karlson, Per Storm, Dan Johansson and Bengt Mölleryd (eds), Erik Dahmén och det industriella företagandet, *Ekonomisk Debatt*, Vol. 38, No. 2, 84–88.

Henriksson, Rolf G.H. (2014a), 'Eli F Heckscher', in: Christina Jonung and Ann-Charlotte Ståhlberg (eds), *Svenska nationalekonomer under 400 år*. Stockholm: Dialogos.

Henriksson, Rolf G.H. (2014b), 'Det ekonomiska tänkandets maxim och utveckling i ekonomisk-historiskt perspektiv'. Review of Martin Kragh, De ekonomiska idéernas historia, *Ekonomisk Debatt,* Vol. 42, No. 1, 59–64.

Henriksson, Rolf G.H. and Eckerlund, Ingemar (1996), Review of Bo Sandelin, Hans-Michael Trautwein and Richard Wundrak, Det ekonomiska tänkandets historia, *Ekonomisk Debatt*, Vol. 24, No. 1, 73–80.

Henriksson, Rolf G.H. and Lundahl, Mats (2003), 'Inledning', in: *Janusansiktet Eli Heckscher: Nationalekonom och ekonomisk historiker*. Texter i urval av Rolf G H Henriksson och Mats Lundahl. Stockholm: Timbro.

Jungenfelt, Karl G. (1966), *Löneandelen och den ekonomiska utvecklingen*. Uppsala: Almqvist & Wiksell.

Kragh, Martin (2012), *De ekonomiska idéernas historia*. Stockholm: SNS Förlag.

Lönnroth, Johan (ed.) (1986), *Den svenska politikens rötter: De ideologiska rötterna till riksdagspartiernas ekonomiska politik*. Stockholm: Studieförbundet Näringsliv och Samhälle.

Lundahl, Mats (2005), *Knut Wicksell on Poverty: 'No Place Is Too Exalted for the Preaching of These Doctrines'*. London and New York: Routledge.

Lundahl, Mats (2018), 'The Inspiration for the Heckscher-Ohlin Theorem', in: Pierre Guillet de Monthoux and Robert Stasinski (eds), *The Heckscher-Ohlin Room*. Stockholm: Stockholm School of Economics Art Initiative.

Lundberg, Erik (1953), *Konjunkturer och ekonomisk politik: Utveckling och debatt i Sverige sedan första världskriget*. Stockholm: Konjunkturinstitutet and Studieförbundet Näringsliv och Samhälle.

Lundberg, Erik (1957), *Business Cycles and Economic Policy*. London : George Allen & Unwin.

Meyerson, Per-Martin (2003), Review of Dan Johansson and Nils Karlson (eds), Den svenska tillväxtskolan, *Ekonomisk Debatt*, Vol. 31, No. 3, 76–80.

Nycander, Svante under medverkan av Jonas Agell, Eskil Wadensjö and Hans Wijkander (2005), *Från värdeteori till välfärdsteori: Nationalekonomin vid Stockholms högskola/Stockholms universitet 1904–2004*. Stockholm: SNS Förlag.

Ohlin, Bertil (1921), 'Växelkursernas jämviktsläge', *Ekonomisk Tidskrift*, Vol. 23, 29–37.

Ohlin, Bertil (1922), *Det interregionala bytets teori*. Licentiatavhandling, Stockholms Högskola.

Ohlin, Bertil (1924) *Handelns teori*. Stockholm: AB Nordiska Bokhandeln.

Ohlin, Bertil (1972), *Bertil Ohlins memoarer. Ung man blir politiker*. Stockholm: Bonniers.

Sandelin, Bo, Trautwein, Hans-Michael and Wundrak, Richard (1995), *Det ekonomiska tänkandets historia*. Stockholm: SNS Förlag.

Schumpeter, Joseph A. (1939), *Business Cycles: A Theoretical, Historical, and Statistical Analysis of the Capitalist Process.* 2 volumes. New York: McGraw Hill.

Schumpeter, Joseph A (1942), *Capitalism, Socialism and Democracy*. London: Routledge.

Wicksell, Knut (1882), *Om utvandringen. Dess betydelse och orsaker*. Stockholm: Albert Bonniers Förlag.

CHAPTER 11

The Peasant Oppressor from Norra Fäladen: Ingemar Ståhl and the Regulation of Swedish Agriculture

Ingemar Ståhl was not an agricultural economist. According to his younger brother Ingolf, the only occasion that he is known to have visited a farm was when he was five years old and managed to unlock the pigsty and let all the piggies out. His contribution to the economic literature on Swedish agriculture is found on a slightly higher level. It belongs to a tradition which began with Gunnar Myrdal and Gustaf Åkerman in the 1930s: a tradition that questioned the wisdom of hiding behind the burka of agricultural policy all kinds of protectionist arms of destruction. '… during the 1930s, the tradition in the agricultural sector that only nominally could be distinguished from social policy was inaugurated,' wrote Lennart Jörberg in 1984.[1] This policy was ultimately founded on the lack of foodstuffs during the First World War, but even more on the overproduction tendencies that had made themselves felt in the world market in the 1920s. In the 'cow trade'—log rolling—of 1933, between the Social Democrats and the Agrarians the principle was laid down that the goal

[1] Jörberg (1984, p. 37). An overview of Swedish agricultural policy from the First World War to the beginning of the 1980s is found in Hedlund and Lundahl (1985). For the two world wars and the interwar period, see also Morell (2001, pp. 157–188), and for the post-war period until the mid-1980s, Flygare and Isacson (2003, pp. 227–249).

M. Lundahl, *Twelve Figures in Swedish Economics*, Palgrave Studies in the History of Economic Thought, https://doi.org/10.1007/978-3-030-94327-1_11

of the Swedish agricultural policy was to protect the Swedish producers. The consumers footed the bill.

During the Second World War, overproduction came to an end, and the problem of how to secure the food supply during a blockade was put into the foreground. During the postwar years, agricultural policy was directed toward three partly incompatible goals: efficient production, preparation for a possible blockade and reasonable incomes for the farming population—the most important goal. Three ambitious government committees were appointed, in 1942, 1960 and 1972. The agricultural sector received tariff protection or subsidies and the economists who formed part of the committees dissented.

Not only that. From the interwar period onwards, the farmer organizations had advanced their positions also in other ways. The agricultural sector was a sector with strong barriers to entry. Anybody could not cultivate the soil. You had to be a 'farmer.' The law on land acquisition from 1945, which had been enacted in order to prevent farmland to be purchased by 'alien capital interests' was gradually sharpened until 1979. At the same time, the agricultural cooperation movement built up a strong power position supposed to keep 'unhealthy competition' away. In the end, it became virtually impossible for the farmers to stay outside the dominant producer organization.[2]

At the beginning of the 1980s, the situation had partially changed. The income objective, which had hitherto dominated Swedish agricultural policy, had begun to be pushed into the background and the blockade problem was pushed forward by the 1983 Committee on Foodstuffs [Livsmedelskommittén]. Like its predecessors, however, this committee failed to discuss seriously the costs imposed by the actual agricultural policy. Those who wanted to know something about them had to read the independent economic studies carried out around the same time.

The most influential study was the one by Odd Gulbrandsen and Assar Lindbeck from 1966.[3] The two compared the different goals and discussed various alternatives to the actual policy. In a later publication they calculated its cost for society.[4] The late 1960s were a period of strife. Sweden had a large excess production, and it cost. Lindbeck had been a

[2] Lindberg (2008, pp. 77–82).

[3] Gulbrandsen and Lindbeck (1966).

[4] Gulbrandsen and Lindbeck (1969).

member of the 1960 committee on agriculture and had filed a reservation against its conclusions. He and Gulbrandsen stressed the efficiency aspect and played down the income target. It was of little avail. Also the next committee on agriculture, from 1972, gave the vaguely formulated income target a prominent position. It was not until more than ten years later that the 1983 food committee was given the task of looking closely into the overproduction problem. The prevailing views on agricultural policy had slowly begun to change.

The Political Economy of the Food Sector

One year later, Ingemar Ståhl together with Olof Bolin and Per-Martin Meyerson published the book *Makten över maten*[5] [English translation, *The Political Economy of the Food Sector*].[6] The background was as follows. The Center for Business and Policy Studies [Studieförbundet Näringsliv och Samhälle, SNS] had a program called *Samhällsorganisation under omprövning* [The Organization of Society under Reconsideration], and in the fall of 1982, the head of the SNS, Bengt Rydén, got in touch with Ingemar for a study that would question Swedish agricultural policy. The idea was that Ingemar should write a public choice analysis of the different actors in the sector. He worked together with Olof Bolin, an agricultural economist at the Swedish University of Agricultural Sciences, and Per-Martin Meyerson, who knew the food sector 'from the inside.' The Meyerson family had owned the vinegar company Winborgs and the confectionery chain Vivels Konditorier.

The authors of *The Political Economy of the Food Sector* posed the blasphemous question of what a completely deregulated agricultural sector would look like. The price regulations imposed in order to reach the income target led to an excess supply that had to be disposed of with the aid of subsidies either of exports or of domestic consumption. In addition, the sector was plagued by a number of other regulations, e.g. via the land acquisition law, the rationalization policy, the environmental policy, the animal welfare act, the food legislation and the taxation of agriculture. Altogether, the Swedish agricultural policy was opaque and

[5] Bolin et al. (1984a).

[6] Bolin et al. (1986).

it was supposed to lead to the fulfillment of three different goals. In his memoirs Per-Martin Meyerson writes:

> In our study ... we opted ... for questioning whether any food policy at all was needed. Based on an analysis of the organization of society we described the creation and development of the agricultural policy and its tasks. The core of our analysis consisted of a demonstration that these tasks can be solved as well as or better by functioning markets than by regulations. We did this from a consumer perspective, in opposition to the dominant producer perspective of the governmental [food] committee.[7]

The authors analyzed the entire food chain, from production to consumption or export. Most of the agricultural produce was marketed via the producer cooperation societies. 'Sweden's 110,000 farmers are usually affiliated with several product-specific cooperative associations; the average farmer is affiliated with nine associations.'[8] These societies covered sixteen different products, and each of them had its own national organization. Together they constituted the Federation of Swedish Farmers [Lantbrukarnas Riksförbund, LRF]. The position of the agricultural cooperative movement was strong. The latter dominated the market. The food chain was strongly vertically integrated and all links in it were regulated. It was not only the producers who were protected. So were the later links in the chain.

The most important contribution of *The Political Economy of the Food Sector* is the public choice analysis of the reasons behind the Swedish agricultural policy. That is where we find the 'agricultural economist' Ingemar Ståhl. This is his contribution to the book. Ingemar had sprung out of welfare theory, influenced by Guy Arvidsson, and he taught welfare courses in Lund. But he was also the Swedish economist who perhaps most consequently adopted the perspective based on the perspective of different interests that constituted one of the pillars of public choice, and there is no doubt whatsoever that he played an important role when James Buchanan received the Sveriges Riksbank Prize in Economic Sciences to the Memory of Alfred Nobel in 1986.

Ingemar's first contribution in the field was a survey of some of the central elements of the public choice theory, applied to the Swedish mixed

[7] Meyerson (1997, pp. 167–168).

[8] Bolin et al. (1986, p. 40).

economy.[9] Buchanan had inspired him, and Ingemar saw to it that he came to Lund and lectured on Wícksell and Cassél, as he pronounced them, in a public choice perspective. Ingemar also invited Mancur Olson who spoke of why his model of how small special interest groups more easily than large ones made their voice heard could be applied to virtually all economic problems.[10] Olson was almost right, at least as far as agriculture in the industrialized countries was concerned. His reasoning was put to use in *The Political Economy of the Food Sector*.

In December 1982, Ingemar wrote a short memorandum about the goals of Swedish food policy, where he discarded welfare economic analysis, the aim of which was to identify relevant policy measures in situations where private and public costs diverged:

> In recent years, a new analytical tradition has been created which does not view political interventions as motivated by a desire to reach socially optimal results but rather views the political game as actions by well-organized interest groups and associations. With this 'public choice' perspective, agricultural policy should not be seen as a policy which aims at the elimination of different kinds of market imperfections but as a game between interest groups.[11]

Thus, the point of departure of the book was defined.

The public choice analysis of *The Political Economy of the Food Sector* was, however, hard-bought. Ingemar Ståhl was not an economist known for punctual delivery.[12] Per-Martin Meyerson recalled:

> Somewhere in the book the new approach had to be described, discussed and compared with the imaginary world of the regulation advocates. This

[9] Ståhl (1977).

[10] Olson (1965).

[11] Ståhl (1982a, p. 4).

[12] When he wrote the book *Miljövård och samhällsekonomi* [Environment and Economics] together with Krister Hjalte and Karl Lidgren (Hjalte et al., 1973, English version 1977), his two co-authors insisted on a contract where Ingemar undertook to pay an indemnity if he did not deliver in time—an indemnity which increased over time. At the time, Ingemar was very interested in contract theory—no problems existed that could not be solved with the aid of some kind of contract. His two co-authors took advantage of this and kept going after him. 'I am working on it', was the perennial answer. Ingemar did indeed deliver in time! (interview with Krister Hjalte, 14 December 2016).

> was Ståhl's job, actually the only thing he had promised to write. In spite of persistent attempts by Bengt Rydén, however, no manuscript arrived from Lund. Time was short. The publication day had already been announced. I had written books with Ståhl before. With the aid of the discussions that we had had in the group I hastily concocted something along the lines of what we wanted from Ståhl. The manuscript was sent to Lund on a Thursday for endorsement. That hurt the pride of the professor. Next Monday, Ståhl showed up in person at the SNS. With few corrections, and with the title 'The Political Economy of the Food Sector—a Synthesis in Terms of the Organization of Society', the study was brought to an end with an elegant display of the theoretical construction upon which our analyses built.[13]

It was obvious that the pace had been fast. The final chapter is a yeast that was thrown in after the dough. It is fine in itself, but it has been loosely grafted on an otherwise integrated exposition and it repeats part of the latter.

Emergency Policy

Ingemar Ståhl, however, did not write simply the final chapter in *The Political Economy of the Food Sector*. In his archive there is a draft from December 1982, 'Några formuleringar kring beredskapspolitiken [Some Formulations of the Emergency Policy].'[14] It was incorporated almost verbatim into the book.[15] The argumentation is strange. In one way it is realistic. While the farmers were busy reenacting the Second World War with its long partial blockade, Ingemar contended that there were many different blockade scenarios, and that the military one was short. At the same time, however, he presented the far-fetched argument that perfect markets would solve the problem. With far-sighted entrepreneurs speculating in a possible blockade no contingency policy was needed. The intrinsic flexibility of the economy would see to it that the needed foodstuffs would be available in suitable quantities. The market system would automatically solve the problem.

[13] Meyerson (1997, p. 168).

[14] Ståhl (1982b).

[15] Bolin et al. (1986), pp. 126–131.

The argument may sound convincing, but such markets do not exist. Stefan Hedlund and I questioned the argumentation in our book *Beredskap eller protektionism?* [Contingency Policy or Protectionism?].[16] The kind of speculation that Ingemar was speaking of assumes that the entrepreneurs have information of the likely prices during a blockade, but if the possible scenarios were short, no hints existed about the probability of each one of them, and in addition, the historic experience was irrelevant and the entrepreneurs would be working on a world of complete uncertainty. There would be no observations that could be used to base price expectations on. If the entrepreneurs do not know either the possible alternatives or their probabilities they cannot be expected to solve the contingency problem. They cannot guess what prices will prevail during a blockade since they have no observations to fall back upon except for the two world wars, and according to Ingemar's own reasoning, these were completely uninteresting.[17]

The Interest Group Analysis

The central question in the public choice section of *The Political Economy of the Food Sector* is whose interests were favored by the design of the agricultural policy in postwar Sweden. The decision situation was characterized by a far-reaching community of interests. The central actors basically shared both the conception of the problem and its solution:

[16] Hedlund and Lundahl (1985, pp. 216–221).

[17] We also demonstrated formally that it was far from certain that the production of foodstuffs would increase during a blockade or, if it did, the increase would be large enough to cover the needs (ibid., pp. 235–240, 265–271)—to Ingemar's great annoyance. He and I collided head-on in the seminar room at the department of economics, to such an extent that Lennart Petersson, who witnessed the fight, preferred to duck and sneak into the nearby kitchen. Ingemar was one of the members of the expert committee when I applied for the chair in economics after Göran Ohlin in Uppsala in 1986. Then course he scolded me for having 'rather uncritically accepted ..., the current contingency arguments' and for having employed 'a formal model based on comparative statics fetched from relatively traditional trade theory', in the analysis of the Swedish problem. This was the model used to refute the argument that the market will automatically solve the contingency problem. 'The presentation seems cosmetic and conceived in order to demonstrate that the author also dominates this more formal analytical technique', wrote a visibly annoyed Ingemar Ståhl. In his defence, it may, however, be adduced that he ranked me first.

the bureaucracy, the farmer interest organizations and the spokesmen in agricultural issues appointed by the political parties.

The LRF had an internally strong position as the self-evident representative of the farmers. The organization exerted an effective control of possible deviators from the right faith and the representatives of the political parties either had a farming background themselves or were country people. The consumers, who had to foot the bill, on the other hand, were a large, heterogeneous group, difficult to organize, who in practice had to be represented by a weak, artificial state consumer representation. The conclusion was obvious: 'That farmers as a group have benefitted from farm price regulations and various types of market intervention—which also support the entire range of farmer cooperative activities—is ... not open to doubt.'[18] A food sector industrial complex characterized by a strong common interest had been created and the latter had pushed for an ever more complex system of regulations.

In the last chapter of the book, Ingemar launched a frontal attack on the traditional analysis of economic policy—the part which builds on welfare theory. His attack displayed a bit of Behemoth[19] vehemence. He called the welfare analysis naïve and pointed to the futility of attempting to find clear-cut relations between ends and means. Our knowledge with respect to the economic system is not good enough to permit social engineering. The alternative is to employ public choice theory and analyze how the economic actors, including the politicians and the bureaucrats, are driven by vested interests and what this leads to. Against these vested interests Ingemar put the market, the dynamic market that works without perfect information and which arrives at contracts by constant experiments which lower the transaction costs and creates a scope for new products and institutions instead of fixing prices and quantities on existing products by regulations. This kind of markets is opposed by special interest groups who stand to lose by the changes. The farmer cooperative movement is a case in point. In addition, it had managed to create an iron triangle with the political parties and the agricultural bureaucracy which had created a deadlock in the Swedish agricultural policy. The few farmers that were still left in Sweden, a maximum of 110,000, of whom

[18] Bolin, Meyerson and Ståhl (1986, p. 74).

[19] *Job* 40: 10–24.

no more than 40,000 obtained half or more of their income from agriculture, provided a pure textbook case of the accuracy of Mancur Olson's thesis that it is easier for small groups than for large ones to organize for a common cause. Against the LRF the consumers were powerless. The only way to reform the agricultural system was to introduce free trade in combination with free entry into the agricultural sector.

The Political Economy of the Food Sector identified four main problems of Swedish agriculture: excess production, high prices, financial difficulties for new units and an opaque agricultural policy. The solution proposals that were available when the book was written were all based on regulations. *The Political Economy of the Food Sector* on the other hand offered a discussion of what a deregulated agricultural sector would look like, based on a large simulation model, that had been developed at the Swedish University of Agricultural Sciences at Ultuna under the direction of Olof Bolin.[20] The surplus production problem would vanish, prices would decrease, the capital requirement of new farms would be reduced and the agricultural policy would become more transparent. The gains from deregulation would be large enough to compensate those who would lose on it.

The simulation model dealt only with the effects at the producer stage, but there were gains to be made from deregulation also at the subsequent stages. The processing stages were characterized by cartel and monopoly elements that it would be advantageous to get rid of. A series of politically determined administrative regulations that made it impossible for Joseph Schumpeter's 'creative destruction' to work had been substituted for competition.[21] Old structures were not replaced by new ones. The dynamic efficiency within the food sector was low and the remedy was deregulation and competition.

Bolin, Meyerson and Ståhl anticipated that their deregulation gospel would be met with skepticism by the orthodox high priests of the organized farmer movement and therefore devoted considerable energy to meeting the most probable counterarguments in advance: the food security would be jeopardized, the excess production could be distributed as grants to developing countries, if world market prices increased in

[20] See, e.g. Rabinowitz (1983) and Sveriges lantbruksuniversitet (1984).

[21] Schumpeter (1934).

the longer run deregulation would eliminate future profitable production, the world market prices were dumping prices, they were not stable, the farmers would make losses, the effects on the environment would be negative, the food standard would be lowered, the countryside would be depopulated, the redundant farmers would not get new jobs, the arguments in favor of deregulation were purely theoretical and had nothing to do with reality.

The Peasants Grumble

The publication of *The Political Economy of the Food Sector*, in June 1984, of course raised hell among the farming community. The book hit the LRF dung heap like a bomb. It was simply blasphemous. It questioned the prevailing orthodoxy. While the earlier interventions from the economists had by and large been limited to the comparison of different regulation alternatives and their costs, all of a sudden, a work had appeared that aimed at sinking the entire regulation ship. It was a shot below the water line. The Ministry of Agriculture cowardly refrained from joining the debate, but the LRF returned the fire using heavy ammunition against the peasant oppressor from Norra Fäladen[22] and his two henchmen.

In the fall of 1985, the journalist Anders Palmgren surveyed the debate, a total of 71 posts, including news articles and the rejoinders from the three economists. His conclusion was that the debate was heavily biased. 'It must be pointed out that while the producers have been very active and well represented in the debate, the consumers are notable by their almost total absence.'[23] This was to be expected. It was completely in line with Mancur Olson's theory. The large, diffuse consumer group could not organize its argumentation. But the LRF could. Fourteen of the posts derived from their representatives or were unsigned articles in its weekly, *Land*. Neither the Ministry of Agriculture nor the Ministry of Defense took part. The debate mainly was carried out between the LRF and the three authors of *The Political Economy of the Food Sector*.

Palmgren also concluded that *The Political Economy of the Food Sector* had 'served as firewood in an already pretty hot debate where gut feelings

[22] Ingemar lived in Nyckelkroken in the Norra Fäladen district in Lund.

[23] Palmgren (1985, s 26).

had been more common than factual arguments.'[24] The attacks began on the very day of the presentation of the book. In a press conference arranged by the LRF, the chairman of this organization, Sven Tågmark, called the book 'erroneous, cynical and not credible.'[25] It rested on 'erroneous premises' which led to 'strange conclusions.'[26] It was simply a 'rehash of ideas from the 60s ... comparable to a unilateral Swedish disarmament ... a murder of the Swedish countryside and landscape.'[27] 'The authors state that their dream may be ridiculed,' said Tågmark. 'That is unnecessary. They are seeing to that themselves.'[28] Already the point of departure for the food committee—the excess production—had aggravated the LRF, and when *The Political Economy of the Food Sector* was produced, the farmers were forced on the defensive, as defenders of a dubious, or even sick, agricultural policy. Bolin, Meyerson and Ståhl argued their case in the press[29] and the LRF had to answer their fire. 'In principle, during the summer [of 1984], each debate article by the authors met a reply from LRF representatives.'[30]

As I have already pointed out, Bolin, Meyerson and Ståhl predicted that the response to their book would be polemical and hence specified the possible points of attack. Their guess had been correct, to say the least. As a matter of fact, the debate would be concentrated on around half of their points: the concentration at the processing stage, the power over the market and over the political decisions, the food security target, the environmental and regional policy, the food prices and the farmer incomes. No new arguments were presented. Most of all, the firing was concerned with the food security argument—the ultimate bulwark of the agricultural policy—and with the argument that everybody else resorted to regulations and around the risk of regional imbalances.[31] In the main, the debate resembled trench warfare. Both sides were firing already familiar

24 Ibid., s 33.

25 Ibid., p. 34.

26 Petzell (1984).

27 TT (1984a).

28 *Svenska Dagbladet* (1984).

29 Their contributions are summarized in Bolin et al. (1985).

30 Palmgren (1985, p. 34).

31 Bolin et al. (1985, pp. 4–6). The survey of the contingency problem made by Nicolaus Rockberger (1985) at the National Defence College in connection to the debate

projectiles. No new solutions to the problems were presented. It was not to be expected.

The debate took place above all in *Svenska Dagbladet*. Per-Martin Meyerson went on the offensive immediately under the heading 'Avreglering måste vara målet [Deregulation Must Be the Aim],'[32] and in a later article he provided the solution to the problems of the agricultural sector: free trade,[33] a thesis underlined by Olof Bolin when the latter in the spirit of the classics argued that free trade would result in a net gain that would make it possible for the winners to compensate the losers.[34] The head of the Swedish Agricultural Research Institute [Jordbrukets utredningsinstitut], Olof Nilsson, claimed that the book contained a 'conspiracy theory,'[35] that public choice theory was a 'fad'[36]and that it seemed as if Bolin, Meyerson and Ståhl 'had received their inspiration from Monty Python.'[37] Olof Bolin replied that Nilsson acted precisely as the theory of public choice would predict and that his factual argumentation was weak.[38] One of the members of the LRF board, Sverker Erlansson, contended that Swedish agriculture was indeed subject to competition.[39] Exactly like the agricultural expert of the Moderate party, Arne Andersson, he contended that the world market was an artificial dumping market.[40] The managing director of the LRF, Thorsten Andersson, called Swedish agriculture 'a rather modest affair,' in comparison to the regulations that existed in the US and the EG and warned that if our policy was changed our entire welfare would be jeopardized.[41]

Olof Bolin had to put up with being attacked by his former boss, the ex-president of the Swedish University of Agricultural Sciences, Lennart

around *The Political Economy of the Food Sector* strangely enough does not deal with the argumentation of the two camps.

[32] Meyerson (1984a).

[33] Meyerson (1984b).

[34] Bolin (1984b).

[35] Nilsson (1984a).

[36] Nilsson (1984b).

[37] Nilsson (1984c).

[38] Bolin (1984a).

[39] Erlansson (1984a).

[40] Erlansson (1984b), Palmgren (1984).

[41] Andersson (1984).

Hjelm, who thought that the proposals in *The Political Economy of the Food Sector* 'partly amounted to sheer demagogy.' Swedish agriculture had to be regulated and protected. Otherwise, it would be outcompeted. There was no better agricultural system on earth than the Swedish one.[42] The debate in *Svenska Dagbladet* ended in November 1984 with an article by Bolin, Meyerson and Ståhl which summarized the flaws of the current agricultural policy and delivered a criticism of the proposal for a new agricultural policy put forward by the food committee.[43]

The LRF also threw one of its worst sluggers, Birger Isacson, into the debate. He wrote a pamphlet on agricultural policy which disapproved of any argumentation which did not come from within the farmer community itself and contended that if you were not a farmer there was no way that you could understand the problems of 'the branch.' With respect to Bolin, Meyerson and Ståhl, he writes: '… the authors have not in any way endeavored to study what Swedish agriculture looks like or how the cooperative agricultural industry works. It is more than surprising, even embarrassing that "eminent economists" think that they can simply make extravagant claims … and that people will believe them.'[44] The trio knew nothing whatsoever about Swedish agriculture. In addition, they made 'fatal errors' in their calculations of how much farm values would be reduced after the introduction of free trade. Isacson boasted: 'You may simply ask whether such arithmetic as the one produced here by eminent economists should be considered a "serious contribution" to the debate on food policy.'[45] As Bolin, Meyerson and Ståhl could, however, easily demonstrate it was Isacson's own calculations that were erroneous. He had managed to impute two different values simultaneously to the farm capital. 'If you break such elementary rules the blame is on you,' commented the trio harshly.[46]

The farmers began a political counteroffensive as well, via the Center Party, which in a motion on agricultural policy demanded that all agricultural land that it was worth to cultivate should remain in production so that Sweden could manage a blockade, the landscape could be kept open

[42] TT (1984a). Cf. Hjelm (1984).

[43] Bolin et al., (1984b). The final report of the committee is found in i SOU 1984:86.

[44] Isacson (1985, p. 97).

[45] Ibid., p. 101.

[46] Bolin et al. (1985, p. 7).

and Swedish foodstuffs could be sent to developing countries in the event of a catastrophe. The land that was responsible for the excess production would get new crops at the expense of the state.[47]

And then the agricultural interest groups resorted to a classical weapon: a farmers' march, in May 1985. In the largest farmer demonstration since 1941, between 20,000 and 25,000 farmers marched to the political party headquarters in the Old Town of Stockholm, with such slogans as 'Send Palme to Siberia' and 'Put Feldt under the roller [Lägg Feldten under välten]'. The LRF boss, Sven Tågmark, made a speech and demanded the end of the 'dictatorial agricultural policy' of the state as well as income increases. 'At times, the attacks on the Minister of Agriculture turned rather aggressive. —Quit, Svante [Lundkvist], quit Svante, screamed many of those assembled. Or, jump Svante, jump, when the politicians gathered near a window on the first floor …'.[48]

The attacks also came from the rank and file. Ingemar received an offer from a tenant farmer in Dalarna of 'a farm workers' wage and free lodging so he can bring his family. He does not have to do anything. But he must follow every step I make during my work for a week. Then we will see if his opinion will remain the same as now.'[49]

Bolin, Meyerson and Ståhl refuted the contingency argument as being inconsistent with the military opinion and concluded that the current policy did not meet the food security need, and did not fulfill the efficiency goal or meet the demand for regional balance, The number of farmers was becoming ever lower while the regulation machinery was growing. The income problem of the farm households had not been solved by the regulations. The farmers had either had to obtain supplementary incomes or leave agriculture. The price policy employed did not equalize domestic demand and domestic supply but led to an excess supply of agricultural goods. The steering system used in the market

[47] TT (1985a).

[48] Silberstein (1985). When the LRF shortly thereafter had its general meeting, the organization jumped on Olof Bolin. *Expressen* (1985) reported in an editorial: 'Olof Bolin is to be reminded of the fact that he is mortal. The meeting commissioned the board to find out "what kind of research is being carried out recently at the department of economics [at the Swedish University of Agricultural Sciences] and of what use this research has been when it comes to improving the difficult situation in agriculture". The LRF is watching you, Olof Bolin.'

[49] TT (1984b).

for agricultural produce reduced the ability to adapt to the changes that would take place sooner or later. It did not facilitate the search for new business alternatives in a dynamic world.[50]

Deregulation

The battle over *The Political Economy of the Food Sector* was the last big battle of the farmer cooperation movement. Time had rendered LRF's ideas obsolete. In the Ministry of Finance, a deregulation of agriculture had been a subject of discussion for a long time. Already after the 1982 elections, Kjell-Olof Feldt wanted it in order to get rid of the excess supply and dampen the inflation, but this came to nothing because of the resistance of the Ministry of Agriculture, which instead favored establishment control and limitations on investment. The Minister of Agriculture, Svante Lundkvist, did not dare to take the fight with the farmers.[51] It would be another eight years before the reform was decided.

The reform was preceded by a number of investigations which had in common that they left less room for the agricultural special interest groups and more for economic considerations. In 1986, Svante Lundkvist appointed an commission of inquiry to find out why food prices were so high and which impact the regulations had on the efficiency within the agricultural sector.[52] Gunnar Wetterberg in 1988 finished a report with the title *Alternativ i jordbrukspolitiken* [Alternatives in Agricultural Policy] for the Expert Group on Public Economics [Expertgruppen för studier i offentlig ekonomi—ESO].[53] The year before, the Nordic ministers of finance had appointed a work group to investigate the economic effects of the agricultural policies of the Nordic countries.[54] Finally, Per Molander at the Swedish National Defence Research Establishment [Försvarets forskningsanstalt—FOA] reviewed the Swedish contingency planning.[55] The conclusions of these studies were similar. The agricultural

[50] Bolin et al. (1985).

[51] Feldt (1991, pp. 113–114).

[52] The report of the inquiry is found in SOU 1987:44.

[53] Wetterberg (1988).

[54] Nordiska Ministerrådet (1989).

[55] Molander (1989)

policy led to unnecessary costs. It was inefficient and did not contribute to the fulfillment of its goals.

In parallel with the investigations, the Ministry of Agriculture underwent important changes in personnel. Mats Hellström became Minister of Agriculture and Michael Sohlman, from the Ministry of Finance, Secretary of State. They had a mandate from the Prime Minister, Ingvar Carlsson, to deregulate the agricultural sector and were considerably more sensitive to the independent criticism that had been directed at the agricultural policy than what the ministry had been during the preceding decades.[56] Per Molander was appointed main secretary for the investigation upon which the deregulation decision would be founded.[57] Exactly like *The Political Economy of the Food Sector*, the document which was produced concluded that the actual policy had not contributed to the fulfillment of the most important goal: that of food security. The deregulation had also been prepared by the entry of the Ministry of Agriculture into the general debate, in opposition to the LRF and other regulation advocates.[58] Finally, the OECD had published a report on Swedish agriculture and recommended its member states to change their policies and make them more market-based.[59]

The incredible happened. The special interest groups were neutralized. Even the LRF found that it had to embrace the deregulation policy.[60] 'The new policy coalition that was gradually formed little by little obtained the prerogative of formulating the problem,' writes the economic historian Henrik Lindberg:

> Investigators and researchers with the new deregulation attitude were linked to the Ministry of Finance and later to the Ministry of Agriculture and were given the task of formulating proposals and produce information that would make a reform possible. Instead of discussing *agricultural* policy and take the needs of the sector as the starting point, the agricultural regulations were put into a wider economic perspective.[61]

[56] Lindberg (2008, p. 103).

[57] Ds 1989:63.

[58] Lindberg (2008, p. 103).

[59] OECD (1988).

[60] Flygare and Isacson (2003, pp. 250–253).

[61] Lindberg (2008, p, 107).

That the agricultural policy was reformed was largely due to *The Political Economy of the Food Sector*, and then, as Per-Martin Meyerson has pointed out, not least to the effort of Ingemar Ståhl:

> I do not hesitate to contend that the publication of 'The Political Economy of the Food Sector' became a turning point for agricultural policy. At the same time, I want to stress that this was mainly due to one person, namely Ingemar Ståhl. The new analytical approach that made it possible for us to undress the special interests behind the regulation policy and demonstrate their ugly nakedness was forged under his leadership in a stimulating atmosphere.[62]

You may perhaps ask whether the reform would not have come anyway, sooner or later, whether the deregulation idea had not sunk in. The share of the farming population of the total population diminished steadily and the number of votes that could be obtained through deregulation would sooner or later outcompete the farmer special interest. But sometimes catalysts are needed. At any rate, in July 1991, a new food policy was in place. The subsidies had been phased out. Market prices were substituted for negotiated prices. The agricultural sector had to work under the same conditions as other sectors. The tariff protection of the sector, however, continued for the time being.

CAP

The deregulation story was a short story. In November 1994, Sweden held a referendum about entry into the European Union and the following year we became a member. We were then faced with an even more incomprehensible agricultural policy than before: the Common Agricultural Policy, CAP, with goals like income levels, market stability, food security and at the same time productivity increases and reasonable consumer prices. The regulation apparatus was formidable:

> The different goals are to be realized with the aid of different market regulations, supplemented with structural policy, regional policy and environmental policy measures. The internal tariffs are abolished, as well

[62] Meyerson (1997, p. 168). The quote is not as presumptuous as it sounds. It is confirmed by the analysis in Lindberg (2008).

> as import fees and subsidies which distort the competition among the member countries. At the same time, the EU farmers are protected against foreign competition by import fees and quotas. The Council of Ministers of the EU fixes target prices and intervention prices (a fixed lowest price level at which the EU commits itself to buy) for the producers, The market price may vary from country to country depending on the balance between supply and demand, transportation distances and the consumer choice of goods.[63]

Sweden was back at square one, with an agricultural policy that guaranteed continued milk lakes and meat mountains and which in the collective mind was symbolized by French farmers demanding subsidies who emptied their dung carts on the stairs of the Élysée palace, in protest against foreign imports. The CAP share of the EU budget when Sweden became a member was almost 60 percent. Thereafter, the share has gradually diminished to less than 40 percent,[64] as the agricultural policy of the EU has been gradually deregulated. The competition *within* the EU has hardened, something that the Swedish farmers had hardly reckoned with. The result is seen in the shelves of our food stores.[65]

Epilogue: This is 2017

Wonderful is short. The CAP put an effective end to the Swedish deregulation line in agricultural policy. The intense debate that characterized the 1980s abated. Other issues than deregulation were given more space, not least the question of how agriculture could be made more ecological.[66] The debate may, however, flare up again. This is the case not least with the contingency issue. The world we live in in 2017 is characterized by all kinds of threats. The new millennium has so far been a millennium of terrorism, but unpredictability has increased also in other ways. Vladimir Putin's Russia wants to reestablish the geopolitical position of the former Soviet Union. The United States has elected an impulsive fake president who is badly oriented about the world he lives in and who could easily be made to commit fatal strategic mistakes. In Europe, populism is on the

[63] Flygare and Isacson (2003, p. 255).

[64] European Commssion (2016).

[65] Hamilton (2016).

[66] See, e.g. Rydén (2003).

rise and with that the risk increases that the edifice of peace that is the EU will in the end be torn down and polarization will experience a new spring.

In Sweden, the will to defend the country has increased in recent years, under the pressure of the provocations from the East. This points to the need for a coordinated contingency policy. The Royal Swedish Academy of War Sciences [Kungliga Krigsvetenskapsakademien] is involved in a multi-year project on contingencies.[67] Among the latter, agricultural policy has a given place. Swedish agriculture is highly specialized and with high specialization comes high vulnerability, higher than in the 1980s.[68] When the present is being written, the Swedish government, with wide support from the political opposition, has produced a bill to the parliament on a new food strategy to increase domestic agricultural production, which aims at increased production, sustainable, environment-friendly development, decreased vulnerability, growth and employment and production that corresponds to the demand of the consumers.[69]

Will the debate on agricultural policy flare up again? If so, one important debater is missing.

Acknowledgements Thanks for constructive comments on an earlier draft to Lena Ekelund Axelson, Carl B. Hamilton, Christina and Lars Jonung, Bengt Jönsson and Sven-Arne Nilsson.

Swedish version published in *Ekonomisk Debatt*, Vol. 45, No. 6, 2017.

References

Andersson, Thorsten (1984), 'Därför har vi LRF', *Svenska Dagbladet*, 6 July.

Bolin, Olof (1984a), 'Olof Nilsson har inte läst på!', *Svenska Dagbladet*, 13 June.

Bolin, Olof (1984b), 'Alla skulle kunna vinna på en avreglering', *Svenska Dagbladet*, 3 August.

Bolin. Olof; Meyerson, Per-Martin and Ståhl, Ingemar, under medverkan av Kjell-Åke Brorsson, Ingemar Haraldsson och Ewa Rabinowicz (1984a),

67 Hildebrandt (2016).

68 See Eriksson et al. (2016).

69 Regeringens proposition 2016/1:104.

Makten över maten: Livsmedelssektorns politiska ekonomi. Stockholm: Studieförbundet Näringsliv och Samhälle.

Bolin, Olof; Meyerson, Per-Martin and Ståhl, Ingemar (1984b), 'Ett kostsamt självbedrägeri', *Svenska Dagbladet*, 16 November.

Bolin, Olof; Meyerson, Per-Martin and Ståhl, Ingemar (1985), *Makten över maten – än en gång*. Företag & samhälle. SNS Orientering, No. 4/85.

Bolin, Olof; Meyerson, Per-Martin and Ståhl, Ingemar, with contributions by Kjell-Åke Brorsson, Ingemar Haraldsson and Ewa Rabinowicz (1986), *The Political Economy of the Food Sector: The Case of Sweden*. Stockholm: SNS Förlag.

Ds 1989:63, *En ny livsmedelspolitik*. Stockholm: Allmänna förlaget.

Eriksson, Camilla; Sollén Norrlin, Sofia and Heed, Josefin (2016), *Hur skulle Sveriges lantbruk drabbas vid en avspärrning?* Uppsala: Framtidens lantbruk, Sveriges lantbruksuniversitet.

Erlansson, Sverker (1984a), 'Lantbruket har konkurrens', *Svenska Dagbladet*, 15 June.

Erlansson, Sverker (1984b), 'Realistisk politik eller teoretisk?', *Svenska Dagbladet*, 7 July.

European Commission (2016), *CAP Post-2013: Key Graphs and Figures*. April. http://ec.europa.eu/agriculture/sites/agriculture/files/cap-post-2013/graphs/graph1_en.pdf. Downloaded 2 March 2017.

Expressen (1985), 'Billigare mat? Kollaps, sa LRF', 1 July.

Feldt, Kjell-Olof (1991), *Alla dessa dagar … I regeringen 1982–1990*. Stockholm: Norstedts.

Flygare, Iréne A. and Isacson, Maths (2003), *Det svenska jordbrukets historia: Jordbruket i välfärdssamhället 1945–2000*. Stockholm: Natur och Kultur/LTs förlag.

Gulbrandsen, Odd and Lindbeck, Assar (1966), *Jordbrukspolitikens mål och medel*. Stockholm: Industriens Utredningsinstitut.

Gulbrandsen, Odd and Lindbeck, Assar (1969), *Jordbruksnäringens ekonomi*. Stockholm: Almqvist & Wiksell.

Hamilton, Carl B. (2016), 'Kött-eliten driver svenska köttbönder ur marknaden', *Dagens Nyheter*, 16 February. http://www.dn.se/debatt/repliker/kott-eliten-driver-svenska-kottbonder-ur-marknaden/. Downloaded 2 March 2017.

Hedlund, Stefan and Lundahl, Mats (1985), *Beredskap eller protektionism? En studie av beredskapsmålet i svensk jordbrukspolitik*. Malmö: Liber Förlag.

Hildebrandt, Johanne (2016), 'Hur kunde vi göra oss så sårbara?', *Svenska Dagbladet*, 19 December.

Hjalte, Krister; Lidgren, Karl and Ståhl, Ingemar (1973), *Miljövård och samhällsekonomi*. Lund: Studentlitteratur.

Hjalte, Krister; Lidgren, Karl and Ståhl, Ingemar (1977), *Environmental Policy and Welfare Economics*. Cambridge: Cambridge University Press.

Hjelm, Lennart (1984), 'Jordbrukarna skulle få bära stora förluster', *Svenska Dagbladet*, 27 August.

Isacson, Birger (1985), *Den vilseförda konsumenten – en debattbok om priset på maten*. Stockholm: LTs förlag.

Jörberg, Lennart (1984), *Den svenska ekonomiska utvecklingen 1861–1983*. Lund: Meddelande från Ekonomisk-historiska institutionen, Lunds Universitet, No. 33.

Lindberg, Henrik (2008), *Korporativa karteller – en studie av byggsektor och jordbruk i den svenska modellen*. Stockholm: Norstedts Akademiska Förlag.

Meyerson, Per-Martin (1984a), 'Avreglering måste vara målet', *Svenska* Dagbladet, 15 May.

Meyerson, Per-Martin (1984b), 'Fri handel lösningen', *Svenska Dagbladet*, 24 june.

Meyerson, Per-Martin (1997), *Sockerbagare i doktorshatt*. Stockholm: Fischer & Co.

Molander, Per (1989), *Säkerhetspolitiska aspekter på livsmedelsförsörjningen*. Stockholm: Försvarets Forskningsanstalt.

Morell, Mats (2001), *Det svenska jordbrukets historia: Jordbruket i industrisamhället 1870–1945*. Stockholm: Natur och Kultur/LTs förlag.

Nilsson, Olof (1984a), 'Makten över maten knappast seriös', *Svenska Dagbladet*, 8 June.

Nilsson, Olof (1984b), 'Jag har läst på för bra, Olof Bolin', *Svenska Dagbladet*, 15 June.

Nilsson, Olof (1984c), 'Mjölk ännu oreglerad', *Svenska Dagbladet*, 4 July.

Nordiska Ministerrådet (1989), *Jordbrukspolitiken i de nordiska länderna: målen, medlen och konsekvenserna*. Nord 1989:15. København: Nordisk Ministerråd.

OECD (1988), *National Policies and Agricultural Trade. Country Study. Sweden*. Paris: Organization for Economic Co-operation and Development.

Olson, Mancur (1965), *The Logic of Collective Action: Public Goods and the Theory of Groups*. Cambridge, MA: Harvard University Press.

Palmgren, Anders (1984), 'Ingen marknadsekonomi inom jordbruket', *Svenska Dagbladet*, 20 June.

Palmgren, Anders (1985), 'Debatten kring Makten över maten', in: Olof Bolin, Per-Marin Meyerson och Ingemar Ståhl (eds), *Makten över maten – än en gång*. Stockholm: Företag & samhälle. SNS Orientering, nr 4/85.

Petzell, Sohie (1984), 'LRF-storm mot nedskärningar', *Svenska Dagbladet*, 6 June.

Rabinowitz, Ewa (1983), *En simuleringsmodell för svenskt jordbruk i samspel med nationell och global ekonomi: Produktion – konsumtion – utrikeshandel – politik*. Uppsala: Institutionen för ekonomi och statistik, Sveriges lantbruksuniversitet.

Regeringens proposition 2016/17:104. *En livsmedelsstrategi för Sverige – fler jobb och hållbar tillväxt i hela landet*. http://www.regeringen.se/490897/

contentassets/256cc25ab5a84db7a76730abb9cc3773/en-livsmedelsstrategi-for-sverige-fler-jobb-och-hallbar-tillvaxt-i-hela-landet-prop-2016-17-104.pdf. Downloaded 2 March 2017.

Rockberger, Nicolaus (1985), 'Beredskapsargumentet i jordbruksdebatten', in: Olof Bolin, Per-Marin Meyerson and Ingemar Ståhl (eds), *Makten över maten – än en gång*. Företag & samhälle. SNS Orientering, nr 4/85.

Rydén, Reine (2003), *Medvindens tid: Ekologiska Lantbrukarna och jordbrukspolitiken 1985–2000*. Ekologiskt Lantbruk nr 36, January. Uppsala: Centrum för uthålligt lantbruk, Sveriges lantbruksuniversitet.

Schumpeter, Joseph (1934), The Theory of Economic Development: An Inquiry into Profits, Capital, Credit, Interest, and the Business Cycle. London: Oxford University Press.

Silberstein, Willy (1985), 'Uppretade bönder tågar igen', *Svenska Dagbladet*, 24 May.

SOU 1984:86, *Jordbruks- och livsmedelspolitik. Huvudbetänkande av 1983 års livsmedelskommitté*. Stockholm: Liber.

SOU 1987:44, *Livsmedelspriser och livsmedelskvalitet. Betänkande av 1986 års livsmedelsutredning*. Stockholm: Allmänna förlaget.

Ståhl, Ingemar (1977), 'En ekonomisk teori för blandekonomin', in: *Erfarenheter av blandekonomin. Uppsatser och diskussioner vid Dahmén-symposiet om den svenska blandekonomin, Saltsjöbaden 18–19 oktober 1976*. Stockholm: Skandinaviska Enskilda Banken.

Ståhl, Ingemar (1982a), 'Mål i livsmedelspolitiken'. Unpublished manuscript, December.

Ståhl, Ingemar (1982b), 'Några funderingar kring beredskapspolitiken'. Unpublished manuscript, December.

Svenska Dagbladet (1984), 'LRF utmanat', 6 June.

Sveriges lantbruksuniversitet (1984), *IAASA:s livsmedelsprojekt och den svenska modellen. Projektets slutrapport*. Rapport 237. Uppsala: Institutionen för ekonomi och statistik, Sveriges lantbruksuniversitet.

TT (Tidningarnas Telegrambyrå) (1984a), 'Rättelse', 5 June. Retriever. https://www.retriever-info.com/. Date plus keyword: Ingemar Ståhl.

TT (Tidningarnas Telegrambyrå) (1984b), 'Utmaning', 8 June. Retriever. https://www.retriever-info.com/. Date plus keyword: Ingemar Ståhl.

TT (Tidningarnas Telegrambyrå) (1985a), 'Centern', 12 April. Retriever. https://www.retriever-info.com/. Date plus keyword: Ingemar Ståhl.

TT (Tidningarnas Telegrambyrå) (1985b), 'Bondetåg, 23 May. Retriever. https://www.retriever-info.com/. Date plus keyword: Ingemar Ståhl.

Wetterberg, Gunnar (1988), *Alternativ i jordbrukspolitiken: Rapport till ESO*. Ds 1988:54. Stockholm: Allmänna förlaget.

CHAPTER 12

My Friend Villy

Villy Bergström (1938–2018) was by far one of the most colorful Swedish economists. He had his education from Uppsala. Later he was attached to the Industrial Institute for Economic and Social Research [Industriens Utredningsinstitut—IUI] and the National Institute for Working Life [Arbetslivscentrum], before becoming the first director of the Trade Union Institute for Economic Research [Fackföreningsrörelsens Institut för Ekonomisk Forskning—FIEF], editor in chief of the daily newspaper *Dala-Demokraten* and deputy governor of the Riksbank. He defended a doctoral dissertation on industrial investment, but his main interest was economic policy—an area where he could combine his knowledge of economics with his strong political engagement in the Social Democratic party.

I met Villy Bergström for the time in 1981. Bo Södersten turned fifty and I edited a festschrift where Villy participated with a chapter on industrial investment policy in Sweden during the postwar period. He came to the fifty-year party in Lund. We hit it off immediately, for Villy was easy to deal with—straightforward and no hypocrisy. He spoke his mind even if it was not politically correct and laughter was always lurking around the corner. Villy always had a new story to tell about some economist colleague and he loved to do it.

M. Lundahl, *Twelve Figures in Swedish Economics*, Palgrave Studies in the History of Economic Thought, https://doi.org/10.1007/978-3-030-94327-1_12

Villy Bergström was born in 1938. He got his Master of Science in Politics and Economics [politices magister] in 1963 and his licentiate degree in 1973, both in Uppsala. In the meantime, he taught in the economics department there. Between 1965 and 1969, he was also attached to the Industrial Institute for Economic and Social Research. Villy defended his PhD thesis in 1981, on Swedish industrial investment during the postwar period—a compilation thesis consisting of separate articles, before this became common.[1] The same year he was appointed associate professor [docent]. His supervisor was Ragnar Bentzel—'Naja'—about whom he wrote a tender portrait in the book that was published on the occasion of the seventieth anniversary of the IUI in 2009.[2]

The first chapter of the dissertation consists of an institutional survey of the rules and the underlying political philosophy that regulated capital formation, taxation and depreciation within the industrial sector. In the second chapter, Villy constructs a model of the capital cost of the firms and presents a few summary calculations of the costs of different funding options. In the third chapter, he estimates production functions and factor demand functions for the Swedish industry. In the final chapter, investment demand is estimated with the aid of a model where the capital variable has been disaggregated into machines and buildings.

Villy's dissertation was 'technical.' However, he did not consider himself a theorist. 'I have to work hard with the mathematics,' he said. What interested him most in economics was rather economic policy, steering and macroeconomics, naturally enough, since he was an engaged Social Democrat and a Keynesian, and he wanted to turn his knowledge of economics into practical action. His licentiate thesis, written at the IUI, dealt precisely with Swedish economic policy.[3] Villy begins with an overview of the policy from the mid-nineteenth century until the 1960s. He thereafter presents the theory of economic policy and ends with 'an attempt to evaluate' the results of the policy during the interwar and postwar years.

Villy kept his interest in economic policy his entire life. Between 1975 and 1977 and 1982–1983 he was a member of the Economists' Expert

[1] Bergström (1982).

[2] Bergström (2009).

[3] Bergström (1969).

Group of the Center for Business and Policy Studies [Studieförbundet Näringsliv och Samhälle, SNS] which every year issued a publication about the Swedish economy and economic policy. He was also a member of the editorial team of *Ekonomisk Debatt* 1977–1979. Villy had been recruited by Hans Tson Söderström, who with time would become his very good friend, hunting companion and ideological sparring partner.

Villy deviated in a fresh and sound way from today's prestige publication hunting article Stakhanovites. 'When I defended my dissertation, I was in my forties and I had never had any fixed employment,' he writes in his memoirs, but in those days, 'conditions were so favorable in the labor market that there was no reason to worry.'[4] The times were different, but I don't believe that Villy would have fallen prey to the present-day fads. He considered that kind of exercises pointless. 'When I have written an article I publish it in the *Scandinavian Journal of Economics*,' he said.

Childhood and Studies

Erik Lundberg coined the Horndal effect concept when he discovered that the ironworks at Horndal during a fifteen-year period steadily increased its productivity without making any investments: what later would become known as learning by doing, total productivity or the residual factor.[5] When the concept was mentioned in some international context where Villy was present, he loved to tell that he came from Horndal. He spent his first eight years there with his parents, in a one-room apartment. Villy acquired an interest in politics at home. His father, Abel, who worked at the ironworks, had written minor articles for *Dala-Demokraten* from Horndal, until, in 1946, he received an offer to become the local editor of the newspaper in Grängesberg. There, Villy became the classmate of Bo Södersten's nephew Lars Ramqvist, who would later become the managing director of Ericsson. He attended junior high school in Grängesberg and high school in Ludvika.

In 1959, Villy began his studies at the university in Uppsala, for the degree of Master of Science in Politics and Economics. Statistics was no fun. The boss of that department was the eccentric Herman Wold.

[4] Bergström (2015, p. 56).

[5] Lundberg (1961, p. 130).

Economics was marginally better, His seven-year older friend Bo Södersten had inspired Villy to study that subject. In his memoirs, he relates how he saw knowledge about economics as an important weapon in the political debate. The economists won all the battles that they are engaged in.[6] (Of course, Villy joined the Social Democratic student club Laboremus.) The department of economics, however, was not an easy department either. Tord Palander had exactly as many eccentric features as ever Wold and in addition was conflict prone, but he gave both brilliant and charming courses and he was generous. To what extent Palander contributed to Villy's decision to go on to higher studies in economics, I don't know. It was probably rather his successor, the incredibly friendly Ragnar 'Naja' Bentzel, who became professor in Uppsala in 1965, who tipped the scales.

The Social Democrat

Villy was strongly engaged in the fight for equality. 'Like so many others who had grown up in ironworks and mining communities, Bergström had an almost physical engagement against the lack of equality,' writes Hans O. Sjöström in *Klassens ljus eller hur man hamnar i arbetarregeringen* [First in Your Class or How to Make it into the Labor Government].[7] He did not hesitate to criticize the party when the growth enthusiasts threatened to take over. When he was a member of the editorial team of *Tiden* [the Social Democratic ideological journal] he whipped the Minister of Finance Gunnar Sträng in an editorial for having made statements during a budget presentation which indicated that he had lost contact with important moods and tendencies within the labor movement. The shit of course hit the fan. Villy was badly scolded by the faithful party supporters. '... the outstanding characteristic of this Villy Bergström, who had a PhD in economics, was that that he also had the temper of a class fighter from Grängesberg,' writes Göran Greider in his obituary of his predecessor as editor in chief of *Dala-Demokraten*.[8]

Villy was, however, not a person who could have left Social Democracy. He was never tempted to follow suit in the journey from the left

[6] Bergström (2015, p. 44).

[7] Sjöström (1987, p. 98).

[8] Greider (2018).

to the right that many of his colleagues—e.g. Assar Lindbeck, Ingemar Ståhl, Nils Lundgren, Carl B. Hamilton and Bo Södersten—embarked on during the 1970s and 1980s, but he remained faithful to his origins and the Socialist conviction of his youth. Hans O. Sjöström calls Villy an 'ideologue,' a Social Democrat who warned that the party was losing its long-run goals and was concentrating on sundry day-to-day insignificant issues.[9]

This included Gunnar Sträng as well. Villy was not particularly impressed by the latter-day leaders of the party. In his memoirs, he labeled Göran Persson 'intelligent but ignorant,' a man who 'could humiliate minister after minister and in front of the entire people.' Persson, 'with his mistaken judgements epitomizes the embarrassing breakdown of Social Democracy as a popular movement.'[10] That would have been inconceivable when the leading Social Democrats were called Rickard Sandler, Ernst Wigforss, Östen Undén, Gustav Möller or Tage Erlander, but since people of that stature had been wanting in the top party hierarchy, persons like Göran Persson had been able to 'rampage.' In a 2012 interview, Villy stated that the Social Democracy had lost the initiative in such central areas for the party as labor market issues and social insurance. Mona Sahlin had just stood there and done nothing, Håkan Juholt had been busy defending his many blunders and Villy had no hope that Stefan Löfven would be able to inject any energy into the ideological debate.[11]

One of Villy's idols was Ernst Wigforss, with whom he carried on a correspondence. Wigforss—an eager advocate of socialization—had written about industrial democracy.[12] Socialism (collective ownership) was not enough, but firms must also be democratized in a way that made it possible for the employees to feel solidarity toward them. Villy regularly visited him in his home in Stora Hult on the Bjäre peninsula. Full of admiration, he told the story of how Wigforss had served coffee in some elegant porcelain tableware that was a gift from the party and then, embarrassed, had apologized because it was so expensive. The equalization of wealth was part of his ideology also on the micro-level. It was no coincidence that Villy formed part of the editorial committee that

[9] Sjöström (1987, p. 100).

[10] Bergstrom (2015, p. 94).

[11] Sköld (2012).

[12] Wigforss (1948, 1980).

prepared the publication of Wigforss' selected works in nine volumes in 1980.

Economic democracy was an issue that was close to Villy's heart as well. He wrote a book about capital wage-earners' funds formation and industrial democracy when the debate began after the congress of the Swedish Trade Union Confederation [Landsorganisationen—LO] in 1971. The LO proposal was not ready until 1975, Villy's own variety two years earlier. *Kapitalbildning och industriell demokrati* [Capital Formation and Industrial Democracy] links his old interest in capital formation and financing in industry with his equality pathos.[13] Like Wigforss, Villy wanted to advance the position of the working class within industry. 'I am trying to concretize a way of solving today's problems by making the transition from private capitalism to socialism,' he wrote.[14] Capital formation was weak at the beginning of the 1970s, For Villy it was self-evident that the stimulation of investment and growth had to go hand in hand with income equalization and democratization of the workplace. Jaroslav Vanek had published his books about the labor-managed economy a couple of years earlier and Villy had been inspired by them.[15] However, the labor-managed firms had a weakness: it could be demonstrated that they tended to shed workers when the price of their products increased. Then, this theory lost its interest wrote Villy in his memoirs.[16] Nevertheless, it was labor management or at least increased worker influence in the firms that was the goal, and the road went through industry funds (what a few years later would be known as wage-earners' funds). That was where the saving should take place and where the physical capital should be rented to the companies from.

The Political Economy of Hemoptysis

Since Villy Bergström was both an economist and a Social Democratic political activist it was only natural that he would write about the attitude of economists toward the labor movement. This he did in a chapter of the commemorative book that was published in 1977, on the occasion of

[13] Bergström (1973).

[14] Ibid., p. 6.

[15] Vanek (1970, 1971).

[16] Bergström (2015, p. 91).

the centenary of the Swedish Economic Association [Nationalekonomiska Föreningen].[17] He dealt with four historic occasions, 'when the bourgeois part of the population and the bourgeois [center-right] parties had had a strong feeling that essential features of the existing society had been threatened': the introduction of the new unemployment policy in 1933, the publication of the postwar program of the labor movement, where the planned economy was put into the foreground, the ATP pension fight 1955–1959 and the fight over the wage-earners' funds 1975–1976. Villy looked into the positions of economists who were not attached to parties or interest groups as they were mirrored above all in the debate in the Swedish Economic Association. 'Have the economists stuck to a scientifically founded analysis of proposals and counter-proposals or have they made it into some fold as party supporters or spokesmen for group or class interests?'[18] He then contrasted the dominant neoclassical theory and the doctrine of the labor movement which rested on conflicts between different groups in society, what he saw as a liberal, individualistic view against a Socialist, collective one.

Villy's conclusion was drastic. '... the survey of the positions assumed by the leading economists vis-à-vis the policies of the labor movement during a 44-year period has left a compact impression of antagonism. Only the younger generation of economists of the so-called Stockholm School constitute an exception to the extent that these economists fought for the new unemployment policy.'[19]

Thereafter, however, Villy saw a complete darkness. Most of the 'independent' economists had been against the policies cherished by the labor movement. This could hardly be explained by their social background. It was their education that got in the way: the economic study of the individual utility-maximizing man and the profit-maximizing firm. An economist was a person with a doctoral degree in 'Liberalism,' and the labor movement had developed in opposition to the consequences of Liberalism. Hence it was not so strange that the nominally unattached economists opposed the labor movement. They had been partial and often not objective. Heckscher, Cassel, Lundberg and Lindbeck had appeared 'as some kind of prophets or oracles. Grandiose forecasts about

[17] Bergström (1977).

[18] Ibid., p. 116.

[19] Ibid., p. 154.

the political development' had been presented 'in scientific gear.' 'But the economists are of course charlatans (or should we be content by calling them jesters?) in the market square of political forecast making, like most citizens from the nuclear physicist to the cleaning lady.'[20] Without mentioning it explicitly, Villy had taken up the heritage from Gunnar Myrdal's *The Political Element in the Development of Economic Theory*.[21]

Erik Lundberg, Bertil Ohlin and Assar Lindbeck reacted against Villy's thesis. Lundberg responded tongue-in-cheek: 'I miss the lofty distance of Villy Bergström and hence his ability to look down on the tentative debates of the old economists from the high but reclining tower of ideology.'[22] He agreed with Villy that the economists had a Liberal bias, but the group of economists was not homogeneous. It offered many ways of looking at life. Myrdal, Ohlin, Ingvar Svennilson and Lundberg himself had not been alien to political interventions in the economy, even though they might have changed their opinions about some issues over time: Bertil Ohlin widened the perspective beyond the economists who have spoken at the debates of the Swedish Economic Association.[23] Where were Gunnar Myrdal, Karin Kock, Dag Hammarskjöld, Alf Johansson and Svennilson? The economists that Villy had picked all had a negative attitude toward the labor movement but were they representative of the profession as a whole? The one who took most offense was Assar Lindbeck. He could not possibly ever had been as close to a hemoptysis as then. The essay should have been refused, he thought. It was not objective and the argument was low-level. (I can see and hear Villy in front of me chuckling and laughing, telling this.) Villy had made a selection which fit his purpose. His 'independent' economists all opposed the interests of the labor movement. Lindbeck was so upset by Villy's 'distortions of reality' that he filed his exit from the Swedish Economic Association. The freedom of the press could not serve as an excuse for publishing 'distorted generalizations about Swedish economists in general.'[24]

To quote Viktor Rydberg, Villy's essay was 'a spear that ... [he] had thrown against the enemy ranks with the commendable purpose of the

[20] Ibid., p. 157.

[21] Myrdal (1953).

[22] Lundberg (1977, p. 160).

[23] Ohlin (1978).

[24] Lindbeck (1978, p. 39).

warrior to wound and kill.' It was not strange that it generated opposition, above all from Lindbeck. 'Many decades have passed since an economist in our country has debated a political proposal with such arguments and in such a high pitch as Lindbeck.'[25] Villy thought that as far as the wage-earners' funds were concerned, the economists were far more high-pitched than both the politicians, the general public and the interest organizations, and this was due above all to Lindbeck's many contributions.

In the Scientific Service of the Labor Movement

Already before his thesis defense in 1981, Villy moved to the National Institute for Working Life [Arbetslivscentrum] which had been set up in 1977. As he said himself, he got his position without anybody asking for his CV. It was enough that he had a cemented reputation as a good Social Democrat. Villy stayed until 1984 but never felt at home there. The place was completely politicized. It was led by discarded politicians with zero knowledge of research. 'Among other things, they were doing something called action research, which meant that if there had been a strike in some daycare center around Stockholm, half the institute went there to study it,' writes Villy in his memoirs.[26] In due time, he recommended Kjell-Olof Feldt to close the institute, but it was not until 2007 that it was liquidated, and then by the new bourgeois government.

When Villy left the National Institute for Working Life he got his own fiefdom: the Trade Union Institute for Economic Research [Fackföreningsrörelsens Institut för Ekonomisk Forskning—FIEF]. People in the Swedish Trade Union Confederation [LO] had found out that all the research institutes outside the universities were funded by the business community. This called for action. FIEF, however, was not politicized, but in the same way as, e.g. at the Industrial Institute for Economic and Social Research [IUI], the researchers were completely free to formulate their research tasks themselves within the area of interest to the LO, without any union interference. Villy led and built the institute between 1985 and 1995. He concentrated the research agenda on labor market problems, macroeconomics, stabilization policy and structural economics.

[25] Bergström (1977, p. 152).

[26] Bergström (2015, p. 57).

The latter he defined as technological development, international trade and competitiveness. He made sure that the institute did not get involved in LO investigations. FIEF was a research institute. The research staff was strong: Bertil Holmlund, Lars Lundberg, Jonas Agell, Per Lundborg and Magnus Henrekson.

Editor in Chief, Deputy Governor at the Riksbank and the LO Once More

Between 1995 and 1999, Villy Bergström was the editor in chief of *Dala-Demokraten*. The newspaper was in dire straits. The competition for readers in Dalarna was stiff. The managing director of *Dala-Demokraten* got rid of the losses by cutting down on staff and by changing the organization in a way that made it possible to receive major government subsidies. Villy did not think that he had any say. 'Actually, I was some kind of hired editorial writer and columnist, nothing else,' he concluded when the time had come to look back. It was difficult to get any insight into local politics, you had to write about many new topics, and Villy managed to lose forty subscribers when he wrote that Sweden did not need a king. In the Advisory Council on Foreign Affairs [utrikesnämnden] he could easily be replaced by the Parliament speaker or 'a bum.'[27] Villy perceived the environment at *Dala-Demokraten* as bad, split and full of intrigues. It was therefore easy for him to accept when the chairman of the Board of Governors of the Riksbank [Riksbanksfullmäktige], Sven Hulterström called and asked if he was available for a position as deputy governor of the Riksbank. He was.

Villy was appointed in 1999 and he would remain at the Riksbank until the end of 2005, when the time had come for him to retire. The bank had just become formally independent, and the Board of Governors was irremovable. It set the inflation target itself, based on vague indications from the Riksdag. Villy liked the arrangement. It made for stability with respect to the monetary policy and the inflation expectations. Villy liked it at the bank. The competence of the board of governors was high, with some exception, Urban Bäckström was an easy-going and charming leader, and the staff at the bank was extremely competent. 'Leading Swedish economists have traditionally had a strong interest in economic policy and

[27] Ibid., p. 110.

have hence also willingly let themselves be engaged in advisory activities of various kinds,' wrote Erik Lundberg in his chapter in the commemorative volume of the Swedish Economic Association.[28] It is hard to find someone who fits the quote better than Villy. When he summarized his years at the Riksbank, he concluded that 'none of my former jobs can be compared to the Riksbank. My time there was the best of my career.'[29]

The seven years at the Riksbank forced Villy to shelve a book project. In connection with the centennial of the LO, in 1998, and a project on the Swedish labor movement after the Second World War, he had been invited to write the history of the different proposals on economic policy presented by the organization. The book was not finished until 2007, when Villy had left the Riksbank.[30] There, he presents the contents of the economic policy advocated by the LO during the postwar period up to 2000. The book connects with *Kapitalbildning och industriell demokrati*. Villy stressed that what he was interested in was those of the proposals on economic policy advanced by the trade union movement which aimed to change the economic system: the collectivization of capital formation, the planned economy and regulation. He analyzed the solidarity wage policy and stabilization policy advocated by Gösta Rehn and Rudolf Meidner[31] and how it was received within the LO, the analysis of the EFO [Gösta Edgren, Karl-Olof Faxén and Clas-Erik Odhner] report on competitive and protected sectors,[32] the pressure on employment and wages caused by increasing inflation, the introduction of the inflation goal as the most important goal for economic policy during Carl Bildt's center-right coalition government and the reaction to this from the labor movement. Distribution policy, especially wage equalization, and the internal debate on this, was given plenty of space. The discussion of savings and capital formation naturally enough concentrated on the wage-earners' funds. One chapter dealt with technological change and the need for an active industrial policy. Finally, Villy surveyed the ideological debate on the desirability of socialism, focusing on the skepticism of

[28] Lundberg (1977, p. 159).

[29] Bergström (2015, p. 136).

[30] Bergström (2007).

[31] Landsorganisationen i Sverige (1951).

[32] Edgren et al. (1970).

Nils Karleby[33] and the more indecisive attitude of Wigforss, on the one hand, and the pragmatic attitude of his own contemporaries. Kjell-Olof Feldt,[34] Ingvar Carlsson and Anne-Marie Lindgren, on the other.[35]

Moose and Ellington

Villy's great leisure time passion was moose hunting. He was a formidable hunter—the equal of Nimrod. I once had a tie with ducks on it. Villy called it a duck-hunting tie. He told me how, when he was to become the director of FIEF, he told Stig Malm, the LO boss, that he accepted provide that he could take time off during the moose hunting season. It was OK. When, in 1999, at the Stockholm School of Economics, we celebrated the centennial of the birth of Bertil Ohlin, the Riksbank offered a reception for the participants in the symposium. I could not resist asking the governor, Urban Bäckström, whether the deputy governor Villy Bergström possibly had a similar clause in his employment contract there as well. He did. Once when I visited Villy in his home in Uppsala I was forced to admire his fine hunting weapons. It did not help that I told him that I was completely uninterested in hunting. Villy opened his weapons locker. Next to the guns there was an original manuscript by Hermann Hesse which Villy's wife Eva had acquired for her antiquarian bookstore. I asked whether we could not rather look at that. We couldn't.

Villy had another great passion, in addition to hunting: Duke Ellington. Naja Bentzel, who was also a jazz fan, but whose great idol was Jack Teagarden, thought that he should listen to other things too, but Villy disagreed. Duke was enough (and I almost agreed—Duke was also my absolute favorite). Villy wrote about Ellington in the cultural supplement of *LO-Tidningen*,[36] when James Lincoln Collier's biography of him had been translated into Swedish in 1988.[37] Already during his schoolboy days, he had understood that Duke would become a life-long interest. In his article, Villy mainly writes about his first golden age, 1927–1929, and the second, greatest, one, 1940–1941. Those were his favorite epochs,

[33] Karleby (1926).

[34] Feldt (1991).

[35] Carlsson and Lindgren (1996).

[36] Bergström (1989).

[37] Collier (1988), the original English version is Collier (1987).

especially 1940–1941. But he also writes about Ellington's weakness for dubious vocalists, the lack of discipline in the band and his method of composing, with the band as his notepad and guinea pig. When Villy was a guest researcher at Stanford University in 1974, he had bought tickets for two Ellington concerts for the entire family, but a few days before the concert, on 24 May, Duke died. Villy kept coming back to it.

Socialism for Real

Villy's great contribution to world literature is his depiction of North Korea. He went there in 1971 together with Arne Hjorth from the Swedish Vietnam Groups and Kurt Wickman from KFML [The Communist Alliance of Marxist-Leninists] (who later defected to the right-wing of capitalism), invited by the North Korean regime, which worked arduously on improving the image of the country in the West. Villy had just been the editor of *Tiden* (1965–1970), or as the North Koreans defined it, the editor of the ruling party ideological journal. This guaranteed a hearty welcome, but when the Swedes (for the sake of courtesy) were asked what they wanted to do and Villy answered 'I want to meet Kim Il-sung!,' their guide sank into the ground and started babbling about something that had nothing to do with his answer. A few days later, Villy received the message that the Great Leader unfortunately was busy with state affairs and did not have the time, but the Swedes were welcome to visit his native village.

The North Koreans only displayed what stood out as favorable, but it didn't quite work. Upon their return to Sweden, Villy and Kurt Wickman wrote a book where they demasked the country, that is, Wickman wrote about what it was like seen through the collected works of Kim Il-sung, while Villy wrote about what he saw and about the discrepancy between reality and propaganda—a largely hilarious and completely revealing account.[38] When the book, on the initiative of Magnus Henrekson, was issued in a second edition in 2010, Villy had made an addition to his original text, while Wickman's opus had been replaced by a critical, analytical part written by the Korean specialist Benjamin Katzeff Silberstein.[39]

[38] Bergström and Wickman (1972).

[39] Bergström and Katzeff Silberstein (2010).

Villy told me about the departure from Pyongyang, an adventure in itself. The three musketeers had traveled with Aeroflot, and the travel conditions included a three-day stopover in Moscow on the way home, in order to increase the Soviet supply of foreign currency. Firstly, however, a visa had to be obtained which allowed this, and it had to be obtained in Pyongyang. The Russians probably perceived the leftist delegation as nothing but capitalist swine so the three had to wait in the antechamber outside the visa section of the embassy almost a full day before they were admitted and finally received their documents. The three days in Moscow passed—vodka made it easier for some of the members of the delegation to stand the workers' paradise—and in the end, the journey to Stockholm was about to commence. In the emigration control waited a huge, uniformed inspector with a tall cap of the standard pompous Soviet model. He took the passports and looked at the Swedes: 'Visa expired! Back to Pyongyang!' The trio squatted, waiting for the inevitable deportation, when the Russian looked at them once more, slapped his thighs and roared with laughter before he waved them through. Obviously, he had some kind of experience of the Communist sister nation.

Finally, Villy's autobiography, *Från banker, bruk och lärosäten* [About Banks, Iron Works and Universities], urged by his son Örjan—thanks a lot!—is extemely sympathetic, no dry enumeration of parts of his CV, no look how great I am, but Villy offers a full-scale portrait of himself, in all ways.[40] Like Villy himself, it is humorous, intellectual and colorful. Whatever your political views, the more Villy Bergströms, the better. Anno 2018, the economist community looks bleaker than it has done for a long time.

Swedish version published in *Ekonomisk Debatt*, Vol., 47, No. 2, 2019.

References

Bergström, Villy (1969), *Den ekonomiska politiken i Sverige och dess verkningar*. Stockholm: Industriens Utredningsinstitut and Almqvist & Wiksell.

Bergström, Villy (1973), *Kapitalbildning och industriell demokrati. Socialdemokratiska perspektiv*. Stockholm: Tidens förlag.

[40] Bergström (2015).

Bergström, Villy (1977), 'Nationalekonomerna och arbetarrörelsen', in: Jan Herin och Lars Werin (eds), *Ekonomisk debatt och ekonomisk politik: Nationalekonomiska Föreningen 100 år*. Stockholm: Norstedts.

Bergström, Villy (1982), *Studies in Post-war Swedish Industrial Investments*. Uppsala: Studia Oeconomica Upsaliensia.

Bergström, Villy (1989), 'Ellington – orkestern var hans instrument', *Ackord, LO-Tidningens kulturbilaga*, No. 4, 8 December.

Bergstöm, Villy (2007), *Rättvisa, solidaritet och anpassning: Landsorganisationens ekonomiska politik under fem årtionden*. Stockholm: Atlas.

Bergström, Villy (2009), 'Ragnar Bentzel: Forskaren, handledaren, vännen', in: Magnus Henrekson (ed.), *IFN/IUI 1939–2009*. Stockholm: Ekerlids Förlag.

Bergström, Villy (2015), *Från banker, bruk och lärosäten*. Stockholm: Premiss förlag.

Bergström, Villy and Katzeff Silberstein, Benjamin (2010), *Bilder från Nordkorea*. Stockholm: Bokförlaget Atlas.

Bergström, Villy and Wickman, Kurt (1972), *Bilder från Nordkorea*. Stockholm: Tidens förlag.

Carlsson, Ingvar and Lindgren, Anne-Marie (1996), *Vad är socialdemokrati? En bok om socialdemokrati*. Stockholm: Sveriges socialdemokratiska arbetareparti.

Collier, James Lincoln (1987), *Duke Ellington*. New York and Oxford: Oxford University Press.

Collier, James Lincoln (1988), *Duke Ellington*. Stockholm: Rabén & Sjögren.

Edgren, Gösta; Faxén, Karl-Olof and Odhner, Clas-Erik (1970), *Lönebildning och samhällsekonomi*. Stockholm: Rabén & Sjögren.

Feldt, Kjell-Olof (1991), *Alla dessa dagar ...: i regeringen 1982–1990*. Stockholm: Norstedts.

Greider, Göran (2018), 'En intellektuell som kunde bli förbannad', *Dala-Demokraten*, 26 November.

Karleby, Nils (1926), *Socialismen inför verkligheten*. Stockholm: Tidens förlag.

Landsorganisationen i Sverige (1951), *Fackföreningsrörelsen och den fulla sysselsättningen, rapport till LO-kongressen 1951*. Stockholm: Landsorganisationen i Sverige.

Lindbeck, Assar (1978), 'Förvanskningar om ekonomerna och arbetarrörelsen', *Ekonomisk Debatt*, Vol. 6, No. 1, 34–39.

Lundberg, Erik (1961), *Produktivitet och räntabilitet. Studier i kapitalets betydelse inom svenskt näringsliv*. Stockholm: Studieförbundet Näringsliv och Samhälle.

Lundberg, Erik (1977), 'Ekonomernas debatt om ekonomisk politik. Strödda synpunkter', in: Jan Herin and Lars Werin (eds), *Ekonomisk debatt och ekonomisk politik: Nationalekonomiska Föreningen 100 år*. Stockholm: Norstedts.

Myrdal, Gunnar (1953), *The Political Element in the Development of Economic Theory*. London: Routledge & Kegan Paul.

Ohlin, Bertil (1978), 'Nationalekonomernas hållning till samhällsproblemen', *Ekonomisk Debatt*, Vol. 6, No. 4, 253–260.
Sjöström, Hans O. (1987), *Klassens ljus eller hur man hamnar i arbetar-regeringen*. Stockholm: Norstedts.
Sköld, Maria (2012), 'Tre frågor till Villy Bergström', *Göteborgs-Posten*, 5 February. http://www.gp.se/nyheter/sverige/tre-fr%C3%A5gor-till-villy-bergstr%C3%B6m-1.692849. Downloaded 30 November 2018.
Vanek, Jaroslav (1970), *The General Theory of Labor-Managed Economies*. Ithaca, NY and London: Cornell University Press.
Vanek, Jaroslav (1971), *The Participatory Economy: An Evolutionary Hypothesis and a Strategy for Development*. Ithaca, NY and London: Cornell University Press.
Wigforss, Ernst (1948), *Ekonomisk demokrati*. Stockholm: Natur och Kultur.
Wigforss, Ernst (1980), *Ernst Wigforss skrifter i urval. II. Agitatorn*. Stockholm: Tidens förlag.

CHAPTER 13

Social Clauses, Harmonization and Transition Economies: The World of Göte Hansson

Göte Hansson (1950–2012) was born in Kristianstad in 1950. At the age of nine, he moved with his family to Nässjö. His father worked as a railroad conductor at the Swedish State Railways and had received an order to transfer. Göte lived in Nässjö until he graduated from high school in 1969. Thereafter, he studied mathematics, information processing, especially numerical analysis and economics in Lund, where he received his B.A, in 1972, before pursuing a PhD in economics, specializing in international economics—especially trade policy—and development economics. Göte first had Bo Södersten as his supervisor, and thereafter, when Bo became a Member of Parliament in 1979, me. He defended his dissertation in 1981 and became a professor in 1997.

Thanks are due Yves Bourdet, Benny Carlson, Lina Maria Ellegård, Hans Falck, Mikael Falk, Peter Gavelin, Tarmo Haavisto, Britt-Marie Hansson, Magnus Jerneck and Leif Johansson for all kinds of assistance.

M. Lundahl, *Twelve Figures in Swedish Economics*,
Palgrave Studies in the History of Economic Thought,
https://doi.org/10.1007/978-3-030-94327-1_13

The First Publications

Göte wrote his first book already when he was a research assistant,[1] a high-school textbook that dealt with the Swedish economy, its history and composition, the connection between different sectors and the different production factors. The book also put the Swedish economy into an international context and discussed spatial aspects, ownership and power structures, the relation between politics and the economy as well as the future of the economy.

In 1981, Bo Södersten turned fifty and I edited a festschrift for him. Göte contributed a chapter on liberalization and protectionism in the postwar trade policy,[2] where he surveyed the institutional framework for the liberalization of the 1950s and 1960s: the creation of GATT, the UNCTAD conferences, the trade preferences for developing countries and the switch to increased protectionism in the 1970s. He concluded that the reform of GATT had to be given maximum priority in order to protect free trade.

The Dissertation

The festschrift chapter was the first result of a larger project, 'International Trade, Protectionism and Social Clauses.' A social clause is a condition written into agreements on international trade. The exporting countries undertake to guarantee that working conditions are up to a certain minimum standard. If they aren't, the importing countries have the right to introduce different obstacles to trade which make it more difficult for the exporters to sell their products. The possibility of introducing social clauses was subject to a vivid discussion within the trade union movement at the time. Bengt Säve-Söderbergh at the International Center of the Swedish Labour Movement [Arbetarrörelsens Internationella Centrum] (today the Olof Palme International Center) and Roland Svensson at the National Institute for Working Life [Arbetslivscentrum] were interested in the question and got in touch with Bo Södersten in Lund for an investigation. Bo recommended Göte.

The investigation turned into a doctoral dissertation. In 1981, Göte Hansson defended his *Social Clauses and International Trade*, which was

[1] Hansson (1978).

[2] Hansson (1981).

published internationally.[3] The book begins with a historical survey of the debate on social clauses. The rest of it is analytical. The first issue dealt with is the possible desirability of social clauses as a tool for ensuring fundamental union rights. Göte brings up anti-union arguments. Does the existence of unions work as a brake on economic development? A common argument against monopolistic unions is that they favor wage increases at the expense of employment, compared with free competition in the labor market.[4]

Göte, however, questions whether it is free competition that is the most adequate comparison to a situation with monopolistic unions. In the absence of unions, it is more likely that the labor market is characterized by monopsony. If unions are then formed, the effect may instead be that the employers will hire more people. Employment will approach the one under free competition and an economic gain will arise. Göte also argues that unions may give rise to positive social effects: improved relations between employers and employees, better work morale and better working conditions.

Social clauses that address specific working conditions probably stand a better chance of being incorporated into trade agreements than the right of unionization per se. In the main chapter of the dissertation, Göte hence analyses a number of such cases: minimum wages, child labor and health and safety in the workplace. He does it with the aid of a general equilibrium model of a small, open economy with three sectors: manufacturing industry, extractive industry (mining) and agriculture. He distinguishes between full employment economies and economies with an unlimited supply, i.e. economies where the wage is given by circumstances outside the three formal sectors of the model. The analysis is comparatively static and reveals what happens to resource allocation and factor incomes when a social clause is directed against the export industry (manufacturing).

Göte's model demonstrates that social clauses have complicated effects and that hence they may not be an efficient means to reach the postulated goals. What determines their efficiency is which groups that are affected negatively and the political clout that these groups possess. Social clauses have been discussed in connection with trade agreements between developed and developing countries. Consequently, it is important to specify

[3] Hansson (1983a).

[4] Cf. also Hansson (1982).

the economies of the latter countries as realistically as possible. In Göte's view, many were economies with surplus labor where the wage could be taken to be constant.

The differences between full employment and labor surplus economies are not trivial. As Göte himself notes, it is obvious that a traditional approach, with full employment as the basic labor market characteristic, may be inappropriate in the case of less developed economies with surplus labor. In fact, the traditional analysis may lead to conclusions that are contrary to those obtained from an analysis where surplus labor is explicitly included.[5]

Göte also investigates under which circumstances, and in which senses a social clause is equivalent to protectionist trade policy in the form of tariffs, import quotas or voluntary export restraints, given that all measures produce the same import quantity from the countries potentially subject to social clauses. He ranks the welfare effects for the importing country of the different interventions and discusses what is preferable for the country confronted with the threat of a social clause: to change working conditions or be subjected to trade policy restrictions on exports.

Finally, the implications of the study for economic policy are discussed. The importing countries may want to protect their own manufacturing, display solidarity with the workers in the exporting countries and improve their working conditions and avoid traditional obstacles to trade. In the former case, the price of imported goods has to increase, which is not the case unless a sufficiently large share of imports is hurt. If the purpose is to improve the conditions for the unions, the social clause should be incorporated in multilateral agreements covering as much as possible of world trade. Social clauses may lead to a decrease in the use of traditional protectionism, especially when the latter rests on arguments about competitiveness based on bad working conditions. Social clauses were at least as good, and sometimes better than the 'voluntary' export restraints that during the 1970s had begun to be substituted for tariffs.

The introduction of social clauses into trade agreements was an infected question. The political debate to a large extent consisted of cocksure statements and assumed conclusions. Göte's major contribution consisted in his raising of the complexity of the question and his nuanced discussion. The book is a pioneering effort. 'This dissertation should

[5] Hansson (1983a, p. 125).

become an international standard work,' wrote Ingemar Ståhl when Göte applied for a lecturership in 1983.[6] 'It is as good, ever, as anything written at Assar's institute,' said Jagdish Bhagwati to me on one of his numerous visits to Sweden.[7] When Victor Norman, his thesis opponent, evaluated Göte's qualifications for an associate professorship he concluded: 'The dissertation contains interesting and original results in a field that has not been so much explored in the professional literature. Its professional level, especially the analytical chapters, is high.'[8] When, nine years later, he examined Göte's merits for a professorship, he referred to the book as 'a classic.' Ronald Findlay, in turn, on the same occasion called the book 'an outstanding contribution,' at least ten years ahead of its time.[9] It is Göte's *magnum opus*. The issue has not lost its interest today. On the contrary: Western consumers have become ever more aware of working conditions in low-wage countries during the forty years that have passed since the book was published, and at the same time the integration of the world economy has increased.

Discrimination

When Göte was writing his dissertation on social clauses, I was myself involved in a project about economic discrimination.[10] Together, we published two articles about social clauses as a weapon against racial discrimination in the labor market, one in a labor surplus economy,[11] and the other in a full employment economy.[12] In the labor surplus case, we

[6] Ståhl (1983).

[7] Göte presented his conclusions in an article in *Ekonomisk Debatt* (Hansson 1983b), which provoked criticism from Carl B. Hamilton (1983), who contended that it was not legitimate, as Göte did, to compare social clauses and voluntary export restraints, since the two differ completely with respect to their purposes and character. Göte (Hansson 1983c), however, replied that of course it is possible to compare the effects of a social clause and a voluntary export restraint that have the same effect on imports. This is precisely what he does in this dissertation. He also refuted Hamilton's argument that voluntary export restraints were limited in time, but not social clauses. In practice, that was not the case.

[8] Norman (1988).

[9] Lunds Universitet (1997, pp. 16, 14).

[10] Lundahl och Wadensjö (1984), Lundahl (1992).

[11] Hansson and Lundahl (1984).

[12] Hansson and Lundahl (1987).

dealt with two types of discrimination, in an economy with whites and blacks, on the one hand crowding, where some blacks are barred from qualified jobs, and on the other hand wage discrimination, where whites receive higher salaries then blacks in qualified jobs. We demonstrated that a social clause stands a better chance to be efficient in the former than in the latter case, but also that it is not an infallible weapon. It is possible that capital owners and landowners both prefer a social clause to trade restrictions, while the preferences of white workers are the opposite, but not with certainty, and in the end, the results are determined by which groups dominate the political scene.

The wage discrimination case is more complicated. Both white and black qualified workers are fully employed but the former have a higher wage than the latter. Göte and I postulated that the share of white workers of the total labor force was given in both sectors. Again, the result is that a social clause is not likely to be an efficient weapon against wage discrimination in economies where land owners and white workers are the politically strongest groups (as was the case e.g. in South Africa around that time).

In the full employment case, we only dealt with crowding. Exactly like in Göte's dissertation, this case tends to be more complicated than when you have an unlimited supply of labor. The conclusion is that a priori it is more uncertain than in the labor surplus case whether social clauses are an efficient weapon against crowding.

A third article, co-authored by Göte and me,[13] deals with the Rybczynski theorem.[14] This theorem states that in a model with two goods and two factors, where the production of both goods displays constant returns to scale, growth of one of the production factors will lead to an increase of the production of the good using this factor intensively, while the production of the other good decreases. Göte and I could demonstrate that with decreasing returns to scale in one or both sectors (diseconomies of scale) the theorem continues to be valid provided that the difference in factor intensity between the two sectors is of a certain minimum size.

[13] Hansson and Lundahl (1983).

[14] Rybczynski (1955).

The Practical Level

The last publication by Göte on social clauses is a survey of diplomatic and other international efforts to establish international agreements on working conditions.[15] He posed the question what it was that made it so hard to agree. Social clauses could be interpreted as a threat about protectionism and the practical difficulties were great. The developing countries could easily contend that the agreements served as a means for the developed countries to dump their domestic problems on the developing countries and that this would act as a brake on their development and hence interfere with their political sovereignty.

An alternative was to make foreign aid dependent on improved working conditions, either targeting the sectors where you wanted to interfere or by linking the improvements to general budget support. This method, however, would not necessarily succeed either. Possibly you could make the issue one of human rights, but in the end, both social clauses and aid clauses were connected with costs for the developed countries, either higher import prices or increased aid.

Harmonization

In 1990, Göte Hansson published his second important book, about international harmonization of economic policy.[16] It connected with his dissertation, both thematically and methodologically. The purpose of harmonization of economic policy between countries is to increase the efficiency of the international allocation of resources by eliminating distortions in production and trade, reducing the risk of trade conflicts and stabilizing the international macroeconomic environment. Exactly like in the social clause book, Göte worked with a combination of partial analysis in order to establish equivalences between different measures and general equilibrium analysis to establish the effects of harmonization on different groups in the economy. Six different areas of harmonization were dealt with: trade policy, technical standards, working conditions, environmental policy, fiscal policy and monetary policy.

[15] Hansson (2009).

[16] Hansson (1990a).

Trade Policy and Technical Standards

The chapter on trade policy concentrates on what happens if free trade, discriminatory or non-discriminatory tariffs are substituted for voluntary export restraints and on the abolition of abuse of anti-dumping tariffs and countervailing duties. Harmonization increases the global efficiency of the resource allocation, but some groups gain and others lose, both in the protectionist countries and in the countries which at the outset are subject to protectionist policies and in countries that are not. Göte demonstrates that there were good reasons for being pessimistic with respect to the creation of a harmonization of trade policy which would abolish voluntary export restraints and lead to free trade, since this would hurt the producers in the importing countries and, in the short run, the workers whose wages would decrease, as well as the industrial capitalists. These groups were not particularly large and hence easy to mobilize in the struggle against harmonization, while the consumers, the winners, were a large and diffuse group. Also those exporters that were not subject to the voluntary export restraints could be expected to be against their abolition, since they would get a lower price for their products and sell less. A harmonization of trade policy hence tends to be difficult to introduce, unless it results in growth which increases the demand for factors which in the comparative static perspective are losers.

Harmonization of technical specifications can be carried out for different reasons and in different ways. Officially, the purpose is often to protect the consumers, but frequently it is rather a question of producer protection. The technical level can lie anywhere between the highest and lowest levels. Göte analyses universal harmonization at the low and the high level, respectively, and in addition voluntary high-level harmonization when simultaneously low-level producers are prohibited from exporting their products. The point of the departure of the analysis is a situation with two types of countries before the harmonization: low- and high-quality producers. The latter can export to all countries, the former only to other low-quality countries. If harmonization implies that all countries have to accept low-quality production, a conflict will arise between the low-quality producers who receive a higher price for their goods, and the high-quality producers whose prices will be lowered. The same conflict materializes in the case of harmonization at the high-quality level. The same groups who in one type of countries are in favor of harmonization are against it in the other type of countries. It becomes difficult to reach an agreement. In the voluntary case, things may be easier. There, the possibility remains of keeping a lower standard for the domestic market remains.

Working Environment Quality and Environmental Destruction

Göte's third harmonization case deals with the working conditions within the industrial sector, i.e. the same case that he dealt with in his dissertation, and he simply summarizes his result from there. Social clauses have effects which often can be compared to those of traditional protectionism, but they may constitute a way of getting away from the discrimination between countries connected with voluntary export restraints. They are, however, dubious if the purpose is to show solidarity with the workers in countries with bad working conditions, since they tend to increase unemployment and lower the wages in the countries which must change their working conditions.

Harmonization has also been recommended as a weapon against environmental destruction. The debate about the environment had acquired a momentum at the time when Göte wrote his harmonization book, and he concluded that it was above all in this field that you could expect harmonization efforts, since environmental destruction was a genuinely international problem. He analyses two types of measures: legislation and taxation of environmentally damaging production. The usual conclusion of environmental economics is that taxation is to be preferred from the efficiency point of view since then each firm can choose the combination of environmental destruction and taxes that suits it best, and Göte demonstrates that the same is true when the destruction extends across national borders. He also derives the effects on the factor incomes and shows that both the capital owners and the workers in the industrial sector—potentially well-organized groups risk to be hurt by both types of sanctions and that hence it may be difficult to arrive at any agreements.

Fiscal and Monetary Policy

When it comes to fiscal policy harmonization, the discussion has mainly centered on tax policy. Göte concentrates on this as well: commodity taxation on the one hand and capital and labor taxes on the other. He discusses the choice between taxation of production and taxation of consumption. Harmonization of taxes on production will be supported by all factor owners in high-tax countries in the short run. In low-tax countries which henceforth will have higher taxes the situation is the opposite. As always, the relative political strength of the different groups will decide whether any harmonization will take place or not.

Göte also analyses harmonization of taxes on capital and labor. The effects of a harmonization of factor taxes differs between labor and capital. A uniform tax on labor will have negative effect on all factor incomes in the former low-tax countries and positive effects in high-tax countries, while a corresponding tax on capital in the short run will only affect the return on capital negatively in the former and positively in the latter, while other factor rewards are not affected. In the long run, the return on capital and the wage rate will fall in low-tax countries while they will increase in high-tax countries. Altogether, Göte was of the opinion that harmonization of taxation stands a better chance to succeed if it encompasses relatively large changes in high-tax countries and relatively small in low-tax countries.

The last measure analyzed by Göte is the harmonization of capital markets, turning them into perfectly working markets, so that interest rates are equalized. This leads to higher interest rates and lower wages in former low-interest countries and, conversely, to lower interest rates and higher wages in high-interest countries. The conclusion is what you would expect: the effects of harmonization continue to be asymmetric. A certain category of factor owners in a certain category of countries oppose the same group in the other category of countries.

The overall conclusion drawn by Göte of his analysis of harmonization is that the latter is no infallible means for increasing the efficiency of resource allocation between and within countries, even in the case (the one analyzed by him) where the only distortion that exists at the outset is the one removed by harmonization. The analysis demonstrates that it is politically difficult to reach an agreement on harmonization, for the simple reason that such an agreement will affect different groups asymmetrically. Those hurt tend to oppose harmonization efforts and they are often groups that are easy to mobilize.

The reception of the harmonization book met with less enthusiasm in expert opinions than the one on social clauses. The book makes tough reading. Göte was criticized because the mathematical expressions were long and cumbersome. The discussion of taxes and monetary policy ought to have been carried out with the aid of a macroeconomic model instead of a model concentrated exclusively on the real side and the analysis of technical standards would have benefited from acquaintance with the literature that was being developed in the field of industrial organization.[17]

A Practical Application: The Car Industry

Göte demonstrated that his analysis of the harmonization issue had practical relevance in an article co-written with Yves Bourdet, about the passenger car industry in the EG,[18] a subject treated by Yves in his doctoral dissertation,[19] Yves and Göte argue that harmonization of trade policy against non-EG countries was a necessary condition for such a market to function. They analyze the welfare effects and the effects on different groups within the EG of a harmonization of a market not characterized by perfect competition.

Three instances of harmonization are dealt with: (a) the same number of cars as before are imported into the union, (b) imports may only amount to a given share of the total sales of cars within the union, (c) the permissible import share also includes cars produced within the union but sold by subsidiaries from a third country. Yves and Göte demonstrate that consumers are likely to prefer the a alternative to the b and c ones, but that the ranking by the producers will be the opposite one. This, in turn, means that it is not certain that it is the kind of harmonization most favorable for the consumers that will be established, since the car market is strongly concentrated and hence the produces within the union easily organize and exert pressure on the decision makers within the union.

Exactly like the book on social clauses, the harmonization issue remains hot. International integration and trade associations touch very many more fields than thirty years ago.

Internationalization

Göte Hansson was also interested in international trade and international politics in a wider context. In 1984, he participated in an anthology about Swedish policy vis-à vis developing countries with a chapter on trade and

[17] Lunds Universitet (1997, pp. 2–3).

[18] Bourdet and Hansson (1991).

[19] Bourdet (1988).

the Third World.[20] Thee, he penetrated the development of international trade and the place of developing countries in it from 1950 to 1980, how the international trade system handled the developing countries (GATT and UNCTAD) and the principal and empirical connection of trade and development. The following year, he wrote about multinational companies in a similar context.[21] He discussed the situation of international research and held out the gaps, above all the effects of multinational companies on the countries of origin and the question of an international rule framework for these companies.

In 1985, the Swedish government appointed a sovereign investigation committee under the chairmanship of the political scientist Olof Pettersson for the study of issues of distribution of power and democracy, the so-called power study. Together with the political scientist Lars-Göran Stenelo in Lund, Göte Hansson edited a book on power and internationalization.[22] He contributed two chapters himself, one on the problems and possibilities of the international economy and one on the autonomy of the international economy. The former is a simple account of the reasons for international trade and international enterprises. Göte enumerates the factors which determine the international competitiveness of a country, including its economic policy, and the effects of internationalization for consumers, producers, capital owners and wage earners.

In the second, more deep-probing, chapter he poses the question of which possibilities a small country like Sweden has to reconcile internationalization with sovereign economic and political decision making. Göte stresses the importance of political action in international circles to ensure that Swedish values and goals have an impact. When the chapter was written, Sweden had just scrapped currency regulation (1989) and our future relations with the EG were high on the agenda. Göte describes how the increasing internationalization limited the domestic sphere of action, so that protectionism easily gains terrain, and based on his harmonization book, he discusses the existing possibilities of coordination of economic policies and the political difficulties likely to arise if you opt for harmonization.

[20] Hansson (1984).

[21] Hansson (1985).

[22] Hansson and Stenelo (1990).

Another internationalization theme associated with Göte's work on social clauses and harmonization was the creation of the WTO in 1995. He analyzed what the transition from the GATT to the WTO would imply for the developing countries.[23] The results were mixed. The Uruguay Round, which began in 1985, led to the creation of an organization which would see to it that global trade would operate within a framework of stable rules and that the extent of protectionism would decrease. Increased multilateralism and harmonization would be substituted for bilateral trade agreements. The Multi Fiber Agreement, which discriminated against the textile exports of developing countries would be discontinued, but at the same time, the option of production and export subsidies would disappear. In addition, Göte argued, the developing countries would need foreign assistance in order to cope with the adjustment to the new set of rules.

Göte Hansson would return to the theme of internationalization and harmonization,[24] At the end of the 1990s, Poland was about to apply for membership in the EU, and in that context, a Polish-Swedish conference on the theme of globalization and change was arranged in Warsaw. Göte's contribution dealt with the connection between internationalization and domestic incentive systems and the need for coordination and harmonization of economic policy. This was a central part of the EU project. International harmonization, however, was a highly political question. Different interests faced each other, it took time to agree, and it was important to analyze who stood to gain and to lose on the agreements.

Göte surveyed the different areas of harmonization, using his book as his point of departure, and cautioned that harmonization does not guarantee an efficient allocation of resources. At the outset, the world is full of distortions, and in the cases where gains can be made, there may be a strong political resistance to change. The harmonization to be prioritized is the deregulation of international capital flows, since it limits the scope for action of individual countries and makes it more difficult for anti-harmonization lobbies to be formed and hence opens the road to harmonization in other fields as well.

The theoretical conclusions were applied to the EU case, measure by measure. The conclusion, again, is that different interests face each other.

[23] Hansson (1996a).

[24] Hansson (2000a).

Göte stressed the importance of growth. The probability of reaching an agreement increases when economies grow, and it becomes easier to adapt your own economy to the requirements of international competition. Finally, with explicit reference to Poland and its efforts, he discussed the importance of liberalization initiatives from individual countries as a prerequisite for economic integration and harmonization.

In 2000, Göte Hansson participated in a conference on genetic engineering and economics in Lund, where he presented a paper on how technology might impact the economic relations between North and South.[25] Technological development in general was heavily concentrated to the North, to the developed countries. This was true for agriculture too. The Green Revolution increased yields, also in many developing countries, however, far from all. One of the problems was to make private companies undertake research in the area, something that brought up the issue of patent and property rights. Another was that the research tended to be concentrated on capital-intensive methods suited to developed countries, but not to developing ones, which in turn might tie the latter to old, less productive, methods. Göte noticed the risk that the development of genetically engineered crops would increase the gap between rich and poor countries and that the paradoxical situation might arise that the developing countries would consume genetically engineered food produced in the developed countries, while the latter might prefer food produced in developing countries with traditional techniques.

Göte Hansson's last publication is from 2011. It was written together with Lennart Petersson for a festschrift to Bo Södersten on his eightieth birthday.[26] The two discuss why efforts of economic integration tended to be frustrated in Africa. The participation of the African countries in international trade was lagging behind that of other developing countries, not least the Asian ones, in spite of having increased during the recent decade, Africa remained outside the global production chains. Lennart and Göte surveyed the existing African integration agreement and the composition of the exports of the African countries: mainly raw materials. The share of inter-African trade in total African foreign trade was insignificant, a mere ten percent, but important for some individual countries.

[25] Hansson (2002).

[26] Petersson and Hansson (2011).

Many factors contributed to keep African foreign trade low, both the inter-African share and the trade with countries outside the continent. Lennart and Göte list a dozen causes, ranging from lack of confidence and border conflicts, undeveloped infrastructure and deficient institutions to protectionism and distrust in free trade in general. Finally, they point to a number of strategic policy issues: build-up of knowledge about the effects of trade and trade policy measures, concerted action, creation of confidence between different African countries and the need for effective support from the rest of the world.

The topic is still on the agenda, not least after the creation of the African Continental Free Trade Area (AfCFTA), in 2018.

Ethiopia

At the end of the 1980s, SIDA (the Swedish International Development Authority) initiated cooperation in the area of macroeconomics with three Swedish universities in order to build up an independent Swedish research capacity with respect to the economies of the most important countries that received Swedish aid. One of these universities was Lund, where Göte Hansson was in charge of the activities. He handled Ethiopia himself, and subsequently also Eritrea. Göte wrote nine country reports for SIDA about Ethiopia, a number of book chapters and, not least, a monograph about the Ethiopian economy during the years when the country was ruled by a single-party system and a Socialist government, 1974–1991, and the reform attempts that were made thereafter, He followed the development of the Ethiopian economy for more than fifteen years.

Göte's first country report was the first macroeconomic study ever published in SIDA's new series.[27] He visited the country in May 1989, under slightly dramatic circumstances. A coup attempt on the 16th forced him to cut his visit short. He, however, managed to interview the Planning Minister of the country, an important interview, since Ethiopia had just launched a new development strategy.

In his study, Göte deals with the most important characteristics of the Ethiopian economy: the factors which made the country the possibly poorest in the world. The growth rate was far below the average for developing countries, mainly because of the low agricultural production. After

[27] Hansson (1989).

the military coup that deposed Hailie Selassie in 1974, the economy had been linked into a Socialist path: production and service cooperatives, which had proved unable to deliver what they had promised, population movements and concentration of the rural population in villages. The individual farmers were discriminated, since the cooperatives were given the best land, priority when it came to inputs and higher prices for their products. Foreign trade was regulated, and the currency was overvalued.

The new development strategy was a mixture of good and bad initiatives. Unfortunately, the latter prevailed. Reaching the Marxist-Leninist political goals stood out as more important than to increase the efficiency and production capacity of the economy. Central planning was extended also to the private sector: an efficient way of reducing productivity there.

Göte was back in Ethiopia a year later, in March 1990, for another report.[28] At that point, the country had initiated a process of change. The regime had announced a reform program which at least formally looked promising. A mixed economy was to be substituted for the planned one and private initiatives were to be encouraged. The large companies were to be exposed to competition, and in agriculture individual cultivators were no longer to be discriminated. A political opposition would be permitted.

Göte analyzed the probable effects of the reform program, given that it would really be carried out. Overall, you might expect the efficiency to increase in the Ethiopian economy when competition was substituted for central planning. This was true not least for the agricultural sector which had been subjected to lots of compulsion. Both production and exports ought to increase. The reform program, however, was incomplete. Göte pointed to the importance of straightening out foreign trade. The Ethiopian birr should be devalued, the link to the American dollar ought to be broken and a basket of currencies that reflected the composition of Ethiopia's foreign trade should be used instead. Trade should be deregulated. Central direction and licensing had to be abolished. Furthermore, it was necessary to reduce public spending. Since the country was involved in a civil war, the military absorbed gigantic sums. To end the war was the number one priority. Göte was optimistic with respect to the possibility of reforming the Ethiopian economy, but continued warfare might frustrate the effort.

[28] Hansson (1990b).

Göte's first published essay on Ethiopia[29] built on his 1992 SIDA country report.[30] It was written soon after the fall of the dictatorship of Mengistu Haile Mariam. A transition government had been appointed and democratic elections were planned for 1993. Göte analysed the economic and political reform program that the transition government had announced and which was to turn the economy away from public ownership and monopolies, state control, central planning and protectionism—a policy which had led to an economic catastrophe—and toward a mixed economy with plenty of scope for private ownership, markets, competition and international trade. The fall of the old regime offered a unique opportunity to break with the completely failed Socialist system, and the prospects for foreign aid were good, but the program was not risk-free. The urban poor risked losing their jobs when the public companies were dismantled, and ethnic and interregional conflicts might flare up.

The next essay dealt with foreign trade and economic growth during the Mengistu period.[31] Göte analyzed the Ethiopian economy with the aid of a model of a dualistic economy with one agricultural and one non-agricultural sector. The focus was on the perverse incentive system which had been built up in the Socialist economy, with its collectivization, public ownership, forced concentration of 35–40 percent of the population in villages. The negative incentives reduced the agricultural production and, together with the high rate of population growth, made GDP per capita fall. To this, you had to add a trade policy with regulated exports and an overvalued currency which created a huge gap between imports and exports. Trade did not work as an engine for growth, since the policy did not allow for imports of the necessary capital goods. Both the domestic economy and the trade policy were in desperate need of reform.

Ethiopia Tikdem

In 1995, Göte Hansson published his most important work on the Ethiopian economy, the book. *The Ethiopian Economy 1974–1994*.[32] It

[29] Hansson (1993a).

[30] Hansson (1992).

[31] Hansson (1993b).

[32] Hansson (1995b).

dealt with the Ethiopian economy during the Socialist dictatorship which followed the fall of Hailie Selassie in 1974 and which lasted until the dictator, Mengistu, was force into exile in 1991. The period ended with a deep economic crisis.[33] The slogan had been *Ethiopia Tikdem*: Ethiopia First. Officially, the issue was about combining nationalism and equality, but in practice it was about preventing Eritrea and Tigray from becoming sovereign states and make a centrally directed command economy which discriminated against the peasants.

Göte demonstrates efficiently that *Ethiopia Tikdem* was a policy in strong opposition to virtually all sound rules of economic policy. He describes the creation of the Socialist economy and its main characteristics. The entire economy was to be in the hands of the state and virtually all private initiatives were opposed. All damaging foreign influences were to be kept out. Collectivization, forced movements of people and their concentration in villages as well as distortions of all incentives and strong control of foreign trade characterized the economy.

With the aid of a mathematical model of an economy with four sectors—subsistence agriculture, non-peasant farming, manufacturing and a public sector which also encompasses the military—Göte derives the effects of the actual policy on the economy. Agriculture was kept down and the public sector, notably the military, was favored. These results corresponded well to the actual development of the civil war. It went bad, soldiers had to be obtained by forced conscription, and the army was demoralized. In order to compensate for that, military spending had to be increased.

The model analysis is followed by an empirical investigation of the Socialist policy. The results of the two approaches confirm each other. The effects of the new policy were negative. In 1987, the per capita income of Ethiopia was the lowest registered one in the world, less than half the average figure for low-income countries. The growth rate of the agricultural sector was gradually reduced until it turned negative between 1980 and 1987. The current account of the balance of payments turned increasingly negative as a result of reduced agricultural exports on the one hand and increases imports of military equipment, food and fuel, on the other. The foreign debt increased dramatically, and the aid donors, with

[33] The contents of Hansson (1993c, 1993d, 1995a), which deal with the economic and political reform initiatives put forward 1991–1993, are worked into Hansson (1995b).

the exception of the Soviet Union, which provided military assistance, were niggard.

The last two chapters in the Ethiopia book deal with the reform efforts that were undertaken from 1988. Mengistu had then been in Moscow and had been told by Gorbachev that he could not count on more support unless he liberalized the economy and brought the civil war which had been going on during virtually the entire Socialist period to a peaceful end. Hence, in November 1988, Mengistu had to announce a reform package, followed by another, more far-reaching one in March 1990. The content of the latter, however, was strongly contradictory. The resolutions stressing liberalization were opposed by others advocating increased centralization and continuation of the centralized economic policy. As Göte demonstrated, the reform document was inconsistent. In 1990, many within the civil service hoped that reforms would really be carried out. One year later, pessimism was widespread. The war had escalated, and the military expenses threatened to nullify the reform eandeavors.

The reforms were slow, so the donors pushed. In addition, the war went bad for Mengistu. In May 1991, he was forced to leave the country and a transition government took over. The latter issued yet another reform program, *Ethiopia's Economic Policy During the Transition* (TEP). The principle of the mixed economy was cemented, and the task of the state was to promote decentralized decision making, private ownership and the market economy instead of the command economy. The solution of the agricultural problem was postponed, but the villagization program was scrapped, and outside agriculture, private actors were allowed to compete with the public companies. Banking would, however, continue to be a government task. The foreign trade would be gradually liberalized, and the rate of exchange would be adjusted.

Göte analyzed the expected and real effects of the transition policy. The point of departure was that you should not expect any drastic changes in such a short time by a country which had just been involved in a long civil war. Nevertheless, argued Göte, the effects of the reforms, according to his model analysis, should be the exact opposite of those of the Socialist policy. His presumption was borne out by the available statistics for the 1991–1994 period, in spite of the fact that the agricultural sector had been exposed to drought. The macroeconomic situation was mixed. The budget deficit had increased, and imports had increased more than exports, as a result of the reconstruction needs.

What did the future look like? Göte was not quite sure that a political majority electoral system was to be preferred. From the democratic point of view, a proportional representation would have been better. Decentralization was another problem. The lack of competence in the regions acted as an obstacle. Democratization, however, was underway. The need for foreign assistance remained, both in order to finance imports and to reform the public sector. Both factor and commodity markets were undergoing strong liberalization. The public enterprises which dominated the economy were being dissolved, but new, smaller, public enterprises were created. The privatization problem remained unsolved. Foreign trade was relieved of a number of obstacles. In 1992, the birr was devalued, and the following year, foreign currency auctions were introduced. Altogether, Göte concluded that much had been done to reverse the negative effects of the Socialist regime, but also that much remained to be done, above all in the area of foreign trade and in the financial sector.

More Sida Reports

Göte Hansson continued to write about Ethiopia for (the reorganized) Sida (Swedish International Development Cooperation Agency) also after his book had been published. The 1995 report[34] focused on the continuing implementation of the economic and political reforms in 1993–1995. In addition to the macroeconomic indicators, Göte discusses the most important issues in the new, 1994, constitution: the possibility for regions to break out and become independent, landownership and the right to cultivate the land. He notes that the political reforms had been consolidated, even though the 1995 elections had strengthened the position of the governing party and that foreign trade had been liberalized, in spite of that Ethiopia hesitated to join the WTO and needed assistance in this process.

The theme for the 1996 report, later reworked into a book chapter,[35] was the legitimacy of the government, sustainable development and aid. Göte poses the question whether the Ethiopian reforms should be regarded as a strategy for sustainable development in the country. Much had been done, but much still remained to be done, as shown by the

[34] Hansson (1995c).

[35] Hansson (1997a, 2001), respectively.

macroeconomic indicators. The question of sustainable development was related to the question of which legitimacy the Ethiopian government possessed. Lack of legitimacy could risk the economic development. Göte examined a number of legitimacy criteria, for the performance of the government, and concluded that, while things had turned out well in the economic field, including decentralization, the results were more mixed when it came to peace, democratization, human rights and social improvements. Finally, he also discussed the role of aid for sustainable development. In that context, legitimacy was important. After the fall of the Mengistu government, an active opposition had taken shape, which in itself was positive, but there was also a risk that the opposition would succeed in discrediting the government and thus jeopardize further aid.

In 1998, Göte discussed problems of regional development and the private sector of the economy.[36] The share of the government budget dedicated to the regions had increased, but the allocation was far from satisfactory. The cities were favored over the rural areas in terms of both investment and education. Göte thought that the future of the countryside looked bleak. The privatization of the public enterprises was underway, but mainly in the trade sector and less in manufacturing. Ownership in the private sector was concentrated and it was problematic that the dominant political party owned companies. The land redistribution which had taken place in the Amhara region in 1996 rested on dubious premises. Göte was concerned that political considerations played too important a role in relation to commercial ones in the economy.

Göte Hansson's last work on Ethiopia, another Sida report, was published in 2004.[37] His point of departure is the situation of the economy in 2003: drought and border conflict with Eritrea. The transition to a market economy with private ownership had slowed down. The critics blamed the government. Agriculture continued to dominate the economy completely. Diversification was necessary, but this in turn required promotion of the private sector. Göte discussed the business climate in Ethiopia, above all the lack of competence in central fields like accounting, auditing, project evaluation, commercial law as well as the deficient financial system, which made it difficult especially for small and medium-sized firms to obtain credits.

[36] Hansson (1998).

[37] Hansson (2004).

Göte's book on Ethiopia was published at the right time. It was written precisely when the country was making the transition from a Socialist economy, driven by compulsion, to an economy based on free market principles. The book is still of interest, not just as far as Ethiopia is concerned, but also because it sheds light both on the processes developed in most economies that have carried out such a transition and of the mechanisms that continue to operate in countries that have not had the sense to abandon economic systems based on nebulous ideologies.

Eritrea

In 1996, Göte Hansson extended his interest in Africa to Eritrea as well. The country had broken away from Ethiopia in 1993 and had become a recipient of Swedish foreign aid. Since Göte knew Ethiopia, he was the logical choice for Sida reports about Eritrea as well. His first contribution dealt with the transition to peaceful democracy and the creation of a market economy.[38] The lack of quantitative data and the short time that had passed since the declaration of independence forced the analysis to be tentative and qualitative.

A commission had been created to draft a constitution for the new country, but it had not advanced very far. The low level of literacy (20 percent) and the lack of administrative capacity meant that it would take time to build democracy. The economic system was undergoing extensive change in virtually all areas, toward a market economy and liberalization. A recovery and rehabilitation program, which also included a number of social goals, had been worked out and was slowly beginning to be implemented. It was too early to say anything about the effects, but the indicators for the first year were pointing in the right direction. The macroeconomic situation was much better than during the Ethiopian period. The main bottleneck was the lack of competent personnel on all levels.

In four publications from 2000 to 2001 Göte discusses how the political tension between Ethiopia and Eritrea threatened the economic progress that had been made in the two countries.[39] Both economically

[38] Hansson (1996b).

[39] Hansson (2000b, 2000c, 2001a, 2001b).

and politically Eritrea had developed favorably until 1997, with the exception of a conflict with Yemen about the Hanish islands. In the same years, however, the country had introduced its own currency, the nakfa, instead of the Ethiopian birr, and insisted that it should be used in the transactions between the two countries, at par with the birr, which Ethiopia had opposed. This led to acute friction and in practice the free trade between the two countries ceased. Ethiopia demanded hard currency and began shipping goods through Djibouti instead of through Assab in Eritrea. The differences of opinion escalated until it came to an open military border conflict in 1998. Two years later, a ceasefire was agreed after the conflict had inflicted huge economic costs on both countries. The macroeconomic indicators were eloquent.

The Horn of Africa and Tanzania

Göte Hansson did not write just on Ethiopia and Eritrea. In a few papers he extended the analysis to encompass the entire Horn of Africa, in addition to these two countries, Djibouti, Somalia, the breakaway republic of Somaliland and the Sudan. With the exception of Djibouti, the situation in the area had been characterized by internal conflicts and breakaway attempts, internal tension, drought and poverty, dictatorship and centralized government. Eritrea had liberated itself from Ethiopia. Somaliland had broken away from Somalia, however, without receiving international recognition. The Sudan risked being split into one northern and one southern part. After the end of the Cold War, the aid flow had been reduced. The Horn of Africa was no longer strategically interesting. The region displayed a depressing and complex political situation.

Göte was interested in the conditions for economic development in the region as a whole.[40] A liberalization of the economy had taken place in some countries: Ethiopia, Djibouti and Eritrea. One possible road to development went through economic integration in the region, but this lay far into the future. Political breakaway tendencies posed other obstacles. Ethnicity was another problem. All the countries in the region were characterized by mixed populations and the ethnic borders did not always coincide with the political ones. Loyalty to the own ethnic group often conflicted with loyalty to the nation state. The risk of ethnic conflicts

[40] Hansson (1997b, 1999).

both inside and between the states of the region was high, and so was the probability that ethnic tensions would trigger migration across national borders. Göte also noted the risk of future religiously based wars as well as conflicts due to different perceptions of what the distribution of the water resources of the Nile ought to be. Both the political and the economic problems of the region were huge. Economic development was sluggish, and the population was growing rapidly. The Horn of Africa was in desperate need of economic resources in the near future.

In 2006, the professor of political science in Lund, Lars-Göran Stenelo, went into retirement. He was then presented a festschrift on the theme of leadership, where Göte contributed an essay on leadership on the Horn of Africa.[41] The essay dealt with how the new government which had been formed in Ethiopia after the fall of Mengistu in 1991 had succeeded. A number of reforms had been introduced, but the political opposition in Ethiopia remained strongly critical. Not least the relations with Eritrea remained bad. Ethiopia and Eritrea had not managed to straighten out their border relations and the risk of war was imminent, which had had a negative impact on the economies of both countries. The money went to defense instead of to economic development efforts. The leadership on both sides stood out as bad. The Ethiopian government enjoyed little support in the capital and the confidence between the political and economic actors was weak.

Göte Hansson was deeply engaged in the African economies. Another example was Tanzania. The department of economics in Lund had an education cooperation project with the corresponding department and the Economic Research Bureau at the University of Dar es Salaam, initiated by Sida. Kighoma Malima and Robert Mabele had come to Sweden to identify a suitable cooperation partner and had opted for Lund. I administered the program from the Swedish side from 1981 to 1987, when I left Lund for the Stockholm School of Economics. Thereafter, Göte took over, until 1995.

After a few years, the education cooperation program also led to research cooperation between the two universities, among others with the future governor of the Tanzanian central bank, Benno Ndulu. Göte never participated in this, but he wrote a popular article together with Stefan Hedlund and me on how the Tanzanian Socialist ideology had created

[41] Hansson (2006).

economic problems in the country.[42] The 'African Socialism' stressed the importance of self-reliance and defined capitalism and what was perceived as neo-colonialism as enemies. In the Socialist spirit, Tanzania was to 'run while others walk.' The reality, however, was different. The Ujamaa villages, the foundation of which was to be equality and cooperation in agricultural cooperatives, had little in common with the ideology. They worked as bad as ever the Soviet kolkhozes. Too many people had been gathered in villages that were too big, in a forced community which was completely unnatural. The entire agricultural policy had misfired. The public marketing boards did not work. The centralized pricing simply aimed at keeping consumer prices down. The farmers had to pay the cost and the policy did not take the differences in transport costs between different parts of the country into account. A number of misdirected interventions in the market mechanism precluded Tanzania from realizing its equality ideals.

A Disputed Chair

Göte Hansson was appointed professor of international economics in Lund in 1997. The chair had been announced in 1995. Lars Ljungqvist had been ranked first by the three members of the expert committee: Ronald Findlay from Columbia University, Victor Norman from the Norwegian School of Economics in Bergen and Niels Thygesen from the University of Copenhagen, but he preferred a position at the Stockholm School of Economics. Göte had been placed after Per Lundborg and Johan Torstensson by Norman and Thygesen. Findlay had only ranked Ljungqvist and Lundborg. When Ljungqvist had withdrawn and the issue was brought up again, Göte was appointed with the motivation that when scientific, pedagogical, supervisory and administrative merits were all weighed together he was superior to the other applicants. The permanent members of the academic appointments board and Findlay voted for Göte. Norman and Thygesen stated a dissenting opinion.

Lundberg and Torstenson appealed. (Torstensson, however, died before the issue was settled.) Simultaneously the people from the bleachers rushed into the playing field. Under the leadership of Assar Lindbeck, a we-who-know-better posse was mobilized with the aid of

[42] Hansson m fl (1983).

sticks and carrots: twenty-three professors in Stockholm, Uppsala and Umeå who interfered with the handling of chair by Lund University. They protested against the disavowal of two of the experts by the academic appointments board. The wording of the diatribes sent to Lund was identical—centrally planned—with the single exception that in Umeå the ranking of the applicants had been confused. Lund University rejected the appeal and so did the highest instance, the Higher Education Appeals Board.

The dispute about the professorship got an epilogue. In an article in *Ekonomisk Debatt* with the title 'One Letter Too Many,' Agneta Kruse and Lars Söderström in Lund attacked the action by the professors. 'It is difficult to free yourself from the suspicion that it is something else than the concern about Lund University and the discipline of economics that has motivated the letter witers.'[43] They took issue with the fact that the letter insinuated cronyism—Göte had received his education in Lund, the same university as the one where he held his position—and pointed out that several of the signatories themselves held positions in the universities where they had been educated.

Kruse and Söderström also revealed important inconsistencies in the actions of the professors. In 1989, another righteous, partly overlapping group, also convened by Lindbeck, had protested against the decision by the board of SAREC (the Swedish Agency for Research Cooperation with Developing Countries) to *follow* the recommendations by three unanimous experts with respect to two chairs in development economics and had requested new appointment criteria and new experts.[44] The year before, 1988, a chair in economics in Uppsala had been filled in Uppsala. There the academic appointments board had *disavowed* the three unanimous experts. 'On that occasion there were no concerned professors who felt the need to fly the academic flag. And it is certainly notable that the person who then received the position is found among today's letter writers. He is concerned that in Lund Göte Hansson is chosen, who is backed by one expert, while he himself was backed by none.'[45]

Kruse and Söderström finished with a broadside:

[43] Kruse and Söderström (1998, p. 301).

[44] Possibly it had something to do with the fact that none of the positions went to Lindbeck's institute.

[45] Kruse och Söderström (1998, pp. 301–302).

> So it is not the first time that a number of professors in our discipline offer an opinion on an appointment decision, Maybe not the last either. Let us hope that the latest letter does not set the pattern for the future. It is shameful for the profession that so many highly qualified colleagues sign letters and back allegations the correctness of which they have apparently not bothered to control. To this comes the deeply unfortunate fact that individual persons are being defamed. Those who apply for a position in our discipline should not risk having their appointments questioned with unconfirmed or directly erroneous accusations of irregularities in the appointment procedure.[46]

Oh, dear ...

The Faculty Man

Göte Hansson had solid administrative merits. He enjoyed administrative work and he was skilled. Göte was study director and head of the department of economics in Lund, subdean (1993–2000) and dean (2000–2003) of the faculty of social sciences there before the School of Economics and Management broke away from it, something which he was against.[47] He had expressed a strong opinion long before that economics was a subject which did not only have business administration as its natural partner but which was of relevance for many parts of society.[48]

Göte had an extremely good cooperation with the political scientists, not least Lars-Göran Stenelo, who was dean when Göte was subdean. He regularly formed part of their thesis examination committees. Another practical result of the collaboration was the courses in international relations where the students had at least two semesters of both political science and economics and where classes were frequently given with

[46] Ibid., p. 302.

[47] Sunesson (2015).

[48] Göte had difficulty hiding his enthusiasm for the university administration. He often spoke on behalf of the faculty: 'We, in the faculty ...'—and he often spoke at length-some of his colleagues thought that he spent too much time on administration and that there was talk scrap in the corners of his office. They referred to him as 'Göte Mote [Meeting],' and when he resigned as chair of the department somebody put a sign on his door which instead of Chairman read 'Citoyen.' Maybe there was something in it, but the attitude was rather a manifestation of the somewhat brutal but warm mood that prevailed in the department.

teachers from both departments present simultaneously in the classroom. Göte and the political scientists also visited Swedish high schools and trained the teachers in politics and economics.

One thing that was also dear to Göte was collaboration with other universities. During 2004, the historian Keith Nelson from Irvine, who had led the University of California Education Abroad Program in Sweden and Denmark, initiated a prestigious interdisciplinary summer school on global relations in Lund, focusing on the relations between Europe and the United States. All the campuses of the University of California sent teachers to Lund for a two-month course for a hundred American students and somewhat fewer Swedish ones. The program lasted between 2004 and 2008, with Göte and the political scientists Christer Jönsson and Magnus Jerneck as the driving forces on the Lund side.

I have already mentioned the cooperation between Lund and Dar es Salaam. In 2006, another Swedish-African cooperation program, the Trade Policy Training Centre in Africa, in Arusha, was launched with aid money from Sida. The program offers master's courses in international economics, trade policy and international trade law for students from the poorest countries in Africa south of the Sahara, with teachers from Europe, the United States and Africa. Göte Hansson built the institution, administered the program from the Swedish side and was academically responsible for the activities. According to what he said himself, this was one of the most thrilling tasks he had ever undertaken.

* * *

Göte Hansson was an extremely good friend of mine. You could always go to him and get advice if you were pondering something or had trouble—good advice, for Göte was wise and thoughtful. We worked closely together for a decade and a half. I supervised him, we wrote together, supervised together and confided in each other. It was extremely rewarding. Göte had the ability to find topics which turned out to be hot for a long time and he was driven by his conviction about the wealth-promoting force of international trade.

Unfortunately, Göte's time on earth was far too short. In 1992, he was diagnosed with carcinoid, an intestinal tumor which metastasized to the liver. He was treated successfully, but the experience went deep into his mind and for a long time, he spoke of nothing else. Thereafter, however, the disease went into a more or less stable state. Göte learned to live with it and was exactly as he used to be. Still, he was living on borrowed time for twenty years. When he was in Arusha around Advent 2011, he had become seriously ill and in January 2012, it was over. I miss him tremendously.

References

Bourdet, Yves (1988), *International Integration, Market Structure and Prices.* London and New York: Routledge.

Bourdet, Yves and Hansson, Göte (1991), 'The Economics of Trade-Policy Harmonization—With Special Reference to the Passenger Car Industry', *World Competition*, Vol. 15, No. 2, 25–41.

Hamilton, Carl (1983), 'Arbetsvillkor, frivilliga exportbegränsningar och handelspolitik – en kommentar', *Ekonomisk Debatt*, Vol. 11, No. 6, 436–439.

Hansson, Göte (1978), *Näringslivet: Resurser och samband.* Lund: Studentlitteratur.

Hansson, Göte (1981), 'Efterkrigstidens handelspolitik – Liberalisering och protektionism', in: Mats Lundahl (ed.), *Ideologi, ekonomi och politik: Tankar i tiden.* Stockholm: Rabén & Sjögren.

Hansson, Göte (1982), 'Do Trade Unions Really Give Rise to Social Losses?', *Statsvetenskaplig Tidskrift*, Vol. 85, No. 1, 21–25.

Hansson, Göte (1983a), *Social Clauses and International Trade.* London and Canberra: Croom Helm; New York: St. Martin's Press.

Hansson, Göte (1983b), 'Arbetsvillkor och handelspolitik', *Ekonomisk Debatt*, Vol. 11, No. 2, 105–112.

Hansson, Göte (1983c), 'Svar till Carl Hamilton: Visst kan man jämföra ekonomisk-politiska åtgärder med olika syften och karaktär', *Ekonomisk Debatt*, Vol. 11, No. 6, 440–444.

Hansson, Göte (1984), 'Världshandelns utveckling och tredje världen', in: Christian Andersson, Lars Heikensten and Stefan de Vylder (eds), *Bistånd i kris: en bok om svensk u-landspolitik.* Stockholm: Liber Förlag.

Hansson, Göte (1985), 'Multinationella företag och internationell ekonomisk politik', in: Lars Engwall and Jan-Erik Vahlne (eds), *Multinationella företag: En utmaning för ekonomisk forskning.* Lund: Doxa.

Hansson, Göte (1989), *Ethiopia, Macroeconomic Performance, Economic Policy and Swedish Aid.* Macroeconomic Studies 1/1989. Stockholm: SIDA.

Hansson, Göte (1990a), *Harmonization and International Trade.* London and New York: Routledge.

Hansson, Göte (1990b), *Ethiopia 1990: A Change of Economic System? A Critical Assessment of the Economic Reform Programme of March 5th, 1990*. Macroeconomic Studies 9/1990. Stockholm: SIDA.

Hansson, Göte (1992), *Ethiopia – Away from Socialism?* Macroeconomic Studies 29/92. Stockholm: SIDA.

Hansson, Göte (1993a), 'Ethiopia—Away from Socialism', in: Magnus Blomström and Mats Lundahl (eds), *Economic Crisis in Africa: Perspectives on Policy Responses*. London and New York: Routledge.

Hansson, Göte (1993b), 'International Trade and Economic Growth: The Experience of Ethiopia', in: Göte Hansson (ed.), *Trade, Growth and Development: The Role of Politics and Institutions. Proceedings of the 12th Arne Ryde Symposium, 13–14 June 1991, in Honour of Bo Södersten*. London and New York: Routledge.

Hansson, Göte (1993c), 'Ethiopia Towards the Year 2000—Prospects for Economic Development', in: *Changing Realities in the Horn of Africa: The Challenges of Political Pluralism and Economic Reconstruction*. New York: Center for the Study of the Horn of Africa.

Hansson, Göte (1993d), *Transition in Ethiopia 1991–1993*. Macroeconomic Studies 45/93. SIDA: Stockholm.

Hansson, Göte (1995a), *Ethiopia 1994: Economic Achievements and Reform Problems*. Macroeconomic Studies 61/95. Stockholm: SIDA.

Hansson, Göte (1995b), *The Ethiopian Economy 1974–94:* Ethiopia Tikdem *and After*. London and New York: Routledge.

Hansson, Göte (1995c), *Ethiopia 1995: Consolidation of Reforms—Implications for Foreign Aid*. Macroeconomic Report 1995:64. Stockholm: SIDA.

Hansson. Göte (1996a), 'From GATT to WTO: A Potential for or a Threat to LDC Development?', in: Mats Lundahl and Benno J. Ndulu (eds), *New Directions in Development Economics: Growth Environmental Concerns and Government in the 1990s*. London and New York: Routledge.

Hansson, Göte (1996b), *Eritrea 1996: Struggle for Sustained Independence*. Macroeconomic Report 1996:12. Stockholm: SIDA.

Hansson, Göte (1997a), *Ethiopia 1996: Government Legitimacy, Aid and Sustainable Development*. Macroeconomic Report 1997:5. Stockholm: SIDA.

Hansson, Göte (1997b), 'The Horn of Africa Beyond the Year 2015: Poverty or Prosperity?', in: *West and East Africa: Regional Studies*. Stockholm: SIDA.

Hansson, Göte (1998), *Ethiopia: Regional and Business Sector Challenges*. Country Economic Report 1998:3. Stockholm: SIDA.

Hansson, Göte (1999), 'The Political Economy of the Horn', in: Steve Kayizzi-Mugerwa (ed.), *The African Economy Policy, Institutions and the Future*. London and New York: Routledge.

Hansson, Göte (2000a), 'Internationalisation, Economic Integration and National Autonomy: General Comments with Some Brief Implications for

Poland', in: Bogdan Wawrzyniak (ed.), *Globalisation and Change: Ways to the Future*. Warsaw: Leon Koźmiński Academy of Entrepreneurship and Management.

Hansson. Göte (2000b), *Eritrea 1999: A Bleeding Country That Never Kneels Down*, Country Economic Report 2000:5. Stockholm: SIDA.

Hansson, Göte (2000c), 'Economic Potentials and Political Threats in the Horn of Africa', *ICEIDA [Icelandic International Development Agency] Newsletter*, No. 11, 10–12.

Hansson, Göte (2001a), *Building New States: Lessons from Eritrea*. WIDER Discussion Paper No. 2001/66. Helsingfors: United Nations University/World Institute for Development Economics Research.

Hansson. Göte (2001b), 'Eritrean Reforms: A Struggle for Sustained Independence and Economic Growth', in: Mats Lundahl (ed.), *From Crisis to Growth in Africa?*. London och New York: Routledge.

Hansson, Göte (2002), 'Genetic Engineering and Economics: A Challenge to North-South Inequalities', in: Susanne Lundin and Lynn Åkesson (eds), *Gene Technology and Economy*. Lund: Nordic Academic Press.

Hansson, Göte (2004) *Ethiopia: Economic Performance and the Role of the Private Sector*. Country Economic Report 2004:4. Stockholm: SIDA.

Hansson, Göte (2006), 'Ledarskapets problem och möjligheter: Iakttagelser från Afrikas Horn', in: Christer Jönsson and Magnus Jerneck (eds), *I ledande ställning. Vänbok till Lars-Göran Stenelo*. Lund: Studentlitteratur.

Hansson, Göte (2009), 'Diplomacy, Trade, Aid, and Global Working Conditions', in: Karin Aggestam and Magnus Jerneck (eds), *Diplomacy in Theory and Practice. Essays in Honor of Christer Jönsson*. Malmö: Liber.

Hansson, Göte; Hedlund, Stefan and Lundahl, Mats (1983), 'Tanzania—Socialistland med bekymmer', *Tiden*, Vol. 75, No. 2, 91–99.

Hansson, Göte and Lundahl, Mats (1983), 'The Rybczynski Theorem under Decreasing Returns to Scale', *Scandinavian Journal of Economics*, Vol. 85, No. 4, 531–540.

Hansson, Göte and Lundahl, Mats (1984), 'A Social Clause Against Discrimination in the Labor Market', *Journal of Development Economics*, Vol. 14, No. 3, 395–405.

Hansson, Göte and Lundahl, Mats (1987), 'International Trade Sanctions Against Occupational Discrimination: The Full Employment Case', *Zimbabwe Journal of Economics*, Vol. 1, No. 4, 48–55.

Hansson, Göte and Stenelo, Lars-Göran (eds) (1990), *Makt och internationalisering*. Stockholm: Carlssons Bokförlag.

Kruse, Agneta och Söderström, Lars (1998), 'Ett brev för mycket', *Ekonomisk Debatt*, Vol. 26, No. 4, 299–302.

Lundahl, Mats (1992), *Apartheid in Theory and Practice: An Economic Analysis*. Boulder, CO: Westview Press.

Lundahl, Mats and Wadensjö, Eskil (1984), *Unequal Treatment. A Study in the Neo-Classical Theory of Discrimination*. London and Sydney: Croom Helm; New York: New York University Press.

Lunds Universitet, Faculty of Social Sciences, Appointments Board (1997), *Minutes*. 3 April. Dnr I E 311 4030/95.

Norman, Victor (1988), Vurdereing av Göte Hansson til dosent i nasjonaløkonomi. 12 April. Bergen: Norges Handelshøyskole.

Petersson, Lennart och Hansson, Göte (2011), 'Utmaningar för ekonomisk integration i Afrika', in: Mats Lundahl (ed.), *Den orädde debattören: En vänbok till Bo Södersten på 80-årsdagen den 5 juni 2011*. Stockholm: Ekerlids Förlag.

Rybczynski, T.M. (1955), 'Factor Endowment and Relative Commodity Prices', *Economica*, N.S., Vol. 22, No. 4, 336–341.

Ståhl, Ingemar (1983), Yttrande över sökande till tjänster som extra universitetslektor i nationalekonomin (5578–5579/83), 30 januari 1983. Lund: Nationalekonomiska institutionen.

Sunesson, Sune (2015), 'Fakulteten var redan delad', in: Gunnar Andersson and Magnus Jerneck (eds), *Samhällsvetenskapliga fakulteten i Lund – en vital 50-åring. En jubileumsskrift*. Lund: Samhällsvetenskapliga fakulteten, Lunds Universitet.

Index

M. Lundahl, *Twelve Figures in Swedish Economics*, Palgrave Studies in the History of Economic Thought, https://doi.org/10.1007/978-3-030-94327-1

Y

The manufacturer's authorised representative in the EU is Springer Nature Customer Service Centre GmbH, Europaplatz 3, 69115 Heidelberg, Germany. If you have any concerns regarding our products, please contact ProductSafety@springernature.com

Printed and bound by CPI Group (UK) Ltd, Croydon, CR0 4YY
30/09/2026
02225499-0017